T0385717

FLYING CAMELOT

A Volume in the Series

Battlegrounds: Cornell Studies in Military History
Edited by David J. Silbey

Editorial Board: Petra Goedde, Wayne E. Lee, Brian McAllister Linn, and Lien-Hang T. Nguyen

A list of titles in this series is available at cornellpress.cornell.edu.

FLYING CAMELOT

THE F-15, THE F-16, AND THE WEAPONIZATION OF FIGHTER PILOT NOSTALGIA

MICHAEL W. HANKINS

CORNELL UNIVERSITY PRESS
Ithaca and London

First published 2021 by Cornell University Press

Library of Congress Cataloging-in-Publication Data

Names: Hankins, Michael W., 1982– author.
Title: Flying Camelot : the F-15, the F-16, and the weaponization of fighter pilot nostalgia / Michael W. Hankins.
Description: Ithaca [New York] : Cornell University Press, 2021. | Series: Battlegrounds : Cornell studies in military history | Includes bibliographical references and index.
Identifiers: LCCN 2021023404 (print) | LCCN 2021023405 (ebook) | ISBN 9781501760655 (hardcover) | ISBN 9781501760662 (pdf) | ISBN 9781501760679 (epub)
Subjects: LCSH: Fighter planes—United States—History—20th century. | Fighter pilots—United States—History—20th century. | Eagle (Jet fighter plane)—History. | F-16 (Jet fighter plane)—History.
Classification: LCC UG1242.F5 H3559 2021 (print) | LCC UG1242.F5 (ebook) | DDC 358.4/30973—dc23
LC record available at https://lccn.loc.gov/2021023404
LC ebook record available at https://lccn.loc.gov/2021023405

However primitive or sleekly modern the machinery of war, the idiosyncratic beliefs of the men of every time and place play their role in how war is fought.

—J. E. Lendon, *Soldiers and Ghosts: A History of Battle in Classical Antiquity*

"You can't repeat the past."
"Can't repeat the past?" he cried incredulously. "Why of course you can!"
He looked around him wildly, as if the past were lurking here in the shadow of his house, just out of reach of his hand. . . .
He talked a lot about the past, and I gathered that he wanted to recover something, some idea of himself perhaps. . . .

—F. Scott Fitzgerald, *The Great Gatsby*

Contents

ACKNOWLEDGMENTS

When I was working at the Air Force Academy, Brian McAllister Linn visited for a guest lecture. Before the event, he took time to meet with the history faculty. Instead of presenting his own research, he wanted to hear about ours. When I explained my project, he told me it might be a good fit for a series on which he was working at Cornell University Press. That is how I luckily happened upon an amazing, fruitful professional relationship. Emily Andrew has been kind, gracious, encouraging, and patient, guiding me through the process, and so has Allegra Martschenko. Brian Linn and David J. Silbey, general editor of the Battlegrounds series, provided wonderful support and encouragement, as well.

In terms of the research on which this manuscript was based, I need to thank Don Mrozek, an inspiring mentor, who continues to provide insight. I have also benefited from the feedback of Michael Krysko, Albert Hamscher, Andrew Orr, and Joseph Unekis. I was fortunate to have worked closely with aviation historian Robin Higham, only a few months before he passed away. Many others helped with the writing process, including General Richard Myers, David Vail, Ted Nagurny, Jennifer Zoebelein, and Kate Tietzen. I am grateful to Kansas State University's history department, which supported me emotionally and financially.

No historian's work would be possible without the archivists who make primary source documents accessible to us. I had help from many, but Mary Elizabeth Ruwell at the Air Force Academy's Special Collections went above and beyond—when I found myself stuck in Colorado Springs without a car, she not only helped me find research material for the project, but personally drove me to and from the archives. I also had great help from the Air Force Historical Research Agency (especially Dan Haulman and Mary Dysart), the University of Texas at Dallas Special Collections, John O'Connell at the President Gerald Ford Library, Mark Nankivil at the Greater St. Louis Air and Space Museum, Heather Anderson and Sarah Musi at Boeing, Carla Krivanek at Lockheed, and the wonderful staff of the Smithsonian National Air and Space Museum Archives, especially Elizabeth Borja, Melissa Keiser, and Kate Igoe. I am particularly indebted to novelist Robert Coram, author of *Boyd: The Fighter Pilot Who Changed the Art of War*. Coram graciously made his research material for that work available at the Marines Corps History Division Archives Branch at Quantico, Virginia. The thousands of pages of correspondence, interview notes, and official documents in that collection were invaluable. Although our interpretations of John Boyd and the surrounding subject matter may diverge, Coram assembled an amazing body of work, and I am very grateful for it and for his generosity.

A number of years ago, I told Don Mrozek that I wanted to study the post-Vietnam Air Force, specifically its changes in training and technology. He said it was a good idea, but one on which someone else at Kansas State had already been working. That person turned out to be Brian Laslie, who I am lucky to say is now a good friend. Not only has he given incisive feedback on numerous versions of this text, but he has walked me through many questions and worries. Many others have provided useful feedback on this text or its supporting materials. I am deeply grateful to Angelica Aboulhosn, James and Emilie Tindle, Mary Elizabeth Walters, Roger Launius, John Terino, Steve Fino, Roger Connor, Jeremy Kinney, Margaret Weitekamp, Angela Riotto, Doug Kennedy, Bob Wettemann, Jennifer Weber, Craig Morris, David Stone, Larry Burke, Sean Seyer, John Krige, and Paul Martell-Mead.

Finally, I would like to thank my friends and family, who have been through a lot with me, and been supportive of me as I worked on this project. I don't know if I got into this more because of all those times my father brought home test footage of Paveway bombs being dropped from F-4 Phantoms, or because of the time Ryan English casually suggested, "You can pursue research in military history focusing on air power, right?" Either way, this whole thing is probably their fault.

While I have tried my best to ensure the text is free of errors, if any remain, they are mine alone and have nothing to do with any of the wonderful people listed above.

ABBREVIATIONS

ACEVAL	air combat evaluation
ADC	Air Defense Command
AFSC	Air Force Systems Command
AIM	air-intercept missile
AIMVAL	air-intercept missile evaluation
APGC	Air Proving Ground Center (Eglin Air Force Base)
ASD	Aeronautical Systems Division
AWACS	Airborne Warning and Control System
BVR	beyond visual range
CAS	close air support
CFP	concept formulation package
CSAF	chief of staff of the Air Force
DCP	development concept paper
DCS	deputy chief of staff
DCS/R&D	deputy chief of staff for research and development
DDR&E	director of defense research and engineering
DOD	Department of Defense
EMT	energy maneuverability theory
EWO	electronic warfare officer
FBW	fly-by-wire
FDL	Flight Dynamics Laboratory
FIG	Fighter-Interceptor Group
FTD	Foreign Technology Division
FWS	Fighter Weapons School
GAO	General Accounting Office
GIB	guy in back
IAF	Israeli Air Force
LWF	lightweight fighter
MAC	Material Airlift Command
MRC	Military Reform Caucus
NASM	National Air and Space Museum

OSD	Office of the Secretary of Defense
PACAF	Pacific Air Forces
PA&E	Program Analysis and Evaluation
QOR	qualitative operational requirement
RFP	request for proposals
RIO	radar intercept officer
RMA	revolution in military affairs
SA	systems analysis
SAC	Strategic Air Command
SAM	surface-to-air missile
SECAF	secretary of the Air Force
SETP	Society of Experimental Test Pilots
SPO	Special Projects Office
STOL	short takeoff and landing
TAC	Tactical Air Command
TFW	Tactical Fighter Wing
TRADOC	Training and Doctrine Command
USAF	United States Air Force
USAFE	United States Air Forces Europe
V/STOL	vertical/short takeoff and landing
WSO	weapons system officer

Introduction

In the early hours of February 6, 1991, Captain Thomas "Vegas" Dietz of the United States Air Force sat inside a McDonnell Douglas F-15C Eagle, one of the most advanced machines human beings had yet devised, soaring through the skies at thirty thousand feet over the deserts of the Iraq-Iran border at hundreds of miles an hour—and he was bored out of his mind. Operation Desert Storm had been raging for three weeks, and Iraqi forces had put up little airborne resistance to US operations. Dietz passed the time that particular morning by singing along to "Hold On Loosely" by 38 Special, when an E-3 AWACS (airborne warning and control system) operator interrupted with the news that an unknown number of Iraqi fighters were sixty miles away at low altitude. Dietz and his wingman, First Lieutenant Robert "Gigs" Hehemann, took their F-15s down through a deck of clouds and punched the throttle, quickly smashing through the sound barrier. Using the Eagle's long-range AN/APG-63 radar, the pair "sorted" their enemies, locking onto them from eighteen miles behind the closest plane, a MiG-21. After closing to about eight miles, Dietz fired an AIM-7 Sparrow, but the missile's motor failed. A second later, Hehemann fired a Sparrow. Dietz later described how he felt as that missile screamed toward the target: "I remember being pissed. The thought of cheering 'Gigs' on while he carved up this group of MiGs like Eddie Rickenbacker against a bunch of Fokkers was more than I could handle." But Hehemann's

Sparrow missed; each man fired another AIM-7, both of which also failed to hit. The Iraqi fighters, now splitting into two groups, didn't bother maneuvering but just increased their speed. Dietz took his Eagle into a roll, putting him a mile and a half behind two MiG-21s as he launched a heat-seeking AIM-9 Sidewinder missile at each of them. Hehemann, chasing the other group—two Su-25s—also switched over to Sidewinders, his headset ringing with the telltale "growl" that told pilots their seeker had a lock from two miles away. Launching two AIM-9s, he turned both Su-25s into fireballs crashing into the desert. Inside fifteen seconds, Dietz and Hehemann had destroyed four enemy fighters, whose lack of action indicated they might not have even been aware of the Eagles' presence.[1]

The engagement was revealing. Dietz felt some sort of connection with World War I, seeing his wingman as a modern-day Eddie Rickenbacker (the top-scoring US ace from World War I) and the MiGs as counterparts to Fokkers (the main German fighter aircraft used in that war). But this fight was nothing like aerial combat from 1914 to 1918. The Gulf War engagement occurred at hundreds of miles per hour, with little to no maneuvering. The F-15 pilots had integrated communication with other air assets like AWACS, using long-range radar in addition to their own on-board radars that allowed them to sort targets and call their shots from beyond visual range (BVR), despite the missile failures. These were not close-turning dogfights with pilots circling each other as their white scarves flew in the wind.

Yet, the F-15—and the smaller, lighter F-16 Fighting Falcon, built shortly after the Eagle—were designed with such close-turning dogfights in mind. Fighter pilot culture held remarkable continuity from its origins in World War I through Dietz's time. The F-15 and F-16 were products of that fighter pilot culture, but, as Dietz and Hehemann's encounter demonstrated, by the time the USAF flew those planes in combat, aerial warfare had changed.

A Breed Apart

"Fighter pilots are a breed apart," claimed F-16 pilot Lieutenant Colonel Dan Hampton. "The uninitiated or envious often call them arrogant, but that's not really *it*. It is an absolute belief in their own invincibility, aggressiveness, and skill."[2] Military culture is different from civilian culture, military aviation culture is distinct from both, but fighter pilot culture is a world unto itself. It began in World War I, when the fighter pilot became a symbol, a collection of ideas that did not always reflect reality—but the romantic, heroic idealization of the fighter pilot meant a great deal to the American public and the pilots themselves. Many of these conceptions were a transfer of older ideas of heroic, masculine, civilized, noble combat that had captured the American mind in previous generations, regardless of how unrealistic such notions may have been.

During World War I, a collection of ideas, beliefs, and behaviors formed, constituting fighter pilot culture and establishing what can be called the "fighter pilot myth" or "knights of the air myth." Historians such as John D. Sherwood and Steven Fino have defined this culture as an informal one marked by confidence and pride, even arrogance, in which individual pilot skill and air-to-air kills were the currency of status, and women were objectified, if they were regarded at all.[3] Their definitions are useful and accurate, but I argue that the mythic construction of an idealized fighter pilot consists of five core elements:

1. Aggressiveness. This includes an eagerness for battle and a strong sense of competition and is tied to what many pilots call the "warrior ethos." Fighter pilots tend to throw caution to the wind and are less likely to trust those who urge restraint.

2. Independence. Fighter pilots guard their individuality. They tend to see flying as a freeing adventure, an escape from normal life, even a game, but mostly they want to make their own decisions—to sit in a single-seat aircraft and alone be responsible for their fate. This leads many to be skeptical of leadership, sometimes disdainful or even hostile to authority—unless that authority figure is an accomplished fighter pilot.

3. Heroic imagery. Many depictions of fighter pilots—in fiction and nonfiction, in prose and poetry, in art and film—tend to include romanticized heroic symbols. Pilots are aware of these images and make purposeful use of them. They see themselves as analogues to Arthurian knights, ancient historical figures like King Leonidas of Sparta, mythological heroes such as Achilles or Samson, and even gods, such as Zeus and Mercury. Later analogies include pilots comparing themselves to aces of the World Wars.

4. Technology. Fighter pilot culture is naturally centered on the technology of the airplane, which pilots see as an extension of themselves—their aircraft of choice becoming a defining aspect of their identity. That is true of most aviators, but what sets fighter pilots apart is their tendency to advocate for the types of aircraft in line with the fighter pilot myth: planes that enhance their individuality or aggressiveness or are designed for air-to-air combat. They don't want just any airplane; they want specific technology that supports their values.

5. Community. Fighter pilots are competitive with each other, but they also form a tight-knit community that exhibits mutual respect and deep admiration. But this community can be suspicious, jealously guarding itself from outsiders. Those who are not "true" fighter pilots are unworthy and unwelcome. By the late twentieth century, members of the fighter pilot community held most leadership positions in the Air Force, but they remember a time when they were a small subculture, feeling persecuted. This perception that their exclusionary traditions are under threat influences their thinking.[4]

Concepts of masculinity are intertwined in all five elements. Fighter pilots coded these traits as masculine, and failure to express them often resulted in one's manhood being called into question by the community. Fighter pilots were expected and encouraged to perform their masculinity through sexual promiscuity or using sexualized language. Rather than constituting a sixth element, masculinity is more properly understood as embedded in all the other five.

These five elements formed the core of fighter pilot culture—the main qualities that most fighter pilots valued most highly—but not every pilot fully embodied all of them. The degree to which individual pilots adhered to this myth forms a spectrum. Some took it to cartoonish extremes, exhibiting radical versions of stereotypes. Others sought a balanced expression, holding on to some elements more than others, or understanding that they were only one type of flier within a larger force. Some fighter pilots did not adhere to the myth at all.

This culture was not entirely new. Other military figures in other branches sometimes espoused similar views. Historian Brian Linn, in a study of schools of thought within the US military tradition, identified a strain he called "heroes." This group espoused a way of thinking about war that "emphasized the human element, and defined warfare by personal intangibles such as military genius, experience, courage, morale, and discipline. Heroes reduced war to its simplest terms." Heroes view warfare as "chaotic, violent, and emotional" and reject attempts to systematize it. They insist, as General George Patton did, that "wars are fought with men, not weapons." They emphasize aggressive, reductive slogans such as "War means fighting and fighting means killing," and insist that the military's role "is to kill people and break things." Although this school of thought promotes adaptability and innovation, it "lends itself to emotional posturing, to elitism or selfishness. . . . And it can produce muddy-boots fundamentalism [and] anti-intellectual reductionism."[5] The role of fighter pilot tended to attract individuals already in line with Linn's "heroes" school. Those who became lightweight-fighter advocates, influencing the design of the F-15 and F-16, not only embodied these attitudes (and used many of the same slogans that Linn identified) but took them to further extremes.

"The Camelot of Aeronautical Engineering"

On January 20, 1974, in the dry desert of Southern California, Lieutenant Colonel Phil Oestricher was fulfilling "a great boyhood dream" of being a test pilot: his job that day was to test the YF-16 prototype, which Oestricher called "a pure air-to-air fighter airplane." Stripped to its essentials, it was smaller, lighter, and unencumbered by the modifications the Air Force later installed on the production models of the F-16. It was, in Oestricher's words, "the Camelot of aeronautical engineering."[6] The creation of an aircraft that could recall the image of chivalrous, knightly warfare of days gone by was not a coincidence. It was a deliberate, hard-fought effort by a group of fighter pilots and their allies to recapture the spirit of the knights of the air myth.

This book argues that military technology is not developed solely as a solution to an operational problem, nor does it have a mind of its own. Humans make choices—humans that are steeped in specific cultures, with specific beliefs, assumptions, behaviors, and values. The F-15 Eagle and F-16 Fighting Falcon, originally designed to focus on air-to-air combat, are the strongest examples of the influence of culture on technology within the US Air Force. Many of the individuals who advocated for those aircraft and guided their development had a specific vision for what they wanted—a vision that was firmly rooted in the beliefs and assumptions inherent in fighter pilot culture. Understanding that culture and how it evolved are key to understanding the development path of those aircraft.

This linking of culture and technology has been explored in other areas, but not often applied to military hardware. It may be tempting to view military hardware as developing linearly, as a response to the needs of a mission. But all technologies, including military aircraft, are the results of humans making specific choices in a particular historical moment and context. Historian David Nye has shown that technologies are the products of larger systems, shaped by social, economic, governmental, and cultural factors, and that culture then shapes the use of new technologies. Any specific technology is more than a machine that does a job; "it is an expression of a social world." Nye demonstrates that, in inventions from telephones, computers, radios, to high-performance fighter jets, "these technologies were not 'things' that came from outside society and had an 'impact'; rather, each was an internal development shaped by its social context."[7]

But technologies are also embedded in cultural narratives; they are expressions of stories that people tell about themselves. From the early colonial period onward in North America, technologies from the ax to the railroad were woven into a cultural narrative about the expansion of the frontier. Those technologies were core elements in the narrative of how people imagined their place in history.[8] In the same way, fighter pilots internalized a narrative of their own place in history, as noble, chivalric warriors engaging in aerial duels with the technology of the airplane—specifically small, light, agile airplanes designed for acrobatic one-on-one jousts. The F-15 and F-16 should be understood as artifacts of that cultural narrative. The YF-16 prototype was the ultimate expression of that culture in physical form. For the knights of the air, the YF-16 was the ideal steed, or castle.

The Air Force bought the plane but modified it into the production model of the F-16A, and later into further altered variants. These added new features, increasing size and weight—anathema to some of the plane's designers who wanted a "pure" air-to-air fighter. These decisions speak to the power of technological momentum, described by Thomas P. Hughes, in which the development of technology along a particular path accrues powerful inertia to continue in that path.[9] The Air Force had long held a preference for multi-role aircraft that could perform many types of missions rather than be optimized for only one job. Subsequent generations of aircraft almost always increased in size, weight, and cost. A group of former fighter pilots and their allies in the 1960s and early 1970s fought hard to stop the F-15 from going further down that path, and they fashioned the YF-16 and YF-17 as exceptions to the rule: smaller, lighter, and cheaper than the fighters coming before them. These advocates saw themselves as rebels fighting against the system, but they were also fighting the institutional force of technological momentum.

To understand the culture of these fighter advocates, this book stands on many shoulders. Studies of military culture abound, although most of these works attempt to link cultural characteristics to warfighting. The works of Wayne Lee and Isabel Hull have been particularly influential in examining how military cultures influence behavior on and off the battlefield.[10] I first encountered the notion that some militaries' approach to warfighting is guided by nostalgia in J. E. Lendon's study of the culture of Greco-Roman warfare, but it is a theme that presents itself in many studies of late nineteenth and early twentieth-century warfare.[11] These ideas have less often been applied to the development of military hardware and rarely to aircraft design and procurement. Two notable exceptions are Fino and Timothy Schultz, who examine the intersections of pilot and crew cultures with changing technologies. These studies are valuable for understanding how military pilots throughout the twentieth century navigated rapid changes in technology, adapting their culture along the way.[12] Air Force culture specifically has been an attractive topic for many historians, as well as Air Force officers themselves. The most comprehensive and influential of these is Carl Builder, who defined the distinct personalities of US military services as well as the various subcultures within the US Air Force, tracking how they changed over time.[13] Speaking specifically of fighter aviation, Linda Robertson's thorough study of World War I shows how the fighter pilot mythology was created, fostered, and used for propaganda purposes, creating a powerful cultural resonance that lasted for many generations.[14]

The F-15 Eagle and F-16 Fighting Falcon specifically are popular aircraft and the subject of many enthusiast books.[15] Scholarly works discussing them tend to fall into a few camps: First, that they are part of a more or less linear narrative of technological progress, best explained by Kenneth Werrell. Second, that they represent a shift in the Air Force's conception of warfighting and organization, as best explained by Brian Laslie.[16] A third camp emphasizes a paradigm of a genius inventor—crediting an individual or small group with being primarily (or largely) responsible for both aircraft. That individual is Colonel John Boyd, and that group is his associates known as the Fighter Mafia. Boyd is a lightning rod in any discussion of Air Force technology and doctrine during this period. He is a controversial figure who is passionately revered in some circles and despised in others. He did contribute to the F-15 and F-16 design process and went on to become an influential military theorist who influenced all the US military services to some degree. No work on the F-15 and F-16 can avoid discussing him in depth.

Much mythology has built up around Boyd, which has led to an exaggeration of some of his contributions as well as legends about his own record. Most of the writing on Boyd, scholarly and otherwise, presents him heroically—but these works are also either written by Boyd's friends and associates or heavily influenced by them. No one has done more to popularize the heroic image of Boyd than novelist Robert Coram, whose biography was based on testimony from Boyd's closest friends and tended to downplay Boyd's detractors. Coram praises Boyd as a genius, comparable to Moses and Sun Tzu. This attitude is common for fans of Boyd, some of whom have written other works examining specific aspects of Boyd's career. Grant Hammond's biography is more measured, but only to a degree. Hammond was somewhat close with Boyd and presents him as an unappreciated genius.[17]

Works that present a different interpretation of Boyd are rare, and none of them are monographs or books. John Andreas Olsen has attempted a more nuanced take on Boyd, while David Metz's review of Coram's work provided a more critical appraisal. James Hasík was also critical but focused on Boyd's later career.[18]

After retiring from the Air Force, Boyd was influential both for his briefings on military matters and his participation in what became known as the Military Reform movement, a large group of active and retired military officers, journalists, and politicians that attempted to change personnel policies, procurement practices, and military doctrine and strategy throughout the 1980s.[19] Almost everything written about this movement has been from the Reformers themselves.[20] Their critics debated them in the popular press and service journals, producing one book in the process, but noncontemporary historical analysis of the movement that is not written by the Reformers themselves is almost nonexistent.[21]

The most dramatic claims about Boyd's career tend to originate from himself or his close friends. In the literature on the F-15 and F-16, Boyd often overshadows the contributions of many other key figures, and those who dispute or criticize claims about Boyd have had less of a voice in the discourse. This book attempts to correct some of that imbalance, but its purpose is not to criticize Boyd or anyone associated with him. These men are neither messianic heroes nor dark villains. They are people—people with strengths and weaknesses, who made valuable contributions as well as mistakes. Some of Boyd's theories changed the way air combat was understood, and his importance is impossible to deny. But many of his ideas were rejected for understandable reasons, and his aggressive personality limited his ability to serve in leadership roles and earned him enemies throughout his life.

This book presents a more balanced view of Boyd and the Reformers, placing them in a broader historical context, but that is not its primary purpose. Rather, this book views the development of military aircraft technology through a cultural lens, demonstrating that from the 1960s though the 1980s, fighter pilot culture and its nostalgia for an imagined past exerted a large influence on the technological development of the F-15 and F-16 fighters. The latter's prototype, the YF-16, was the ultimate expression of the mythic fighter pilot cultural narrative.

To that end, the first chapter establishes a working definition for fighter pilot culture and how it operates, describes how and why the fighter pilot emerged as a distinct cultural category during World War I, and explains the key mechanisms by which that culture was able to persevere and evolve for over sixty years, through the Vietnam War and beyond. The second chapter then explores the five elements of fighter pilot culture in more detail, the various ways in which they expressed themselves, and how the culture evolved through various contexts.

The remaining chapters tell the story of the development of the F-15 and F-16 fighters, beginning in 1964 with a small group of fighter pilots advocating for a new aircraft. These individuals were imbedded in the fighter pilot tradition, and many were established heroes of the fighter pilot community. Emphasizing individuality and aggressiveness, these pilots advocated for a dedicated air-to-air fighter that could re-create the glory days of fighter combat— an idealized vision of World War I, which they sometimes referred to as "the white scarf stuff." That aircraft would need to be small, lightweight, single-seat, maneuverable, and emphasize the role of man over machine, using advanced technology only in ways that enhanced its nimble air-to-air role.

One segment of this community took these ideas to extremes, zealously arguing for their version of a lightweight fighter. This group, a mixture of pilots and engineers, began calling themselves the "Fighter Mafia." They took the knights of the air myth to radical extremes. They were aggressive, competitive, and confrontational in their everyday dealings with fellow officers and coworkers. They saw themselves as rebels within a corrupt organization, and they spoke of trying to tear down the system using guerrilla tactics in the halls of the Pentagon. They used religious imagery, referring to themselves as doing "the Lord's work" in trying to break a corrupt "orthodoxy." The leaders of their movement became holy, messianic saviors of what they judged to be the "true" role of air power. In their advocacy for a "pure" lightweight fighter plane, they approached cultlike fanaticism. They exaggerated fighter pilot culture almost to the point of caricature, becoming self-radicalized and distanced from others in the fighter community. In the late 1960s and into the 1970s, many former allies began to oppose the Fighter Mafia's work.

Disappointed in the Air Force's modifications to the F-15, the Fighter Mafia advocated for a pure air-to-air combat aircraft to fulfill their vision. That plane was the YF-16. The Fighter Mafia were disgusted when their pure fighter was distorted by adding weight, size, more advanced electronics, and air-to-ground bombing capability to the production model. Frustrated, they gave up trying to create new aircraft and instead became politically active, partnering with other military leaders, journalists, and politicians, creating the reform movement. They argued that American defense was in a state of crisis because of an overreliance on complex, expensive weapons. They advocated weapons and doctrines that tended to exemplify the values stemming from their cultural beliefs of agility, individualism, and superiority of man over machine. Speaking to a sense of crisis and loss in the wake of Vietnam and after the failure to rescue hostages in Iran, the reform movement resonated powerfully with a certain segment of the defense industry and the public. After the US success in the Gulf War of 1991, the reform movement dissipated, but some of its members remained politically active, and their ideas lingered in the discourse around American defense.

Fighter pilots are not the first group to look to a constructed, imagined version of the past and attempt to emulate it; the ancient Greco-Roman armies looked to their mythologized pasts to inspire and guide their military practices.[22] Just as Greek military planners were haunted by the ghosts of Homeric epic, and the Romans by their construction of Greek heroic combat, sixteen centuries later the US Air Force was haunted by the ghosts of the knights of the air. Fighter advocates longed to re-create the deeds of exemplary ancients, to turn with Rickenbacker, to duel with the Red Baron—the air-to-air combat pilots of World War I, or, at least, a constructed memory of them. Some might call this antiquarianism, although the fighter advocates themselves would likely deny such a charge. But their push for simpler, cheaper weapons to capture disappearing modes of combat spoke more to nostalgia than to realistic war planning.

This book is not just a history of Air Force technology but of a belief system: a biography of an idea. It is the story of how a subculture with its own values grew to become one of the most influential voices within the US Air Force and how it created multimillion-dollar weapons that were expressions of its own nostalgic beliefs. For many fighter pilots, the mythologized knights of the air in their imagined version of World War I was the Camelot of air power. In designing the F-15 and F-16, they sought to re-create that ideal and build a new flying Camelot.

They almost succeeded.

A Note on Sources

Although records exist for the design process of aircraft, many of them are still classified at the time of this writing. Such official documents are useful but can obfuscate the underlying attitudes of the designers: their beliefs, their biases, their assumptions. There are fewer records kept of conversations at bars, angry phone calls, discussions over fast food, and arguments in hallways. Yet these may best reveal the attitudes and beliefs of the players involved. In addition to the official documents available, I have relied on oral histories, interviews, correspondence, memoirs, and recollections. Such sources require caution. People often misremember, obfuscate the truth, or disagree on key events. The same individual can tell the same story in different ways at different times. I strive to present these differing perspectives as much as possible. Although some of these recollections may be inaccurate in some details, the way these individuals remember events (or want events to be remembered) can reveal their underlying attitudes, and their specific language is often telling.

Military aviation has generated a robust secondary scholarly literature that this work is indebted to, but the topic has also engendered many non-scholarly works aimed at a popular or enthusiast audience. Many of these works are valuable contributions to the field, although some are limited; some are methodically researched, others less so. For the purposes of this book, the enthusiast literature provides a useful window into cultural attitudes of the aviation community, but for matters of fact, this book will more often rely on primary or scholarly secondary sources.

CHAPTER 1

The Fighter Pilot with a Thousand Faces

> The American Fighter Pilot is a rare sort: part rebel, part intellectual, part athlete—all kid. If you don't ever want to grow up, become a fighter pilot.
>
> —Major Robert Burgon, *Piano Burning and Other Fighter Pilot Traditions*

In the early twenty-first century, the F-22 Raptor was the United States' most advanced operational air-to-air fighter plane. It was fast, stealthy, used thrust-vectoring engines, and carried radar and electronic warfare equipment, with powerful computer processors to analyze and sort incoming sensor data. The Raptor, in most ways, was nothing like the open-cockpit wood-and-canvas planes of World War I, nor their metal-skinned counterparts from World War II, and it bore only passing resemblance to jet fighters from the years of the Korean or Vietnam Wars.

Perhaps that is why F-22 pilot Major Robert Burgon spoke of his "euphoria" at flying it for the first time nearly one hundred years after the start of World War I. Yet he also noted of that flight, "Once I was safely on the ground, my thoughts returned to the fighter pilots of yesterday." When he joined the US Air Force, he said, "My desire to study history surged, and I started learning about the aerial warriors of an era gone by. The more I learned about those crusty old pilots and compared my story to theirs, the deeper the connection I felt to them." According to him, "Everything in my career seemed to link back in time to those first, brave airborne soldiers who took to the skies in the cutting-edge technology of their day."[1]

Burgon is not the only fighter pilot who has felt culturally connected to his historical counterparts. The culture of fighter pilots first formed as several mutually reinforcing reactions to the harsh realities of World War I.

That culture was then passed down to subsequent generations for over a century, evolving over time but remaining centered on the five elements of aggressiveness, independence, heroic imagery, technology, and community, all coded with masculinity. To explore these elements and their evolution in detail, it is first necessary to define what "culture" is and how it affects decisions and behaviors, particularly in a military context.

Military Culture and the US Air Arm

Culture is a powerful force, but it is also a broad concept subject to a variety of definitions and interpretive lenses. Historian Wayne Lee's definition (adapted from that of anthropologist Clifford Geertz) is useful: "'culture' refers to the patterns of meanings and beliefs expressed in symbols and actions, by which people communicate, perpetuate, and develop their knowledge about and attitudes toward life."[2] Historian Isabel Hull, influenced by anthropologist Clyde Kluckhohn, added the key clarification that much of what constitutes culture is beneath the surface, and that "military culture" consists of "habitual practices, default programs, hidden assumptions, and unreflected cognitive frames."[3]

Culture and behavior are interrelated—one does not cause the other, strictly speaking. But culture consists of assumptions, interpretations, and patterns of thinking that shape behavior and are shaped by those behaviors. Most importantly, most of this process is not conscious, "it is unexamined and unverbalized." Thus, cultural beliefs and behaviors can often contradict a group's goals or beliefs, and members might not be aware of that contradiction. From the outside, cultures can often appear irrational.[4]

Militaries are large organizations, which generate culture in specific ways. Organizational culture is "the total of the collective or shared learning of that unit as it develops its capacity to survive," according to social scientist Edgar Schein. "Culture is the solution to external and internal problems that has worked consistently for a group and that is therefore taught to new members as the correct way to perceive, think about, and feel in relation to those problems." Schein clarifies: "The power of culture is derived from the fact that it operates as a set of assumptions that are unconscious and taken for granted."[5]

Behavioral scientists Alan Wilkins and Kerry Patterson agreed, arguing that "the real power of culture resides in the tacit assumptions that underlie it. These habitual ways of seeing and thinking about the world are like automatic pilots. They are powerful because people rarely think about them, though they influence almost everything people do."[6] Culture can create limits on the options that are available to a group. In large organizations with pressure to conform—such as militaries—the unconscious nature of culture "can lead to rigid thinking . . . to a reluctance to seek further information, and to unrealistic assessments," all of which "short-circuit the process" of decision making.[7] As Schein summarizes, "Not only does culture limit the strategic options that are conceivable to an organization, but strategies cannot be implemented if they run against powerful cultural assumptions."[8] Cultural power also comes from the strong connection between organizational culture and a sense of personal identity. Organizational theorists Mary Jo Hatch and Majken Schultz posit that members of an organization form distinct identities "in relation to what others say about them, but also in relation to who they perceive they are." Identity and culture are caught in a feedback loop, in which each continually reinforces the other.[9]

Military cultures are not monoliths. In the United States, the uniformed services have distinct service cultures that in turn contain subcultures. RAND analyst Carl Builder argued that each of the US military services has a distinct "personality." "The Air Force," he specified, "could be said to worship at the altar of technology," especially the technology of the airplane.[10] Builder asserted that throughout the Cold War, Air Force leaders "revealed— through their decisions more than their words—that their true affection was not for the theory of air power, but for the airplane."[11] As a service, that meant the airplane generally, but individuals got more specific. "Air Force pilots often identify themselves with an airplane," Builder observed. "'I'm a 141 driver.' 'I flew buffs [B-52s].' Sometimes this identification goes right down to a particular model of an airplane: 'I fly F-4Cs.'" He concluded, "The pride of association is with a machine, even before the institution. One could speculate that, if the machines were, somehow, moved en masse to another institution, the loyalty would be to the airplanes."[12]

This devotion to specific airplanes and an inherent otherizing of crews of different aircraft contributed toward the formation of subcultures in the Air Force. These subcultures centered broadly on the two main "families" of aircraft: large, crewed bombers, and single-seat fighters. There are, of course, other types of missions such as close air support (CAS), transport, intelligence, and a multitude of support roles (logistics, search and rescue, refueling, electronic warfare, to name a few), as well as an overlap regarding the planes that perform these missions. But strategic bombers and tactical fighters made up the largest, most distinct groups. Each group evaluated itself by different measures; strategic bombers need to carry massive payloads and thus need to be large, less maneuverable, fast, and have crews that are trained for coordinated teamwork, while fighters emphasize maneuverability, smaller size, and the autonomy of the individual fighter pilot. Each group tends to see itself as important—if not paramount—to achieving decisive success in warfare.

Hull and Schein have noted that institutional culture is most powerfully formed at an organization's founding or when facing an existential threat, especially if those moments are associated with an influential leader.[13] The late 1940s and early 1950s were both foundational and threatening for the Air Force. During and after the Second World War, when the Air Force became an independent institution, the bombers ran the Air Force and were cultur-ally dominant.[14] Most of the Air Force's early leaders were former bomber crew members who felt a need to protect the new service from being folded back into the Army. The Air Force at that time was marked by insecurity and suspicion of other services treading on its turf. Hence the bitter rivalry for air assets between it and the Army, as well as a reluctance to coordinate tech-nological development with the Navy. To maintain this bomber identity and prevent cultural shifts within the service, the Air Force style of leadership tended to be "monarchic."[15] Of the many charismatic leaders associated with this foundational moment of bomber dominance, none was as prominent as General Curtis LeMay, the second commander of Strategic Air Command (SAC) and later Air Force chief of staff (CSAF), who allegedly said, "Flying fighters is fun. Flying bombers is important."[16]

The division between bomber and fighter culture was a hallmark of the Air Force for most of its existence, at least through the late 1960s. Fighter pilots in those years tended to be marginalized, or at least felt so. Some schol-ars have referred to the intense "tribalism" between the two groups, seeing them as dividing the Air Force into "clans," or asserting that the Air Force operated under a "caste system."[17] In a superficial sense, the conflict was typified by the split in the Air Force between its two largest subcommands: SAC, which handled strategic bombing missions, and Tactical Air Command (TAC), which handled air superiority, interdiction, and CAS. However, even TAC attempted to legitimize itself by focusing on bombing missions and adopting elements of the nuclear delivery mission, so that many fighter pilots (especially those that valued air-to-air combat) saw themselves as mar-ginalized within their own branch.

These fighter pilots maintained a distinct subculture within the service, and that culture had a large effect on all aspects of the service: doctrine, train-ing, organization, and technology development. As the fighter subculture gained more of a voice and more influence within the Air Force, the service began to produce technologies that were more in line with that culture's values.

This book is less concerned with how US fighter pilots fought and more with how they wished to fight—what they thought their ideal role in war should be. Those cultural assumptions regarding the prediction of future war and what they wanted to do in those hypothetical wars are what guided their technological decision-making processes. The evidence for defining those cultural assumptions includes what Schein called "artifacts": "the visible behavior manifestations of underlying concepts," as well as professed values and beliefs, actions motivated by basic assumptions, and common interpretations of the past and shared history.[18]

Much of this book analyzes fighter pilot behaviors, stated beliefs, speech that indicates patterns of thinking, actions that reveal specific assumptions, and interpretations of the past that reinforce those assumptions. There is remarkable continuity of these typical cultural expressions among US fighter pilots, from the introduction of military aircraft in the early twentieth century to the late 1980s and into the early twenty-first century. However, it must be emphasized that fighter pilots exist on a spectrum regarding the degree to which they conform to this culture. Not all fighter pilots agree with the stereotypes and assumptions of this culture, and some actively resist it. Most fighter pilots do express and participate in at least some, if not most, elements of it, perhaps tempering certain aspects. A small group of fighter pilots take these cultural characteristics (behaviors, patters of thinking, etc.) to extremes. The fighter community often holds up those radical individuals as examples for other fighter pilots to follow.

This book refers to "fighter pilots" broadly, including crews of fighter-type aircraft in a variety of missions. Air-to-air combat (air superiority) was the preferred role for most fighter pilots, who tended to measure their worth by their count of aerial victories—the number of enemy planes they allegedly shot down.[19] This book focuses on fighter pilots in the air-to-air role, but not exclusively. Many who are not fighter pilots by strict definition still exhibit fighter pilot cultural characteristics. The best examples are those flying in the backseat. In the two-place fighter jets of the Cold War, such as the F-4 Phantom, the backseaters—in the Air Force, weapons systems officers (WSOs, pronounced "whizzos"), and in the Navy, radar intercept officers (RIOs, pronounced "ree-ohs), or often simply the GIB (guy in back)—often saw themselves as real fighter pilots, at least culturally.

Until 1969, the Air Force required F-4 backseaters to be pilots. This often caused tension between the crew, and some front-seat pilots ordered their backseaters to not do or say anything on flights, while some GIBs resented the front-seaters, who were often less experienced. Once the Air Force changed its policy, it took through 1972 to fully transition the pilot backseaters into front seats while replacing them with navigators as WSOs. This seemed to ease some of the tension.[20]

These WSOs were proud of their role and, in terms of cultural assumptions, behaviors, and rituals, thought of themselves as fighter pilots. As Lieutenant Colonel Dick Jonas, also an F-4 GIB, said, "There isn't a GIB in the 8th Fighter Wing that won't fight you if you call him a copilot, or a navigator, or some other dirty word. He's a GIB, and that's what you'd better call him. Just ask any AC [aircraft commander, i.e., front-seater] that ever flew the Phantom and he'll tell you that some of the world's best fighter pilots fly the back seat of the Phantom."[21] Many WSOs saw the pilot seat as a step forward and tried to move. By the 1970s, WSOs who were eager to move to the front seat could reapply to transition to a pilot slot every six months, although the Air Force usually made them stay in the back for a number of years.[22]

Some backseaters, including the electronic warfare officers (EWOs) in the post-Vietnam period, wore a different set of wings from those of the pilots but donned the same flight suits and patches. Some pilots resented this and bristled at being given advice or instruction from a backseater. Some EWOs were proud of their position, while others seemed to wish they were pilots. They may have sat in the backseat, but GIBs often observed the same rituals, held the same beliefs, made the same assumptions, and carried the same swagger that many of their fighter pilot companions did, and they are just as valuable of a window into the nature of fighter pilot culture.[23]

The type of mission a fighter pilot flew also carried status implications. Air-to-air combat was the preferred role, partially because it resembled the dueling nature of older combat, as opposed to ground-attack missions, which did not. "Fighter pilots dream of victory in aerial combat," said revered ace Brigadier General Robin Olds; "it's the be-all and end-all of the fighter profession."[24] World War II ace Major General John Alison explained, "Ground attack [was a] mission which fighter pilots generally did not like because you got shot down. Air-to-air combat was relatively safe. We had some almost unexplained losses on ground attack. You never knew who was shooting at you."[25]

Aerial victories mattered, as fighter pilot and subsequent CSAF General Merrill McPeak noted: "What fighter pilots want to do is chase MiGs, make ace and sleep between clean sheets." Yet McPeak also emphasized, "MiG killing is not all there is to it," that ground-attack roles of defense suppression, interdiction, and CAS are all essential for tactical fighters.[26] Olds himself said, "You're not going to win a war by shooting down a damn MiG, you're going to win a war by bombing the bejesus out of whatever you were sent to bomb."[27]

Many fighter pilots performed both roles. For example, Colonel James Hagerstrom, one of the seven men who achieved ace status in both World War II and Korea, achieved many aerial victories while flying as a ground-attack pilot in Korea, although he considered MiG-killing his true passion.[28] Many ground-attack pilots who flew fighter-type aircraft considered themselves just as much true fighter jocks as the air superiority crews and participated in the same culture to a large degree. For example, F-4 Phantom ground-attack pilot Lieutenant Colonel David Honodel said, "I believed, no I KNEW, that I was a shit-hot fighter jock." He summarized a song sung by his fellow ground-attack Phantom drivers: "With my hand around its throttles, I'm in a separate class. I'm a fighter-bomber pilot, let the others kiss my ass."[29]

Fighters flying as forward air controllers, or "fast FACs," such as the pilots of Operation Commando Sabre in Vietnam (code named Misty) who marked targets for other fighters and engaged in a variety of ground-attack roles, also considered themselves true warrior fighter jocks. Misty pilot Major General Don Shepperd argued, "Rarely have fighter pilots performed such exciting work" as FAC missions.[30] McPeak, also a Misty pilot, said that the FAC unit "became a haven for the hardcore," and he described individual members as "seasoned fighter pilot" or "warrior type."[31] Misty's first commander, Brigadier General George "Bud" Day, emphasized that the fast FACs were "men selected because of their expertise as fighter pilots."[32] While aerial victories were the most important status symbol, one could still revere and participate in fighter pilot culture by flying fighters in other roles, being in a backseat, or in some cases through exemplifying fighter pilot beliefs and behavior while working as a desk jockey at the Pentagon.

New Knights?

Before World War I even began, popular author H. G. Wells linked air-to-air combat with medieval heroism. "Every man who goes up and destroys either an aeroplane or a Zeppelin in the air should," he said, "have a knighthood."[33] American pilot Lieutenant Bennett Molter, who had volunteered to fly for the French Air Service, took the concept further in his 1918 memoir, saying that he wanted to become a pilot partly because of his "boyhood love of adventure and an avid appetite for the tales of chivalry recounting the deeds and exploits of the knights of old." He clarified: "Instead of faring forth clad in shining armor and mounted on a fiery charger I would . . . ride a steed of metal, wood, and linen. . . . [A] felt padded leather helmet would replace the one of steel . . . gloves of wool instead of gauntlets of mail, a machine gun in lieu of a lance, goggles in place of a vizor."[34]

Many fighter pilots of World War I saw themselves as this new breed of heroic warrior. Cloaking oneself in childhood nostalgia and taking on the role of a noble warrior hero is an attractive idea, although it was far from the reality of the situation in World War I. Flying wood-and-canvas aircraft was often a harrowing, dangerous experience that ended in horrific death. Psychological trauma was common, and air-to-air combat in that war had little, if any, measurable effect on the war's outcome. Despite this, the experience of flying such aircraft and engaging in exciting dogfights could feel exhilarating and important for those participating—contributing to the formation of fighter pilots as a distinct culture. Thus, as historian Steven Fino put it, "The Fighter pilot myth was not an outright lie but a purposeful opaquing of historical events."[35]

If the fighter pilot image was not fully representative of reality in World War I, how then did it form? And how did it come to create such a distinct culture that has lasted over a century? The most common explanation historians have given is that piloting aircraft offered a direct contrast to the more grisly type of warfare seen in the trenches, which was a negation or violation of Victorian values and the military culture of glory that had allegedly been evolving over the previous few centuries. This argument often implies that there had been a previous sense of chivalrous combat, epitomized, perhaps, in the popular memory of Theodore Roosevelt leading the charge up San Juan Hill in the Spanish-American War of 1898. Although the horrific conditions of trench warfare in World War I obliterated the possibility of such heroic images, fighter pilots engaging in exciting aerial duels seemed to revive the possibility of this romantic image of chivalrous war.[36]

This contrast only goes so far. The trenches of World War I were certainly horrible conditions, and on a much greater scale than that of previous conflicts, but those earlier wars were hardly marked by chivalry, heroism, and Victorian ideals. Just a few examples, such as the Russo-Japanese War, the Wars of German Unification, the American-Philippines War, and centuries of military atrocities associated with European colonialism and American frontier expansion certainly do not accord with a romanticized view of honorable combat. Furthermore, discussions of shock at the horrors of trench warfare often assume tropes of Victorian culture that, if true at all, might have applied only for a certain class. James Hamilton-Patterson has noted that the hardships of trench life may have shocked the upper-class officer corps, but for the common working-class soldiers such conditions were not that far removed from the hardships of Britain's factories in the age of industrialism.[37]

The degree to which the stalemate and high casualty rates of combat in World War I shocked the participants must be tempered by the fact that most military theorists in the belligerent nations did not expect future wars to look like San Juan Hill charges. Throughout the last few decades of the nineteenth century, European and American military theorists wrote extensively about the crisis of infantry in the face of changing technologies that allowed for the industrialization of warfare and the massive increase in the scale of battles. These theorists were well aware of the potential for modern warfare to devolve into brutal wars of attrition and had been searching for new methods to create breakthroughs and restore movement to the battlefield. However, the gulf between theory and practice was large, and many ideas of the theorists had not been fully disseminated or incorporated into actual use.[38]

One of the aspects of military theory that came to the forefront before World War I—and became especially relevant to air power—was the spirit of the offensive, closely linked to the perception of a sociocultural crisis at the advent of the modern industrial world. Many military leaders at the time thought that improving living conditions were weakening society and reducing the warrior spirit of the general population. German *General-leutnant* William Balck summarized his view of the problem: "The spirit of the times looks upon war as an avoidable evil and militates directly against the kind of courage that despises death. The fast manner of living at the present undermines the nervous system; and the fanaticism, the religious and national enthusiasm of yesterday are gone." He concluded, "The physical powers of the human being are also on the wane."[39] Almost seventy years later, Balck's son Hermann, after serving in many command positions in the Wehrmacht in World War II, befriended and mentored a US Air Force officer, Colonel John Boyd, who was influential in designing the F-15 and F-16. Boyd argued many of these same points that William Balck had argued before World War I.

The idea that previous wars had been exemplars of chivalrous, honorable values is of course a myth unto itself, and the degree to which World War I was a huge break from previous conflicts has perhaps been overstated. Nonetheless, there is merit to the idea that fighter pilots in World War I became glorified because their role offered an alternative to President Woodrow Wilson's observation that "war had lost all of its glory."[40] There are several reasons why the role of the fighter pilot appeared so different and glorious (although in many ways it was not), but the most important was that aerial combat was, as historian Lee Kennett explained, "a resounding affirmation of the individual." Victory in air-to-air combat "was in itself a small thing," Kennett said, "but it was a victory with an identifiable victor, a flesh-and-blood 20-year-old who was the sole author of his triumph."[41] Turning those individuals into heroes had obvious propaganda value that many governments seized on immediately, but such lionization was not exclusively top-down. The public wanted individual heroes—at least according to press outlets and at least one member of the British Parliament, who demanded that their governments be more forthcoming with names of individuals and details of aerial battles, which the media then used to regale the public with exciting tales of aerial adventures.[42] Naturally these lionized pilots became mass celebrities, bombarded with fan mail and chased by admirers seeking autographs. Their place in popular culture was more like that of Hollywood movie stars than of military veterans.[43]

The focus on individuality not only made it easy to render pilots as heroes, but, combined with the allure of their bird's-eye-view, helped make the sprawling, massive scope of industrial warfare more comprehensible. Historian Peter Fritzsche noted that "their exploits also localized the war for all combatants, allowed it to be seen in miniature, and thereby made the sprawling conflict more graspable." While this was likely true for the general public following the press coverage of famous aces, it was certainly true for many infantry soldiers, some of whom were among the first to submit their accounts of aerial battles to the press. These stories were often laden with a tone of glorious, chivalric combat. Fritzsche noted that in these tales, pilots were often portrayed "as a mythic creature who restored perspective, consequence, and willfulness to the war as a whole."[44]

In addition, the airplane itself brought a sense of excitement that separated pilots from other combatants—if only in the sheer novelty and wonder of new technology that made possible their (relatively) fast, maneuverable, controlled flight. The years leading up to the war had spurred what historian Antulio Echevarria called "public mania" about flying that captured the imagination of the press, the public, fiction authors, and military theorists, all of whom imagined a variety of ways that aircraft could dramatically change society and the future of warfare.[45] For many both at home and serving in the trenches, the technology of the airplane had an inherent heroic quality that other new technologies of industrial warfare lacked. As Fritzsche noted, "In an otherwise unromantic war of machines, Boelcke [one of the most prominent German aces] had mastered an art, not simply a technique as a means to an end; his contests resembled knightly tournaments and thereby restored a human and heroic measure to the content."[46]

But the creation of fighter pilot mythology and culture was not simply a heroic celebration; it was also a coping mechanism to deal with the horrific realities of air combat, which, according to top-scoring US ace Captain Eddie Rickenbacker, was "not a sport, it is scientific murder."[47] Fighting in the air could be as brutal as on the ground, with death coming as quick and as horribly. Life expectancies for fighter pilots were short—only eleven days for RFC (Royal Flying Corps) pilots in April 1917—and while the chances of being shot in the air or crashing were nightmare-inducing enough, the chances of burning to death while streaking across the sky were high. Manfred von Richthofen, Germany's famed ace known as "the Red Baron," seemed to take a perverse joy in causing and watching his enemies burn to death, which he did in over two-thirds of his kills. He took efforts to always find out and note in his logs whether his victims had been lit on fire or not. "One's heart beats faster," he noted, "if the opponent, whose face one has just seen, plunges burning from four thousand meters."[48]

In the face of such psychologically traumatizing horrors, it was likely comforting to paint oneself as participating in a knightly, chivalric, civilized tradition harking back to an imagined knightly past that recalled childhood nostalgia. Many pilots struggled with guilt and disgust at the killing they participated in, and, as aviation author Mike Spick noted, "tended to play up the chivalric and sporting image as a result, probably as a form of mental self-protection."[49] Media analyst Linda Robertson noted the same trend when pilots or other authors wrote public-facing works about the war, explaining, "The emphasis on the combat pilot as a lone warrior made it easier not to mention the grim realities of air combat."[50]

The image of chivalrous knights of the air also had value outside of combat itself, both for recruitment purposes and as propaganda to build support for the war effort. But that meant purposefully covering up the brutality. Robertson has argued that the constructed image of heroic, noble fighter pilots was "potent and seductive," and "as a tool for propaganda, the image of the combat pilot was the most significant contribution to the war effort."[51] This overstates the value of both propaganda and of combat pilots to the war generally, but does explain another reason why the mythology of heroic fighter pilots took hold both among the public and the pilots themselves.

It must be emphasized that the image of the knights of the air that formed and took root during World War I was, even as acknowledged at the time, a constructed mythological image that did not reflect reality. As W. E. Johns summed up his experience, "Only politicians saw the romance in it then, with their beautiful speeches about 'our boys.' . . . You know the stuff. Glorious victory, my hat. With most of us the war was a personal matter."[52] Fritzsche noted that famous aces like "Boelcke, Immelmann, and the others were not prototypes of a new twentieth-century aerial chevalier." Many of the mythological elements simply did not describe the majority of pilots in World War I. Most pilots did not fly single-seat fighters; many flew in other roles, and even for those in fighter roles, solo missions were rare compared to larger formations. Dogfights were rarely one-on-one duels but frequently involved over a dozen aircraft, or, in at least one case in the Third Battle of Ypres, up to ninety-four planes.[53] French pilot Pierre de Cazenove de Pradines wrote that it was "impossible to speak of chivalry in that relentless pursuit."[54] British ace Arthur Rhys-Davids agreed: "All you can think of is pumping lead into any machine you see, and looking out and avoiding collisions, just missing each other by perhaps a couple of feet."[55]

Many pilots flatly rejected the romanticized stereotypes and went in the opposite direction, embracing fatalism and the image of themselves as "nothing but hired assassins," as British ace James McCudden said, using a phrase that became somewhat common among World War I combat pilots.[56] Others suffered psychological trauma, a common element mentioned in diaries and memoirs. Captain Arthur Gould Lee of No. 46 Squadron RFC recalled several occasions of dreaming of machine guns firing at him as he flew, and he woke up screaming and shaking, covered in sweat. Captain Harold Wylie discussed instances of fellow officers who had nervous breakdowns. A Lieutenant Oliver from No. 66 Squadron noted that "this flying job is rotten for one's nerves, and although one is supposed to last months with a fortnight's leave half way, quite a lot of people's nerves conk out."[57]

American lieutenant Walter L. Avery's diary demonstrates how quickly some pilots became disillusioned. His early entries are laden with the stereotypical aggressiveness and lust for combat of fighter pilot culture—that is, until he actually encountered combat. In his first dogfight, he shot down *Oberleutnant* Carl Menckhoff, who was only bruised. Avery took a few souvenirs from Menckhoff's plane and later saved the *London Daily Mail*'s colorful account of the fight. Avery's own diary shifted to a dry, matter-of-fact style. He began to express skepticism about his chances of survival. Later aerial victories were mentioned briefly—and the early romanticism had dissipated almost completely. After his first combat encounter, the most excited he became was when he ate ice cream. The deaths of his fellow pilots began to bother him less. "Funny, how things go along just the same," he noted after the death of one of his colleagues. When his friend Bill Taylor was shot down while flying Avery's plane, Avery made no comment about his friend's life but merely expressed frustration that one of the souvenirs from his Menckhoff battle was destroyed.[58] It could be that Avery was simply too busy to write in more detail, or had lost interest. Or it could be that he was growing disillusioned with how the brutal realities of combat failed to live up to the idealized construction of the knights of the air.

Perhaps the most potent example of the contrast between the idealized construction of the fighter pilot myth with the more brutal reality is the case of fighter ace Henry Clay, who flew for both the RAF and the US Air Service. When writing to his sister in-law, Clay expressed the typical enthusiasm for combat and individualism. "Here's hoping that before they do get me though that I can have about fifty [aerial victories] to my credit," he wrote. "That is my first wish and then my second is that they do not get me at all!" Yet, a few weeks later, Clay wrote separately to his brother, who was considering becoming a pilot: "I'll tell you it isn't all sunshine and flowers—more flowers than anything else though. We all joke about pushing up daisies but it is more of a reality than a joke. . . . The whole thing may be summed up in a few words 'don't be a damn fool.'" Two months before that letter, when one of Clay's friends was killed in combat, Clay wrote to his brother: "This game of war is the greatest game of chance you ever played. I'm a fatalist through and through. So is everybody else in this game." He concluded: "Sherman was right—[war is] hell and I don't know the half of it at present. There isn't any hell hot enough for those who contributed toward the beginning of it."[59]

The mythological image of the knights of the air was born of a confluence of mutually reinforcing factors of World War I: the seeming contrast with trench warfare; the sense of inspiring heroism that came from focusing on individuals; the fascination with new technology; the pure sense of excitement that aerobatic flight engendered; a coping mechanism for dealing with the trauma of warfare; and that image's value for propaganda and recruitment. For these and perhaps other reasons, the image took hold among the public and pilots themselves. This was passed down to subsequent generations through a variety of mechanisms, despite its dissonance with reality. The notion that earlier wars had been chivalrous and honorable was mistaken to begin with; the idea that World War I fighter pilots recaptured this noble way of war further skewed reality. But that idea became imbedded in the way the public and pilots themselves thought about World War I and air combat, trivializing or minimizing many aspects of the war. The knights of the air myth continued fostering misunderstanding for over a century.[60]

Passing the Torch

"It is entirely up to the current group of fighter pilots to ensure subsequent generations are properly indoctrinated," said Burgon, reflecting on the connections between his flying the modern F-22 and the experiences of other, earlier fighter pilots. "The aggressive fighter pilot attitude is preserved and passed on through the observance of *tradition*."[61] These traditions involve games, songs, ritualized meetings and ceremonies, patterns of speech, call-and-response actions, the encouragement of particular behaviors, and choices of clothing, accessories, and grooming. All of these are designed to promote the five characteristics of fighter pilot culture, coded in masculinity and looking back to the past. It is through these mechanisms, among others, that fighter pilot culture has been passed down from one generation to the next, evolving over time but with its core tenets remaining intact.

"The process of indoctrinating a fledgling fighter pilot is a lengthy one that can span the pilot's career. It starts by teaching the young pilots history." Eventually, these recruits "are permitted to participate in rituals like Roll Call and piano burnings. Their acceptance into the fold is culminated by a naming ceremony where they receive a tactical call sign by which they'll be known throughout their career." Burgon explained that maintaining the heroic image of former fighter pilots was key: new pilots should strive to "honor those who have gone before us by emulating their noble characters and adopting their attributes." This constructed history of past fighter pilots often relies more on myth and less on sources and evidence. History is passed down in a "mostly word-of-mouth nature."[62]

Much of the word of mouth came directly from previous generations, as US airmen frequently served in multiple wars, with experienced veterans from previous conflicts serving alongside newly arriving pilots. Many airmen in command positions in World War II had flown in the previous world war. In the Korean War, the connection was even stronger. Of the 355 coalition pilots who earned aerial victory credits against MiGs, 56 of them had scored kills in World War II, and 7 had earned ace status separately in both wars. The top five highest-scoring aces in Korea also served in World War II, three of them as combat fighter pilots with victory credits.[63] Similar patterns existed in the Vietnam War. Famed fighter pilot Brigadier General Robin Olds, who commanded the 8th Tactical Fighter Wing (TFW) during the Vietnam War, earning four victory credits in the process, had also been a double ace in World War II with twelve kills. He felt the connection to the earlier war so strongly that on every mission over Vietnam he wore the same socks he had worn in World War II—at least until they got too malodorous for his deputy commander of operations, Colonel Daniel "Chappie" James, who threw them out. James had served in World War II and flown fighters (in ground-attack roles) during the Korean War. Olds's vice commander was Colonel Vermont Garrison, one of the seven who had earned ace status in

World War II and Korea.[64] Some fighter pilots flew in all three conflicts: World War II, Korea, and Vietnam. For example, Brigadier General Charles McGee flew with the Tuskegee Airmen during World War II, shot down a Focke-Wulf 190, then went on to fly fighters on ground-attack missions in Korea and flew F-4 Phantoms as commander of the 16th Tactical Reconnaissance Squadron during the Vietnam War. These are just some of many examples of this pattern.

Many fighter pilots sought out connections to the past on their own or had early brushes with men who became their heroes. Major General Frederick Blesse, who became a double ace in Korea and held command positions in several TFWs during the Vietnam War, spoke frequently about being inspired by Captain Eddie Rickenbacker, the top-scoring US ace of World War I. "'Captain Eddie' was my hero, now joined by World War II aces like [Colonel Francis] Gabreski, [Colonel Walker] Mahurin, [Major Richard] Bong, [Major Thomas] McGuire, [Brigadier General Harrison] Thyng, and others," he said, emphasizing the mythological aspects of dogfighting: "The picture was always in the back on my mind—fighter pilots diving, climbing, turning, finally destroying the enemy aircraft; bringing honor and glory to themselves and their country."[65] One of the pilots Blesse mentioned, Walker Mahurin, also counted Rickenbacker as a personal hero. Olds recalled, when he was a child, meeting Rickenbacker in person but being "too awed to say anything."[66]

Another major vector for passing down fighter pilot culture to later generations was popular culture. Depictions of fighter pilots in popular media tended to focus on and reinforce the stereotypes of the knights of the air, and among the consumers of that media were existing or future pilots. Indeed, some pilots participated in creating this media, contributing to a feedback loop of cultural expectations. Early on, silent adventure films made use of aviation; these included Blanche Scott's *The Aviator and the Autoist Race for a Bride* (1912); *Marriage by Aeroplane* (1914); *An Aerial Revenge* (1915); the Keystone comedy short *Dizzy Heights and Daring Hearts* (1915); Harry Houdini's *The Grim Game* (1919); and *The Flying Ace* (1926)—the latter being part of a trend of "racial uplift" films, in this case imagining a world in which the US Army permitted African Americans in the elite role of fighter pilot, which at the time was reserved for whites only.[67]

Charles Lindbergh's cross-Atlantic flight in May 1927 generated enthusiasm for aviation, leading to an influx of aviation fiction across a variety of media, including the new pulp magazines—collections of short stories often accompanied by a few illustrations—devoted solely to aviation tales. The first of these was *Air Stories* that August, but within five years dozens of others emerged, with titles like *Air Trails*, *Sky Fighters*, *Dare-Devil Aces*, *Flying Aces*, and *Sky Trails*, to name a few. These stories tended toward adventure, detective, and crime-story plots, but many of them emphasized typical fighter pilot culture stereotypes. Some publications were based directly on historical examples, such as Terry Gilkison's *Famous Sky Fighters*, a comic strip series running in issues of *Sky Fighters* starting in 1933. Each month, Gilkison told stories of famous aces of World War I.[68]

Some of the stories, films, and comic strips during the interwar years were cocreated or influenced by World War I fighter pilots who emphasized the excitement of air-to-air combat and the stereotypes of fighter pilot culture. Captain Elliot White Springs, a triple ace who flew with the British and the US in World War I, wrote a series of aviation stories that became popular after the war.[69] The silent film *Wings* (1927) was directed by William A. Wellman, who had flown as an American volunteer with the French, achieving several aerial victories. This was followed shortly by the talking films *Hell's Angels* and *Dawn Patrol*, both released in 1930. The latter was directed by Howard Hawks, who did not see combat during World War I but had served as a flight instructor in the US Army. For *Hell's Angels*, director Howard Hughes hired former World War I aviators as stunt pilots for the flying sequences. In the world of comics, Rickenbacker collaborated with illustrator Clayton Knight, who had himself participated in air-to-air combat while flying with the RFC and RAF during World War I. The duo created two comic strips that ran from 1933 to 1939, with Rickenbacker receiving a writing credit and Knight as the artist: *Ace Drummond* became so popular it generated movie serials, and *Hall of Fame of the Air* told tales of historical World War I fighter pilots.[70]

One of the most dramatic examples of the reciprocal relationship between comics and real pilots was the work of Milton Caniff, creator of *Terry and the Pirates* and *Steve Canyon*. *Terry* debuted in 1938, but in 1941 Caniff met with First Lieutenant Philip G. Cochran, a P-40 pilot and commander of the 65th Pursuit Squadron, who wanted to commission Caniff to draw an insignia for his unit. Caniff was so taken with Cochran's stories and what historian John Correll described as "the picturesque vernacular of the fighter pilot" that he changed his *Terry* stories to focus on fighters in the Pacific, with the character "Flip Corkin" based on Cochran. In 1947, Caniff launched a new strip, *Steve Canyon*. Although a transport pilot by trade, Canyon embodied many of the rugged individualist and heroic adventure stereotypes associated with fighter pilot culture. During the Korean War, Canyon transitioned to an F-102 fighter. These strips (and the television shows, movie serials, and radio dramas they spawned) were popular in the Air Force and with government officials in general. Pages of *Terry* were entered into the *Congressional Record*, and General Henry "Hap" Arnold, chief of the Army Air Forces, assigned an officer to assist Caniff. After World War II, the Air Force gave Canyon an official serial number, and CSAF General Nathan Twining said that Canyon was "an officer in my command."[71] Years later, Major Ed Rasimus, a fighter pilot during the Vietnam War, insisted that the defensive tactics used by North Vietnamese MiGs could be easily explained: "Since the enemy hadn't grown up with Steve Canyon, Terry and the Pirates, or Sky King in their comic books, they didn't much care about daring dogfights."[72]

One of the best-known instances of fighter pilots in comics is the *Peanuts* character Snoopy, who frequently embarks on imaginary adventures in which he is the unnamed "World War I Flying Ace," searching for the Red Baron. This character-within-a-character exhibits many of the stereotypical knights of the air traits: aggressiveness, individualism, and an emphasis on air-to-air combat. To further adhere to the myth, Snoopy's combat was always a one-on-one joust. Snoopy as the flying ace was popular among actual fighter pilots and became a symbol for depicting their cultural values, featured on patches, unit insignias, and in training materials.

For famed fighter ace Robin Olds, Snoopy was not just a comic strip character, but an ideal to strive toward: "Give me a little plane with a great big gun; Snoopy flying alone on his doghouse shaking his fisted paw at the sky, shouting, 'Curse you, Red Baron!' I was Snoopy in my dreams, but only in my dreams."[73] Olds was also influenced by World War I films like *Wings* and *Dawn Patrol*, as well as pulp novels, especially *G-8 and His Battle Aces*, a series about a fighter pilot in World War I that exemplified the sense of adventure and heroism typical of the knights of the air mythology but also included fantasy, science fiction, and horror elements.[74] The series had been created in 1933 by Robert Hogan, who had joined the US Air Service in 1918 and become a flight instructor but was struck with influenza during the 1918 pandemic before he could go overseas to fly in combat.

Olds was not alone. Blesse also recalled the effect of pulp fiction and comics: "I grew up reading *G-8 and His Battle Aces* and *Tailspin Tommy* in the funny papers," he said, "dreaming of the fighter pilot's life."[75] *Tailspin Tommy* was an aviation-themed adventure comic strip that began in 1928 and spawned radio serials and movies, written by Hal Forrest, who did serve as a fighter pilot in World War I but did not leave the States. Although not a war comic, the strip did rely on many stereotypes of fighter pilot culture, emphasizing exciting aerial maneuvering and heroic adventures.

One exception to the trend of romanticized fiction was the character of Major James Bigglesworth (known as "Biggles"), created by W. E. Johns.

Johns, who piloted British two-seater DH.4s in World War I, became the editor of *Popular Flying* magazine in 1932. Perhaps because of his experience of being shot down and held as a prisoner of war, Johns's Biggles stories attempted to demythologize the air war by avoiding the more typical jingoistic, chivalrous tone. Biggles was so burned out from the trials of combat that he was a depressed, nihilistic alcoholic suffering from post-traumatic stress. Nonetheless, the focus on flying combat and the rate at which Biggles and his fellow pilots downed enemies amounted to a sort of romanticization. Yet compared to other media from the period, it did not play into typical fighter pilot cultural stereotypes nearly so much.[76]

After World War II and into the twenty-first century, the more typical depictions of brash, heroic pilots continued to be a theme in popular culture and increasingly merged with science fiction. Hollywood films such as *The Hunters* (1958), *The Blue Max* (1966), and *Top Gun* (1986) are but a few popular examples, the latter earning a sequel in 2020. The trend of fighter pilots as comic book superheroes remained a trope, recurring in examples ranging from *Blackhawk*, first appearing in 1941, to *Green Lantern* (the 1959 reboot introducing Hal Jordan), to the 2012 reboot of the *Captain Marvel* series (the basis for the 2019 film), which writer Kelly Sue DeConnick said "can pretty much be summed up with 'Carol Danvers as Chuck Yeager.'"[77] Similar depictions of pilots exhibiting fighter pilot cultural stereotypes appeared in *Star Wars* (1977) and its numerous sequels; *Iron Man* (2008); *Guardians of the Galaxy* (2014); *Wonder Woman* (2017); and many others. All these examples were vectors to perpetuate the culture of fighter pilots through subsequent generations.

The promulgation of fighter pilot culture was not only an ad hoc affair; it was also supported institutionally and systemically. In the years before and during World War II, the US air arm consulted psychologists to construct tests to discriminate between ideal candidates for bomber pilots and ideal candidates for fighter pilots. Former fighter pilot and historian Major General Mike Worden described the distinction: "Bomber pilots needed to be more deliberate and orderly in their thinking, with slower, but dependable decisions and actions. Also, they were expected to be more mature team players." By contrast, air leaders "wanted fighter pilots to show more alertness, respond quicker, and display higher motivation and controlled aggressiveness than other single-engine and multiengine pilots." One of the psychologists noted that in fighter squadrons a "status system pervades everything [a pilot] does, as there is no way to get away from it." Worden concluded, "Fighter pilots were cliquish combat elites, self-reliant and aggressive, who valued technical knowledge over education. . . . They took pride in being men of action and of decision." Even outside these tests, flight instructors tended to assign students to particular roles based on instinctual judgment of these traits. Arnold insisted that fighter pilots be "individualists . . . with quick agility and facility."[78] Again, fighter culture became a self-reinforcing feedback loop. Incoming pilots were told that to be an effective fighter pilot, they needed to have certain traits. Those who had these traits were both selected for the fighter role by the Air Force and self-selected to attempt to be placed into that role, perpetuating and ingraining cultural stereotypes.

The systemic inculcation of fighter pilot culture continued during and after the Vietnam War. In August 1966, the Directorate of Defense Research and Engineering (DDR&E) instructed its Weapons Systems Evaluation Group to conduct a study of air-to-air encounters in Vietnam for the primary purpose of guiding the development of future fighter aircraft. By the end of 1967 alone, the project had conducted over 330 interviews with the goal of "reconstructing" each air-to-air battle in detail. The effort was aided by psychologists from the Institute for Defense Analysis and graphic artists from the Boeing Corporation who translated a pilot's memories into drawings. The effort continued into the mid-1970s, chronicling virtually every air-to-air encounter of the Vietnam War. Revealing the pervasiveness of the knights of the air myth, the project was code-named Red Baron.[79]

A similar effort began in 1976: Project Corona Ace, a series of oral history interviews with former ace pilots. In late 1976, CSAF General David C. Jones (who had served as a bomber commander and operations planner before commanding a TFW of F-4 Phantoms) initiated the project. Its goal was to "attempt to develop an *ace profile* for the selection and training of future fighter pilots."[80] Clearly, at least some segment of the Air Force leadership believed in the knights of the air myth—first, in thinking that the service was deficient in air-to-air combat and that part of the solution was to identify potential aces, and, second, in thinking that aces could be identified by their personalities. The interviewers tended to express belief in many of the core components of the knights of the air myth, especially aggressiveness and competitiveness.

For example, in Major General John Alison's interview, the questioner, Lieutenant Colonel John Dick Jr., asked many leading questions: "Are you a fatalist at all?" "[Was your motivation] competition, to be better than anybody else? To match your skills against someone else?" "Why if you got four you want five; you got five and you want six. You become a single ace and you want to get ten?" "If there is a kind of personality that you and other aces have is there some basic personality for whatever reason, aggressiveness or competitiveness. And if we can identify those kinds of people, aren't they still the most important ingredient in this weapons system?"[81] Some pilots agreed with these sentiments, and others dissented, yet the majority of interviews were conducted under the implication or the assumption that the personality of the pilot—especially the qualities of competitiveness, aggressiveness, and individuality—were the most important determining factors in becoming an ace.

The interviewers at times goaded their subjects when discussing those traits, such as in the interview with General Frank Everest, who commanded the Fifth Air Force in Korea and later served as deputy commander of TAC. When Everest argued that TAC pilots were superior to bomber pilots because one individual, instead of a crew, handled each plane, questioner Dick exclaimed, "Hear! Hear!"

"One guy and he does the whole goddam bit," Everest said.

Dick continued: "And loves doing it."

"Loves to do it, yes," Everest agreed.

Dick explained, "There is the perfect authority and responsibility stuck together—flying is just something else. If you are good, you want to do the toughest thing there is to do and the most fun."

"Yes," Everest confirmed.

Dick concluded, "There are different kinds of folks, you know. You get around Nellis [Air Force Base] around those young fighter pilots—they are just vibrant, smart people. They can do anything."[82]

This was far from an unbiased assessment. The interviewer agreed heartily with everything Everest was saying, encouraging him to draw these points out further. Both parties celebrated the knights of the air mythology, proud of their view that fighter pilots were inherently superior to other types of fliers.

Through these ad hoc and formal mechanisms, from both within and outside the military, fighter pilot culture passed from generation to generation, despite the tenuous relationship between that culture's mythical elements and reality. Technology and the ways pilots used it changed over the years; flying an F-22 Raptor had little in common with piloting a Fokker *Eindecker*. Yet as Fino noted, "the myth of the fighter pilot remained remarkably consistent despite the pilots' ever-changing relationships with their machines and their fellow aviators."[83]

The notion that pursuit aviation was a heroic form of combat, whether through its seeming differences with ground combat, its façade of nobility, its propaganda value, or its usefulness as a coping mechanism, became entrenched in the minds of pilots and the general public during World War I.

This culture was passed down through word of mouth, behavioral expectations, peer pressure, training, popular media and fiction, shared rituals, and institutional structures. This newly formed culture of fighter pilots remained intact for decades, passed from one generation to the next, though it did evolve particular expressions as technology and circumstances changed. Through the Vietnam War and beyond, the five key characteristics of that culture remained powerful.

CHAPTER 2

"You Can Tell a Fighter Pilot (But You Can't Tell Him Much)"

> Fighter pilot is not just a description, it's an attitude,
> it's cockiness, it's aggressiveness, it's self-confidence.
> It is a streak of rebelliousness and competitiveness.
>
> —Brigadier General Robin Olds, *Fighter Pilot*

The people responsible for the creation of the F-15 and F-16 existed within a cultural context. Some were commanders, engineers, technicians, or designers, but some of the most influential voices were fighter pilots or allies of fighter pilots who exhibited similar cultural characteristics. Their cultural context began in World War I but evolved in the years before the F-15 began its development. That culture consists of five key elements or tenets: aggressiveness (including emphasis on competition); individualism (including a resistance to authority figures); technology (which enhances the fighter pilot's preferred roles, particularly air-to-air combat); heroic imagery; and a close sense of community. All these traits are imbued with a sense of masculinity.

Culture, although powerful, is not prescriptive. Not all fighter pilots are the same. The degree to which they adhere to the stereotypical behaviors, thought patterns, and assumptions of fighter pilot culture forms a spectrum. Some do not adhere to the stereotype at all, or only to a certain degree. Others take it to cartoonish extremes, making Tom Cruise's "Maverick" character from *Top Gun* look like a documentary. Of the thousands of fighter pilots who have flown for the US over the years, each has a unique story, and although the examples outlined here are representative of many, they are not universal. This curated list of examples illustrates the key tenets of fighter pilot culture and its various evolutions from World War I through the Vietnam era.

Aggressiveness

"There is no question, you will find that the one word that will always run through all of the people that you talk to, I am sure, will be aggressiveness," said World War II ace Brigadier General Frank Gailer, a P-51 Mustang ace, when asked what makes a good fighter pilot. "He has to be an aggressive individual. . . . The great ones tend to be, in most cases, a pretty wild bunch." He continued: "I hate to use the term reckless, but to some degree, that's what makes a successful fighter pilot. He has got to be willing to take a chance." Comparing fighter pilots to bomber and transport plane pilots, he argued, "They are just a different breed of cat. A banker is just not the same kind of a guy as Evil Kenievel [*sic*]."[1]

No other single trait is cited as often as aggressiveness as the element that sets fighter pilots apart. The celebration of a lust for battle and the notion that warrior spirit can be decisive in air combat dates back to World War I. Kiffin Rockwell, the first American pilot to shoot down a German aircraft, had the reputation of a man "who attacked so often that he has lost all count, and who shoves his machine gun fairly in the faces of the Germans."[2] Kenneth W. Clendenin of the US 14th Aero Squadron argued that Germany's most successful ace pilot, Baron von Richthofen (the "Red Baron"), would have stood no chance against US fighters had he faced them, owing to "the individual's 'make-up,'" which consisted of *"Courage, 'grit,' enthusiasm, 'elan,' pride*—name it, they had it!"[3]

Aggressiveness meant risking death. To be killed in combat was, for some, glorious and inspirational. Victor Chapman was the first US pilot to be killed in aerial combat, at age twenty-six. Rockwell wrote to Chapman's family, "He died the most glorious death, and at the most glorious time of life to die. . . . I have never once regretted it for him."[4] Lieutenant John G. Agar expressed similar thoughts at the 1920 memorial ceremony for lost pilots of the US 22nd Pursuit Squadron: "Do we not envy them both the living and the dying?" he asked the surviving veterans in the audience. "The eagerness with which they seized their first opportunity; the spirit with which they trained; the fortitude with which they said goodbye; the valor with which they fought; the courage with which they endured, and the glory with which they died! All their qualities single them out to be loved, admired, envied, and followed."[5]

Few fighter pilots were as aggressive as First Lieutenant Frank Luke, who was determined to "make myself known or go where most of them do."

Luke earned a reputation not only for his dogfighting skill and his preference for "balloon busting"—attacking the heavily defended observation
balloons—but for his lone-wolf attitude and frequent instances of insubordi-
nation, recklessness, and lack of discipline. He routinely disobeyed orders and
peeled away from formations to hunt on his own. Even when ordered to take
leave, he refused to comply and continued to go into combat without per-
mission from his commanders. Luke's seemingly death-wish-inspired recklessness is contrasted with the relative moderation of Eddie Rickenbacker.
Both were competing for the spot of the top-scoring US ace, but they had
markedly different approaches. Rickenbacker exhibited aggressiveness as
well but was much more deliberate than Luke, not taking unnecessary risks,
carefully planning his tactics, and showing a more marked concern for his
fellow pilots. Luke and Rickenbacker's careers demonstrate how fighter pilot
attitudes exist on a spectrum and can be expressed in distinct ways, although
it is unsurprising that Luke came to a more tragic, violent end.[6]

Competition like Luke's and Rickenbacker's was a common outlet of
aggressiveness. "I had a reasonably competitive attitude and I wanted to
excel in flying school," recalled Major General John Alison, a World War II
fighter ace. "I had a lot of confidence that I would. It may have been misplaced confidence, but I had it. I think for a fighter pilot this is important."
Speaking of his training, he said, "I prided myself that I could outturn anybody in the group. I believed I could. I could take the airplane off and land it
in a shorter distance than anybody in the group."[7]

Some US pilots looked to aviators from other nations, even their adversaries, as exemplars of fighter culture. Gailer held up the memoir of German
fighter ace Adolf Galland, *The First and the Last*, as an inspirational ideal.[8]
Like many US pilots of the 1940s, Galland looked to World War I for inspiration. He described himself as the next incarnation of Richthofen, with his
colleague Werner Mölders as the new Oswald Boelcke. Galland's frequent
verbal sparring with Luftwaffe commander Hermann Göring mirrors the
disdain American fighter pilots had for some commanders. Galland, credited with 104 aerial victories, also emphasized eagerness and aggressiveness:
"Only the spirit of attack borne in a brave heart will bring a success to any
fighter aircraft, no matter how highly developed it may be." He decried
defensive tactics, holding that for the best pilots, "their element is to attack,
to track, to hunt, and to destroy the enemy. Only in this way can the eager
and skillful fighter pilot display his ability to the full." Galland said that any
limits on the individual agency of a fighter pilot would "rob him of his initiative, and you take away from him the best and most valuable qualities he
possesses: aggressive spirit, joy of action, and the passion of the hunter. The

fighter army cannot be manacled."[9] Gailer took these ideas further when asked if ace pilots all have "a killer instinct." Gailer affirmed, "The taste of blood makes it greater."[10]

One of the most celebrated US fighter pilots, and among the clearest examples of their cultural stereotypes, is Brigadier General Chuck Yeager. "You're whipping through a desert canyon at three hundred miles an hour," he said, describing an early training flight. "Your hand on the throttle of a P-39 fighter. . . . The joy of flying—the sense of speed and exhilaration twenty feet above the deck—makes you so damned happy that you want to shout for joy. . . . You feel so lucky, so blessed to be a fighter pilot." He claimed that encountering 150 Luftwaffe fighters was not frightening, but thrilling: "We couldn't believe our luck. . . . We began to dogfight, happy as clams," he said. "I knew the dogfighting was what I was born to do. . . . It's as if you were one with that [P-51] Mustang, an extension of that damned throttle." He continued: "Up there, dogfighting, you connected with yourself. That small, crammed cockpit was exactly where you belonged. . . . When he [the enemy] blew up, it was a pleasing, beautiful sight. There was no joy in killing someone, but real satisfaction when you outflew a guy and destroyed his machine." He concluded, "For me, combat remains the ultimate flying experience."[11]

Colonel David Lee "Tex" Hill, a squadron leader with the Flying Tigers who earned over eighteen victories during World War II, also expressed a longing for combat. "Six or seven combats in one day" against "as many as a hundred [enemy] fighters" was "just a fighter-pilot's dream," he said. Of aerial combat against Japanese fighters, he said, "They began to dogfight with us and there were so many planes in the air that the chance of collision was pretty good. In those early days, it was really beautiful." A desire for combat was essential to Hill: "The real fighter pilots, who are good at anything, will try to think of ways to get there [into combat] instead of ways to not get there." Regarding aces, Hill said, "They are all very aggressive. Usually anything they get into, they go whole hog." Some fighter pilots emphasized the role of luck in earning aerial victories, but Hill insisted that his own kills were due to his personal eagerness and skill.[12]

Colonel James Hagerstrom had made ace in P-40 Warhawks in World War II, but getting recalled to fly F-86 Sabres in the Korean War (where he made ace again) was "the assignment I had spent my life preparing for."[13] The technology was new, but the culture of the knights of the air remained in place, especially the focus on aggressiveness. The 4th Fighter-Interceptor Group (FIG) instructed its pilots, "When in doubt, attack—be a determined, aggressive killer—thats [sic] what you're flying a fighter for." The 51st FIG took a similar approach: "Every man's a Tiger! The aggressive spirit must always be foremost if the pilot and his organization are to enjoy a successful career in the fighter business."[14] Major Frederick "Boots" Blesse certainly pushed that envelope, in one case ignoring that his Sabre was too low on fuel to return to base, and continued fighting MiGs, getting one victory before having to bail out when he ran out of fuel, risking his life and sacrificing an airplane just to down one MiG.[15] Blesse later wrote an influential air tactics manual whose title summarized his attitude: "No Guts, No Glory."

Captain Joe McConnell, the top-scoring US ace in Korea with sixteen aerial victories, expressed a typical eagerness for battle. When engaging a large group of MiGs over the Yalu River, his wingman called out, "My God, there must be thirty of them!" McConnell responded, "Yeah, and we've got 'em all to ourselves." That spirit led him to take risks, including dangerously luring in MiGs, or disobeying orders to return to base when his plane experienced a hydraulics failure. Historian Kenneth Werrell has noted, "In his eagerness for combat and MiG kills, [McConnell] violated policies and certainly put himself and his wingmen in peril."[16]

The first US pilot to achieve ace status in Korea was Colonel James Jabara, who exhibited stereotypical aggressiveness. He defied orders by engaging in combat after one of his fuel tanks failed to jettison, going on to dogfight with a hanging tank and making ace during the battle anyway. He disputed kill claims with his wingman and was known for his eccentricity and discipline issues. His colleagues described him as an "aggressive scrapper" and an "arrogant little bastard." His commander labeled him a "hot shot Charlie type . . . the guy who sang the loudest in the club and made more noise than the other people and dressed on the extreme side for the military."[17]

The clearest example of these pilots' willingness to bend the rules to get victories was their habit of violating Chinese airspace to hunt for MiGs. Fearing escalation and widening of the war, Washington forbade pilots from crossing the Yalu River and flying over China. Many F-86 pilots routinely disobeyed this order, at times under the insistence of their commanding officers. For example, General Frank F. Everest, commanding the Fifth Air Force at the time, recalled, "I told these lads that if they were really on the tail in the killing position they could cross the Yalu to make that kill and they didn't need to make any official report of it. I didn't want to know about it."[18]

Aggressiveness and disdain for regulations extended to life outside the cockpit and continued into the Vietnam War. "Fighter pilots are not happy unless they are stirring the pot," recalled C. R. Anderegg, who flew F-4 Phantoms in over 170 combat missions in Southeast Asia. "Many crews were nonconformist and frequently disregarded regulations about uniforms, flying, and social behavior." The most skilled fighter pilots earned the monikers "good sticks" or "good hands," and they tended to be the students and graduates of the F-4 Fighter Weapons School at Nellis Air Force Base, Nevada. The school had a reputation for dogmatically emphasizing fighter pilot skills and attitudes, with the instructors known for being "overbearing and egocentric." Anderegg wrote of one student's complaint that the instructors "'were just so damn intimidating' with their cocky attitude and seeming indifference to standard grooming practices." Anderegg summarized, "It was clear that the instructors were more concerned with proving that they were better than the students than they were in teaching them how to be weapons officers."[19]

In the years before and during the Vietnam War, F-4 Phantom pilots received little formal air-to-air training. Some pilots took their own initiative to remedy this. Colonel Robin Olds, as a fighter wing commander in Thailand, partnered with a Royal Australian Air Force detachment of F-86 Sabres and had his own pilots "tangle with them almost every day" after returning from their combat missions.[20] Captain John Jumper, stationed at RAF Bentwaters after his combat tours in Vietnam, recalled similar ad hoc mock dogfights between US and British pilots, despite the fact that US Air Forces Europe (USAFE) rules prohibited air-to-air practice. "We had no idea what we were doing," Jumper said. "It was just a free-for all. Sometimes it was so dangerous it wasn't even fun. It was plain stupid."[21] Fighter pilots valued aggressiveness so highly that it blurred the line between fun and stupid.

Individualism

"Single seat, single engine, baby. It's a great motto," said F-16 pilot Lieutenant Colonel Dan Hampton. "In short, rely on yourself, because if you don't do it then it won't get done. This had been preached to us, fed to us, mixed in our drinks, and by now was habit."[22] This preference for solo flying and self-reliance reflected a key component of fighter pilot culture that dated back to World War I and had remained intact, even throughout the years of the Air Force's premier fighter being the two-seat F-4 Phantom.

In World War I, the act of being aloft created a sense of physical, mental, and perhaps spiritual separation from ground soldiers. Encased in an airplane, a pilot could feel more autonomous than an infantryman, even when flying in formation with others. Many early reconnaissance airplanes had a crew of two—a pilot and an observer who controlled the gun.

A French pilot, Roland Garros, became so annoyed at this that he worked with his mechanic, Jules Hue, to mount a machine gun directly in front of the pilot's seat, protecting the propeller with metal deflectors. This single-seat design soon became the preferred aircraft of the fighter pilot, closely identified with the image of the knight of the air, as it represented the "promise of unprecedented aerial autonomy."[23] Oswald Boelcke, the celebrated German ace pilot and tactician, loved the concept as well. "I believe in the saying that 'the strong man is mightiest alone,'" he said. "I have attained my ideal with this single-seater; now I can be pilot, observer and fighter all in one. . . . My little single-seater possesses the advantage of giving me complete independence."[24] American pilots felt the same way, but often assumed this trait was unique to them: "It was fortunate that the Germans were so well trained as formation flyers that they were to follow the leader," Colonel Livingston Irving said. "They weren't individuals like the Americans. I used to lose the leader, the hell with the bastard, go off by ourselves."[25]

The 1918 British tactical manual *Fighting in the Air* agreed. Although group formations and tactics were more commonplace by that time, the manual minimized them, because "fighting in the air . . . even when many machines are involved on each side, tends to resolve itself into a number of more or less independent combats." The manual insisted, "Fighting tactics vary with the type of machine and with the powers and favorite methods of the individual pilots. No hard-and-fast rules can be laid down." Individual intuition was key. "A pilot who has full confidence in his own powers can put his machine in any position suitable to the need of the moment, well knowing that he can regain control whenever he wishes."[26]

"The work of the flier as an individual is more than that of any other," American ace Henry Clay wrote in a letter to his sister in-law. "In other branches one is just a small part of a big machine and the individual does not count for much. But in the Air Service the individual is something. . . . In scout work the individuality of the pilot shows up only in his fighting, that is his job." Expressing to her why he thought their younger brother should become a pilot, he said, "In these fights it is man against man instead of a division of an army against another division. That is why I like the Air Service. The individual counts for something."[27]

Lieutenant Walter L. Avery, an American pilot with two aerial victories, reveled in the solitude of flying in World War I fighters: "Some isolation for the hours altitude!" he wrote. "Nothing but me and the sun and an endless sea of ice! Far from the maddening crowd."[28] His diary repeated this theme often, including copying lines from "The Twelfth Floor" by Mary B. Mullett, with sentiments such as

> Only your call, like the beating of waves, in dim, half forgotten, subterranean caves,
> Comes up to me here.
> Comes up and I hear,
> I look down and listen and watch you go by,
> And am free of you all, alone in my sky![29]

In World War II, air combat tactics had evolved, and most fighter missions involved coordinated formations that required communication and cooperation with other pilots or crews. Yet a fighter pilot could easily feel isolated, encased in the cockpit, alone at the controls of a powerful machine of war. Individualism remained a core, celebrated trait. Gailer asserted, "A guy that goes into the fighter business ought to be a specialist in it because what he does he does by himself."[30]

General Frank Everest, who held a variety of command positions in the Air Force, made a similar point: "A fighter pilot, a single man, with a multimillion dollar vehicle between his legs, has got to exercise judgment, a hell of a lot of it, because there isn't anybody there to tap him on the shoulder and say, 'Son, I think you had better turn right instead of left.'" Everest allegedly argued with General Curtis LeMay, the commander of SAC and later chief of staff of the Air Force, about whether fighter or bomber pilots were superior. Everest challenged LeMay to "come down to Myrtle Beach sometime and stand there and watch young, 22-year-old kids take off with a ring of thunderstorms surrounding them with two over-the-sea refueling contacts to make and the first landing at some airbase in France." He concluded, "One man to do all of the instrument work, all of the refueling. Christ, you have a crew of eight to do the same job! Now tell me which is the better pilot."[31]

In the post–World War II United States, the individualized freedom and the status associated with flying fighters proved a powerful alternative to the increasingly bureaucratized and homogeneous business world. "The reward of the Air Force," said Colonel George Berke, who piloted F-86s and F-4s, "was not a large office and all the bureaucratic stuff, but your own airplane; that's what people want: a plane with your name on it so wherever you go people know who you are!" In Korea, the need for radio silence, the fact that flight formation leaders could rarely see their wingmen, and the frequency with which formations broke apart during battle all contributed to the sense of air combat being an individual role. Colonel Walker "Bud" Mahurin, a quadruple ace in World War II who also earned victory credits in Korea, urged his wingmen to "make any attacks as he saw fit" if separated. He recalled, "A jet-fighter pilot is responsible to himself alone."[32] Mahurin experienced just how far individualism could go on one mission in Korea when he heard a fierce dogfight playing out over the radio. Mahurin made several calls asking for a location so he could help before he finally got an angry response: "To hell with you, Colonel. Find your own damn Migs."[33]

James Salter's first novel, *The Hunters*, is a revealing look into the culture of fighter pilots in the early Cold War. Under his given name, Major James Horowitz was an F-86 pilot in Korea and credited with shooting down a MiG-15. His novel, partly inspired by his experiences, exemplifies typical fighter pilot traits. It depicts their culture as obsessed with killing in air-to-air combat, and that to be a successful ace, pilots must become, as historian Seve Call suggested, "grotesque caricatures of depravity."[34] The individual nature of flying fighters was important to Salter: "You lived and died alone, especially in fighters," he wrote. "You slipped into the hollow cockpit and strapped and plugged yourself into the machine. The canopy ground shut and sealed you off. . . . You were as isolated as a deep-sea diver, only you went up, into nothing, instead of down." Salter dismissed the idea that formation flying mitigated this isolation: "They [wingmen] flew with you in heraldic patterns and fought alongside you, sometimes skillfully, always at least two ships together, but they were really of no help. You were alone. At the end, there was no one you could touch."[35]

Call has suggested that *The Hunters* was likely meant as a critical rebuke of fighter pilot culture—exposing its ugliness. Indeed, when Twentieth Century-Fox began producing a film adaptation, they radically changed the story, presenting the lead character as a hero who learns the value of teamwork and finds redemption in working together with his fellow pilots. The Air Force objected to the changes, arguing that the movie studio had undermined "what was fundamentally an honest fictional study of jet aces and what made them effective 'Hunters' in the Korean War." Call implied that the Air Force, even at the height of the bomber-dominant years of the early Cold War, was so enamored of fighter pilot culture that it failed to recognize when that culture was being exaggerated for the purposes of critique. "To characterize as 'fundamentally honest' a novel portraying successful fighters as twisted and unscrupulous, while everyone who possesses any normalcy and decency fails . . . and either dies or goes home in disgust indicates the air force either did not understand the deeper meanings or did not find them repulsive," said Call. "It objected to excessive drinking and adultery but accepted promoting those who obtained glory by getting their leaders killed."[36]

The celebration of individualism often led to frustration with leadership and regulations. One popular fighter pilot song, "Air Force Lament," sung to the tune of "Battle Hymn of the Republic," began during World War II, criticizing rules placed on fighter pilots from commanders. As the song was passed down over the years, more verses were added, combining a sense of loss of individualism with a powerful nostalgia for the past. The song opens with "My eyes have seen the days of men who ruled the fighting sky / with hearts they laughed at death, who lived for nothing but to fly. / But now those hearts are grounded and those days are long gone by / the Force is shot to hell!" The song complains that "now we're closely supervised," longing for "the days when men were strong," and when "we were cocky, bold, and happy." In air-to-air combat over Korea, the song says, "The pilots then were fearless men and not afraid to die / but now the regs are written, you can kiss your wings goodbye." The conclusion is the hearty chorus ending with "Let us fly like hell!"[37]

During the Vietnam War, the Air Force's front-line fighter was the two-seat F-4 Phantom II. Historian and pilot Steven Fino observed it was "anathema to the myth of the fighter pilot," in part because having two crew members threatened a pilot's sense of individuality. As the pilots of single-seat F-105 Thunderchiefs sang in their mocking song "F-4 Serenade," "I'd rather be a pimple on a syphilitic whore, than a backseat driver on an old F-4."[38]

Until 1969, the Air Force required that Phantom backseaters be rated pilots. Everest, then the commander of the first F-4 training unit, noted "it was demoralizing" for those pilots, who wanted to fly the plane. Lieutenant Howard Hill, disappointed by his backseat assignment, recalled how GIBs tried to hold on to the typical "fighter pilot's bravado and the swagger" as much as possible and tried to work their way into a pilot slot. As for those front seaters, many did adapt and learned to work well with their GIBs, but many insisted they "didn't need anybody back there." Some pilots told their backseaters, "Shut up, go cold mike, and when I need you I'll tell you." F-4 pilot General Larry Welch argued that the presence of the GIB threatened a pilot's "manhood."[39] This might explain the popular song "Fighter Pilot's Lament," which, to the tune of "She'll Be Coming Round the Mountain," mocks non-pilot roles: "Oh, there are no fighter pilots down in hell, / Oh, there are no fighter pilots down in hell, / Oh, that place is full of queers, navigators, bombardiers, / But there are no fighter pilots down in hell."[40]

Not all pilots felt this way. Some welcomed the backseater as an enhancement, especially once the Air Force filled backseats with specialist WSOs. "Rather than compete for control of the plane and lobby for an upgrade to the front seat," recalled Major Ed Rasimus, an F-105 driver who transitioned to Phantoms, "the WSO formed a team with the pilot, supporting rather than challenging." He continued: "Two heads, two sets of eyes, and two pairs of hands could increase the effectiveness of the total weapons system. It was a good solution. Not perfect, but much better than before."[41] Some front seaters were still skeptical but could be swayed to appreciate their partners. Joseph Tuso, an F-4 navigator, explained, "Many fighter pilots prefer to fly alone in a single-seat aircraft; others don't mind flying with another pilot; but some are hesitant about flying with a navigator, especially in combat." Tuso recalled flying with one fighter pilot on a dangerous mission. After they landed safely, Tuso recalled the pilot telling him, "'What had me worried was flying a mission like that with a *navigator* in my backseat!' He shook my [Tuso's] hand, winked, and said, 'I'm damned glad you were there.'"[42]

Some pilots accepted the idea of teamwork and became close with their backseaters, but the Air Force's two-seat fighter era was an anomaly. Many fighter pilots tried to hold on to a sense of individualism, and even when the next generation of fighters, the F-15 and F-16, returned to a single seat, the culture of fighter pilots tended to remain hostile to former GIBs, even if they had risen to command positions. F-16 pilot Dan Hampton explained: "I was dumbfounded that the military could find a guy to ride along in the back of a fighter with absolutely no control over his destiny." When an instructor, a backseat EWO, admonished Hampton about flying outside the EWO's line of sight, Hampton shot back, "'You're not a pilot so why does it matter if you see me or not? . . . I mean, aren't you busy doing something in the backseat?' Like winding the clock? I didn't say that but I was thinking it."[43]

Heroes

Whether through references to knights, or mythological heroes, or simply connecting oneself to earlier generations of revered aces, fighter pilots tended to talk of themselves in heroic terms. For example, Major General William "Billy" Mitchell, often called the father of the Air Force, claimed that a fighter pilot must be "an individual who possessed the highest qualities of courage, judgment, intelligence, and endurance known to the human race." He clarified: "Horatius at the bridge and Leonidas at Thermopylae had no greater odds against them than these aviators." Successful fighter pilots required "the heart of a lion, the wisdom of a serpent, and the speed of thought of Mercury. . . . [They are] imbued with the spirit of 'do or die.'" Those who self-selected for pursuit flying "were those in whom the instincts of combativeness and daring bequeathed by warrior and pioneering ancestors showed in undiminished force."[44]

Gailer took his arguments further into mythological territory, shifting the analogy away from European knights and toward uniquely American mythological heroes: "I think bomber pilots, from my experience with them, kind of look up to the fighter pilot. They like him. He is kind of like the cowboy. He is manifest destiny. He is the pony rider going across the country delivering the mail. He is that kind of a guy."[45]

The association of fighter pilots with knights was common throughout World War I when it originated but continued into the jet era. Recruiting advertisements made frequent use of such imagery, such as a 1954 Air Force ad showing a jet fighter pilot holding up his goggles in the same position as a medieval knight holding up his visor. Below the title "America's Knights of the Sky" ran the poem: "The Spartan Band that held the pass, / The Knights of Arthur's train / The Light Brigade that charged the guns, / Across the battle plain / Can claim no greater glory than / the dedicated few, / Who wear the Wings of Silver . . . / on a field of Air Force Blue."[46]

Connections to heroism were not always mythological. Connecting oneself to the original World War I generation of fighter pilots was a form a heroic imagery. This attitude was so common among some fighter pilots that others ridiculed them for it. When Olds was working at the Pentagon in the early 1960s, his boss was frustrated at the number of fighter-based projects Olds submitted. The bomber general told Olds, "You're not going to put on your leather jacket, your scarf, your helmet and goggles and go out and do battle with the Red Baron."[47] Within a few years, Olds was in an F-4 shooting down MiGs and dreaming of Snoopy.

Technology

Pilots are inherently tied to the technology of the airplane. But fighter pilot culture is tied specifically to technologies that enhance the role of air-to-air combat. That culture emphasizes agility and maneuverability over other characteristics such as range or payload. Speed plays a changing role, as speed and acceleration were valuable for dogfighting in the years of both World Wars, but moving into the supersonic era, fighter pilots de-emphasized high speeds as interfering with their ability to maneuver.

In World War I, pilot preferences were fickle, changing often owing to the rapid pace of development. New designs could render the current ones obsolete within six months, and, as Hamilton-Patterson observed, "WWI pilots often found a new type [of aircraft] wonderful and exhilarating to fly, usually because it was so much better than the machine they were used to." Maneuverability and responsiveness were especially prized, which is why aces such as Rickenbacker, Billy Bishop, Albert Ball, and Charles Nungesser all preferred French-built Nieuports.[48]

Clendenin made a similar argument for the Nieuport-28 in contrast to the SPAD fighters (also French built), "for its ability to maneuver quickly enabled us to 'carry on' with the type of fighting we had developed. Our style was the so-called 'dog-fight,' in which we stayed until the fight was over." He continued, "We never favored the game of 'shoot and dive for home,' the style so popular among the French Spad pilots."[49] Irving praised the maneuverability of specific planes: "The British SE5 was a peach of an airplane. . . . The Soph [Sopwith] Camel was what the British termed as 'a Split-[S]-ing Fool' [referring to the "split-S" maneuver in which an aircraft flips, dives, and reverses direction quickly], it would turn on a dime."[50]

Walter Avery also showed a fascination with aircraft that were optimized for air-to-air combat. He was excited to have access to Nieuports and SPADs, although after getting some flying experience by the summer of 1918, he preferred the latter and protested against his commanders when he was sent out in Nieuports.[51] Which plane each pilot preferred is less important than the fact that pilots had strong emotional ties to specific planes—and that their choices were based on which one they thought was better at air combat.

One thing was certain: fighter pilots did not want to be caught dead in bomber aircraft. Alison, speaking of the World War II years, said, "My heart would have been broken if I had been put in bombers." Part of this preference was his sense of pride. He admitted that "I would have hated to be a bomber pilot because I would have hated to have my co-pilot see me tremble."[52]

Contributing to these technological preferences was an insistence that man was more important than machine. For some pilots, if the aircraft were made too complex, then it would take something away from the pilot and somehow make flying the aircraft less pure. Fighter pilots "don't need all that sophisticated an airplane," said Gailer. "I think we try to make the state of the art much too complicated, and war just is not all that complicated." Gailer expanded that idea: "It has got to be simple and easy to use. We have lost the simplistic approach, which used to be one of the great strengths of this society. Good, simple, effective equipment and great pride in it, and he [the pilot] will do the rest."[53] This argument ignores that the fighter planes of the previous wars were always complicated, state-of-the-art machines for their time. Gailer's nostalgia for an idealized past America that had been built on "simple" equipment was a common theme among some fighter pilots, especially after the Vietnam War. Perhaps the frustrations of that conflict prompted a rosy view of the past.

Fighter pilots tended to grow attached to their planes, praising those with good air combat characteristics and deriding those that lacked them. For example, Colonel Clarence "Lucky" Lester, a Tuskegee Airman with three aerial victories, said "P-39s were dogs if I ever saw one, rickety old things, just lousy airplanes. . . . It was lousy for air-to-air combat but pretty good for ground support." The P-38 Lightning was slightly more liked. Fighter pilot Harold Rosser noted, "It was a 'Hollywood' plane . . . beautiful in flight but fragile in combat, like the beauty who had been made uncomfortable by a pea under her mattress."[54] Robin Olds, who became an ace in Lightnings, noted, "I loved the P-38 but I got those kills in spite of the airplane, not because of it."[55]

The fighter of choice for most US fighter pilots during World War II was the P-51 Mustang. When converting to it, Olds said, "I was falling in love all over again with a new girl." Olds, like many fighter pilots, coded their relationship with their airplane through a gendered lens, with romantic or even sexual overtones. He recalled the first time he started the engine: "Unlike the P-38, which seemed a quiet lady by comparison, the Mustang began with a snarling earnestness, vibrating through my body and telling me, 'I'm ready! You're ready! Let's go!'"[56] Tuskegee Airman Captain Louis Purnell agreed about the Mustang: "If that plane had been a girl, I'd have married it right on the spot. Damn right! It was like dancing with a good partner," he said. "Speed, maneuverability, climb rate, reliability? We had it in the P-51. Anyone who has flown a P-51 will agree with me. And those who haven't, wish they had."[57] Lieutenant Colonel John Dick Jr., when interviewing Gailer, suggested that one key element of a good pilot was "knowing your airplane and putting it on like a coat—" Gailer interrupted: "Or a glove." He concluded, "They [aircraft] are all different, just like women, just as ornery."[58]

F-86 Sabre pilots in Korea had similar experiences; Major Douglas Evans explained it as the "very personal relationship each fighter pilot must establish alone with a single-seater." Fighter pilots longed to get assigned to an F-86 unit. Evans noted it was "the hottest assignment in Korea," which gave those pilots superiority over "jealous prop and straight-wing pilots." When he went to Japan, he noted that "everybody just gaped in awe at us. After all we were the only 86 Sabre outfit in the war, the big MiG hunters, and considered very hot stuff wherever we went—especially heading back for combat."[59] Colonel Frank Tomlinson noted the same thing: "Everybody that wanted to fly a fighter wanted to fly the hottest, fastest, best thing, and that was the F-86 at that time." As for the F-84 and F-80 pilots doing ground-attack missions, "they were trash haulers, you know, I mean we were the elite. We were the crème de la crème."[60]

The two-seat fighter era of the Vietnam War years did not fundamentally alter the relationship between pilot and plane. Olds argued that the nature of dogfighting heightened the connection between man and machine, even in the two-seat F-4 Phantom. Speaking of the F-4, he said,

When the tracers from an enemy's guns flick past your canopy and your bird shudders as others strike home; when you twist and turn in mortal combat, outnumbered and far from help; when you strike with savage, thunderous power and wheel in white-hot anger toward another foe; when your bird responds to your impossible demands, slamming you into near unconsciousness with crushing g-force, leaping like a cat when you unleash the full energy of 40,000 pounds of thrust, beating the earth below with one rolling thunderclap as you exceed the speed of sound, hurling iron bolts of destruction with deadly accuracy, and then quietly, serenely lifts you home, physically battered, emotionally spent, and numb with weariness, then that bond is as solid and as personal as any relationship you will ever experience.[61]

He also noted the F-4's limitations. "As marvelous as our Phantoms were in air-to-air combat, they were no match for the MiGs," he said. "Our first hard turn put us at the speed where the MiG-17, as old as it was, was at its best. He could intercept and close with us." The MiG-17's "wing loading was so light that his turn capability was fantastic. There was no way to turn an F-4 with a MiG-17 and no way to battle with it in a classic World War II dogfight. I liked to think that if I'd been a North Vietnamese pilot, I would have been an ace ten times over."[62]

Olds, in reflecting on what he looked for when assigning new pilots, summarized the deep connection pilots had with their aircraft. "A pilot is a man in love, a man whose emotional ties with a piece of machinery run deep," he said. "Man merges with machine; he doesn't simply use it. You strap the machine to your butt, become one with it. Hydraulic fluid is your blood; titanium, steel, and aluminum, your bones; electrical currents, your nerves; the instruments, an extension of your senses; fuel, the food; engine, the power; the control surfaces, the muscle." The end result of this "love affair" for Olds was a transfiguration: "You are something more than earthbound man. You are augmented and expanded by the miracle of the machine. You are tied to it physically and you are a part of it emotionally. Together you conquer the bonds of earth."[63]

Community

"Fighter pilots are secretive and superstitious creatures. We don't like outsiders digging into our business," said Robert Burgon. "The process of being allowed entrance into our exclusive club is required to get everyone on the same page mentally and emotionally." That process consisted mostly of the rituals, songs, and games of the fighter pilot community. Most of these traditions had "the intent of fostering brotherhood."[64] Fighter pilots make up a tight-knight community that often sees itself as under threat from outsiders and is carefully guarded.

This defensiveness became more pronounced in the interwar years as bomber advocates gained influence and dominance in the Army Air Corps and into World War II with the Army Air Forces. For fighter pilots like Gailer, maintaining the fighter subculture was important in creating aces: "The peer group bit is important in the fighter business. He wants to do better because he knows everybody else knows how good he is or how bad he is or where his weaknesses are." Gailer claimed that the fighter community "is not supported from on high. . . . You are constantly being pushed aside. Instead of the Air Force being proud of its glamour boys . . . they are not. And they know it all the way down." The community relied on itself to create an identity for what its members felt was a marginalized subculture: "A guy has to feel like he is a part of an outfit. Most fighter pilots do. Most fighter squadrons . . . are a close-knit group, very close-knit. . . . It's not really encouraged, however, from the higher-ups." For many fighter pilots, their sense of persecution and their aggressiveness were expressions of insecurity. Gailer said that many a pilot was "trying to prove something, whether it is to himself or to his peers. . . . Maybe he doesn't even know what it is, but whatever it is he has to have that ambition and aggressiveness and recklessness to a degree."[65]

However, inside the fighter community bubble, close bonds could form. Wingmen grew attached to one another, and it was not uncommon to see fighter pilots share a loving, tear-soaked embrace. P-51 pilot Captain Robert Powell recalled, "There was brotherly love. We knew our lives depended on each other. Pilots developed some fantastic camaraderie."[66] This continued into the jet era. F-4 Phantom pilot Captain J. W. Smith, after switching to fighters from previously flying C-130s, reveled in both the sense of freedom and belonging. His mother asked him, "Tell me, J.W., what's it like being in one of them thar fighter squadrons?" He replied, "Well, momma, it's like bein' paid $30,000 a year to be a Hell's Angel." Flying jet fighters certainly bore some similarity to cruising on motorcycles, but the infamous club was known for its sense of belonging, ritual, and wild, even antisocial antics. Anderegg added, "The supreme lesson from combat was that the only people one could trust were the other members of the flight and squadron peers."[67]

Being a part of that community was a prize to be held. Rasimus emphasized the importance of maintaining status within the fighter community, which could be lost at any time. Quitting or failing to step up to one's duty brought dishonor from one's peers that was unfathomable in the crucible of wartime. As historian John D. Sherwood summarized, "However sophomoric this may sound to the uninitiated, Rasimus and others cherished their membership in the elite brotherhood of fighter pilots more than even their marriages. . . . They would sacrifice just about everything, including their lives, to retain this status."[68]

As the community took shape in World War I, many pursuit pilots were frustrated at taking orders from leaders who were not experienced in air combat. Those with air-to-air credentials earned loyalty or even reverence. Kenneth W. Clendenin of the US 14th Aero Squadron described his squadron leader, Major Geoffrey H. Bonnell, as "a real flying man" who knew "the flying game."[69] Leaders who lacked fighter pilot experience or knowledge could be ridiculed, have their masculinity questioned, or be outright disobeyed. Author William E. Barrett's history of the 90th Aero Squadron recounted how the pilots disapproved of replacing their Sopwith aircraft with the SPAD fighter, saying the decision was made by "some diplomat in a brass hat [who] spoke softly."[70] Many preferred that their commanders be proven fighter pilots. Gailer noted that a fighter pilot was unwilling to show deference to others unless "they can fly his ass off." Otherwise, he said, "How does he know what they ought to be able to do? He has never been in the airplane. It's wrong, basically wrong." For Gailer and some other fighter pilots, higher rank was inherently poisonous: "The wing commanders are big stuff guys. They . . . have begun to believe their own reviews. That's the problem with senior rank. . . . It's a very common disease."[71]

Many fighter pilots wanted to fly in agile acrobatic maneuvers in the style of the knights of the air, but this often put them at odds with commanders who discouraged the practice. Alison recalled the training he had in 1937: "Penalties were pretty severe if you were caught doing acrobatics in the airplane. So I practiced my acrobatics at night. Then I wouldn't get caught."[72] From pilots crossing the Yalu in the Korean War to flying low-altitude, high-speed "bubble checks" over friendly radar sites, fighter pilots in the jet era consistently flew carefully when protecting each other in combat, but looked for opportunities to showboat, to the chagrin of leaders trying to enforce safety rules. As Anderegg described it, "a contradiction existed in the fighter force [of the 1970s]. Within fighter culture there was unquestioning loyalty to one's mates that demanded total discipline in the air. But there was also a common disregard, even disrespect, for authority above the squadron level."[73]

Masculinity

Masculinity was intertwined with all five of these defining elements. Pilots coded the expressions of these characteristics as masculine, and failing to adhere to them could cause peers to question the transgressor's masculinity, or mock him for being too feminine. Whether owing to the stresses of a combat environment, or the pressure of being surrounded by large groups of men who encouraged rowdiness, many performative displays of manhood became what Robertson called "hypermasculinity."[74] This emphasis on masculinity was at least in part because in the United States, women were banned from military flying for much of the twentieth century. No American women flew military aircraft in World War I. In World War II, the US Army and Navy allowed women pilots in certain limited roles: primarily ferrying newly constructed aircraft but also towing gunnery targets and instructing male pilots. After that war, women could not fly for the military until the Navy allowed women pilots in 1973, followed by the Army later that year. The Air Force followed with a test program for women pilots that began in 1976. None of the US services allowed women to fly in combat until 1993.[75]

The association of combat aviation with hypermasculinity began in World War I, with the association of ace pilots with stereotypically masculine qualities and associations with sex. For example, as author William E. Barrett described, "Prospective Aces became bulky across the chest and shoulders, brown in the face and tough—very tough."[76] Many pilots developed superstitions and attached good luck charms to their aircraft or bodies. One of the most common was women's lingerie—which pilots strapped to their plane or stretched over their head.[77] In linking his fighter pilot identity to hypermasculinity, Major General Frank O'Driscoll Hunter went to absurdist lengths later in his life, when the entryway to his home was lined with mementos of his flying career on one side, and on the other, mementos of women he had slept with.[78] The coding of aircraft as feminine and the sexual imagery often used to describe flying them was common. Many pilots used the sobriquet "weak sisters" to insult and question the masculinity of pilots who were not sufficiently eager for combat or otherwise failed to measure up to fighter pilot stereotypes.[79]

F-86 pilots in the Korean War often linked aggressiveness to masculinity and used sexualized language to describe combat.[80] Outside the cockpit, Sabre pilots were expected to be sexually outgoing. "Chasing women," said Berke, "was one of the things you did as a fighter pilot—it was part of the caché [sic] and mark of things." The *Air Force Times* went as far as to outline the type of woman that pilots were attracted to. "Brunettes with light blue eyes and healthy tans have a slight edge, but physical characteristics are not so important to him as, first, a sense of humor, and second, the ability to 'mix' well." The article continued, "One characteristic of the pilot of yesteryear he will retain—he's something special. Something unique—and he wants his date to match him. He wants her to have, for him, something no one else has or could have. . . . That's not too much to expect for a young man with worlds to conquer, is it?"[81]

Sexually charged language was common in Vietnam as well. Fighter pilot Mel Porter wrote a "Credo" in which each stanza juxtaposes concepts of pilots "touch[ing] the face of God," or pondering deep philosophical questions or the inherent beauty of the sky, with subsequent references of "pulling girls' pants down." The poem ends, "If there is one thing to remember, it will be that sweet memory that transcends them all, the little boy, the go-to-heller, the philosopher, the realist; it will be the ineffably beautiful picture of a girl . . . with her pants down."[82] F-105 and F-4 pilot Ed Rasimus noted of combat in the Vietnam War, "Fighter pilots in Thailand built a fantasized reality around the machismo of it." Aircraft were sexualized, but in a way that related to their status among pilots. Rasimus spoke of his training flights: "Flying a T-37 was like masturbating. It was fun while you were doing it, but afterward you were slightly ashamed." He recalled that in his graduating class, nine pilots got slots in the single-seat F-105, while 140 got backseater assignments in F-4s: "Nine guys got laid by a queen of the prom," Rasimus said, "and 140 got sloppy seconds with a fat, smoky, double-breasted ex-Navy airplane that didn't even have a gun."[83]

Fighter pilot culture and its elements had been firmly established early on and passed down through generations. By the time of the Vietnam War, the fighter community had generated an ingrained set of values and a select group of heroes that embodied them. Although not all fighter pilots exemplified all these elements, many did, and some of those began to be increasingly frustrated with the direction that fighter aircraft development had been taking throughout the Cold War. By 1964, they started doing something about it.

CHAPTER 3

What We Mean When We Say "Fighter"

> I had felt for years we went the wrong direction in the Air Force when we decided guns no longer were necessary. . . . It was a disease.
>
> —Major General Frederick "Boots" Blesse, *Check Six: A Fighter Pilot Looks Back*

As America sank deeper into conflict in Vietnam, a cultural shift began in the Air Force. Fighter pilots, previously viewing themselves as marginalized within the service, gained more leadership positions and a louder voice. The "space race" with the Soviet Union created leverage to push the boundaries of state-of-the-art technology, and since many test pilots were former fighter pilots, they were able to advocate more strongly for an emphasis on traditional fighter roles in the design of new aircraft. More so, the perception of failure in Vietnam, particularly in air-to-air combat, gave fighter pilots space to push the knights of the air mythos into the mainstream discussion of Air Force doctrine, force structure, and technological planning.

Throughout this period, a small, tight-knight community of fighter advocates gained influence on the future direction of the Air Force. One major result was the F-15 Eagle fighter, which itself was the result of a long and tumultuous development process in which fighter advocates fought not only against the Air Force establishment, but among themselves, while the more extreme among them pushed for a plane that would be the ultimate expression of their knights of the air culture.

White Scarf Stuff

"No event since Pearl Harbor had such a profound effect on our country and our industry," said Neil Armstrong of the 1957 launch of the Soviet *Sputnik* satellite.[1] According to Navy test pilot Lieutenant Charles "Chuck" E. Myers Jr., after *Sputnik*, neither the Air Force nor the Navy was interested in manned aircraft at all, especially tactical ones.[2] This is an overstatement. Both services had large inventories of piloted craft and were in the process of acquiring a substantial number of new F-4 Phantoms throughout the second half of the 1950s. But Myers was not alone. In 1955, a group of seventeen test aviators created the Society of Experimental Test Pilots (SETP), "dedicated to assist in the development of superior aircraft."[3] After becoming president of this organization, Myers went to San Diego, California, in 1960 to speak at a symposium held by the Institute of Aeronautical Science. Myers had flown most of the United States' fighter and attack aircraft and thought they were more capable than the military realized. For example, he insisted that the F-106 Delta Dart was a much better fighter than the newer F-4 but had not been properly exploited. But, he recalled, "people weren't really much interested in that in 1960."[4]

Myers took a position at Lockheed, selling F-104 Starfighters to the Air Force. When he encountered a lack of interest from his potential customers, Myers was convinced that the Air Force (and the Navy's aviation element) had given up on the concept of air-to-air combat, which he identified with the romanticized image of World War I pilots. "People had forgotten about the mission of air fighting," he argued. "That was a thing of the past; it was 'white scarf' stuff. It was fun to sit around barrooms and talk about it with the few guys who had done it. But the DOD [Department of Defense] experts and whiz kids were convinced it had never really contributed to the outcome of any military activity. . . . A number of generals/admirals felt the same way." He took issue with the aircraft themselves: "If you're going to sell a fighter airplane, first of all people have to understand what you mean when you say 'fighter.' . . . The air-to-air portion of a limited war might be important." Although at that time the US was shifting toward President John F. Kennedy's concept of "flexible response," which called for a wider variety of aircraft types and missions, Myers thought that discussion of air-to-air roles "was only token."[5]

The problem, Myers thought, was that the definition of the term "fighter" had changed. For him, a true "fighter" should excel at the "white scarf stuff": air-to-air dogfighting at close range. In the Cold War context, air superiority came to mean, for the most part, interception of large, non-maneuverable enemy bombers: a role requiring a high top speed and launching guided missiles—not dogfighting. Air superiority, according to Air Force doctrine, would not be achieved through air-to-air attrition but by destroying enemy planes and bases on the ground. A new fighter plane was unnecessary, according to the massive 1963 study, Project Forecast. Dogfighting was a relic of a bygone era.[6]

Myers—along with a large segment of the fighter pilot community—rejected these doctrines and began advocating for a redefinition of the fighter role to emphasize dogfighting. He had to do more than just speak romantically about the glory days of gentlemanly duels in the air with scarves flapping in the breeze; he needed evidence. He traveled across the United States and Europe, meeting with pilots and engineers and with a wide variety of military, government, and industry leaders. Myers interviewed pilots about fighter combat and the capabilities of new weapons such as the F-4 Phantom and the AIM-7 Sparrow radar-guided missile. Other meetings were about advocating his position, which met significant resistance. The Air Force and Navy had just committed to a shift away from gun-based air combat. Both services were buying large numbers of F-4s, a multi-role interceptor that could excel at ground attack yet carried no gun. Myers pushed ahead anyway. By his own recollection, he was so adamant that he was nearly thrown out of the offices of several generals. For Myers, this was a holy cause. He recalled, "The whole 'free' world had to be re-educated about the possibilities of air-to-air combat."[7]

In 1964 he compiled his efforts into a briefing: "The Requirement for an Air Superiority Fighter in Limited War," which he presented to approximately five hundred civilians, military officers, Defense Department personnel, and members of Congress. His main argument was that interceptors could not handle dogfights and should not even be called fighters to begin with. He used an analogy to make this clear: "Two adversaries in a telephone booth, one has a rifle and the other a hand gun. It illustrates the dilemma of the all-weather interceptor pilot with his long-range weapon engaged in close combat against a fighter equipped with a cannon." He continued: "There were only two fighter airplanes in the United States inventory. One was the Navy's F-8 and the other the Air Force's F-104. In the all-weather interceptor category we had F-101's, F-102's, F-106's, F-4B's and F-4C's." He concluded, "DOD was saying, '[the F-4 is] the greatest fighter in the world.' I was saying, 'It's not a fighter at all; it's an all-weather interceptor and there's a hell of a difference.'"[8] His briefing included a poster that included a cartoon of the phone booth analogy, as well as images of the *Peanuts* comic strip character Snoopy as the "World War I Flying Ace" engaged in an aerial duel against the Red Baron.[9]

One area where Myers struggled was in being able to define specific performance parameters that he desired. At the time, the DOD viewed top speed and altitude as the most important metrics. Myers argued that "these considerations . . . have of course little to do with air warfare. . . . 'Mach 2' has no relevance to air combat." Instead, Myers wanted "not speed. We *should* be asking for *quickness* and *agility*. We want to be able to accelerate rapidly, and maneuver and have good flying qualities."[10] Myers's problem was that "agility" was too abstract of a concept, not a measurable metric. Unknown to him, this problem was in the process of being solved elsewhere.

Others within the Air Force agreed with Myers. One of the most prominent was Lieutenant General Arthur C. Agan, who spent World War II as a tactical operations chief, fighter group commander, and P-38 Lightning pilot. Despite being shot down and held prisoner, Agan thought that "shooting from a fighter is the greatest sport" and that maneuverable fighters had been the key to the success of World War II bombing campaigns. He shared Myers's view that the Air Force had corrupted the meaning of the word "fighter." "We *didn't* have fighters in development," he later recalled of the years leading to the Vietnam War. "So we showed up without any fighter aircraft under development."[11] In addition to Myers and Agan, another former fighter pilot, a major at the time, was working elsewhere on a new way of thinking about fighter combat. His name was John Boyd.

John Boyd

John Boyd is one of the more controversial figures in the history of the US Air Force. Historian Grant Hammond called him "legendary," "a military genius," a "prophet," and "loved by many . . . for his character and integrity."[12] Novelist Robert Coram's best-selling biography claims that Boyd was "the best fighter pilot in the U.S. Air Force," "the most influential military thinker since Sun Tzu," and likens him to the biblical figure of Moses.[13] On the other hand, Boyd was hated by others, including former fighter pilot and CSAF General Merrill McPeak, who said, "Boyd is highly overrated. . . . In many respects he was a failed officer and even a failed human being."[14] General Wilbur Creech, former commander of TAC, called Boyd "a 24-carat PAIN IN THE ASS!"[15]

Regardless of what one thinks of him, Boyd is important, if for no other reasons than his advocacy for fighter aircraft and his concept of "energy maneuverability" as a quantifiable way to aid in the evaluation and design of fighters. He played an important role in the F-15 development process, and a key role in designing the F-16 Fighting Falcon. Later he and his associates became activists pushing for a different approach to weapons procurement. Overriding all these accomplishments was Boyd's personality. He presented himself (and his followers presented him) as the exemplar of the ideal fighter pilot: all the elements of the knights of the air culture taken to extremes. Whether or not he was the "best fighter pilot" is debatable, but in many ways he was the ultimate expression of fighter pilot culture stereotypes.

Boyd expressed the typical fighter pilot individualism and denigration of other flying roles. "You know, you get in there and the whole load is on you alone—'Can you or can you not do it?' I was convinced I could do it, and it triggered a lot of excitement within me," he said. "Bomber pilots are a bunch of truck drivers or Greyhound bus drivers," he added. "I did not want to . . . have a bunch of crowded buses and people continually telling me what to do. . . . There was a kind of esprit, some freedom about being a fighter pilot."[16]

Fiercely competitive and individualistic, Boyd often clashed with his superiors and enjoyed bragging about it. For example, after enlisting in the Army in April 1945, Boyd spent a few months as a structural engineer, then was stationed in Japan from January through October of 1946, serving as the athletic instructor for the 8th Fighter Squadron under the 49th Fighter Group.[17] During this time, Boyd claimed to have gotten so frustrated at having to sleep in tents while the officers slept in quarters that he cannibalized two US Army hangars and burned them for warmth. He claimed to have been threatened with a court-martial but argued his way out of this by accusing the officers of not sufficiently caring for the troops under their command.[18] No official records of this incident have been found—which does not necessarily mean it is false. But it was part of a pattern. Boyd wanted to be seen as a rebel who was more clever than his superiors.

In his early flight training, Boyd complained of having to practice "stupid gliding turns." Bored, he allegedly found a copy of an air combat textbook and taught himself how to do Immelmann turns. He claimed that his instructors were impressed but his training was holding him back, and that even though he refused to learn some of the more basic maneuvers, fighter tactics came to him intuitively.[19] This was all part of the persona Boyd created for himself, forming a pattern repeated for most of his life—that he was a natural combat pilot whose superior abilities continually shocked those around him.

In the stories Boyd continued to tell about himself, he displayed stereo-typical fighter pilot confidence spilling into arrogance. He depicted himself as the smartest person in the room—especially if there were others present that were "supposed" to be smarter, such as scientists, academics, or engineers. Allegedly he shocked his superiors with his skills and claimed to defeat any of his instructors in simulated combat, forcing them to recognize his greatness. He insisted that the extent of his intelligence, prowess, and flying skills was beyond belief. Certainly, some people were impressed. Many of his colleagues began speaking of him in the same hallowed ways, but others found Boyd's braggadocio obnoxious.

In 1953, while stationed at Suwon Air Base in Korea with the 25th Fighter-Interceptor Squadron under the 51st FIG, Boyd finally saw real combat. From April through July he flew almost forty-four combat hours during twenty-nine missions in F-86 Sabres and engaged in aerial combat. Perhaps his largest battle involved him flying wing for RAF exchange pilot Squadron Leader Jock Maitland. They crossed the Yalu and encountered approximately fourteen MiGs, but Maitland experienced an electrical failure, and the formation scored no victories. Boyd found the experience thrilling and later recalled the event with hand gestures and sound effects. "Jesus Christ," he said, "I really like this stuff. If I could only get five on a mission (ping! ping! ping! ping! ping!)." But he did not get even one. Boyd never shot down a MiG, but he did receive credit for damaging one on June 30, 1953.[20]

In 1954, after the war ended, Boyd was transferred to Nellis Air Force Base in Nevada. After refusing an assignment on a maintenance squadron, he began working as an instructor at the Fighter Weapons School (FWS), staying in that role until mid-1960. Holding to his notion of true fighter pilots, Boyd insisted that his students must be treated as individuals, with their training experiences matched to their personality. Perhaps ironically, when Boyd trained students who displayed a cockiness much like his own, his competitive drive kicked in. He targeted those students, going out of his way to show them how much better he was at combat. Using gestures and sound effects when telling the story years later, he recalled, "as soon as I would spot him [a cocky student], I would cut his balls off in 10 seconds, and I would do it (bing!bing!bing!bing!bing!) five in a row, then the guys would be ready to learn."[21]

Aggressiveness, independence, and individual initiative were the key traits Boyd looked for in student pilots. For Boyd, tactics and flying ability were details that could be taught, while the true determinant of victory was attitude and lust for battle. The best pilots "reeked with the essence of flying. They knew when to move, how to move, they were very confident, very

outgoing and very aggressive," he said. "Even though other guys could perform the maneuvers, they would do it in a passive fashion, which meant the
end result was not too good." He insisted a fighter pilot "has to have—well,
blood in his eyes. So much of it is attitude. . . . He doesn't necessarily have
to be a real good pilot initially, you can teach him to be." When asked how
to identify potential aces, Boyd said, "They are killers, and they love it. . . .
Guys who like war."[22]

Boyd strongly preferred air-to-air fighting. With ground attack, he said,
"I just do not feel that I am in control of the situation. . . . In the air, I can
kind of mark the cards. . . . You are in direct competition with the other guy,
and you know when you are better than he is. But with air-to-ground, some
guy out there is pumping something at me and I don't even know if he is near
me." It all came down to a sense of individuals in aggressive competition:
"I mean if you think like an air-to-air pilot; who is the best man?—The fighter
pilot knows all the time because he can beat the other guy no matter what
the situation. . . . I just like air-to-air better."[23]

His time at Nellis was the origin of his nickname "forty-second Boyd,"
for claiming that he could defeat anyone in air-to-air combat inside of forty
seconds. Boyd and his followers maintain that he was undefeated.[24] Like
many Boyd stories, the forty-second stories come almost entirely from
Boyd himself or his close friends, and there are many claims to the contrary.
Boyd developed a reputation for repeatedly using the same maneuver—
the "high-G barrel roll"—as his preferred method for beating opponents.
This maneuver, if performed while being chased by an enemy from behind,
decreased speed and usually caused the chasing opponent to dart out in
front and become vulnerable. The Marine Corps' Major General Hal Vincent claimed that although he did not defeat Boyd, he was able to counter
this maneuver by performing a similar maneuver of his own, and eventually the two men came to a draw. Vincent, who was a friend of Boyd's
and complimentary of him, said that "no one was better slow speed than
John." Vincent clarified: "John was one of the best I ever fought. Although
there were others, over the years, in the high speed ACM environment, that
I found better." He named the Marine Corps' General Mike Sullivan and
Navy F-8 pilot Duane Varner as being "as good or better" than Boyd and
explained "there are now [April 2000] several of the top instructors . . . that
are better than all of us."[25]

In addition, General Wilbur Creech, later commander of TAC, maintained that he defeated Boyd.[26] Creech claimed that he advised Boyd that the
high-g barrel roll would not be effective against skilled opponents. To prove
it, Creech alleged that he flew a mock dogfight against Boyd, and that when

Boyd attempted his typical maneuver, Creech countered with a roll in the opposite direction, after which "it was a fairly simple matter to place the pipper on John's aircraft."[27] Creech dismissed the whole "forty second" claim as a fabrication: "Boyd carried no such fighter pilot reputation . . . among the instructor cadre. And he simply was not 'called out' by the best fighter pilots from throughout the military as is claimed—there simply was no opportunity for that in the FWS mission—or any record of any kind for that."[28] Many other pilots who served or flew with Boyd doubt the truth of the story as well.[29] Whether or not Boyd was "undefeated" is impossible to prove, but it matters little. What is clear is that in his roles as pilot and instructor, and in the ways that he wished others to think of him, stereotypical fighter pilot cultural elements defined his thinking.

During Boyd's years at Nellis, the school primarily flew the then-new F-100 Super Sabre, which Boyd claimed to have quickly mastered better than his peers. "I could beat the best instructors only after four rides in the F-100s because I figured out how the ailerons worked," he asserted. "All I have to do is use a cross control technique for the goddamn thing to really hook around or just neutralize; the rudder being the primary control. . . . I was the first guy to accomplish that, to develop those techniques. The company engineers said it could not be done. I told them, 'I do not care what you say, this will work.'"[30] As part of his work at Nellis, Boyd and other instructors published their tactical concepts in the school's journal, the *Fighter Weapons Newsletter*. Boyd eventually condensed his lessons on air combat into a manual called *Aerial Attack Study*.[31] Boyd's emphasis on air-to-air combat frustrated some other leaders. Creech, who took over as director of operations and training for the FWS for the last few months that Boyd was there in the summer of 1960, recalled, "I was at times exasperated because of his [Boyd's] single-minded focus on 'turn and burn' air-to-air combat—to the exclusion of virtually everything else." Creech implied that Boyd's aerial dueling tactics were not suited for new types of aircraft: "Most of it made no sense at all for aerial combat in the F-100, and that's what the Air Force was flying at the time!"[32]

Aerial Attack Study generated some debate because Boyd had written it on his own without asking or notifying anyone in command but wanted the FWS to adopt it as an official textbook. But the school had already created a new textbook and saw no need for *Aerial Attack Study*. Boyd claimed that he gave a copy to a friend, LeCroy Clifton, who worked in the tactics division of TAC, and asked him to conduct an independent review of both books. TAC decided to use *Aerial Attack Study* as the official training prospectus at FWS. Allegedly Boyd rubbed this in the face of his commander and told him, "You ought to be glad. This way you are ending up with the better book. It is a better reflection on you as the commander. Why are you protecting a bunch of goddamn losers over there . . . who cannot even do their homework? You know they did not do as good of a job as me. They are losers."[33] This quote is likely apocryphal, recalled by Boyd almost two decades after the fact. Yet it represents a common mode of thinking for him and his allies: a binary view that divided people and ideas into "winners" and "losers," depending on how much they agreed with Boyd.

Mathematical Language

The Air Force selected Boyd for its education program that sponsored officers to obtain technical degrees through civilian universities. From the fall of 1960 through 1962, Boyd earned a bachelor's in industrial engineering from Georgia Tech (the Georgia Institute of Technology), where he developed the concept that came to define much of his career and exerted a huge influence on the development of future Air Force fighter aircraft and pilot training. That concept was "energy maneuverability theory" (EMT). Boyd claimed he came up with the idea during a night of hamburgers and beer with his fellow students. He realized that his study of thermodynamics could be a useful way to understand how fighter aircraft maneuver. He could use thermodynamics equations to describe maneuverability in terms of transferring energy from one state to another—altitude as potential energy and airspeed as kinetic energy. He expanded the concept from that starting point.[34]

After completing his bachelor's at Georgia Tech, Boyd was assigned to the Air Proving Ground Center (APGC) at Eglin Air Force Base, Florida, as a division chief of its research, development, and test and evaluation projects. Boyd wasted no time spreading the word about his energy maneuverability theory, developing it into a method by which computers could run performance comparisons of fighter aircraft. He briefed his methods to two panels of Project Forecast and assisted in designing tests of his ideas with both SAC and Air Defense Command (ADC), based on data supplied to him from contactors, the Foreign Technology Division (FTD), and the Navy. In addition, he won the support of many engineers and computer specialists at Eglin who volunteered for additional duty to work on energy maneuverability, and made favorable impressions on some officers, particularly APGC vice commander Brigadier General Allman Culbertson.[35] Boyd's recollection of this time only recalled the negative reactions, however, and revealed his tendency to disdain both scientists and academics while also demanding recognition from them.[36]

One of the academics that Boyd met was Tom Christie, a mathematician working at the APGC Ballistics Division. They met at the officers' club bar, where Boyd allegedly sketched out the basics of EMT on a napkin. Christie saw the project as a chance to put his degree to use and do something new, and Boyd saw that Christie was not only a good mathematician but had access to aircraft performance data. More important, Christie had access to one of the Air Force's room-size supercomputers, the IBM 7094. Use of this advanced computer was tightly regulated. Christie could not use the machine himself but had to submit requests for engineers to run programs, and their time was then charged to a specific project. But Boyd's EMT project had been denied more than once. Christie, who was working on several approved projects, submitted EMT studies and fraudulently charged them to other projects, essentially stealing government computer time.[37]

These EMT programs provided a way to quantifiably measure the fighter pilot's most prized characteristic: maneuverability. At the time, aircraft were primarily measured by set points such as top speed, rate of climb, or thrust-to-weight ratios. "It will go so far, so high and so fast," Christie explained. "It didn't tell you anything unless your aim was to fly faster and higher which might or might not have anything to do with your ability to do the mission."[38] EMT changed that, making maneuverability a measurable metric. "EM theory," as historian Jacob Neufeld summarized, "expressed in numbers what fighter pilots had been trying to say for years by moving their hands."[39]

The Air Force quickly realized the value of EMT for aircraft design, evaluation, and comparison (especially against enemy aircraft). Although Boyd and Christie (and other writers such as Hammond and Coram) have emphasized the subterfuge involved in their analysis, that did not last long. After Boyd's first year at Eglin, his superiors already recognized and encouraged his work. In 1964, the Air Force had created an "Energy Maneuverability Program" and placed Boyd at the head of it, with special recognition of the "fundamental tools" that his computer programs represented. That May, the APGC published a two-volume technical data report by Boyd and Christie outlining EMT in full detail. By September 1965, Boyd had authored an official paper on the subject for presentation at the 1965 Air Force Science and Engineering Symposium, as well as given briefings to the President's Scientific Advisory Board and Secretary of the Air Force (SECAF) Eugene Zuckert.[40] The APGC published a three-volume technical report expanding on EMT concepts applied to air-to-air combat in March 1966, coauthored by Christie and First Lieutenant James E. Gibson. The APGC commander, Major General J. E. Roberts, and the Air Force Armament Laboratory director, Colonel Walter P. Glover, noted the program's magnitude, and that many unnamed individuals contributed to the EM project. They gave special recognition to mathematician Carl Davy as well as two women, programmer Mrs. Anthony Bicle and graphic illustrator Betty Jo Salter.[41] Despite the institutional support and accolades, Boyd and others usually described strong resistance to his ideas during this period. Although there likely was some, the degree of resistance may have been exaggerated over time. Boyd liked the compelling image of being seen as a rebel pushing against the system.

Boyd was not the first person to come up with EMT. Christie stated that Boyd's EMT "had been done before and there wasn't anything new to it."[42] Even Boyd admitted that his ideas were influenced by others. Although in interviews Boyd frequently misremembered the names of authors and titles of papers, other scholars had applied thermodynamic ideas to aircraft performance. The most prominent was Edward S. Rutowski, an aerodynamics engineer at Douglas, who published a paper titled "Energy Approach to the General Aircraft Performance Problem" in the *Journal of the Aeronautical Sciences* in 1954. In this work, Rutowski argued that aircraft performance should not be measured by speed, climb rate, or range, but by how quickly aircraft can shift from one characteristic to another. Rutowski created a series of equations to measure that shift. Boyd's later work was almost identical but differed in its application. As a fighter pilot, Boyd used the same concepts as Rutowski to measure maneuverability and translate the concept of aircraft agility into mathematical terms that engineers could work with. Rutowski used the concept to solve problems regarding fuel use and range in aircraft performance.[43] Others, including Grumman scientist Henry Kelley in 1960, and Harvard University physicist A. E. Bryson and Raytheon researcher W. F. Denham in 1962, had published papers making use of EMT concepts for studying flight characteristics, but none of these applied the idea to fighter aircraft maneuverability.[44]

One of the most useful aspects of Boyd and Christie's work was its presentation. The output of their computer programs was just a long list of numbers cataloging how a plane reacted to certain conditions. Boyd and Christie turned these into a chart that allowed pilots and engineers to "see" how aircraft performed across a variety of situations. Christie explained that these were "diagrams wherein you are able to look across an aircraft's performance envelope which in the past might have included just lines depicting maximum speed and altitude." These graphs answered questions of interest to fighter pilots: "Could it sustain maneuvers? What could it do against the enemy? Could it turn tighter? . . . Now we had enough of a map across the whole aircraft steady state and that's really what was new about it."[45]

Boyd lifted the concept of these charts from Rutowski's article. "The fact is I liked the way he [Rutowski] laid it out and the way he expressed his charts," Boyd admitted in a 1977 interview. "I liked his charts so well that I borrowed them."[46] Boyd did cite Rutowski, Bryson, Denham, and others in his APGC reports.[47] This is not to imply that Boyd's work was fraudulent or insignificant. Although Rutowski and others had developed EMT earlier, Boyd most likely came up with it independently. Multiple independent discovery is a frequent phenomenon in the history of science and technology. His application of EMT to fighter aircraft maneuverability—filtering EMT concepts through his knights of the air mentality—was also unique. The idea of visualizing EMT data in his charts was borrowed, but the work of creating all the charts for various aircraft was still important and influential.

Another new element that Boyd contributed was using EMT to compare US aircraft to Soviet fighters. The results surprised him. "I expected to see our airplanes, like the F-4 and all of those, look a lot better than the Soviet airplanes," Boyd recalled. "Then we ran our first plots off. I said, 'Gee, Tom, wait a minute. The Soviet airplanes are better. I think we made a mistake.' . . . It never even occurred to me at that particular moment that the Soviet airplanes could actually be better than ours."[48]

Boyd was worried that he had been given faulty data from the technicians at Wright-Patterson, so he flew to Ohio and retrieved more recent information. According to Coram, even on this research trip Boyd could not help but indulge his stereotypical fighter pilot impulses. Boyd approached the Eglin runway in a T-33 to find a B-52 taking off. He allegedly flew head-on at the giant nuclear bomber, inverted and swept under it, then came back around for a second pass from behind. During both passes Boyd broke through the radio, shouting, "Guns, guns guns!" Afterward, Boyd was grounded.[49]

With new data for Soviet planes in hand, Boyd made graphs that could "match up" American planes against their Soviet counterparts by overlaying the two charts, visually depicting the situations in which one plane had an energy advantage over the other. The graph showed that at particular altitudes and speeds, one plane could potentially accelerate faster or turn tighter. Boyd used color to drive his point home, shading the areas of American advantage in blue and Soviet advantage in red.[50]

By 1964, fighter pilot advocates, especially Myers and Agan, advocated a return to classic air-to-air combat fighters that could perform the "white scarf stuff." Boyd's and Christie's EMT gave them a mathematical language to express that stuff quantitatively. Their efforts would result in a program for a new aircraft unknown to Boyd at the time but which he would have a large hand in developing.

A Rebirth of Air Fighting

On July 1, 1964, Agan became the director of plans, deputy chief of staff (DCS) for plans and operations at the Pentagon. He was already familiar with Boyd's EMT concepts and, that fall, commissioned a committee of experienced fighter pilots, especially aces, to study the state of tactical aviation capabilities. The chair of the group was Brigadier General Harrison Thyng, and others on the committee included Brigadier General William Dunham, Lieutenant General Winston Marshall, Colonel Francis Gabreski, Colonel George Laven, Colonel Woody Davis, Lieutenant Colonel John Burns, and Lieutenant Colonel Jack Holly.

The majority of these men had become aces in World War II or Korea. Davis, Burns, and Holly were not aces, but Davis and Burns had extensive experience both flying fighter aircraft and commanding fighter groups, squadrons, and wings. Thyng and Gabreski stood out further—they were two of only seven US pilots to achieve ace status in both World War II and Korea. The assembly of this panel reflected Agan's interest in dogfighting expertise, and it may have reflected the ongoing pattern of fighter pilots looking to heroic individuals of the past to help define the future. Myers recalled that Colonel Jim Hagerstrom, another one of the seven to become an ace in both World War II and Korea, was also instrumental in this effort. Agan hoped the prestigious group could give leverage to his arguments both for placing a gun on the F-4 Phantom and for starting development on a new true fighter plane.[51]

The panel concluded what Agan and Myers hoped—that there was an urgent need for a new fighter plane agile enough to handle new Soviet threats. However, the group hedged its recommendations. "We concluded that we were diverging from the Russians in some very important parameters mostly having to do with fighter maneuverability," Burns recalled. "A new tactical fighter was required that emphasized air combat." However, he clarified, "we were very seriously concerned that this would not be well received in the Air Staff and also could have an adverse impact on the F-111 program." Instead of arguing for a new fighter, the panel merely "expressed concern" and "request[ed] a study of the need for a new tactical fighter."[52] Myers claimed that the only reason the panel went as far as it did was the advocacy of Thyng and Gabreski.

As the US became more involved in Vietnam, events there influenced the shift toward a more air-to-air focused fighter. In March and April 1964, two pilots were killed as the result of wing failure in two T-28 Trojans, which triggered a wider discussion in the Air Force about force structures. That December, SECAF Zuckert requested $50 million to expand and update ground-attack and reconnaissance planes. Secretary of Defense Robert McNamara granted only $10 million and instructed the Air Force to consider developing a new ground-attack plane—because, he thought, they could assume that the US would have tactical air superiority in Vietnam.[53]

Zuckert and other members of the Air Staff disagreed with the assumption but were also concerned at how a new plane would affect the tactical force structure. The Air Staff initiated a study of that question in August 1964, led by Lieutenant Colonel John W. Bohn Jr. "Force Options for Tactical Air," which concluded in February 1965, argued that the latest planes that the Air Force was pursuing—especially the F-111—were too costly to be risked in limited wars and should be saved for the higher-stakes nuclear conflict. The Bohn study examined low-cost alternatives, including modifications to the A-1E Skyraider, the A-6 Intruder, the F-104 Starfighter, and the F-4 Phantom to make them cheaper and, by implication, more expendable. The study rejected all these options. The cheaper planes could not perform well enough, and the more expensive planes were too expensive to risk, even when stripped down. Instead, the Bohn study recommended a mix of high- and low-cost airplanes, recommending either the Navy's A-7 Corsair II or Northrop's F-5 for the "low" support role. The A-7 could handle a larger payload, but the F-5 was more effective in air-to-air roles.[54] This marked the beginning of a long debate regarding procurement of the A-7 versus the F-5, an argument that later influenced the development of the F-15 Eagle.

Less than four weeks before the Bohn study was released, General John P. McConnell took over as CSAF. Agan had convinced McConnell that a dedicated air-to-air fighter was necessary. McConnell was concerned that new Soviet interceptors were more than a match for the Air Force's current inventory and worried that US planes were vulnerable to antiaircraft fire. This was especially so after the first strike of Operation Rolling Thunder on March 2, 1965, when three F-105 Thunderchiefs and two F-100 Super Sabres were shot down by ground fire over North Vietnam. Zuckert mostly agreed with McConnell, and on March 16, he forwarded the Bohn study to the Office of the Secretary of Defense (OSD) and asked for authorization to purchase two wings of F-5s as a temporary placeholder while the Air Force pursued a medium-cost tactical fighter. In April, Zuckert specified to McNamara that this new fighter should have "significant air-to-air fighting capability."[55]

On April 2, 1965, work on a new fighter began in earnest, partly spurred by Lieutenant General James Ferguson, deputy chief of staff for research and development at Air Force Headquarters. He had extensive fighter experience both as a pilot and as a group commander during World War II before serving as vice commander of the Fifth Air Force in Korea. Ferguson convinced the director of defense research and engineering (DDR&E) Dr. Harold Brown of the need for dedicated air-to-air fighters. Brown agreed to a purchase of F-5s as a placeholder and also authorized the development of a new fighter, the Fighter-Experimental, or F-X.

Ferguson established a working group in the Air Staff led by Brigadier General Andrew J. Evans Jr., the director of development, and science adviser Dr. Charles H. Christenson. This group conducted a series of studies on a possible new fighter, envisioned as a single-seat, twin-engine craft emphasizing maneuverability over speed, with superior air-to-air and all-weather (radar) capability, but that could still excel in a ground-attack role with assistance of a ground-looking radar system. Representatives from Brown's office warned Ferguson, as well as the director of operational requirements, Major General Jack J. Catton, that funding such an experimental fighter would be difficult if the craft was too specialized. Catton and Ferguson surmised that the Air Staff preferred multi-role planes to specialized ones. Their solution was—as historian Jacob Neufeld termed it—to "disguise" the F-X as a "close support fighter" that gave top billing to its ground-attack capability, although the working group intended to make a dedicated air-to-air fighter.[56]

Burns, working in the TAC Directorate of Operations at the time, remembered this period a bit differently, noting that there was a "contradiction," a "dichotomy" between the Air Staff and TAC in 1965. Burns alleged that Ferguson and the rest of the Air Staff considered air-to-air fighting "frivolous," partly because it was more difficult to measure air-to-air performance than ground attack, which could be quantified. TAC took its position clearly: "No. We need an air-to-air airplane. Then whatever air-to-ground capability falls out, okay." He recalled that over time the issue became more polarized.[57]

Interviewed in 1973, Ferguson claimed the opposite, that he felt the need to develop an air-superiority fighter "about as strongly as you can feel," and fully disagreed with the assertion that an air-to-air craft was not "sellable."

He did emphasize that any air superiority aircraft, including his idea for the F-X, should be flexible, because once air superiority is achieved, those same airplanes should be used for attack roles, and that was even more to the point in a war like Vietnam in which MiG engagements were rare. Yet his concept for the F-X, which he remembered as starting in the fall of 1962, was far different. He wanted "to keep things as simple as possible. . . . We needed a relatively cheap, relatively unsophisticated, airplane that we could produce in large numbers." He specifically differentiated the F-X from other interceptors and linked it to the First World War: "The FX, as we were talking about, was the one that maneuvers with and really fires at the opposite airplane that has equal maneuvering capability . . . and dogfight, if you want to use a World War I expression."⁵⁸

Another member of the working group, Heinrich Weigand, scientific adviser to the director of development, agreed with Ferguson: "There was no dichotomy on the Air Staff," he stated; "the Air Staff supported air superiority," and any concessions toward multi-role features was only to appease OSD. Weigand emphasized that "the air superiority fighter should be the cleanest possible. . . . I never believed in the multi-role fighter aircraft." The working group's original definition was for "a lightweight air superiority fighter" costing $1 million each, later raised to $1.5 million. This stance, as he recalled, was a direct reaction to Soviet capabilities. Weigand also indicated that EMT played a role in their evaluations, but that "energy maneuverability was not a revolutionary theory at the time. It was just another way of comparing performances of airplanes."⁵⁹

Fighter advocates such as Burns and Myers tended to portray themselves as "voices in the wilderness," yet they were not as alone as they imagined.⁶⁰ They had won authorization and funding for a new fighter, and leaders within TAC and the Air Staff supported the idea of a dedicated, lightweight air superiority fighter. Some leaders remained unconvinced of their view of the importance of the "white scarf stuff," particularly OSD. The debate regarding a focus on air-to-air or ground-attack roles would remain the defining aspect of F-X development.

Events in Vietnam gave fighter advocates more ammunition for their case. Only two days after Brown authorized studies on the F-X, on April 4, 1965, a group of forty-eight F-105s, organized into flights of four planes, flew on a mission to destroy the Thanh Hóa bridge, escorted by F-100s. Four MiG-17s emerged from the mist, and their cannon fire tore through the Thunderchiefs. During what became a tight maneuvering gun battle, two F-105s were hit. One was heavily damaged, and the pilot announced his intention to eject, but weather prevented his wingmen from verifying, and his body was never found. The other damaged Thunderchief attempted to return to base, but the damage to its hydraulic systems forced the pilot to attempt an ejection—a chute failure claimed his life. A third F-105 was lost to ground fire, as was an A-1H Skyraider flying a search and rescue mission for pilots who had been shot down the previous day. During the fight, two flights of four F-100s entered the area and became tangled in their own dogfight with the MiGs. One of the Super Sabres barely escaped being shot down as another F-100 damaged a MiG. One of the Super Sabres fired an AIM-9 Sidewinder missile after carefully maneuvering to ensure it would not hit one of the F-105s, but the missile failed to hit, and the MiGs escaped.[61]

The surviving pilots' reports blamed a variety of issues: the time-consuming control switch procedures, lack of radio discipline, lack of experience and training for the F-105 crews, and the thick mist that covered the battlefield and limited situational awareness. Some pilots also mentioned the same problems that fighter advocates warned about: poor maneuverability of their aircraft. One F-100 pilot wrote, "F-100 could not match MiG turn." Another elaborated: "Day fighters not too effective over enemy GCI [ground-controlled intercept] environment. MiGs easily slipped around small number of MIGCAP [combat air patrol] aircraft."[62]

The deadly encounter was not bad news to everyone. "Somebody called me from Washington to say 'It happened,'" Myers recalled. "'Just like you said it would happen. A flight of guys in 'tac' fighters . . . were jumped by [MiGs], they flailed around and the [MiGs] shot a couple down and escaped scot-free.' That helped." He noted, "Suddenly there was a rebirth of the air fighting mission."[63]

More help appeared for fighter advocates when Ferguson worked with Air Force Systems Command to conduct studies on another potential new fighter emphasizing STOL (short takeoff and landing) capability. Burns pounced on this as an opportunity to push his fighter concept and immediately drafted a position paper. "This was the opening that we needed," he recalled. "That night we prepared a wire saying . . . what we needed was an improved combat maneuvering fighter with total air combat performance. . . . What we needed, therefore, was a STOL fighter airplane. That was a euphemism to cloak it under the V[ertical]/STOL program." TAC commander General Walter Sweeney was interested in the proposal yet did not issue any formal requirement for a new fighter. According to Burns, Sweeney accepted and wrote a requirement for Burns's proposal for an F-X of thirty to thirty-five thousand pounds that would emphasize agility and air-to-air capability, yet Sweeny refused to sign it because he was about to retire. Neufeld suggested that Sweeney's lack of commitment to major changes could have resulted from his deteriorating health. The commander had been struggling with cancer, which at the time of this incident was only a few months away from taking his life.[64]

Burns claimed that his plan (and that of other fighter advocates) all along had been to first create a plane like the F-15–"a very highly maneuverable airplane with outstanding combat maneuverability that would have somewhat less, or approaching the radar and missile capabilities of the F-4," for service in 1970. Burns asserted that he and fighter advocates always intended to follow up that plane with another new fighter, the F-X2, "which would have more emphasis on avionics and missilery."[65] Although it is possible that Burns was placing this concept earlier than it actually arose or may have been conflating later events, it is also possible that, as early as April 1965, certain members of the fighter community were thinking of a mix of two types of fighters, planning to follow up the F-15 with another new fighter. Even if that is the case, what Burns described is essentially an inversion of what later took place.

Burns's efforts were not unrewarded. In June 1965, TAC created a panel to study the threat of new Soviet fighters. It concluded that to defeat emerging Soviet threats, the Air Force needed a small, lightweight day fighter that emphasized maneuverability instead of speed. Their recommendation paralleled the early F-X working group studies, arguing for a single-seat, twin-engine craft of between twenty and twenty-five thousand pounds.[66] For comparison, a completely empty F-4 Phantom weighs over thirty thousand pounds, with a maximum takeoff weight more than twice that number. Myers recalled a panel taking place about this time made up of TAC leaders and ace pilots from World War II and the Korean War, for the purpose of highlighting "the close combat deficiencies of our *so-called* fighter aircraft."[67] It is unclear if he was referring to this study of Soviet threats or Agan's panel of the previous year.

However, Myers could have been referring to another pertinent study, called "Tactical Fighter Ground Attack Aircraft," completed in June 1965 and led by Colonel Bruce Hinton, the first F-86 pilot to shoot down a MiG-15 in Korea. This panel studied the debate over acquiring the A-7 or the F-5 as a temporary measure until a new fighter was developed. It argued that the A-7 was the preferred airplane for ground attack, but only if air superiority could be assumed—and it could not; thus it recommended the F-5. Some members of the Air Staff resisted the F-5 because of its increased cost—the A-7 was simply cheaper, although Hinton noted that costs could be offset by selling more F-5s to allied nations.[68] Burns recalled that Hinton's work, although it was based on creating a ground-attack plane, was very concerned with achieving the air-to-air capability that he thought was lacking in the Air

Force at the time. Burns also remembered Hinton's study as including the first official use of the F-X designation.[69]

OSD pushed for the A-7, as the office was committed to the concept of commonality: having the Air Force and Navy use the same (if modified) aircraft.[70] Pierre Sprey, then working as a consulting statistician at Grumman, recalled, "The Air Force didn't want either airplane. They didn't want the A-7 because it was a 'goddamn Navy' airplane and they didn't want the F-5 because it was too cheap and not fancy and glamorous enough and it didn't go to Mach 2."[71] Although the Air Force decision makers were typically against procuring Navy aircraft, their objection to the F-5 was not that it was too cheap, but that it was too expensive. During this debate, in July 1965, General Gabriel P. Disosway took over as the commander of TAC. That same month, McNamara called for a joint study between the Air Force and OSD to settle the A-7 versus F-5 issue and, at the same time, endorsed the effort for studies for the F-X.[72]

Just what that fighter would look like was still a matter of fierce contention; the question of whether the F-X should be a dedicated air-to-air platform or emphasize ground attack was not settled in mid-1965. Contractors, eager to get ahead on potential contracts, began preliminary designs on up to six types of planes in order to cover the wide range of what the new F-X could become. For each of the two "families" of aircraft (ground attack and air-to-air), contractors designed three options based on price: low-cost ($1.2 million), medium-cost ($2 million), and high-cost ($3.2 million) options. Burns recalled TAC and the Air Staff disagreeing about top speed. TAC wanted a slower plane, under Mach 2, to emphasize maneuverability, while the Air Staff wanted Mach 2.7, which introduced structural engineering requirements that were anathema to TAC's concept of a light, agile fighter. As a result, contractors had to design several options within each of the six categories. Burns recalled that this "ended up with each company producing several thousand designs." TAC and the fighter advocates became even more hardened in their own view that the F-X should be a dedicated air-to-air platform. Some began to worry that, even if they got the plane they wanted, they would fail in the long term without convincing leaders of the importance of air-to-air. "Godammit, it's time we got the message across to the people that air combat is a very serious business and we've got to prepare for it," Burns said. "We've got to have it recognized. We might win *this* airplane by sneaking it in, but we've got the future to think about."[73]

That fall, Brown was named to be the next SECAF, and he changed his position on the A-7/F-5 debate. He had formerly backed the F-5 but switched to fully endorsing the A-7. Disosway later agreed. He emphasized that cost was the primary factor in his decision but also noted how unpopular his decision was: "The Air Force was pretty damn sick of getting the Navy aircraft, the F-4 and the A-7 and whatnot, and they just had a thing about it."[74]

This decision on the A-7 had lost-lasting implications for two reasons. First, the idea of using F-5s to fill the air-to-air role is one to which fighter advocates returned in earnest many years later. Second, the fact that the Air Force now had an upgraded ground-attack plane left an opening. As Lieutenant General Glenn A. Kent, then working in the Air Force Directorate of Requirements, recalled, "The decision was made to go ahead and buy an A-7, an aircraft designed primarily for air-to-ground. With that decision behind us, there was immediately, and rightly so, greater emphasis on an aircraft designed primarily for air-to-air combat."[75]

On September 30, 1965, on his last day as DDR&E, Brown approved a request from the Air Force for $1 million to go toward further F-X studies. Disosway, six days later, on October 6, issued a qualitative operational requirement (QOR) for an air-to-air fighter. Whether it was based on one that Sweeney had originally written is unclear, although Burns, then serving as Disosway's operations adviser, a position shared with Colonel Gordon M. Graham, claimed to have written the QOR himself.[76] Disosway did make some changes to previous recommendations for the F-X. He increased the weight requirement by ten thousand pounds, included radar capability, and specified that the plane carry guided missiles (both infrared and radar-guided).[77] Despite these additions, which were not in line with what some fighter advocates wanted to pursue, the Air Force now had a requirement to develop a dedicated air-to-air fighter that emphasized maneuverability and dogfighting capability over speed and interception. As Kent recalled, "There was a push toward 'now let's get on with an F-X.'"[78]

Piled On

The first step in "getting on with it" happened on December 8, 1965, when the Air Force sent a request for proposal (RFP) to thirteen aircraft manufacturers to conduct design studies for the F-X.[79] But the question of the F-X's main role—whether it would be focused on air-to-air or air-to-ground—was not fully settled. Agan took the debate to a wide audience in December 1965. In an article for *Air Force / Space Digest International*, Agan called for a "smaller aircraft than the F-111, and possibly than the F-4 . . . because we can plan to use it for air superiority and close air support and thus can accept less range and payload in order to get superior agility. . . . It should be a medium-cost aircraft, because we will need many."[80]

Meanwhile, throughout 1965 Boyd and Christie continued to present briefs on EMT for various figures of influence within the Air Force, Navy, and the Pentagon. In the process they disparaged the F-111, the F-105 Thunderchief, and the F-4 Phantom as inadequate. The Phantom, they said, was especially ill-suited to air-to-air combat because of its size and weight, and they asserted that guided missiles were useless in a dogfighting scenario. According to Coram, Dr. John Foster Jr., then DDR&E at the Pentagon, became a convert to Boyd's way of thinking.[81] Disosway at least agreed with them about the F-111. He hated that the airplane had an "F" designation, arguing it should have been called the A-111 or B-111 because it was suited for attack and bomber roles and lacked the capabilities of a true fighter.[82]

As Boyd grew more influential, he also created enemies. Boyd's fighter pilot mentality went further than the stereotypes and often expressed itself as a penchant for confrontation. For Boyd, interpersonal interactions were dogfights. For example, in late 1965 at Eglin, Boyd happened to run into a civilian who had formerly worked at the computer shop and been skeptical of Boyd's research. Boyd confronted the man, repeatedly shoving him and jabbing his chest, saying, "You didn't think my work was important enough for your goddamn computer and now I got four-stars calling me for briefings." He poked the man's chest repeatedly. "Everybody in the Air Force has heard of energy-maneuverability," he said. "You. Don't. Know. Shit." As the man tried to walk away, Boyd stopped him and pressed his lit cigar against the man's tie. As the man left, Boyd chased him, shouting, "You're a loser. A fucking loser. Go on, get out of here. Run." Boyd shouted after the man, "You're a fucking loser!"[83] The story is possibly apocryphal or exaggerated. Boyd's boss, Lieutenant Colonel Vernon Markham, noted around this time that EMT had gained "wide acceptance" and was "extensively employed throughout the Air Force and Aerospace industry," but that in the process "Boyd has encountered many problems and strong opposition." Further up the command chain at Eglin, Colonel James Lillard Jr. noted that Boyd's ideas were valuable but that "he is an intense and impatient man who does not respond well to close supervision."[84]

Boyd also faced resistance from other fighter pilots, some of whom viewed his EMT ideas as antithetical to the knights of the air mentality. In early 1966, Navy F-8 pilot Cal Swanson heard Boyd speak about EMT and was eager to share the approach with his squadron mates. But the other top pilots in the group—Dick Wyman, Richard Adams, and John MacDonald—rejected EMT. As journalist Zalin Grant described, "They saw themselves as stick-and-throttle pilots in the World War One tradition, white scarfs flowing in the wind. Rick Adams, who was something of a writer, composed romantic fantasies about air combat." When Swanson tried to use EMT against Adams in a simulated dogfight, Adams dominated him.[85] The Navy was more accepting of EMT a few years later.

In 1966, one of Disosway's goals in his new position was to increase the perceived importance and influence of TAC compared with other major commands (SAC and MAC, Material Airlift Command). To do this, he had conferences with TAC theater commanders, specifically General Bruce Holloway, who commanded USAFE, and General Hunter Harris, commander of PACAF (Pacific Air Forces). These conferences often resulted in position statements called the "Twelve Star Letters" in reference to the three four-star generals. The first of these, in February 1966, advocated for a dedicated air-to-air fighter. Burns claimed to have written this letter himself. Whether he did or not, it reflected his views, arguing that air superiority would be "severely jeopardized" if the F-X became a multi-role plane. Instead, the letter urged that the F-X be dedicated solely to air-to-air combat.[86] The battle over the role on which the F-X should focus raged inside the Air Force for over two more years.

One other factor that pushed the F-X toward an air-to-air focus in late 1965 into early 1966 was Project Feather Duster: two studies using F-86 Sabres to simulate the MiG-17 and MiG-21 in air-to-air combat against several USAF planes. Although little effort was made to simulate enemy tactics or doctrine, the project concluded, "The MIG-15/17/21 will all out-perform any of our fighters at Mach numbers below .9 at any altitude." The study advised against engaging in dogfights: "Above all, do not enter into a shin-kicking, G-pulling contest with a MIG."[87] Sprey thought that Feather Duster was powerful evidence for fighter advocates. In his view, it proved that Air Force "hardware certainly wasn't well-suited to air-to-air combat. . . . Anybody who even threw a few antiquated fighters against them [USAF] was going to do pretty well despite all the high technology in their own so-called fighters which weren't fighters, they were bombers."[88]

After judging the eight responses to the December 1965 RFP, in March 1966 the Air Force granted contracts to three companies to begin preliminary studies for their designs of a possible F-X: Boeing, Lockheed, and North American. Grumman also participated in the study, but with no funding from the Air Force. McDonnell also conducted in-house studies on the F-X throughout most of 1966. The guidance for these studies came from the Aeronautical Systems Division (ASD) under Air Force Systems Command, and despite the efforts of fighter advocates, the studies were dominated by the desire to have a multipurpose craft that could challenge the Soviets in maneuverability but also have long range and ground-attack capability. Some thought ASD was trying too hard to make "one aircraft for the generation" that could do everything, while others defended ASD's effort as an honest but misguided attempt to create the best airplane.[89]

Kent described a process in which "requirements got piled on," gradually increasing the F-X's size, weight, and cost. "If someone says I want a low wing loading," he said, "you're going to have a large aircraft. If you now demand that it have a large thrust-to-weight, you've got to have a big engine. If you now demand that it go a long way, you've got to have a lot of fuel. If you put all these together, pretty soon you find that you have an aircraft that weighs a lot more than you anticipated."[90] Myers blamed TAC, recalling that in early 1966 TAC issued the "Preliminary Concept for the FX" that identified air superiority as the "primary mission" but also stipulated a strong ground-attack capability. Myers complained that this "gave license to the air-to-ground advocates to drive the FX toward the all-purpose concept," and that "these zealots" took the avionics too far. He was especially angry about the inclusion of avionics for night operations.[91] Specifically, Myers pointed to Colonel William Whisner, chief of the Fighter Division at TAC, as being preoccupied with top speed, desiring a plane that could go Mach 3.[92] Whisner was one of the seven pilots who had earned ace status in both World War II and the Korean War, demonstrating that some accomplished fighter pilots did not go as far as others in expressing stereotypical fighter culture traits.

After examining about five hundred proposed designs, in July 1966 ASD settled on a design calling for state-of-the-art avionics and radar equipment, a variable-sweep wing (necessitating a heavy hinge mechanism), and a high-bypass engine ratio of 2.2:1.[93] ASD wanted the F-X to have podded engines with horizontal tails mounted on them, a 20 mm gun, four missiles, and four thousand pounds of bombs. The final proposed F-X, then, had a wing loading of 110 pounds per square foot, significantly higher than the F-4 Phantom's 78, increasing the F-X's speed at the cost of maneuverability. The thrust-to-weight ratio (related to acceleration) of 0.75 was much lower than the Phantom's, which was over 1. The proposed F-X's total weight was over sixty thousand pounds, nearly triple Burns's original concept.[94]

Fighter advocates already derided the F-4 as not a true fighter. In almost every measurable factor, the F-X concept was even less of one. At least some comfort could be taken in the fact that the F-X proposal included a gun. As Neufeld summarized, "The F-X then, promised to be a very expensive aircraft resembling the F-111 but which, in no sense, would be an air superiority fighter."[95] Ferguson and his development planners, Kent and Brigadier

General F. M. Rogers, were not happy with the studies. In October 1966, they decided to bring in fresh sets of eyes.

The fighter pilot community within the Air Force had grown influential enough by the mid-1960s that the service was designing a new fighter aircraft. The decision to procure a new plane was not the result of any one person but bubbled up from the ongoing advocacy of several members of the fighter community and their allies, many of whom held to the tenets of fighter pilot culture. But their influence was limited; they did not achieve what they truly wanted: a dedicated air-to-air combat plane that could re-create the "white scarf" aerial duels as in the days of World War I. Old habits were still ingrained in all levels of the Air Force, and the F-X on the drawing board in 1966 did not look much different from the F-111 or even the F-4 Phantom before it. The Air Force's desire to make the plane a versatile jack-of-all-trades was not a malicious one; it showed a desire to maximize effectiveness. But the fighter community wanted more specialization on its favored role of air combat. To break this stalemate, the Air Force needed fresh blood.

CHAPTER 4

"The Right Fighter"

Air-to-ground is bull shit!

—Colonel John Boyd

In the fall of 1966, the F-X program was stuck in a rut. The Aeronautical Systems Division (ASD), the Office of the Secretary of Defense (OSD), and some members of TAC and the Air Staff wanted the F-X to be a multi-role fighter emphasizing ground attack, while fighter advocates coming from the knights of the air tradition fought to make it a lightweight, agile air-to-air machine. The result was a bloated jack-of-all-trades, master of none. The Air Force brought in fresh blood, including General Glenn A. Kent and Major John Boyd. Kent sought to simplify the plane and have it specialize in the fighter role, and Boyd attempted to incorporate his and his followers' ideas about an ideal air-to-air fighter that could recapture the constructed memory of knightly aerial duels. But Air Force service culture, interservice rivalry with the Navy, and fears about the state of the Soviet air force also influenced the F-X, and the program became a battleground for competing interests. While this fight unfolded, the Air Force itself experienced structural changes that influenced the direction of the program and changed the possibilities available to Boyd and his growing group of acolytes.

Practically Useless

"With the last glimmer of hope fading," as Chuck Myers recalled about the F-X program in the fall of 1966, "OSD (SA) [Systems Analysis] came to the assistance of the fighter advocates." The assistant secretary of defense for SA, Dr. Alain Enthoven, wrote a memo to DDR&E John Foster "which essentially rejected the FX described by the CFP [concept formulation package] and insisted that the *fighter* end of the design-spectrum be examined." But OSD also said there was "no urgency associated with the FX program."[1]

At about the same time, Boyd was disappointed that the Air Force canceled his orders to fly fighters in Vietnam and instead called him to Washington, DC. Myers claimed responsibility for this, recalling that when he heard Boyd had been ordered to Vietnam, he contacted the DDR&E deputy for tactical warfare, Dr. Thomas P. Cheatham Jr. At a party, Cheatham spoke with CSAF General John McConnell about his concern for the F-X. A matter of days later, Boyd's orders changed, and he was assigned to the Pentagon.[2]

Boyd was still firmly wedded to fighter pilot culture, which was evident even from a simple visit to the movies. That summer, he and Christie went to see the film *The Blue Max*, which examines fighter pilots from different socioeconomic classes. The film deconstructs the myth of chivalrous pilots, emphasizing the extremes to which one can be driven in the name of an aggressive warrior ethos. But Boyd focused entirely on the accuracy of the air-to-air combat scenes. He shouted at the screen when a character missed a shot or maneuvered in a way that Boyd thought was ineffective. At one point Boyd allegedly stood up in the crowded theater, waving his arms, and shouted, "You missed the goddamn shot! Hose him, you stupid bastard!"[3]

In September 1966 Boyd reported to USAF Headquarters in Washington to work as a research and development director in the Advanced Systems Bureau, Tactical Division of the Directorate of Operational Requirements in the DCS/R&D. He was there to work on the F-X and was immediately frustrated with the existing designs. The requirements for a variable-sweep wing, sixty-thousand-pound plane with its high wing loading, high engine-bypass-ratio, and low thrust-to-weight ratio were the opposite of everything Boyd valued in an aircraft. After his first look, he concluded, "It looks like we're building another F-111."[4] One of Boyd's supervisors was Colonel William D. Ritchie, deputy director for general purpose and airlift forces in DCS/R&D. Pierre Sprey recalled that Ritchie had changed Boyd's orders because he specifically wanted Boyd to apply his EMT ideas to the F-X. Allegedly, after two weeks of analyzing the F-X designs, Boyd told Ritchie, "Sir, I've never designed a fighter plane before. But I could fuck up and do better than that."[5]

Boyd began a series of trade-off studies, evaluating a variety of proposed F-X designs using EMT and computer models. For some time, Boyd kept the variable-sweep wing as part of the design. Although it increased the plane's weight, switching to a fixed wing seemed to provide no difference in performance. At first, much of Boyd's data came from ASD at Wright-Patterson Air Force Base. He soon incorporated data from NASA, particularly in the area of drag polars—graphs that measure the relationship between lift and drag. According to Sprey, these are key to understanding how well an aircraft turns. Sprey thought the researchers at ASD were "never very competent" and claimed they were using standardized drag polars that were not unique to the specific designs Boyd was studying. This issue of the ASD data not matching NASA's caused Boyd quite a bit of confusion for the next two years. As Sprey recalled, Boyd periodically forced ASD to adjust and recalculate its information.[6]

In early 1967, Pierre Sprey was a civilian consultant working in OSD (SA) and had recently completed a study arguing that in the case of a Soviet invasion of Western Europe, the Air Force should give up the interdiction mission altogether and instead focus solely on close air support of ground troops. To that end, Sprey's study called for large numbers of "pure fighters" in the World War I tradition to stop enemy MiGs from interfering. One of Sprey's superiors, Colonel Howard Fish, a plans and programs officer in the Directorate of Plans at USAF Headquarters, disagreed with that assessment. Fish told Sprey to meet with Boyd, presumably thinking that, as an expert on fighter tactics, Boyd would prove Sprey wrong. Instead, the two men found that they agreed on many issues and became close friends.[7] Much like the stereotypical fighter pilot, Sprey valued his independence and enjoyed pushing back against authority figures. He tended to think that the higher one's rank, the less one's intelligence. He also tended to take extremist, all-or-nothing positions on many of the issues he researched. He exhibited many of the same personality traits that were the hallmarks of the stereotypical fighter pilot, especially aggressiveness and independence. This absolutist way of thinking ran through Boyd, Sprey, and some of their other associates, marking this group's approach to problem solving for the remainder of their careers.

Both men were unhappy with the plans for the F-X as they existed when Boyd joined the project. Sprey recalled that "the airplane was practically useless for anything except flying in a straight line because it didn't have enough wing area to provide the lift to make maneuverable turns."[8] He agreed that the Air Force had redefined the word "fighter" in a way that did not connote the "pure" fighter that he envisioned as dedicated to air-to-air combat. As Sprey later said, studies on the F-X had been conducted up to this point "without any clear concept of what a fighter is."[9]

The team expanded in September 1967 when Colonel Robert Titus, a former fighter pilot in the Korean War with extensive squadron command experience, took a position above Boyd in DCS/R&D as chief of Advanced Tactical Systems and project officer for the F-X. Titus recalled that "we were intent on getting a fighter that would be the best 'fighter-fighter' capable of being produced," and that the F-X should have "not one pound for air to ground." Titus agreed with the fighter advocates that an air-to-air focus was necessary, and he was particularly insistent on a high thrust-to-weight ratio, low wing loading, removing a ground-looking radar, and including an internal gun. Although Titus formed a close relationship with Boyd, he was privately skeptical of the legends about "forty second Boyd" and recognized that Boyd's briefings—in which he tended to yell and wave his arms at his audience while insulting them—might be counterproductive. In late 1967, an unnamed general asked that Titus perform all EMT briefings to the military and to Congress, although Boyd could still brief industry figures, at whom he frequently screamed profanity-laden personal insults.[10]

Boyd continued working with Christie, Sprey, Titus, and Ritchie to define the F-X in a way that satisfied their desire for a true fighter. EMT computer programs to look at the trade-offs of various configurations formed the basis for their analysis, as did Boyd's study of Soviet fighters and air-to-air missiles. His supervisor, Colonel John F. Groom, noted the importance of Boyd's EMT-informed methods. In his "pursuit of optimum fighter aircraft performance," Groom said, "[Boyd] is capable of translating fighter system performance into objective and measurable terms."[11] Boyd was particularly concerned with the engine bypass ratio and the wing design, although he had not yet abandoned the variable-sweep wing as of the summer of 1967.

The group sought changes that could make the F-X a more maneuverable airplane. A high thrust-to-weight ratio would help acceleration. Lowering the engine bypass ratio made it less fuel efficient but smaller and lighter. A lower wing-loading ratio made the plane more agile. One major sticking point was the built-in radar. Some designers wanted a large radar dish for tracking enemy planes at long distances. A larger dish, however, required a larger fuselage. Boyd and other fighter advocates were against this.[12]

Boyd and his associates at DCS/R&D were not the only ones frustrated with the F-X. Others further up the chain of command were pursuing a similar path on their own. In September 1966, the same time that Boyd was assigned to the F-X project, there was a large shift in leadership: General James Ferguson became the head of Air Force Systems Command (AFSC). General Glenn Kent, who had been serving above Boyd as assistant for concept formulation to the DCS/R&D, kept the duties of that position in addition to his new role at AFSC as DCS for development plans. The same month, General Felix Michael Rogers, a former fighter group commander and assistant chief of staff to IX Fighter Command in World War II with extensive fighter experience, became Kent's assistant DCS. Underneath Kent and Rogers was Major James Tedeschi, who was very involved with modifying the F-X as well.

This group was frustrated by the long list of characteristics that TAC labeled as "requirements" for the F-X, such as speed, turn rate, payload, range, total weight, and others. Kent felt that many of the requirements were mutually exclusive. "The people at TAC were demanding an aircraft that simply could not be built," he said. "One can achieve any one of these specifications individually but not all of them in a single aircraft. If you want payload and range, you develop a high-wing-loading aircraft. If you want agility—the ability to turn and maneuver—you develop a low-wing-loading aircraft. You cannot have it both ways."[13]

Kent's group independently came to similar conclusions as Boyd, Sprey, Christie, Titus, and Ritchie. They disagreed with having two pilots and were opposed to the high wing loading (126 pounds) and the heavy weight (60,000 pounds). This group was also opposed to the variable-sweep wing, which Boyd had not yet completely rejected. Rogers recalled that "without talking to anybody else except General Ferguson and General Kent, it was quickly agreed that from our viewpoint all of those things were unacceptable."[14]

Kent went as far as to call the requirements "an abomination," but emphasized that they had not been created maliciously. He blamed the process itself, arguing that well-meaning people kept adding additional "wish requirements" that, taken individually, seemed beneficial, but when combined called for a completely different type of aircraft from what was originally intended. For Kent, the best way forward was "by not paying attention to these 'sacred requirements.'"[15] He recommended to Ferguson that "we wait until the 'requirements' had run their course" and later call for an "agonizing reappraisal" that resulted in a new list, not of requirements, but achievable "performance specifications."[16]

What this group wanted to achieve was a dedicated air-to-air platform. Rogers wanted to go as far as to make a single-engine fighter, although that view had little support. Regardless, the team agreed to "resist all attempts to build a 'baby TFX [F-111]'" or anything that had significant air-to-ground capability. The efforts to redefine the F-X involved a wide range of people. Rogers and Kent contributed to a briefing that Ferguson delivered to Disosway, leading to the elimination of many of the more extreme requirements.

Although Boyd and Sprey were often quite critical of ASD at Wright-Patterson, Kent noted that ASD played a part in rolling back those requirements. Rogers specifically pointed to Colonel Robert Daly, a development planner at ASD and first senior program officer on the F-X, as having the "prime responsibility" during the first phase of redefining the plane. Kent and Rogers preferred a general officer in that role, and later requested General Robert White, a fighter pilot in World War II, the Korean War, and the Vietnam War, as well as one of the X-15 test pilots, who became head of the F-15 program at Wright-Patterson in June 1968. Rogers insisted that guidance for the work of redefining the F-X into an air-to-air fighter "was *totally* the work of Glenn Kent," and that there was a significant amount of cooperation from a large group of people working under General Otto Glasser, the assistant DCS/R&D (the head of Boyd's section). He named Al Flax and Cal Hargis as making important contributions, the latter specifically on engines, and noted that large teams at DDR&E and SA were also involved.[17]

Rogers saw himself in the mold of the fighter pilot tradition, if not to the extremes of Boyd. Summarizing their work on the F-X, Rogers said, "What we contributed over there was the push of General Ferguson to get a real fighter which is probably a part of the role that I was supposed to play since I was supposed to be 'a real fighter pilot.'" He felt similarly to Myers, arguing that "we hadn't procured any fighters for quite a long while. . . . We hadn't produced an air-to-air fighter . . . since the F-86, really." He did note the importance of Boyd and Christie's efforts. For Rogers, their EMT work—which Kent extended with additional computer modeling later in the process—helped not only to define the F-X but to convince others above them of the need for a dedicated fighter. Rogers expressed frustration that "nay sayers at every level above us" held back the F-X program by up to two years because the many decision makers did not agree with their view of the importance of a dedicated fighter.[18]

Owing to the efforts of Ferguson, Kent, Rogers, Boyd, Christie, Sprey, and others, by the spring of 1967 the Air Force had worked up a design of a lighter aircraft to weigh forty thousand pounds. Some fighter advocates nicknamed this version the "Blue Bird." At first, the wing loading had been 110 pounds, but, attempting to increase maneuverability, Boyd lowered it to 80 pounds (arguing for a slower but more agile 60 pounds). To increase acceleration rates and combat performance, he lowered the engine bypass ratio to 1.5, although he advocated lowering it much further, all the way down to 0.6. He originally called for a thrust-to-weight ratio of .97, but in the interest of having a bigger wing to increase maneuverability, the ratio was lowered to .9.

This was still a partial compromise, as Rogers recalled that Boyd thought forty thousand pounds was far too large.[19]

Incoming Threats

This version of the F-X was presented to the Air Staff and then to the Defense Science Board in the summer of 1967. At this point, the US Navy became involved. The Navy also presented designs for a new fighter, code-named the VFAX (this project was later canceled in favor of the VFX program—both based on the Grumman 303 series—that eventually resulted in the F-14 Tomcat). The Air Force feared that Congress would approve the Navy's VFAX and reject the Air Force's F-X, forcing it to adopt a Navy-designed plane yet again. Secretary of Defense Robert McNamara had initiated an eighteen-month study in May 1966 to determine if one airframe could meet the needs of both services. To prevent that, the Air Force needed to differentiate the F-X and show that it was superior in some way—such as air-to-air combat. The Navy's design emphasized effective dogfighting, but its specifications also called for ground-attack capability. George Spangenberg, head of aircraft design in the US Navy's Naval Air Systems Command, noted that the Navy wanted the VFAX to be "as capable in bomb delivery as an A-7."[20] Some of those requirements were later dropped, but the Navy's specifications created an opportunity for the Air Force to differentiate its fighter as a pure air-to-air weapon. Boyd also emphasized the competition with the Navy. As he explained, "We had a higher thrust to weight and a lower wing loading. Thrust to weight gives you better climb and acceleration; lower wing loading gives you better turn. So we could out-climb, out-accelerate, and out-turn them—the Navy VFAX."[21] This pressure from the Navy continued to influence the design of the F-X throughout its development.

Another external source of pressure that shaped the F-X toward an air-to-air focus was the Domodedovo air show in Moscow in July 1967. This event revealed a new arsenal of Soviet fighter aircraft for the first time. The variable-sweep-wing MiG-23 (similar to USAF's F-111) drew little worry from fighter pilots. The MiG-25 interceptor was a different story. It was fast, with an attack speed of Mach 2.8 and reported dash capability of Mach 3. The show also unveiled the Su-15 interceptor, which caused a stir in the American military aviation community.[22] These planes could fly higher and faster, and senior members of USAF worried that their forces were inadequate to stop them—especially given the fact that in Vietnam the less advanced MiG-21s were shooting F-4s out of the sky in large numbers throughout 1967.[23] USAF leaders wanted to make sure that the F-X could address these threats.

The Six-Day War in June 1967 also gave fighter advocates ammunition for their arguments about making the F-X dedicated for air-to-air. That conflict opened with a preemptive attack in which the Israeli Air Force (IAF) destroyed 380 Egyptian aircraft—most of them hit on the ground. Some Egyptian planes did get airborne, but twenty of them were shot down, costing the IAF only two losses. The failure of Egyptian fighters was largely the result of poor training—they fought at altitudes and speeds at which their MiG-17s and MiG-21s did not have an advantage, using tactics that were not suited for the strengths of those planes.[24]

Although air superiority had been achieved almost entirely through a ground attack, fighter advocates saw the war as evidence for their case that not only was air combat essential, but the myth of the lone fighter pilot winning aerial victories based on personality traits seemed to be reinforced. One Israeli flight leader, recalling the events, argued that the reason the Egyptians performed poorly was that they lacked "the high degree of our [Israeli] pilots' personal identification with their assignments." He then argued, "A good pilot . . . is not merely a mixture of skill, resourcefulness, discipline and good judgement, but also, even primarily, an outgrowth of the spiritual values and the cultural level which have nurtured him."[25] Titus was especially influenced by the Six-Day War, claiming that a gun was necessary on fighter aircraft because Israeli pilots had achieved all their kills with guns.[26]

In the summer of 1967, the modified F-X proposal underwent further modification both by the Air Staff and by ANSER Analytical Services Inc., a nonprofit Air Force contractor. By August, SECAF Harold Brown presented a slightly modified version of Boyd's changes to OSD, emphasizing the role of air-to-air combat. Brown argued that unless air superiority was decided first, no other tactical air missions (such as interdiction and CAS) could succeed, but the then-current main fighter, the F-4 Phantom, could not prevail in air-to-air combat against newer Soviet planes. Brown and other fighter advocates thought that the air superiority achieved in Korea and in Vietnam (to that point) was possible because US pilots were better trained, and their aircraft had better weapons and avionics equipment. These advantages would not exist, Brown and the fighter advocates believed, if the US had to fight against the more capable Soviet air force.[27]

The result of these pressures and efforts was a new RFP for a tactical fighter issued in August 1967. Boyd's analysis formed a "major part" of that RFP, which represented a shift further toward an air-to-air focus and called for a state-of-the-art approach, noting that the Air Force could not "rely on pilot skill alone to offset any technical inferiority of U.S. aircraft. . . . To win an air war against Soviet forces it is essential that U.S. pilots be given the best aircraft that technology can afford."[28] On December 1, 1967, McDonnell Douglas and General Dynamics won contracts to pursue a six-month concept formulation "point design" study in response to the new RFP and continued to work with the Air Force to refine the designs. Fairchild-Hiller, Grumman, Lockheed, and North American all undertook unfunded studies of their own.[29]

Air-to-Air?

With these studies under way, the Air Force still struggled to define exactly what it wanted the F-X to be. The air-to-air advocates had made significant advances, but there was disagreement. Some desired a multi-role plane with significant ground-attack capability, while various fighter advocates wanted an air-to-air focus to differing degrees. In February 1968, Myers drafted a review of the F-X program to that point, arguing for a move away from "the multi-purpose monster" toward what he repeatedly called "the 'right' FIGHTER." He questioned the need for long range and large fuel capacity, the need for two engines, and the need for radar and missiles. He wanted a gun-based, very light, maneuverable, daytime-only, air-to-air fighter, and argued that a plane designed that way would be effective in ground attack anyway. Myers did not want "to inflict the weight, volume, complexity, manpower, logistics and cost burdens associated with 'all-purpose' on the much needed air superiority *fighter*."[30]

Also in February 1968, Disosway, commander of TAC, issued an updated Required Operational Capability (ROC) for the F-X, citing the need to counter the air threats of the MiG-21 and the newly revealed Soviet aircraft from the recent Moscow air show. However, the new requirements were mixed—some were in line with what fighter advocates wanted, others were not. They included high speed, up to a Mach 2.7 burst, a single pilot, high-energy maneuverability, all-weather capability, and a ground-looking radar.[31]

The issue was further obfuscated on February 29, 1968. In a statement to the Senate Armed Services Committee, Lieutenant General Joseph Holzapple, the DCS/R&D, stated, "The F-X, as we see it, will be a multi-mission tactical fighter with a decided advantage in aerial combat," and emphasized that it would have a variable-sweep wing. As of April 1968, CSAF McConnell and SECAF Harold Brown were both committed to the variable-sweep wing.[32] Despite the advances that fighter advocates had made in pushing their cause for a dedicated air-to-air fighter, the upper leadership remained unconvinced.

The team at DCS/R&D expanded in February 1968. Titus hired a close friend, Colonel Garry Willard, whom he called "a great fighter pilot." Indeed, Willard had extensive fighter experience as an F-86 pilot in the same squadron as Boyd's (the 25th, although Willard had completed his tour before Boyd arrived) and had fighter command experience, including serving as the commander of the first "Wild Weasel" squadron. Titus and Myers later recalled the almost cartoonish atmosphere that this team worked in. Titus described Boyd's eccentricities: "The room turned blue with obscenities and cigar smoke. The young secretaries were reduced to tears."[33] Myers noted that much of the team's work on the F-X was done under the influence of alcohol, reminiscing about "when it was actually fun to work there—lots of three martini lunchs [sic] and cocktail parties at which [Titus] was a star."[34]

This second concept formulation phase ended in May 1968. General Dynamics offered two designs, one fixed-wing and one variable sweep. McDonnell had studied many designs, including variations of podded engines versus fuselage-mounted engines, each combined with fixed and variable-sweep wing concepts. After these comparisons McDonnell settled on a fixed-wing, two-engine, single-seat plane.[35] Fairchild-Hiller, Grumman, Lockheed, and North American also contributed results from their self-funded efforts. At the ASD office at Wright-Patterson, Daly led a team of over one hundred people to pore over these results and incorporate them into a final concept formulation, a process that took some time.[36]

At this point, the debate between air-to-air and multi-mission focus took a further turn toward the former. The competing visions of the F-X consolidated around two leaders. Disosway championed the push for a dedicated air-to-air fighter, while the vice chief of staff of SAC, General Bruce Holloway, argued for a multi-role plane.[37] Although Holloway was a leader in SAC, he was not a champion for bombers. He had been among the first in a new wave of leaders with a predominantly fighter background. Holloway had been the first commander of a US jet fighter group in 1946, and he had coauthored the twelve-star letter arguing for an air superiority fighter. But in his role at SAC, he pushed for the F-X to adopt multi-role capability.

Disosway tried to push Holloway and other multi-role advocates toward his point of view. "We wanted an air superiority fighter, and we didn't want any air-to-ground stuff mixed up in it," he said. Disosway recalled that the pressure to make the F-X a multi-role plane was not coming from Holloway or McConnell themselves, but from their subordinates or from other offices around the Air Force. "I used to go up there and see Bruce Holloway and

McConnell," he said, "and I would say, 'Now look, let's have an air-to-air airplane, nothing else. Remember, air-to-air airplane.' I would make them repeat it, 'Air-to-air airplane, and don't let any of these guys get into it.'" He continued, "There were pressures from everybody you could think of to mess that airplane up, but we wanted to keep it pure air-to-air, knowing full well after awhile that they would use it air-to-ground, but at least we didn't want it designed for that. It had to be designed for just air-to-air."[38]

What brought these disparate voices together was competition with the Navy. The Navy's fighter program was further along in development and had a clearer vision than the F-X. McConnell won many multi-role advocates to his side by arguing that unity against the Navy was necessary, or else the Air Force might be forced to buy another Navy aircraft. "We had a very difficult time in satisfying all the people who had to be satisfied as to what the F-X was going to be," McConnell testified to the Senate Armed Services Committee on May 28, 1968. "We finally decided—and I hope there is no one who still disagrees—that this aircraft is going to be an air superiority fighter." When asked if the plane would be used for ground-attack missions, he retorted, "It would be over my dead body."[39]

Yet not all the fighter advocates were satisfied, and this decision was not as final as it seemed. In June 1968, Pierre Sprey authored a study of air avionics systems. He claimed these systems, particularly combat radar systems, were useless, primarily because they were too complex and unreliable. He implied that pilots should use their eyes instead of radar, and there should be less automation in the cockpit. The report was worded in an accusatory tone, and he suggested that the system responsible for procuring avionics was corrupt and in need of massive reform.[40] The F-15 was not mentioned specifically, although the avionics and radar that current F-X designs contained was a major sticking point for Sprey and his associates. Many of the arguments made in this paper came to define these men for the remainder of their careers.

That same month, General Roger K. Rhodarmer, who had been working in DCS/R&D and had a history mostly in aerial reconnaissance, became the liaison of the F-X program. Rhodarmer's role was to both resolve the remaining differences in requirements and sell the plane to Congress to obtain approval. He was particularly worried about the Navy's fighter program, which he considered "a threat to our concept of the F-X."[41] To help convince Congress, Rhodarmer relied extensively on Titus, Boyd, and Major John Axley, an electrical engineer and F-105 pilot.[42]

Sprey was unsatisfied, and on July 18, 1968, he wrote a memo to Ferguson, head of AFSC. He said he thought the plan for the F-X was "most disturbing and bodes ill for the likelihood of developing a truly superior (and saleable) fighter." He listed specific complaints, first that "there is no evidence of willingness to forego nice-to-have items that do not contribute directly toward shooting down MiGs," such as a tail hook and nose wheel steering. He accused ASD of relying on "abstract and unrealistic analysis," and expressed much concern for the general size of the plane, wanting the F-X to be much smaller than the F-4, which it was not. He then produced a checklist, twenty-three pages long, of specific characteristics for his desired version of the F-X. These included light weight (as low as twenty-nine thousand pounds for a single-engine version or thirty-three thousand pounds for a twin-engine version), a low bypass ratio of 0.6, a maximum range of 260 miles, low wing loading of sixty pounds per square foot, a range-only X-band radar (here Sprey entertained a variety of options but was steadfastly opposed to look-down, pulse-Doppler radars), and as few missiles (preferably only AIM-9 Sidewinders) as possible. To the latter point, Sprey argued that missiles were too easy to dodge, and thus the "proper role" for missiles (if they had one at all) was to force the enemy into a turning dogfight to then be killed with a gun. Like his earlier writing, his tone was frequently aggressive, attacking the Air Force's entire approach to weapons design, which he said in some areas went as far as "mania." He concluded, "Despite all the USAF and DOD forces mitigating against it, we have, for the first time, the opportunity of producing a fighter that will have a real rather than paper dominance over anything in the sky."[43]

About this same time, and possibly related to this memo, Boyd and Sprey proposed a version of the F-X they called the "Red Bird." It used the same engine and same shape, but it was an "attempt to shake all the crap out of [the] airplane." They removed whatever they considered nonessential and brought the weight down to thirty-four thousand pounds. The idea was to "strip down" the plane to make it more agile. When their vision was not implemented, Sprey recalled that they were "disgusted" and they "declared war on the [US]AF."[44]

The Air Force might not have gone as far as the fighter advocates wanted, but it was moving in that direction. In August 1968, General Kent became the assistant chief of staff for Studies and Analysis at Air Staff Headquarters. There, Lieutenant Colonel Larry Welch, a fighter pilot and future CSAF, was working on a computer program called TAC Avenger. The program, coded by Welch and two other fighter pilots working under him, simulated air-to-air combat duels by "flying" aircraft in five degrees of freedom (altitude, sideways motion, forward motion, pitch, and roll), based on Boyd's EMT data, to predict which aircraft could defeat the other in a dogfight. Although

Boyd did not work for Kent, Boyd was present for the running of some of the simulations. Kent saw the potential for TAC Avenger to help with two problems. First, the program could demonstrate whether the Navy's proposed F-14 or the Air Force's F-X was the superior dogfighter. Kent was not only worried that pressure for commonality would lead Congress to cancel the F-X, but about a recent NASA study that argued in favor of the Navy's fighter. Welch ran a series of simulations of both the F-14 and the proposed F-X against MiG fighters, demonstrating that the F-X "was by far the better fighter."[45] Second, Kent used TAC Avenger to supplement Daly's effort to reshape the F-X requirements. The simulation could run various configurations of proposed F-X designs and see how they affected air-to-air combat performance. The Air Force Flight Dynamics Laboratory contributed data on various technological possibilities, and fighter pilots made trade-off studies based on those options. The information produced from Welch's program helped to define the requirements for the F-X.

Bearing Little Resemblance to Fighters

By the end of August 1968, Daly's team at ASD had completed its analysis and issued a new concept formulation package. It stressed the importance of air-to-air combat as the main role and air-to-ground as a secondary mission. It specified a single pilot and retained the variable-sweep wing. Based on this, John Foster, DDR&E, along with his agent Robert O'Donohue, composed a development concept paper (DCP) to finalize what the Air Force wanted the F-X to be.[46]

The document represented some victories for fighter advocates; it diminished some of the requirements that TAC had previously insisted on. The range and length of time of the plane's top-speed dash were decreased. The top speed was lowered to Mach 2.3, with a 2.5 burst capability, meaning less of the airframe needed to be built out of titanium. Lowering the burst speed took three thousand pounds off the airplane. Boyd called for the elimination of variable intake ramps (computer-controlled surfaces that shape the flow of air into an engine to maximize power) and the bellmouth mechanism (which directs air into a jet engine) on the engines—both were complicated features that had allowed the F-4 to achieve its high top speeds. Boyd thought they were unnecessary for combat maneuvering. But the fighter advocates did not get everything they wanted. Boyd called for wing slats, extra surfaces placed on the leading edge of a wing, allowing it to operate at more extreme angles. McDonnell argued for a less complicated (and less expensive) solution in a high-camber (curved) wing. Both solutions increased maneuverability, but the high-camber wing increased drag. Despite Boyd's objections, the leading-edge slats were not used.[47]

In the interest of survivability and the ability to function in rougher forward areas, the DCP called for many features Boyd and Sprey hated, including an auxiliary power unit, soft-field landing gear, a tail hook, a drag chute, an autopilot system, self-sealing (foamed) fuel tanks, armor, and bulletproof glass. Perhaps the biggest loss for fighter advocates was the inclusion of long-range pulse Doppler radar with ground-looking capability. The argument for these larger, more complex avionics systems came from the Feather Duster and Have Donut programs, which had demonstrated the importance of detection of the enemy for determining air-to-air victory. As OASD/SA (Office of the Assistant Secretary of Defense, Systems Analysis) noted in September 1968, "It was formally decided . . . to develop a larger, more versatile aircraft with stand-off weapons rather than a lighter, more specialized visual dog-fighting aircraft."[48] The Air Force needed to choose between building a small plane that was difficult to detect, or a larger airplane that could carry the equipment needed to detect the enemy first. The Air Force chose the latter.[49]

With the F-X concept now defined, in September 1968 the Air Force sent an RFP for contract definition to McDonnell, North American, Grumman, General Dynamics, Lockheed, LTV, Fairchild-Hiller, and Boeing. At this time the F-X was now officially the F-15, the reason being that F-13 was considered unlucky, and the Navy had already claimed the F-14. Four of the eight companies responded: Fairchild-Hiller, General Dynamics, McDonnell, and North American. That December, the Air Force selected Fairchild-Hiller, McDonnell, and North American for competition, asking for full proposals by the end of June 1969.[50]

While contractors prepared their designs, the Air Force was busy convincing Congress of the necessity of the F-X, and it did so mostly in terms that aligned with the fighter advocates. On March 27, 1969, the DCS/R&D, Lieutenant General Marvin L. McNickle, testified to the House Armed Services Committee that the F-15 was "an air superiority fighter to combat the Migs," and that the goal of the program was "to design the best possible single-seat, twin-engine fighter for air-to-air combat." McNickle emphasized the maneuverability and acceleration of the fighter. Testifying to the same committee on May 20, Rhodarmer made it even clearer: "This aircraft will be designed as a single-purpose fighter-fighter. By that I mean, it is not a fighter-bomber, it is not designed to carry bombs. It is not a fighter-interceptor. It is an airplane designed to fight aircraft in air-to-air combat." He added, "We know what we want. . . . This aircraft is not saddled with a multipurpose role."[51]

As Stuart Levin, writing in *Space/Aeronautics* magazine, noted, "There's a superconsciousness (you can taste it in every conversation) that the plane must be optimized for the air-to-air dogfight," but he also noted some ambiguity in that the Air Force "also asks (in muted tones) for air-to-ground strike capability." That added ground capability, Levin noted, "touches a raw nerve underlying USAF's loudly proclaimed identification of the F-15 as a pure dogfighter."[52]

The contractors each produced quite different designs. Fairchild-Hiller emphasized its experience building the F-105 Thunderchief and a focus on survivability. Its design was a single tail with a "three-body" concept involving podded engines placed under each wing, separated from the main fuselage. North American had previously designed the P-51 Mustang and F-86 Sabre—fighters heralded by Boyd and other fighter advocates. Yet, Robert Kemp, the company's F-15 program manager, admitted that "we have a team of folks whose pencils may be rusty when it comes to writing the word 'fighter.'" They enlisted the aid of Northrop, designers of the F-5, and sought to create "a pilot's airplane." They incorporated elements from their previous work on the XB-70, using adjacent inlets slung underneath the body. Their design also incorporated a blended wing-body shape to maximize lift and maneuverability.[53] These choices gave North American's design a look that foreshadowed the later F-16.

If those entries represented opposing ends of a design spectrum, McDonnell's entry was more conventional, with engine inlets against the side of the fuselage and a twin tail. McDonnell was struggling, having recently lost three major aircraft contracts. For the company, the F-15 program was a matter of life or death. "We were dead-in-the-water," F-15 engineer Jack Abercrombie recalled. "In order to survive, a major over-haul of our *modus operandi* was essential." The program manager, Don Malvern, led the efforts to do exactly that. Experienced in fighter design, McDonnell staffed almost the entirety of the F-15 program with the same people who had worked on the F-4 Phantom. The company canceled vacations, and engineers worked over eighty hours a week. They conducted wind tunnel tests of eight hundred configurations, including seventy-four wing shapes and fifty-eight variable wing camber devices. The company created a computer-aided design and evaluation (CADE) program to run simulations and evaluate thousands more options. The final proposal took 2.5 million man-hours and totaled 37,500 pages in 382 volumes.[54]

Rhodarmer served as the focal point of the F-X program in the Pentagon, and his office coordinated disparate departments and dealt with the press, but the details of the design process were directed mostly from the

Air Force Special Projects Office (SPO) at Wright-Patterson. That office had been headed by Colonel Robert White, but on July 11, 1969, shortly after the competing contractors turned in their proposals, Brigadier General Benjamin N. Bellis became the SPO director. Bellis had worked on the Matador and Atlas missiles, managed the development program of the SR-71 Blackbird, and held advanced degrees in both aeronautical engineering and business administration.[55]

Around May 1969, many members of the F-15 group that had been working at the Pentagon were transferred to nearby Andrews Air Force Base to become part of the F-15 Program Element Monitor office at AFSC. This included Boyd, now a temporary lieutenant colonel and R&D director for AFSC. Summarizing his time at DCS/R&D, Titus asserted that Boyd's EMT work was "the single most important link in making the acquisition of the F-15 Advanced Tactical Fighter possible." Although Boyd, Sprey, Myers, and others often complained of resistance within the Air Force, Titus reported that Boyd's work was "enthusiastically received" by Air Force leaders at every level and across various commands, as well as by civilian officials and Congress. Whether this was accurate, or an overstatement Titus made for the sake of official reporting, is unclear.[56]

Boyd remained involved with the F-15 program for three more years, but, according to Coram, Boyd viewed his role as a humiliating "non job," and he basically ignored it. He often came in late or missed days completely.[57] This is perhaps why Bellis barely remembered him, later recalling, "To my knowledge, John Boyd had nothing to do with the design of the F-15," although Bellis did clarify that Boyd's EMT language was important for the program and that Boyd had been involved with concept formulation. Despite all the progress fighter advocates had made on the plane, Boyd was frustrated that the F-15 had not been taken to the extremes that he wanted in his quest for a true fighter, and essentially abandoned it. Bellis claimed that "Boyd became so involved with EM that he never really understood the modern day fighter. He thought that all fighter warfare involved the maneuvering 'DOG Fight.' He liked 'turning and burning' because it all involved EM." Bellis thought Boyd ignored the complexities of wing loading, composite materials, and beyond-visual-range capability, and that "he hated the complexity and sophistication of an on-board fire control system (radar)." Boyd wanted a small, day-only, clear-weather-only lightweight fighter in large numbers but, according to Bellis, refused to consider that such a plan would cause massive increases in pilots, training, maintenance, basing, refueling capability, and command and control. In addition, reliance on an aircraft that could not function at night or in the weather conditions endemic to the

European theater, among other considerations, threatened to make Boyd's more extreme ideas nonstarters. "John really did not support the F-15 program," Bellis concluded. "I did not consider him to be a reliable officer."[58] Some of Bellis's claims are not wholly correct, as Boyd did often discuss some of these factors, such as wing loading. But Boyd was clearly frustrated and already focused on other projects.

Others were frustrated too. In October 1969, Myers sent a scathing memo to DDR&E Allan Simon, saying, "I have little confidence that our aerospace/military community can be guided toward the development and production of a FIGHTER optimized for the close-air combat task." Regarding the competing contractors, Myers said, "All three have designed aircraft which bear little resemblance to air superiority fighters," and he blamed the Air Force, saying the service "would never bring itself to overcome the appetite for sophistication and technology." Myers went as far as to say the Air Force was ignoring the realities of a wartime environment, and that specifically there were three characteristics he thought were being ignored. The "prime" of these was "airplane size," followed by "simplicity" and "numbers" (quantity of aircraft).[59]

Fairchild-Hiller, McDonnell, and North American turned in their proposals for the F-15 by July 1, 1969. The Air Force evaluated them according to eighty-seven different factors split into five categories: technical, operational, management, logistics, and cost. Each area had a different team of evaluators who scored the proposals separately. Thus, there was not any single overriding reason why one design was chosen over another, but McDonnell's entry scored highest in each individual category and had the lowest cost. SECAF Robert Seamans announced McDonnell as the winner on December 23, 1969.[60]

A Real Mess on Our Hands

The F-15 development process happened to occur amid a shift in the Air Force procurement policy. As secretary of defense, McNamara instituted his "Total Package Procurement" policy. It called for contractors to bid for the near-entirety of full weapons systems, including design, development, production, and various subsystems—hence, a "total package." Prior to this, contractors had bid for components or phases separately. Sometimes they sought to underbid on the design and development phase and gain back the spent resources during production, since production contracts usually went to the same designer. McNamara's office thought that production phases were not truly competitive and that their costs tended to become inflated.

Total Package Procurement theoretically encouraged more competition, brought down costs, and could help the Air Force predict and manage long-term costs and production schedules.[61]

The theory didn't always work out. Several weapons platforms in various services experienced major problems using Total Package Procurement, most notably the Air Force's C-5 Galaxy, designed by Lockheed. Misunderstandings about the level of coordination needed between contractor and government and, even more, the inability to predict costs of developing the advanced technologies of the time led to massive cost overruns on the C-5 project.[62]

The F-15 happened to be entering the contractor competition phase during the shift away from this procurement model. Major General Harry E. Goldsworthy, commander of ASD, was assigned to come up with a new procurement approach for the F-15. He thought that emphasizing cost instead of performance was a mistake. He also wanted to place most of the risk on the government, rather than on the contractors, in order to encourage a high level of quality in their work. In January 1969, the incoming administration of President Richard Nixon brought a change to DOD, including a new deputy secretary of defense, David Packard, an electrical engineer and cofounder of Hewlett-Packard. He immediately began an effort to reform what he as well as many in the military saw as the failed policies of McNamara. Speaking to a group of defense managers in August 1970, Packard stated, "In defense procurement, we have a real mess on our hands."[63]

Nixon's newly appointed SECAF was former deputy administrator of NASA and MIT professor of aeronautical engineering Dr. Robert Seamans. Seamans developed a method of creating "demonstration milestones" that could measure a program's development and ensure cooperation and mutual faith between contractor and government. However, John Foster of DDR&E was concerned about price overruns and wanted to save money on the F-15. As a result, some air-to-ground capabilities were cut from the F-15.[64]

The debates about procurement were not the only larger shift happening at the time of the F-15's development. One of the reasons why fighter advocates could make such headway was that the Air Force was experiencing a shift in leadership and in its thinking—a shift that brought more attention to the role of tactical air power broadly and to fighters specifically. Air-to-air combat began to receive greater focus as more and more young officers, known as the "iron majors," pushed for a complete cultural, technological, and training overhaul in the service. Much of this shift was a reaction against perceived shortcomings of the Air Force's performance in the Vietnam War, especially in the realm of air-to-air combat. Planners took steps to address this in several ways, including focusing the F-15 program on air combat, but they also instituted changes in leadership, reevaluated pilot training procedures, and looked to the history of the service for inspiration.[65]

The change in leadership, beginning as early as 1965 and in full swing as the Vietnam War approached its end, was dramatic. After World War II, bomber generals had dominated the service: as Colonel Mike Worden explained, "By 1 October 1961 all major operational commanders, and the vast majority of the Air Staff leadership, had become ardent bomber generals—most of them SAC absolutists. SAC's methods became Air Force methods."[66] In 1965, CSAF General McConnell initiated a change in leadership, hoping more tactical-air-power-minded leaders would lend insight on the Vietnam War. At that point, the only former fighter pilot in a high command position was USAFE commander General Disosway. McConnell promoted him to commander of TAC in August of that year and replaced him at USAFE with General Holloway, a double-ace fighter pilot. In 1966, former fighter ace General William Momyer became the commander of the Seventh Air Force—the senior Air Force commander in the Southeast Asia theater—and in 1968 he took command of TAC. Also in 1966, McConnell brought Holloway in to be his vice chief of staff, before making him commander of SAC.

McConnell did not place only former fighter pilots to major commands, but he did seek a balanced group. For example, he placed the former SAC commander and bomber pilot General John D. Ryan as PACAF commander and then as his vice chief of staff. Although these moves did put fighter generals in positions of power and influence in the Air Force, they did not overturn the service's doctrine, which remained based on strategic bombing primarily through nuclear weapons.[67] Furthermore, while an officer's background may be influential on that individual's later decision making, it does not dictate a particular approach. Although an examination of trends regarding which types of officers rise to high command positions is useful in pointing to institutional culture, many officers, regardless of background, can and do broaden their viewpoint and considerations when they reach that level.

Nonetheless, the role of tactical air power rose during this period, even outside of key leadership positions. By 1965 the fighter force, in terms of numbers of pilots and wings, had doubled in size since 1948 and outnumbered bomber pilots and wings. By 1966, tactical air forces received a larger budget than strategic forces. By 1969, fighter generals outnumbered bomber generals two to one. Because promotions often depended on combat experience, the simple fact that the Air Force flew more tactical sorties in fighter aircraft in Korea and Vietnam meant that most of the airmen eligible for promotion in those years happened to be fighter pilots. "From 1971 to

1982 fighter pilots on average outnumbered bomber pilots by four to one," according to Worden. "By 1982 there were no bomber generals in key Air Staff positions, and fighter generals outnumbered bomber generals in the major commands by five to four."[68]

The Air Force also dramatically changed its training procedures in the years immediately after the Vietnam War. CSAF General Ryan, working with Momyer, conducted surveys of pilots who had flown in Vietnam and concluded that they had been woefully undertrained for air-to-air combat. By 1972, the Air Force created the "Aggressor" squadron—a group of pilots flying aircraft and tactics meant to mimic Soviet tactical air forces in simulated air combat against American pilots. A series of exercises known as "Red Flag" soon became a normal practice for training top USAF pilots in advanced air-to-air combat techniques.[69]

Not all the fighter generals were air-to-air combat specialists wedded to the stereotypes of the knights of the air; many had flown fighters in other roles such as interdiction or CAS. However, fighter advocates who did adhere to that culture had more in common with the new crop of leaders and a louder voice in the institution as a result. The technology development of this period, specifically the F-15 Eagle, reflects that emphasis. Despite some of the mythology regarding Boyd's influence on the F-15, he was not acting alone but was part of a cohort including Titus, Ritchie, Sprey, Christie, Willard, Daly, and White, among others. Without question, Boyd's EMT shaped the design of the F-15, giving engineers a language with which to quantify the performance parameters that fighter advocates desired. However, others working elsewhere, particularly Kent, Rogers, Tedeschi, and Welch, were working toward the same goals and likely would have done so whether Boyd was involved or not. Whether they would have been as successful without Boyd's EMT work is impossible to say.

Despite the F-15's specialization as an air-to-air fighter, Boyd and his associates rejected it as a failure—unable to truly capture the "white scarf stuff" of aerial combat. As they became increasingly frustrated with what they felt were shortcomings of the F-15, they attempted to achieve their vision of a lightweight day fighter with another aircraft—this time, one they would design from the ground up.

CHAPTER 5

"The Lord's Work"

> The F-15 was enormously successful because we had
> a long period of defining what we wanted it to be. . . .
> The F-16 was almost an afterthought.
>
> —General Larry Welch

Lieutenant Colonel John Boyd, Pierre Sprey, and their associates wanted a fighter plane that could live up to their idealized image of knights of the air fighting aerial duels. They attempted to transform the F-15 Eagle into exactly that, and although they achieved many of their goals, they saw their effort as a failure. The Eagle was, in Boyd's and Sprey's minds, too big, too sophisticated, and too expensive, and it had been too heavily modified by the Air Force. Boyd and his associates began advocating for an entirely new aircraft that culminated in the F-16 Fighting Falcon. They saw themselves as guerrilla fighters against the US government, describing themselves with religious metaphors—they were divine messengers saving a corrupt and ineffective Air Force from itself. The F-16 project was guided by the subculture of fighter pilots that dated back to World War I—based on a constructed, idealized image of romantic duels in the sky. The F-16 is an artifact of that culture.

"A Pure Air-to-Air Fighter"

By the start of 1969, the Air Force pressed forward with the F-15 program, confident that it was one of the best fighter aircraft ever devised. Boyd and Sprey seethed with anger. To them, the F-15 was a missed opportunity at best: gold-plating and Air Force bureaucracy had destroyed their vision for a true fighter—a simple, lightweight plane designed for close-quarters air-to-air combat. Test pilot Chuck Myers recalled, "When I say, 'We're not happy with the F-15,' I wouldn't want people to think that I helped spawn *that* airplane, all I helped do was create the need for a new fighter airplane which we haven't yet procured."[1] He said that the F-15 "should have been smaller and better. . . . That's what drove us to try again."[2]

Sprey led the effort to try again. On July 18, 1968, he had written a memo to General James Ferguson, commander of AFSC, outlining the problems with the F-X, proposing large-scale changes to bring down the weight and size, remove most or all of the avionics, and increase its maneuverability. Ferguson took no action. "When it became very clear to me that General Ferguson either couldn't or wouldn't do anything about getting a more rational fighter," said Sprey, "I decided at that point that I would carry this debate into public." He gave a series of briefings at NASA and "all over the Pentagon . . . on behalf of an airplane that I called the F-X2 [or F-XX]."[3]

The core idea of this type of lightweight fighter was not new, nor was Sprey its only advocate. The same initial studies into new fighters that had launched the F-X program in 1965 had also examined the possibility of an "advanced day fighter" (ADF) in the range of twenty thousand to twenty-five thousand pounds, with both a high thrust-weight ratio and low wing loading to create 25 percent more maneuverability than the MiG-21. While the F-X program was still in the early part of the concept formulation stage, the revelation of the new MiG-25 at the Soviets' summer 1967 Domodedovo air show prompted the Air Force to focus away from the ADF and toward the heavier, higher-speed, and longer-range F-X that led to the F-15.[4]

Yet some aircraft manufacturers had been pursuing a concept similar to Sprey's F-XX on their own. In the mid-1960s, Lockheed and Northrop both realized that their lightweight fighters, the F-104 Starfighter and F-5 Freedom Fighter respectively, had sold very well in Europe, and that there might be a large foreign market eager for a replacement. Both companies began in-house studies to pursue that possibility. Lockheed began developing the CL-985, based on the F-104, but with larger wings and a more powerful engine. Northrop did not try to modify its F-5 but instead pursued a completely new craft, starting with the N-300 in 1966, and, through testing and refinement, evolving into the P-530 Cobra program by 1967. In 1968, interested in a lower-cost, single-engine version of the F-X, Alain Enthoven, the assistant secretary of defense for systems analysis (the top of Sprey's reporting chain), instructed General Dynamics and Northrop to study the potential for exactly this type of lightweight fighter.[5]

After his failure to spur change with his 1968 memo to Ferguson, Sprey's goal was to take Boyd's energy maneuverability theory (EMT) approach and design a "smaller, much more austere, and vastly higher performance airplane . . . a pure air-to-air fighter" to excel at agility and dogfighting situations at slower speeds (just below and above Mach 1). He called for a twenty-five-thousand-pound craft with a single seat, a single engine, a high thrust-to-weight ratio, and sixty pounds per square foot wing loading, with a light internal gun and two heat-seeking AIM-9 Sidewinder missiles. He rejected "complex" avionics systems, instead using a "simple visual radar." Sprey also proposed his lightweight fighter (LWF) concept to the Navy, labeling it the VFXX. He claimed his LWF "would really answer the mission of a pure air-to-air fighter as opposed to the F-15 which by now is really a fighter-bomber in classical Air Force tradition."[6] Sprey also gave his requirements to General Dynamics and Northrop, who then provided him with preliminary data to test his concepts and provide potential designs.[7]

On June 9, 1969, Sprey released his vision for the F-XX and Navy VF-XX as an official Office of the Assistant Secretary of Defense (Systems Analysis) staff study. This document was a manifesto of the shared vision for the LWF and also of the underlying philosophy that came to define the remainder of his (and Boyd's and their associates') career. Sprey harked back to dogfights of World War I, arguing that maneuverability and turning performance were the key to victory, and that missiles do not—and will not—change that. He asserted that individual "pilot skill and tactical acumen . . . outweighs all normal technological differences between opposing fighters." Maximizing maneuverability was key, he thought: "It is impossible to identify a level of maneuvering performance that is 'good enough.'" Achieving the necessary agility "can be accomplished *only* by rigorously eliminating every pound of weight associated with equipments and airframe specifications that are not absolutely essential to the mission of shooting down enemy aircraft—*then replacing that weight with more engine and more wing.*"[8]

Sprey based his plans on the existing initial work by General Dynamics and Northrop, the FX-404 and N-700 respectively. For specific requirements, Sprey called for using far less fuel than previous fighters and for using lighter materials, even if that meant relaxing safety standards. Avionics was a sticking point—he argued against forward-looking radars, saying they "have been singularly unsuccessful in tactical air combat," and that ground-based radars should be used instead. Although Sprey allowed for some electronics (such as a ranging gun sight, UHF radio, and a passive electronic countermeasures receiver for warning), he insisted on eliminating as much avionics and computer equipment as possible, including automated navigation and intercept computers, autopilot, digital data links, and identify-friend-or-foe systems. He called for maneuvering capability at speeds from Mach .4 to Mach 1.5 and saw no need to go above Mach 2. He demanded a single, low bypass ratio (0.5) engine, claiming a second engine was a liability. He favored guns over missiles but wanted the smallest caliber gun that was still capable of destroying an enemy plane. He completely rejected the radar-guided AIM-7 Sparrow and infrared AIM-4 Falcon missiles and judged the AIM-9 Sidewinder as "almost acceptable." He also called for deleting other features, including self-sealing tanks, a bulletproof windshield, a powered canopy, nose wheel steering, a tailhook, and nuclear protection.[9]

Sprey's study established design goals and themes that dominated discussion of the LWF and later defense reform topics, and it also showcased the personality that grew to define the careers of Boyd and his followers. The proposal pointed to past examples, repeating the assumption that technological and doctrinal limitations of the past (World War II and the Vietnam War, specifically) would remain valid for the foreseeable future. Sprey's tone was accusatory, indicating frustration that the Air Force (and Navy) had not listened to what he and some other fighter advocates thought was their wise counsel, blaming the services for a host of mistakes as a result.

This tone of the study was not lost on its audience, who fervently rejected it. The Naval Air Systems Command Evaluation Division and Systems Analysis Division, for example, noted that a "Mr. Sprey and Mr. Rosenzweig of OASD(SA) have been suggesting a similar approach, although in less specific terms, for at least the past 3 years." The Navy was frustrated at having to look at the proposal again, noting that "the reconsideration of the concept as a viable alternative [to the F-14 and F-15] should have been turned down before submission to the services." Their evaluation noted that the gun Sprey advocated was considered "obsolete" by its own manufacturer, that his engine proposal was "of doubtful merit," that his arguments on engines in general were "specious," and that Sprey's work contained "many contradictory statements" to the degree that "any precise checking [is] impossible." Sprey's thoughts on radar and avionics might have been appropriate for the mid-1950s but were "completely inadequate" even by 1964 standards, much less the mid-1970s, owing to the increasingly complicated electronic warfare environment. The conclusion was that the F-XX as presented "approaches the absurd." Frederick M. Gloeckler, director of advanced systems, and George Spangenberg, Evaluation Division director, added, "In common with past papers by the same author, this study contains many fallacious assumptions, half truths, distortions, and erroneous extrapolations. Unsubstantiated opinions are presented as facts."[10] Spangenberg later recalled, "The lightweight fighter scheme of course had been promulgated by the 'gum on the windshield' fighter types in and out of the Pentagon for a long time. Those people of course were part of the background noise that confused everything that was going on in the real world."[11]

Sprey was not deterred. In March of 1970, Sprey gave a talk at an American Institute for Aeronautics and Astronautics event in St. Louis, the headquarters of the F-15's manufacturer, McDonnell Douglas. The goal of the event was to celebrate and showcase the new F-15 in front of the defense and aerospace contractor community. Political scientist Grant Hammond, a close friend of Boyd, describes Sprey taking the stage "with malice aforethought and a hint of glee," as he proceeded to criticize the F-15 and the contractors involved for not having "a shred" of discipline. He then laid out his vision for the F-XX (also pronounced "X-squared," a name he chose purposefully "to antagonize" his audience), calling for contractors to submit prototypes to compete in a flyoff.[12]

The services saw little, if any, merit in Sprey's jeremiad. They argued that his LWF had insufficient range and needed avionics to be effective in the complex air defense environment. The Air Force pointed to the F-104 Starfighter's poor performance in escort missions in Vietnam as evidence that lightweight fighters were ineffective—hardly conclusive, since the F-104, unlike what Sprey wanted, was a high-speed interceptor that was not optimized for maneuverability. Both services argued that the F-XX could not defeat the new MiG-25, which was also designed as an interceptor. The fighter community responded to these charges with skepticism, suggesting that perhaps the best way to deal with enemy fighters was for the US to buy MiG-21s.[13] Sprey decided to move forward anyway. He, Boyd, and a soon growing group of associates "had gotten disgusted with it," he said of the F-15, "because it had gotten too loaded up with junk. And so we went off and as kind of bureaucratic guerrillas, an underground started the F-16."[14]

The Fighter Mafia

This underground group, initially consisting of Boyd, Sprey, Myers, and Christie, soon grew. One key member was already present: Harry Hillaker, the chief of General Dynamics' preliminary design division in Fort Worth, Texas. Hillaker and Boyd had first met in 1964 at the Eglin Air Force Base Officers' Club and found they had similar interest in lightweight fighters. They had stayed in close contact over the years. As Boyd grew increasingly frustrated with the F-15, his talks with Hillaker became more frequent. By the late 1960s, the group had regular secret weekend meetings. Hillaker spent full days working up data for Boyd, then took the 5 p.m. Friday flight from Fort Worth to Washington, DC (paid for by General Dynamics), where he met with Boyd and Sprey in hotel rooms and worked on LWF designs through the weekend. He then took the first Monday morning flight back to his job in Fort Worth. These secret sessions were a regular occurrence for months at a time.[15]

The other new key member of the underground was test pilot Colonel Everest Riccioni. He had flown P-38 and P-51 fighters in World War II, then earned an undergraduate degree in aeronautical engineering and a master's in applied mathematics. He finished the coursework for a PhD in astronautical engineering at MIT but dropped out before completing his dissertation. Later, while teaching at the Air Force Academy, Riccioni had written a manuscript called "Tigers Airborne," which was critical of then current Air Force air-to-air tactics.[16] Riccioni had first encountered Boyd in 1964 at Eglin, although Boyd was not aware of him.[17] Yet Boyd's ideas took hold, and Riccioni referenced them in his 1968 Air War College thesis: "The Air Superiority Fighter: A Modern Analysis," in which he looked to the heroes of World War I for inspiration on developing fighter aircraft. He quoted an undated report by World War I air commander Major General Billy Mitchell: "Control . . . is obtained by the air battles of pursuit [fighter] aviation. It can be gained in no other way. . . . [Pursuit] is the branch of aviation which assures victory in the air."[18]

Citing Boyd as "a bright young luminary" whose EMT ideas could help solve the problem of a lack of air superiority fighters, Riccioni's work emphasized the characteristics of the stereotypical knights of the air, advocating for air-to-air combat with small, nimble fighters in close-turning gunfights as the ideal means for achieving air superiority. He referenced World War I aces such as Manfred von Richthofen (the "Red Baron") and argued that aggressiveness and low rank were key to fighter pilot success, lamenting that "senior commanders . . . generally lose their lust for high G, high speed, close-pass maneuvering."[19]

He, like Myers, argued that the US had few "pure" fighters. Only F-104s, F-100s, F-86s, and F-84s fit his criteria, meaning NATO forces had only eighteen hundred fighters against the Soviets' nine thousand (MiG-15s, -17s, -19s, and -21s). Like Sprey, Riccioni also rejected the idea of pilots relying on technology, especially avionics computers and radars. "No amount of electronic or optical equipment can substitute for a pilot's ability to turn his head and see his antagonist," he claimed. He also insisted that fighters must be single-seat with a bubble canopy for 360-degree vision, and that missiles were only necessary to force an enemy into a close-turning fight to end with a gun kill. Agreeing with Boyd, he concluded that maneuverability was of prime importance.[20]

Sometime around either late 1968 or 1969, Riccioni joined Boyd and his growing underground, although the exact circumstances are debated. Colonel Robert Titus recalled hiring Riccioni at DCS/R&D for the F-15 project, most likely around the fall of 1968. Riccioni himself recalled that Titus hired him in September 1969 and claimed he stayed there for six months with Boyd, which cannot be correct unless he misremembered the date and meant 1968. Sprey contends that Riccioni did not work on the F-15 but joined the group later. Hammond claims that Riccioni joined the group at the Pentagon in May 1969. In any case, by January 1970, Riccioni was in Boyd's circle and became chief of development, plans, and analysis.[21]

Around this time, in October 1969, Captain John Michael Loh joined the group. With a background as a test pilot after flying over two hundred combat missions in fighter aircraft during the Vietnam War, he worked for Boyd as a fighter requirements staff officer in the Pentagon. He had met Boyd earlier in 1965 and remained intrigued by his EMT concepts, working to apply them to potential new fighter designs while also balancing what he thought were the competing personalities of each key member of Boyd's group. Loh, who later became a four-star general, commander of TAC and Air Combat Command, and vice chief of staff of the Air Force, recalled that each member had distinct agendas. "Boyd was unquestionably the leader and dominated the crusade," Loh said. "His motivation was to vindicate his EM theory, and he wasn't concerned about any mission beyond close-in air-to-air combat. He spent hours debating anyone who challenged his views." Sprey was different: "a true Luddite, opposed to any advanced technology," Loh noted. "His agenda was to produce the cheapest fighter for daytime air combat in Europe against Warsaw Pact forces." Loh saw Christie as more interested in having a new, lower-cost fighter to complement the F-15 while also concerned with validating EMT. The group was united by cost concerns. Loh recalled, "All of us . . . were concerned about the cost trend in fighters . . . where each generation of fighter was going to be 10 times more expensive than the previous generation."[22]

Loh expressed concern that some of the group's ideas for new fighter designs might endanger the project. "I had to try to channel the agendas away from features that would make the LWF unacceptable to Air Force leadership," he said.[23] The group had allies in high places with similar worries, such as Lieutenant General Glenn A. Kent, head of the Systems Analysis Division in the Air Staff Headquarters. Kent thought that the style of advocacy that

Boyd and Sprey used was frequently off-putting. Riccioni was so alienating in his approach that it threatened to derail his goals. Kent recalled, "Boyd and his acolytes were on a mission, and they could not be persuaded to alter their pitch."[24]

In 1969, Riccioni had coauthored a report recommending the LWF over the F-15, intending to brief it to CSAF General John P. McConnell and his vice chief, General John Meyer, one of the leading aces from the Second World War. Kent spoke to Lieutenant General Otto Glasser, DCS/R&D; both men supported the LWF, but Meyer had made it clear that "he would prefer not to have to listen to the briefing, having been irritated before by the Boyd group and its strident campaign for the LWF," but that if Kent recommended it, Meyer would listen. Kent was concerned because the second half of the briefing "alleges that those who support the F-15 lack a basic understanding of air-to-air combat." Kent told Riccioni he could give the briefing only if he cut out all such material and did not even take the charts from that part of the briefing into the room. Allegedly, almost immediately after the briefing started, Riccioni, who had zero aerial victories to his name, took out the forbidden charts and told Meyer, a fighter pilot with twenty-six victory credits from World War II and Korea, that "a review of the fundamentals of air-to-air combat is necessary." Meyer dismissed Riccioni. Despite Riccioni later apologizing to Kent and mending their friendship, Meyer was so angry that he ordered Riccioni transferred to Korea so that, as Kent recalled, Riccioni "would be in no position to muddy the waters."[25] Riccioni left for Korea in September 1971; until then, he remained at the Pentagon with Boyd, pushing their LWF idea.[26] At least part of the reason for Riccioni's removal was his demeanor and his condescending comments to the vice CSAF, but Riccioni and his associates saw his reassignment as punishment for his views about the LWF.[27]

Another key individual who joined the group at the same time as Riccioni was First Lieutenant Robert Drabrant. He had worked in the Pentagon the previous year on a different project but was aware of what Kent and Lieutenant Colonel Larry Welch were studying with their TAC Avenger program. Although Drabrant did not have combat fighter experience, he shared the view of fighter advocates that "fighter pilot is a state of mind." In February 1970, Drabrant was assigned to Eglin and began working for Christie, running EMT analyses for Boyd, who called several times during the day or night for lengthy discussions about EMT and the LWF.[28]

To get the LWF concepts to the next level, the group needed more design work from contractors, meaning they needed funding. In the summer of

1970, Riccioni made an initial proposal for a project he called "Study to Validate the Integration of Advanced Energy-Maneuverability Theory with Trade-Off Analysis." The name was intentionally obtuse, Riccioni's intent being to masquerade the project as another study of EMT, while using the money to fund contractors to study LWF designs. Despite having some allies around the Defense Department, Riccioni and his partners were not certain that they could obtain funding for an LWF that many in the Air Force saw as a threat to the F-15 program. Riccioni persuaded elements of OSD to support him by arguing that the Navy might be considering a competing LWF and by saying that the F-15 might need a low-cost complement or alternative in case of problems. In the fall of 1970, Riccioni received $149,000 for his study, although his tactics may have been deceptive. Sprey recalled that Riccioni "stole" the money. Herbert Hutchinson, later the chief system engineer for the LWF, said of the money's source, "best not to inquire where and how."[29]

By this point, Hillaker was not the only contractor Boyd and Sprey met with regularly; Lee Begin of Northrop was also involved. The group split the funding between the two, giving $100,000 to Northrop and $49,000 to General Dynamics to work on the LWF. Boyd's group continued to guide the two companies in secret hotel-room meetings. "We just didn't want anyone knowing what we were doing," Drabant recalled. "This was totally illegal since we didn't provide the same opportunity to the other airframe manufacturers." Interviewed in 1987, Hillaker said of their process, "Under today's standards, I would probably be indicted."[30]

Boyd, Sprey, Christie, and Riccioni congratulated themselves on their progress. Riccioni floated the idea of the group calling themselves the "Fighter Mafia," with himself as their "Godfather." However, according to Coram, Boyd still considered himself the leader, fostering "an underground guerrilla movement" against the Air Force. Boyd and Riccioni had taken their stereotypical fighter-pilot individualism and maverick attitude to such extremes that they now saw themselves as enemies of the military, waging an insurgency within the Pentagon. The "mafia" took pained efforts to hide their activities, refusing to speak of their work openly either over the phone or in private conversations, fearing that they might be overheard. Any reference to work on the F-XX was called "the Lord's work," a coded term that reflected the zealous fundamentalism of their goal.[31]

The Fighter Mafia's extremism began to alienate their former allies. In a 1973 interview, Major General John J. Burns, who just a few years previously had been one of the loudest voices in advocating that the F-15 be a dedicated air-to-air fighter, found himself aligned against Boyd and his followers: "Now, if we have any problems, it's with the zealots who say you don't need any-thing but performance and a gun. And now we're trying to hold them back."[32]

To gain support around the Pentagon, Hillaker gave a series of briefings on the LWF. Boyd functioned as a plant in the audience, asking preplanned questions of Hillaker, and fed questions to other skeptical Air Force officers. The officers in the room had no idea that Hillaker and Boyd knew each other. All the answers had been practiced, and although Hillaker was expressing Boyd's own views (as the two of them had all but scripted the performance), the impression was that Hillaker was shutting down Boyd's "objections." The show of the arrogant Boyd being put in his place by a civilian contractor impressed the other officers.[33] Boyd knew he was widely disliked and used that to his advantage.

"We were bureaucratic guerrilla warriors, fighting the system and deploy-ing whatever underground means we could use," Sprey said. "We're a net-work of subversives."[34] To achieve their goals, the Fighter Mafia needed a bigger network. As one of Boyd's closest friends, Colonel James Burton, described, "Quietly, secretly, it [the Fighter Mafia] worked the hallways, back doors, and alleys of the Pentagon and the aircraft industry. Its members probed the establishment everywhere and looked for any signs of support." Through this effort, "they established a network of sympathetic key officials within the Air Force and the Office of the Secretary of Defense, a network that would be instrumental when it came time to strike in the open."[35]

Not all the mafia members were secretive. The godfather himself, Riccioni, was a far cry from the careful, soft-spoken Vito Corleone, instead allowing his aggressiveness to harm his own cause. Around the Pentagon, Riccioni brandished a hunting arrow in meetings, "because I am a warrior," he said. "It never lets me forget that I am a true warrior." Referring to him-self often in the third person, he warned generals that they should beware of the Fighter Mafia, which he bragged about creating. He sent insulting memoranda to high-ranking officers extolling the virtues of the LWF con-cept, including veiled references to the true purpose of the $149,000 study grant, predicting that one day the LWF would embarrass the F-15 and the Air Force along with it.[36] When his argumentative attitude became a threat, Sprey recalled Boyd demanding of Riccioni, "'Take your goddamn pen and break it across your knee.' No more memos."[37]

Proposing Prototypes

In the summer of 1969, President Nixon announced a new policy that included supplying military hardware to allies in Asia.[38] To that end, Secretary of Defense Melvin Laird allocated $58 million for the development of an inexpensive, austere fighter plane for the international market in fiscal years 1970 and 1971.[39] That October, the new SECAF, Robert Seamans, indicated worries about the F-15's cost. The F-15 "will be a substantial improvement over the F-4 and F-111," he said. "The question is, can we buy enough of them?"[40] This gave tacit support to the idea of complementing the F-15 with a lower-cost LWF, an idea known as the "high-low mix."

While the LWF gained support, the DOD's procurement policy was changing. Former defense secretary Robert McNamara's "Total Procurement Package" concept had eliminated the use of prototypes in favor of paper studies. Theoretically, this saved money by allowing for the evaluation of many potential designs before building one. But finished products often failed to perform as well as the studies promised, leading to cost overruns. When David Packard became deputy secretary of defense in January 1969, he worked to revive prototyping—colloquially known as "fly before you buy." In February 1971, Laird agreed to a study, led by DOD researcher Allan Simon, of the LWF program as a tryout for Packard's new process.[41]

With the Air Force now officially spending money on the LWF, many contractors not involved in the larger F-14 or the F-15 programs jumped at the chance. In the first six months of 1971, Lockheed, Northrop, and Ling-Temco-Vought (LTV) all submitted unsolicited proposals. Boyd and Riccioni pressed Boeing to submit one also. General Dynamics, worried about its reputation after the problems with its F-111, chose to wait for further study. LTV proposed a two-seat version of the A-7 Corsair, and a new design, the Super V-1000. Lockheed's famed designer Clarence "Kelly" Johnson offered to build two prototypes of his CL-1200 design for $30 million. Johnson insisted on several terms, such as the Air Force having no management of the development process, yet shouldering most of the cost and component support, as well as allowances for foreign sales. The Air Force was cautiously open to the CL-1200, especially because it used a familiar engine, the Pratt & Whitney TF30-P-100, previously used on the F-111F and a variant of the engine used on other F-111 models, on the A-7D, and on the Navy's new F-14 Tomcat. Negotiations continued, and the aircraft had support within the service, partly due to Johnson's promotion efforts. Boeing's proposal was to put the engine from an F-4 Phantom into a Dassault Mirage F-1 to make it an effective strike fighter. The Air Force evaluation judged that it "does not appear to offer any gain in any way to the USAF."[42]

Northrop's proposal benefited from contact with the Fighter Mafia and their secret funding, which covered extensive wind tunnel testing at the NASA Langley Research Center with Dr. Richard Whitcomb. Northrop had also benefited from research at the Air Force's Flight Dynamics Laboratory (FDL, later folded into the Air Force Research Laboratory) in two areas: a survivable flight control system using hydromechanical controls with electronic backup, and wings with computer-controlled leading and trailing edge flaps. These efforts had allowed Northrop's initial N-300 LWF design to progress to the P-530–3 Cobra. Despite these advantages, the Air Force determined that "Northrop's proposal cannot be considered seriously at this point," because the company's proposal insisted that it would provide prototypes only if Air Force could guarantee a $100 million contract for the European market.[43]

Most of these designs were either influenced directly by the Fighter Mafia or by ideas similar to their own. High altitude and high speed, the previous hallmarks of Air Force requirements, were ignored in favor of agility. The ideas of simplicity, man over machine, and the "white scarf stuff" took center stage.

In July 1971, Packard announced $200 million available for any projects that might be good candidates for his prototyping procurement process. To determine what projects would be best submitted for consideration, Vice CSAF Meyer created a study group consisting of Glasser, Kent, the SECAF's assistant for R&D Grant L. Hansen, vice commander of AFSC Lieutenant General John William O'Neill, a Major General Graham (likely Donald William Graham, DCS for systems and logistics), and Brigadier General Kenneth L. Chapman, assistant DCS/R&D and head of the study group. Four task groups supported this effort. Boyd was the assistant head for one of them, the Project Selection Task Group, which was headed by Boyd's friend and LWF advocate Colonel Lyle Cameron, himself a former fighter pilot who had flown F-84s on attack missions in the Korean War.[44]

Kent, still an LWF advocate himself, recalled that at this point Meyer was still skeptical about the LWF. "His real problem was not with the concept of an LWF per se, but, rather, with the way the concept was being promoted," Kent recalled. "It would help," he added, "if those who favor the LWF would stop acting as if they were the only people in the nation who understood anything about the nature of air-to-air combat." Hansen was unwilling to consider the LWF unless he knew that Meyer supported it. Kent worked with Glasser and Colonel Larry Welch, who had been helping him with EMT studies and the TAC Avenger simulations, to prepare a briefing on the LWF for Meyer. Kent and Welch emphasized the idea of the high-low mix, arguing that complementing a small number of F-15s with a larger number of F-16s would be much more effective in combat than buying only F-15s. Meyer agreed, as did CSAF General John Ryan.[45]

Chapman's study examined 220 proposals, selecting 6 to recommend in August 1971. The majority of these were handled by other offices or agencies, and only two, an advanced transport (resulting in the C-17 Globemaster III) and the LWF, became part of the new Prototype Programs Office run by Cameron. Perhaps showing Boyd's influence, the study group's technical objectives for the LWF prioritized maneuverability and controllability for the pilot.[46]

The LWF prototype program called for a fighter with "outstanding maneuvering performance" but that "will not possess the full spectrum of air combat capabilities of the F-15" and be limited to "a day visual fighter air combat environment." However, the intent was not to create a production airplane, but to build prototypes for use as technology demonstrators to experiment with new ideas in terms of materials, components, flight characteristics, computers, flight surfaces, or other aspects. To that end, the program called for two distinct designs, with the expectation that each would be "significantly different" in order to test a wide variety of technologies.[47]

The Air Force sent an RFP, cowritten by Boyd, for LWF prototypes on January 6, 1972. Differing from the then-typical RFPs in the hundreds of pages, the LWF RFP was radically simple. It asked for two prototypes with a list of performance goals emphasizing air-to-air combat, including weight under twenty thousand pounds, high maneuverability in the transonic speed range (Mach 0.8 to 1.5), only avionics required for clear weather daytime conditions, high pilot visibility (preferably a bubble canopy), and handling qualities suited for air combat. The document made some concessions at odds with the Fighter Mafia's goals, such as providing hard points for some air-to-ground capacity and the ability to upgrade the avionics and radar for all-weather and night conditions. The RFP did not list specific performance requirements but kept these broad goals loose so that contractors could maximize overall performance. This was almost precisely the type of aircraft the Fighter Mafia had wanted for many years.[48]

The RFP also placed strict limits on the length of responses: no more than fifty pages of technical material, plus twenty more for management and cost information. This trend stemmed from one of the major goals of the Prototype Study Group: "replacing paperwork with people." The intent was for close cooperation between Air Force and the contractor, with many decisions happening verbally and quickly with a minimum of red tape. However, the Air Force intended to verify its trust, requiring contractors to deliver wind tunnel test models for independent Air Force testing and IBM punch-card decks of flight data for additional testing by Thomas Christie at Eglin.[49]

The RFP went to nine companies. Fairchild, Grumman, McDonnell Douglas, and North American Rockwell did not respond. The five that did make a submission included the four that had submitted unsolicited proposals a year earlier: Boeing, LTV, Lockheed, and Northrop, plus General Dynamics. Northrop submitted two proposals: a single-engine and a twin-engine design. These were judged by a Source Selection Authority board, led by Lieutenant General James Stewart, commander of ASD at Wright-Patterson. The Air Force awarded contracts for the LWF prototype to General Dynamics and Northrop—perhaps not surprising, as the Fighter Mafia had been secretly working with both companies to design a plane, and members of the Fighter Mafia influenced (perhaps actually wrote) the RFP for exactly that type of plane. However, the circumstances of how the source selection board arrived at its choice have been contested, as many participants have differing stories about what happened.

Historian Jay Miller indicates that the Boeing Model 908–909, General Dynamics Model 401, and the Northrop twin-engine Model P-600 (an evolution of its earlier P-530) were the top three contenders, with Northrop choosing to withdraw its single-engine Model 610.[50] Herbert Hutchinson, the LWF chief engineer, recalls that LTV and Lockheed both chose to withdraw their entries (the Model V-1100 and CL-1200 Lancer respectively), because they were not competitive and did not feature enough technological innovation, noting that the LWF program office considered the CL-1200 "only a lukewarm version of a warmed-over F-104."[51]

Spangenberg, part of the Navy's observation team, remembered events differently, recalling that LTV had approached the Navy afterward, frustrated, claiming that the Air Force had told them that they were the second-choice candidate under General Dynamics but had still not received the contract. He also argued that Lockheed had not withdrawn from the competition but had been eliminated because "it seemed fairly obvious that Kelly Johnson at Lockheed had just ignored all the rules and tried to build . . . a replacement for the F-104." Spangenberg also claimed that Boeing was under the same impression—that they were the second choice, but somehow Northrop's twin-engine P-600 was selected, despite the understanding that "under the ground rules told to us, a twin engine design would not be competitive."[52]

Christie recalled that Stewart insisted that one of the designs must be a twin-engine design, and since Northrop submitted the only twin-engine model, it automatically got one of the contracts. However, Christie also argued that Lieutenant Colonel Jerauld Gentry, who became the program manager for the LWF, was a "devotee of Boyd," and that the decision to go with General Dynamics and Northrop was his.[53]

Drabrant, who was also on the source selection committee, indicated that Major Michael Loh (whom Christie also called a "devotee of John [Boyd]") as well as Boyd himself participated in the source selection committee. Drabrant agreed that it was "determined 'a priori' that one of the contenders would be a twin-engine design," and thus Northrop "was essentially guaranteed as shoo in." However, he claimed that General Dynamics also submitted a dual-engine model that the Air Force "dismissed from the get go," along with Northrop's single-engine P-610, because "they were really only paper designs which were obviously given only lip service by some engineers from the company." He argued that LTV had performed well in the initial analysis, but on closer inspection the Air Force had grown skeptical of LTV's performance claims. Drabant commented "they must be using some exotic materials that we hadn't heard of yet, 'balognium' and 'helinolium' which weighed less, generated more lift . . . and actually converted drag into thrust." He also expressed that the board eliminated Lockheed's entry because "Kelly [Johnson] didn't listen to us or the Air Force RFP . . . since he essentially said I know what they, the Air Force, need and took an F-104, put a large trapezoidal low wing on it along with a conventional tail and a big engine." The real problem with that, Drabrant recalled, was that it relied on internal fuel, making it too heavy and less maneuverable.[54]

If Northrop's P-600 was almost guaranteed a spot, the tough choice then was between Boeing's 908–909 and General Dynamics' 401. These entries had a similar overall shape, configuration, and EM profile. Drabrant recalled that the main difference was the wing design, Boeing's having more sweep. Drabrant was convinced that the decision in favor of General Dynamics was mostly political, due to the contractor working at an Air Force plant in Texas and because they had experience in fighter aircraft (specifically the F-111). Boeing, in contrast, had not had a fighter aircraft in production since the 1932 P-26 Peashooter.[55] Hutchinson, however, noted many more key differences. Compared to the Model 401, Boeing's Model 908–909 lacked wing-body blending, leading-edge extensions for vortex lift, an all-electronic control system, and a rounded inlet. All these innovations were built on research at NASA and the Air Force's Flight Dynamics Laboratory—research that General Dynamics had capitalized on, but, to Hutchinson's eye, Boeing had not, having done the majority of its wind tunnel testing at other institutions such as Cornell University.[56]

In essence, the Fighter Mafia had spent several years in secret, illegal meetings with two contractors (General Dynamics and Northrop) to design an aircraft; then the Fighter Mafia cowrote the RFP for that plane; then they participated in a source selection committee that also contained many of their devotees who shared their values; and finally, amid numerous possible outcomes and other potential factors affecting the selection process, the winners were the two companies the Fighter Mafia had been secretly meeting with all along.

Also around this time, Boyd, Christie, and Drabrant had been conducting a study they called "Maximum Maneuver Concept," another application of the EMT analysis to discover the precise regions in which a given airplane had the maximum amount of maneuverability. The study then recommended tactical approaches for taking advantage of those characteristics in battle and recommended using the concept as both a design aid and evaluation tool for new aircraft.[57] The Fighter Mafia continued their obsession with studying air-to-air combat and attempting to institutionalize it in a more concrete way, yet there is little evidence that this study had any broader influence.

Laird approved the contract for the LWF prototypes on April 13, 1972, and directed the creation of a new development concept paper to guide the program moving forward.[58] The new DCP was completed on November 1, 1972, and reiterated the Fighter Mafia's focus: "superior performance in accomplishing maneuvers and tasks required for the visual fighter air combat environment." The document named four specific design goals, also in line with the Fighter Mafia's description of ideal air-to-air combat: maximum turn rates at Mach 0.9 and 1.2 (at thirty thousand feet), quick acceleration from Mach 0.9 to 1.6 (at thirty thousand feet), and maximum controllable g-force at Mach 8 (at forty thousand feet). Cost was also a key factor, if not the overriding one. The DCP also repeated that the main objective of the prototypes was not to put a fighter into production, but to work as a technology demonstrator only. Deputy Secretary of Defense Kenneth Rush added that if either prototype was chosen for production, it would undergo changes and reconsiderations.[59]

Just a few years earlier, Air Force officials had been afraid they would have to adopt Navy-designed aircraft because they lacked options of their own. With the order for the LWF, the Air Force had three tactical aircraft of its own design in development: the A-10 Thunderbolt II, the F-15 Eagle, and now the LWF prototypes. All three had been influenced or initiated by the Fighter Mafia (Sprey had done extensive work on the A-10). However, four days after Laird's approval, Boyd was reassigned to Nakhon Phanom

Air Force Base to become a vice wing commander at Task Force Alpha, an intelligence-gathering project supporting Operation Igloo White in Southeast Asia.[60]

"Eyeball to Eyeball"

The General Dynamics Model 401 became the basis for the YF-16, and the Northrop 600 evolved into the YF-17. Tracking the technological development of these prototypes is difficult. Not only was Boyd's and Hillaker's early work kept unrecorded, secret, or in coded language, but both the Air Force and the company often eschewed record-keeping and documentation in favor of simplicity. Hillaker said that at General Dynamics' offices and the USAF Prototype Program Office, problem-solving decisions were "most often made verbally and on the spot."[61] Yet many of these decisions reflected the philosophy of the Fighter Mafia. As Hillaker described, "The design objective of the original YF-16 was to maximize the usable maneuverability and agility of the aircraft," and to do so, "emphasis was placed on small size and low weight/cost, on advanced technologies, and on design/aerodynamic innovation."[62]

The most important aspect was the wing shape and overall configuration including tails, inlets, and body shapes. General Dynamics spent 1,272 hours conducting wind-tunnel tests of seventy-eight combinations before finalizing the shape that the engineers believed maximized maneuverability. One of the key aspects was the blended wing-body shape, which provided lift at increased angles of attack while also providing extra internal space for fuel storage and allowing for lower overall weight. However, at those angles, vortices occurred that decreased directional stability. To solve that issue and generate more maneuverability, the YF-16 used forebody strakes— small protrusions along the body or in front of the wings of an aircraft. These direct the vortices, generating more lift—a property that became known as "controlled vortex lift"—allowing the plane to perform at steeper angles.[63] Both companies used these, although Northrop's Model 600 (and the earlier P-530) had much larger strakes that resembled the hood of a cobra snake—the source of the plane's nickname. Another key element used by both contractors' overall designs was the variable-camber wing. Based on extensive research from FDL beginning in 1966, a variable-camber system uses a flight computer to change the shape of the leading and trailing edges of the wings depending on the speed and angle of attack in order to maximize maneuverability.[64]

The Fighter Mafia also prioritized people over machines, which meant they wanted pilots to retain as much freedom and control over the aircraft as possible. The relationship between man and machine in the cockpit had been a contentious negotiation since the early days of flight.[65] By 1972, the issue of flight controls neared a major turning point. The previous generation of aircraft was already difficult to control; the increased g-forces in a turning battle could knock a pilot unconscious. If planes became more maneuverable, they needed simpler controls and a way to allow pilots' bodies to sustain intense physical forces.[66]

To lessen the physical stress, the Air Force conducted centrifuge tests, determining that reclining the body made it easier to stay conscious under high g-forces. The YF-16 thus had a 30-degree reclined seat with heels elevated six inches. Cockpit visibility was also a priority; thus a bubble canopy with only one structural frame behind the pilot allowed for a full 360-degree view at eye level, 15-degree downward visibility over the nose, and 40-degree downward visibility to either side. The cockpit also included a heads-up-display and simplified instrumentation, allowing pilots to rely more on their own senses rather than instruments and to perform tasks using a minimum of motions.[67] The bubble canopy is not aerodynamic, but its choice reveals the prioritization of the Fighter Mafia. As Hillaker explained, "Although the 'full bubble' represents a rather significant supersonic drag penalty, it is not inconsistent with 'eyeball-to-eyeball' combat and the high-maneuver capability of the airplane in the combat arena."[68]

Perhaps the most significant application of new technology on the YF-16 was the fly-by-wire (FBW) control system. FBW was a significant turning point in thinking about flight controls and the man/machine relationship in the cockpit, and it was controversial. In the early decades of flight, pilots held a stick, with their feet on pedals. The stick and pedals were connected to the control surfaces of the plane—ailerons or rudders—via rods or cables. As aircraft grew heavier and faster, hydraulic assistance to these controls became common, but the idea of a pilot's motion moving a specific control surface remained. These hydraulic systems were vulnerable, relying on flammable liquid running through exposed lines. During the Vietnam War, for example, hundreds of fighters were lost to ground fire, often from the damage done to their hydraulic lines.[69]

FBW systems instead fed a pilot's commands through a computer, which interpreted which control surfaces needed to move (and how) in order to achieve the pilot's intent. The Flight Dynamics Laboratory had been working on FBW systems as early as 1956.[70] Not everyone thought FBW was a good idea. It had some support from contractors, such as Douglas and Sperry Flight Systems, as well as from Colonel Charles A. Scolatti, chief of the Air Force Flight Control Division. To sell pilots—and more importantly, the Pentagon—on the idea of FBW, the FDL held a conference on December 16–17, 1968 (the sixty-fifth anniversary of the Wright Brothers' first flight), to gain support and funding for further research. One of the FDL engineers, Major J. P. Sutherland, appealed to the fondness for World War I air combat in his talk, showing a cartoon resembling the beloved *Peanuts* mascot Snoopy as the "World War I Flying Ace," shooting at the Red Baron, with a thought bubble of what critics of FBW were likely thinking: "Security is a mechanical flight control system!" Sutherland emphasized the performance advantages of FBW controls but focused on their greater survivability compared to hydraulic systems. He ended his talk with another cartoon of the World War I canine ace overlooking another *Peanuts*-like character in the pilot seat, who is exclaiming, "Security is a fly-by-wire system!" FDL engineers often used another cartoon featuring the canine ace having three of his four electrical cables shot off by the Red Baron, while shouting "This fly-by-wire is great!" Sutherland further argued that FBW could improve performance while decreasing weight, complexity, and cost.[71]

FDL and NASA, working with McDonnell Douglas, Sperry Rand, General Electric, and Lear Siegler, experimented with FBW systems on F-4s from 1969 through 1972. They concluded that FBW provided "significant maneuvering performance improvements and control techniques not possible with a mechanical control system. This makes mandatory the transition from a mechanical control system to FBW."[72] F-4s that were modified to be intentionally unstable and retrofitted with FBW systems could maneuver at 4-g's up to five thousand feet higher than before and could handle higher angles of attack. The Fighter Mafia had been chasing exactly these performance parameters for their "pure" air-to-air fighter. James L. Dabold, an Aeronautical Systems Division engineer, encouraged FBW and gave McDonnell's F-4 data to General Dynamics, which had been experimenting with the concept on previous aircraft as well.[73]

The YF-16's design rendered it unstable in normal conditions, mostly due to the center of gravity being near the back of the plane. Without the computer adjustments of the FBW system, no human could fly the plane. Use of a failsafe, in which a control surface is locked into a stable position after an electrical failure, was not possible, since the aircraft had no such position. To safeguard against failure, the YF-16 used a quadruple sensor system—four independent electrical channels that provided triple redundancy. Even if the control system suffered two electrical failures, the system could still fly the plane.[74]

Handing control of an aircraft over to a computer could seem antithetical to the Fighter Mafia's core concepts of simplicity and of the value of man over machine. But in a way, FBW reflected their values. Although the pilot was unaware of the computer's adjustments to the flight surfaces, the pilot was free to give simple commands and quickly translate his will into reality. A computer was making thousands of decisions, but control, from the pilot's perspective, was simple. Furthermore, because a plane did not have to be designed to be inherently stable, FBW allowed for less drag, more lift, and tighter turns.[75] Even though FBW seemed to contradict the goals of Boyd and his acolytes, it actually fulfilled them.

Not all the components of the YF-16 were fulfillments of Fighter Mafia ideals; the engine selection presented tradeoffs. General Dynamics considered a twin-engine design, using two General Electric YJ101s, but decided to use a single Pratt & Whitney F100—the same engine used in the F-15 Eagle. They argued that the lower weight of a single engine resulted in a greater thrust-to-weight ratio.[76] Although the Fighter Mafia favored simplicity, the F100 was anything but simple, especially compared with General Electric's J79, used in the F-4 Phantom. The new F100 had thirty-one thousand components, requiring 4.2 man-hours of maintenance per hour of flight. The earlier J79 had twenty-two thousand components and needed 1.7 maintenance hours per flight hour. The complex F100 was also riddled with performance issues, suffering from frequent compressor stalls and higher than expected rates of fatigue.[77]

However, the engine intake, also based on NASA test data, did emphasize the Fighter Mafia's penchant for simplicity and focus on air combat. Many fighter aircraft before this point, including the F-4 Phantom, used a variable inlet system, in which computers detected flight conditions and controlled the shape of the air intake to maximize engine performance. This was especially useful at high speeds. Yet, because the focus of the plane was on air-to-air fighting, which designers argued happened at lower speeds, the YF-16 used a simpler system without a variable inlet.[78]

There Can Only Be One

To evaluate the two prototypes, the General Dynamics YF-16 and the Northrop YF-17, the Air Force planned a series of flights to test each plane independently against criteria that emphasized Fighter Mafia ideals of maneuverability and air-to-air combat. The tests also evaluated logistical issues and general flight characteristics, but the process was designed to be flexible. The Air Force worked more closely with contractors than it had in previous programs and encouraged those companies to design their own tests that could be changed on an ad hoc basis. As one colonel summarized the evaluations, "We don't want to bog down in minor details."[79]

Before these flights occurred, there was contention about the purpose of the tests. "Many outsiders [in government and in the press] misunderstood the LWF Prototype Project objective, and . . . declared the Lightweight Fighter Program to be a head-to-head competition," Hutchinson noted. "There was never a USAF plan to have a head-to-head fly-off."[80] The issue was not misunderstanding as much as competing goals. The Fighter Mafia and their allies wanted the LWF in production; the Air Force was adamant that the prototypes were only technology demonstrators to inform a later decision on an LWF if it decided to procure one at all.

In October 1973, DDR&E Malcolm Currie asked the Air Force about a funding plan for procurement, with the assumption that the test flights were a competition to determine which plane, the YF-16 or YF-17, was suitable for purchasing as a complement for the F-15 force.[81] SECAF Dr. John McLucas responded with frustration: "The primary Air Force objective" for the prototype program "was the demonstration and evaluation of modern technology expected to provide improved performance . . . [and] hardware options applicable to our future fighter requirements." He stressed that the approval of prototypes "did not imply Air Force commitment to follow on or production programs. The selection of two fighter designs was not to infer competition." McLucas was also clear that although there was a need for a new fighter, no official decision had been made on what a new fighter should be. If the service decided it wanted a new fighter, it would start a new program to define it—which would be influenced by the results of the prototype tests—but none of that was guaranteed.[82]

That same month, the 1973 Arab-Israeli War influenced the issue of whether to procure an LWF. The Israeli Air Force faced a dense network of Egyptian SAM (surface-to-air missile) launchers. Despite losing at least eighty-seven planes to ground-based fire, the IAF still performed well in air combat against its enemies, who were not only ill-trained for that role but also relied on aging MiG-17s and MiG-21s. Israeli sources claim that their fighters (F-4 Phantoms) shot down over 240 Arab aircraft. More than half of those kills were with air-to-air missiles. During these fights, the Israelis lost sixteen planes to air combat, a 15:1 kill ratio. Even if these figures are exaggerated, the success of the IAF in air-to-air fighting is clear.[83] American fighter advocates saw this war as more ammunition for their arguments of the "white scarf stuff" being key to victory. However, Air Force leaders saw it as a warning that future wars would involve high losses of aircraft. This came just as the US was shifting toward a force structure based on fewer, higher-quality, expensive aircraft: the F-15 Eagle and the F-14 Tomcat.[84]

Another factor pushing the evaluations toward a competitive flyoff for production, however, was the interest from some NATO allies. Belgium, Denmark, Norway, and the Netherlands were looking to replace their aging F-104s. In 1973 the NATO Conference of National Armaments Directors conducted a study recommending that all four countries should seek the same aircraft as a replacement, and the countries then formed a consortium to select a plane. By the time the LWF tests were beginning, the consortium had narrowed its choices to the Saab Viggen, the Dassault Mirage F-1E, the YF-16, or the YF-17.[85]

The Fighter Mafia and their allies continued to apply pressure and build support for taking the LWF into production. In December 1973, Christie prepared a memo for the director of defense program analysis and evaluation, Leonard Sullivan, urging the assistant secretary of defense (comptroller) to arrange a competitive flyoff to determine procuring an LWF. Complaining that DDR&E Malcom Currie had deleted funding for an LWF from the fiscal year 1975 budget, Christie and Sullivan urged that $40 million be placed back in via cuts to other programs.[86]

Beginning in January 1974, to evaluate the prototypes, the Air Force Flight Test Center created a joint test force led by Lieutenant Colonel James R. Rider, a fighter pilot who flew F-105s in Southeast Asia. Rider and his team coordinated the test plan with General Dynamics and Northrop, focusing broadly on maneuverability and acceleration while also testing the four specific performance tasks stated in the DCP.[87] The first flight of the YF-16, on January 20, 1974, was unintentional. During a ground-taxi test, when the plane reached a speed of about 130 knots, the plane began an oscillating roll, causing the left wing and tail to slam into the ground. With the plane careening out of control and bouncing across the runway, the test pilot, Phillip Oestricher, decided to take off for an unplanned six-minute flight.[88]

Early tests in 1974 led to minor adjustments, often in line with the Fighter Mafia's design philosophy. For example, a higher-rate gyro system was added to increase agility. Also, the YF-16's control stick, located on the right side instead of between the legs like a traditional fighter joystick, was force-sensing; it responded to pressure but did not move. Pilots, accustomed to the tactile sense of moving the stick, often exerted too much force. Some pilots were strongly against the concept of the control stick, instead preferring a traditional moving joystick. One test pilot expressed such vehement opposition to the lack of a joystick that Lieutenant General Stewart, the commander of ASD, thought he was incapable of providing an objective assessment of the plane and fired him. After further flight tests, the control stick was redesigned to move slightly, although that movement was solely to provide tactile feedback and did not affect the control surfaces. Most pilots enjoyed the controls. Rider himself noted that "the YF-16 has been one of the most exciting, dynamic aircraft I have ever flown."[89]

Both planes engaged in simulated air-to-air combat against other USAF and Soviet fighters. The YF-16 flew against the F-106, the F-4E, and the other YF-16 prototype, as well as against a captured MiG-17 and MiG-21. Victory was determined when one plane achieved a position that was likely to result in a "kill" using the gun. Not only did the YF-16 win against all these opponents in direct matchups, but its increased agility allowed it to win using far less fuel. The most dramatic example involved the F-4E. After the YF-16 won three consecutive rounds, the Phantom ran out of fuel and was immediately replaced by a second F-4. Without refueling, the same YF-16 continued against the second Phantom, winning several more consecutive contests.[90]

Northrop's YF-17 had a lot in common with its competition. Although Northrop used more composite materials, the plane was about 9 percent heavier. Its two engines gave it nearly 25 percent more power, and the twin tail fins helped its controllability in high angles of attack. The cockpit of the YF-17 was reclined with elevated feet, although not to the extreme angles of the YF-16. The planes both used fixed geometry inlets, forebody strakes, and the heads-up display in the cockpit. The largest difference other than the engines was that the YF-17 did not use a complete FBW system but retained hydromechanical controls with a computer-controlled augmentation system.[91]

As of spring 1974, Air Force leaders still viewed the prototype program as a "technology demonstrator," not as a basis for procuring another new airplane. That soon changed.

James Schlesinger, who became the secretary of defense in July 1973, supported the LWF right away, most likely because of the increasing interest from NATO allies. If the Air Force refused to procure either the YF-16 or YF-17, however, it seemed unlikely that the European consortium would either. But Schlesinger could not force the plane on the Air Force against its will. As the tests on the YF-16 began, the new CSAF, General George Brown, became more interested in a new fighter. On March 25, 1974, he created a Tactical Fighter Modernization Study Group to plan a force structure strategy for the 1980s, particularly the question of what characteristics new fighters would need. The group concluded that the Air Force should buy an operational version of the LWF as a complement for the F-15, endorsing the high-low-mix concept. However, the study also recommended that although this potential LWF should be "optimized for close-in air-to-air combat with a gun and close-in IR [heat-seeking] missiles," it should also have "ground attack capability . . . greater than the F-4," and be capable of delivering nuclear weapons.[92] With this show of support, on April 29, 1974, Schlesinger ordered that the prototype program was no longer a technology demonstrator, but a competitive flyoff, and that the winner would go into production.[93]

The exact nature of this decision is unclear, partly because the Fighter Mafia took credit for it. Christie said Schlesinger was an "instant devotee" of the LWF and "hellbent" on procuring it, while glowing press coverage of the Fighter Mafia in 1987 referred to Schlesinger as their "most powerful agent." Christie maintained that Schlesinger made a secret deal in March or April 1974 with Brown to gain support for procuring the LWF: authorization for four new operational wings, as long as they were F-16s.[94] Sprey told the same story, but claims it was six wings, and a mix of F-16s and A-10s.[95] Historian Kenneth Werrell, based on interviews with Christie and General David C. Jones, the new CSAF who replaced Brown on July 1, 1974, claimed that Brown had refused the deal, but Jones accepted it—the terms of which were increasing the number of wings from twenty-two to twenty-six, with ten of them as LWFs.[96] Schlesinger and Jones also claim that they had made the deal, not Brown.[97] However, the decision to move to a competitive flyoff for production was made over two months before Jones took his position, while Brown still held the office.

Sprey claimed he was responsible for the decision. He said that Schlesinger was a close confidant of Sprey's mentor, Colonel Richard Hallock. Hallock was a paratrooper veteran of World War II who had worked in OSD and at the time was a defense consultant.[98] Hallock allegedly urged Schlesinger to prioritize Sprey's two pet projects—the LWF and the A-10—as the foundation of his legacy. Sprey then claimed that Boyd, back from Southeast Asia, gave a briefing to a room of four-star generals allegedly intent on canceling the LWF, at which he said that the meeting was "not a decision brief" and the secretary of defense had already decided to go to production.[99]

This story has been retold in many sources in different ways. Christie insisted that the infamous "not a decision brief" moment occurred in "the end of 1971 or very early in 1972" and did not involve Schlesinger at all, but was about convincing DDR&E John Foster to support the LWF as a candidate for Packard's prototype program.[100] This is also unlikely because that decision had already been finalized by August 1971, owing in large part to Kent and Glasser. Other sources written by the Fighter Mafia or their admirers have each told the story with vague details, unclear timelines, and wide variation in the specifics of what happened.[101] It is impossible to say with certainty what the nature of this brief was or whether it even occurred. It mirrors many other tales of the Fighter Mafia that originate only from Boyd, his friends, or his devotees. Their main goal seems to be painting them as noble underdog guerrillas bravely fighting against the system—true to Boyd's fighter pilot cultural roots.

After Schlesinger's decision to procure an LWF, the question of who would win the flyoff remained. At the end of 1974, toward the end of testing, the *New York Times* noted that most Western European air force officers favored the YF-17.[102] The White House also favored it, emphasizing the international significance of the decision as well as the prospects of domestic job creation. Although Texas congressmen urged the Air Force and the White House to choose the YF-16 because of General Dynamics' location in Fort Worth, the executive branch argued that Texas was in a better economic situation than Northrop's home of California. The White House also claimed the YF-17 was more versatile and that the two-engine design led to better economics of production.[103]

Test pilots enjoyed both planes, and the Fighter Mafia's goal of designing a plane to re-create the aerial duels of World War I was well realized. Test pilot Michael Clarke recalled that being in the YF-16 "was like flying in an open cockpit airplane," and he began taking a World War I–style leather helmet with him on flights. The helmet accidentally appeared in a photograph meant for official documentation, earning Clarke a reprimand from the wing commander.[104]

Both aircraft performed well in test flights, although the YF-17 did not meet all of Northrop's predictions. Some of the pilots thought the YF-17 was easier to fly, as Rider recalled: "You had to fly the YF-16 all the time," but, regarding the YF-17, "You could put your daughter in it and it would go fast. It was a piece of cake!"[105] Perhaps more important, the YF-16 not only performed slightly better, but, owing to its single-engine fuel consumption rate, promised cost savings.[106]

On January 13, 1975, the Air Force announced that it had selected the YF-16. McLucas insisted that although other nations had influenced the decision, they did not have a vote. The key factor deciding in favor of the YF-16 was performance. McLucas argued that the YF-16 "had advantages in agility, in acceleration, in turn rate and endurance over the YF-17 . . . better tolerance of high G because of the tilt back seat, better visibility and better deceleration. . . . The YF-16 had lower drag and was a cleaner design."[107]

Clearly, the performance characteristics that the Fighter Mafia valued, especially maneuverability, were the deciding factors.

In the mid-1960s, some leaders in the Air Force feared that the lack of development of USAF aircraft would force the service to accept Navy aircraft as it had in the past. A decade later, the Air Force had three new aircraft in production, the F-15, A-10, and F-16. All of these had been influenced by the Fighter Mafia to some degree, although some mythology has built up around that group. Boyd and his allies continued to push energy maneuverability as a core concept for defining, creating, and evaluating aircraft agility, which for them was key to building a good fighter in the tradition of World War I dogfighting, translated to the modern age.

However, this group was so zealous that they often hindered their own efforts. Without contributions from others, particularly Kent and Glasser, the group might not have been as successful as they were. The Fighter Mafia's efforts also stood on the shoulders of massive amounts of engineering work from NASA and FDL. Hillaker himself recalled, "If it hadn't been for efforts undertaken by the Flight Dynamics Lab in the 1960s on fly by wire, the high-acceleration cockpit, and relaxed static stability, there would not be an F-16."[108] The Air Force was also a different place from what it had been in previous years. More leaders had experience in fighters and were sympathetic to that culture if not the products of it. New Soviet threats and interservice rivalry seemed to indicate a need for the types of planes the Fighter Mafia wanted. Cost considerations and international conflicts drove a reevaluation of needs, as did interest in sales on the international market. Despite Boyd and his associates' habit of portraying themselves as secret warriors, they found a receptive audience and environment, helped along by other like-minded people.

For the Fighter Mafia and some others, their choices were influenced by the stereotypes of fighter pilot values. They wanted an aircraft that exemplified those values, emphasizing the role of the individual man over the machine, and aggressive and agile maneuvering in one-on-one air combat duels. Others agreed to planes with these characteristics for other reasons. Despite their success in securing support for the LWF, once the Air Force began modifying the prototype for operational use, the Fighter Mafia became frustrated with the changes, leading them on a new path of advocacy throughout the entire Department of Defense and later, the general public.

FIGURES 1 AND 2. Two-page spread from the July 17, 1967, *Aviation Week & Space Technology* shows photos from the Domodedovo air show in 1967. It was the first time the American public saw a new generation of Soviet fighters such as the MiG-25 and Su-15.

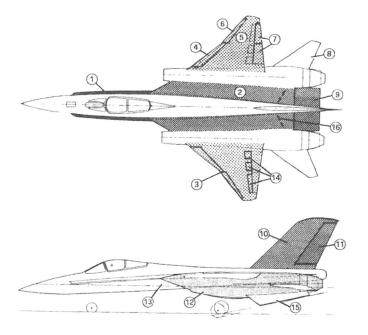

FIGURE 3. An engineering sketch of the Fairchild Hiller design for the F-15. The contract featured a podded engine concept, with engine nacelles separated from the main body. (Greater St. Louis Air and Space Museum)

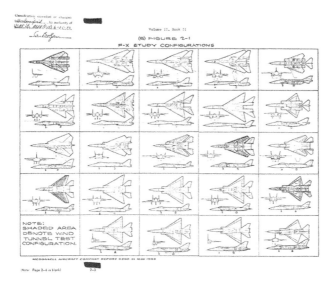

FIGURE 4. McDonnell tested many variations of fuselage, wing, fin, and engine configurations with wind tunnel models before settling on its final design for the F-15 Eagle. (Greater St. Louis Air and Space Museum)

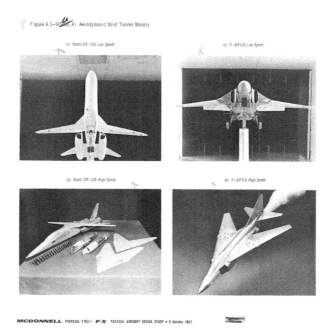

FIGURE 5. One of the largest decision points in the F-15's development was the choice between a variable-sweep wing and a fixed wing. These images are of wind tunnel tests on some variable-sweep wing concepts. The two on the right feature a modified F-4 model. (Greater St. Louis Air and Space Museum)

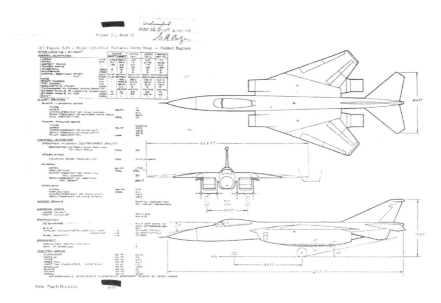

FIGURE 6. This rejected McDonnell design for the F-15 features a variable-sweep wing and a single-tail configuration. This represented a significantly smaller, lighter aircraft than the final version of the plane. (Greater St. Louis Air and Space Museum)

FIGURE 7. Several of the F-15 prototypes at Edwards Air Force Base, participating in a variety of test flights, July 28, 1973 (Greater St. Louis Air and Space Museum)

FIGURE 8. The first McDonnell Douglas F-15A Eagle prototype (YF-15A-1) in flight, most likely near Edwards Air Force Base, California, 1972 (US Air Force photo)

FIGURE 9. The first F-15A being assembled in the McDonnell Douglas factory (Boeing Company)

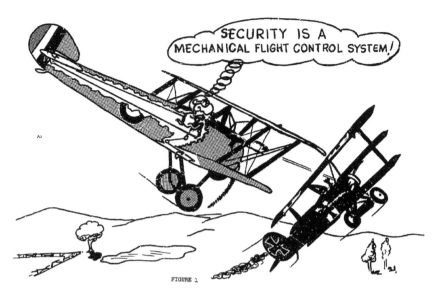

FIGURE 10. The first of a series of cartoons by an unknown artist from 1968 aimed to help convince pilots of the advantages of fly-by-wire controls. The image represented the typical fighter pilot viewpoint of that time, relying on mechanical controls. Subsequent images portrayed the canine "World War I Flying Ace" learning that fly-by-wire systems made him more effective against the Red Baron. (Air Force image)

FIGURE 11. Concept art from a briefing by General Dynamics engineer Harry Hillaker shows two early designs for the lightweight fighter that eventually resulted in the F-16 Fighting Falcon, also known early on as the F-XX (or F-X²). Although many components and visual elements are similar to those of the eventual F-16, these designs call for a much smaller, lighter, simpler aircraft. (Lockheed Martin Corporation)

FIGURES 12 AND 13. The Boeing 908, depicted in this mockup, was the company's entry to the Lightweight Fighter Prototype program. It has many similarities with the General Dynamics entry but does not feature the wing-body blend and has sharper angles throughout, especially on the intake. (Boeing Company)

Three-quarter view of Boeing 908 emphasizes cockpit and pilot configuration. (Boeing Company)

FIGURE 14. The first prototype Northrop YF-17 Cobra. While the YF-17 was originally intended as an alternative technology demonstrator to complement the YF-16, the Air Force decided to create a flyoff competition between the two. Although the Air Force rejected the YF-17, it was the basis for the Navy's F/A-18 Hornet. (Smithsonian National Air and Space Museum)

FIGURE 15. The two Northrop YF-17 Cobra prototypes fly with two McDonnell F-4E Phantom IIs from the 66th Fighter Weapons Squadron. Both the YF-16 and YF-17 performed simulated air-to-air combat against F-4s and other fighter aircraft as part of the flight test procedures. (Smithsonian National Air and Space Museum)

FIGURE 16. Phil Oestricher poses next to the YF-16 in Fort Worth, Texas. Oestricher became the first pilot to fly the YF-16 and referred to it as "the Camelot of aeronautical engineering." (Lockheed Martin Corporation)

Figure 17. The first General Dynamics YF-16 prototype parked for display in Fort Worth, Texas, in December 1973. (National Archives and Records Administration)

Figure 18. The second prototype of the General Dynamics YF-16 Fighting Falcon (Smithsonian National Air and Space Museum)

FIGURE 19. The YF-16 Prototype 2, in a blue-and-gray camouflage paint scheme, flies next to an F-4 Phantom II. Throughout 1974, the YF-16 and YF-17 went through a series of air combat trials against fighter aircraft such as F-106 Delta Darts, F-4 Phantoms, and clandestinely obtained Soviet MiGs. In close air combat, the YF-16 appeared clearly superior. (Lockheed Martin Corporation)

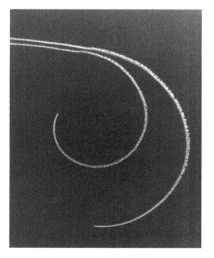

FIGURE 20. This image compares two smoke trails, the outer one left by an F-4 Phantom and the inner one by the YF-16. The lightweight fighter competition compared the agility of the two planes, demonstrating the superior agility of the F-16. (Lockheed Martin Corporation)

FIGURE 21. The General Dynamics YF-16 prototype no. 2 and the first production model F-16A, shown side by side in October 1977, make the differences clear. The production model is slightly larger, especially in the nose area, to accommodate a larger radar. (Lockheed Martin Corporation via Smithsonian National Air and Space Museum)

THE MYTH

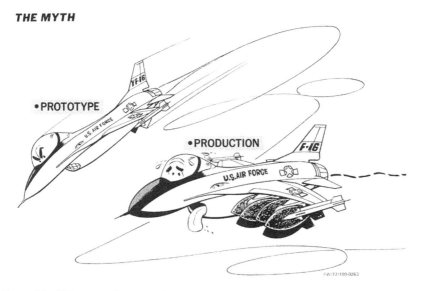

FIGURE 22. This cartoon from an unknown artist was part of a presentation outlining the differences between the prototype and production models of the General Dynamics F-16. The "myth" presented was in line with the Fighter Mafia's complaints that the production model had become too heavy and cumbersome, ruining its performance. The Air Force and General Dynamics worked to counter this argument. (Lockheed Martin Corporation via Smithsonian National Air and Space Museum)

FIGURE 23. F-16 lineup includes the first two General Dynamics YF-16 prototypes and the first two F-16A production models. The modifications from prototype to production are visible, especially the larger noses on the production models to accommodate an internal radar. The first prototype has been modified with extra canards for its use in test flights as the Flight Dynamics Laboratory's Control Configured Vehicle (CCV). (Lockheed Martin Corporation via Smithsonian National Air and Space Museum)

FIGURE 24. YF-16 prototype no. 2 displaying the extensive ground-attack munitions and other auxiliary equipment that the F-16 could carry, shown at Edwards AFB, February 12, 1975. (National Archives and Records Administration)

Figure 25. General Dynamics F-16 Fighting Falcon aircraft undergo final assembly, probably at General Dynamics' Forth Worth (Texas) Division plant, circa mid-1970s. (Smithsonian National Air and Space Museum)

CHAPTER 6

Writing Heresy

> If you study half a war—you will probably become half a warrior.
>
> —Lieutenant Colonel Mark Hamilton

After January 1975, the Air Force modified the F-16 from the prototype into an operational "missionized" fighter, including a ground-attack role. This angered the Fighter Mafia—whose core consisted of John Boyd, Pierre Sprey, Everest Riccioni, Thomas Christie, and Franklin "Chuck" Spinney, an Air Force officer who had been working with the group and soon became a civilian analyst for tactical air power in OSD. This core team had many allies spread across the military and its contractors. Their vision for a pure modern fighter aircraft that could replicate the "white scarf stuff" of their memory of air-to-air combat had been—in their minds—ruined by the Air Force.

The Fighter Mafia considered themselves a counterculture within the Air Force that was actively oppressed by the mainstream establishment. They cultivated the allegory of themselves and the Air Force as competing religious orders. Referring to their efforts as "the Lord's work," they took on the role of religious zealots, fighting against what they saw as a corrupt orthodoxy. The Fighter Mafia "presumed the inherent righteousness of their cause, recognized that there would be martyrs to it . . . and that they would be persecuted, right or not, by the powers that be," said political scientist Grant Hammond, a close friend of Boyd's. "Ultimately, the heresy that they represented to the orthodoxy of the military services and the defense establishment was something that could not, and would not, last."[1]

This zealotry stemmed from the stereotypes of fighter pilot culture taken to extremes. Boyd and his followers were rugged individualists who were not afraid to question authority; and to pursue their righteous cause, they needed to remain aggressive. Until the mid-1970s, their efforts were focused on making aircraft that fit their idealized fighter role—first the F-X, then the lightweight fighter, or LWF. Frustration with the latter drove the group to look beyond the Air Force and attempt to effect change in the entire military.

By the end of the next decade, the Fighter Mafia metamorphosed into a larger group, which would come to be known as the Military Reform movement. The movement was public, publishing conference papers, briefings, newspapers, articles in professional and popular magazines, and books. Its proponents became directly involved with members of Congress, who formed the Military Reform Caucus. The reform movement's concerns went beyond aircraft, encompassing budgets, procurement policy, research and development processes, and doctrine. As this movement grew it became radicalized. Because the reform movement evolved from the Fighter Mafia, it incorporated many of the original fighter pilot stereotypes: strong individualism; distrust or resistance to authority; a focus on specific technologies that addressed the movement's values; protection of its community; use of heroic and religious imagery; and above all, aggressiveness.

Many Pounds for Air-to-Ground

The F-16 Fighting Falcon prototype was the physical manifestation of the Fighter Mafia's ideal. However, after winning the competition in January 1975, the F-16 design went to the Air Force Configuration Control Committee, headed by former fighter pilot General Alton Slay, to produce an operational version of the plane. The Fighter Mafia nicknamed this group the "Add-On Committee," assuming Slay's role was to exact the Air Force's revenge by making sure the F-16 did not threaten the F-15 in any way. That meant turning the Fighting Falcon into a multi-role craft emphasizing ground attack and nuclear delivery.[2]

Christie, and his subordinate Robert J. Croteau, tried to stop this process before it started with a memo to Leonard Sullivan Jr., the director of Defense PA&E. They warned that moving too far away from the single-mission focus of air superiority would "subvert the purpose of the entire LWF/ACF [Air Combat Fighter] program." They insisted that "the radar is the major item" they took exception with, arguing that a small radar such as the APQ-153 used in the F-5 was plenty. Beyond visual range (BVR) threat detection and long-range missile attacks could be handled by ground stations or other aircraft (such as the F-15). They wanted a configuration "based on primary commitment of the ACF to intense high frequency dogfights."[3]

They were not successful. The production version of the F-16 added almost one thousand pounds in structural and equipment changes and additional fuel storage. The landing gear was strengthened, the fuselage increased by ten inches, and the radome size increased by three inches. The wing and tail area grew by about 7 and 15 percent respectively, and a tailhook was added. Chaff and flare systems and improved avionics also appeared, as did more pylons for ground-attack ordnance, with the existing pylons increased for heavier weight. The loading capacity almost doubled, from 7,700 pounds to 15,200 in the production model. Although the acceleration and energy maneuverability of the operational F-16 was slightly less than the prototype YF-16, the production model did have increased range, thrust, and load factor, able to pull nine g's.[4]

Despite the Fighter Mafia's objections, the Air Force added a ground-looking, all-weather, night-capable, medium-range radar to the F-16, the Westinghouse AN/APG-66. The company maintained that this system was "the Fighter Pilot's Radar" and was "designed for easy operation by a one-man crew," thus "allow[ing] the pilot to keep his head up and his hands on the throttle and stick throughout a dogfight engagement." With the flick of a switch, the radar provided ground mapping, improved with a Doppler beam, for both navigation and weapons delivery.[5] The avionics systems incorporated Boyd's EMT work into the cockpit via an "Energy-Maneuverability Display" that gave pilots visual cues to indicate their current available energy, how to maximize their turn rates, the level of g-forces available, altitude and airspeed limits, and how to gain maneuvering energy quickly.[6]

Development problems plagued the radar, however. The system Westinghouse delivered in 1977 had only half the range the Air Force had specified. Its ground mapping was undecipherable, and it had problems tracking targets while the plane performed maneuvers. Some of the units Westinghouse delivered were inoperative from the outset. After more refining and testing, in October 1979 the Air Force rated the radar as "marginally satisfactory" and accepted the system.[7]

Contrary to the Fighter Mafia's intentions, Slay thought that the nature of the F-16 as a complement to the F-15 dictated that it should be a multi-role aircraft. Describing the new plane to the Senate in 1976, he argued, "The F-16 has a capability that the F-15 does not have, deliberately so. We did not choose to burden the F-15 radar with a significant air-to-ground capability. We have engineered the F-16 radar to have very good ground mapping . . . [and] to do an extremely good job of air-to-ground missions."[8] Slay appreciated the

F-16's maneuverability, noting "I almost had a heart attack watching the F-16 do a split 'S' from 2,700 feet. It was fantastic as far as maneuverability is concerned." He argued this made it useful in roles beyond dogfighting: "We also found that the things that made [the F-16] good in an air-to-air role . . . were extremely good in [an] air-to-ground context." He concluded, "We got more than we paid for in having a multipurpose capable airplane."[9]

The move from a dedicated air superiority fighter to a multi-role aircraft played out in the press as well. In the weeks after the F-16 was selected in January 1975, many reporters, officials, politicians, and test evaluators emphasized that the Fighting Falcon was supposed to be a dedicated air combat fighter. The Pentagon echoed some of the Fighter Mafia's main arguments when describing the F-16 to the press, saying the intention of the plane was "to reverse the . . . trend toward more sophisticated and thus costlier air superiority fighters." One reporter covering the announcement emphasized that "the stress in design of the lightweight fighter has been for maximum maneuverability and handling in aerial dogfights."[10]

Seven months later, this line had shifted. David Lewis, the chairman and CEO of General Dynamics, still emphasized the dogfighting aspect of the F-16, arguing that it "can outfight any known competitor." Yet Lewis immediately added, "The versatile F-16 proved to have an exceptional air-to-ground capability with weapons delivery ranges far better than current operational aircraft."[11] By mid-1977, General Dynamics promotional material and press releases ceased referring to the F-16 as an "air combat fighter" as they originally had and instead defined the plane as "the multirole fighter" or as a "multimission fighter."[12] By the fall of 1978, the story had shifted further, to the point of insisting that the F-16 had been designed with ground attack in mind, that it was "designed as a 'multi-role fighter'"—almost the opposite of the Fighter Mafia's intentions. H. F. Rogers, the vice president of General Dynamics and director of the F-16 program, claimed that "the Air Force was looking for a new jet capable of both air-to-air and air-to-ground combat."[13]

Boyd was unhappy with these changes and wrote to Slay several times throughout the opening months of 1975, arguing that "F-16 maneuvering performance has diminished significantly because of engineering necessity and conscious decisions that resulted in a substantial weight increase." To attempt to keep the same level of maneuverability that he desired, Boyd said that the wing area, which had already been increased from 280 to 300 square feet, must be increased further to 320. This plan was rejected because of increased cost and a perception of increased risk with a larger wing.[14]

Boyd remained cordial in his correspondence with Slay, but privately, he and the rest of the Fighter Mafia expressed frustration. Christie recalled that "the so-called 'missionization' was an exercise that went well beyond a suitable radar and other avionics." Major Ray Leopold, who became Boyd's assistant and mentee about this time, described the group as worried that the F-16 would be "a disastrous compromise" and "fall prey to the same vagrancies of the bureaucracy" as had the F-15. Leopold recalled Boyd complaining about the addition of armor plating, arguing that "it was mor[e] important to be maneuverable and less likely to get hit in the first place." He railed against the increase in bombing capacity, claiming that "the original concept of designing for energy maneuverability was compromised." Sprey was frustrated as well, claiming that the Air Force "degraded" the F-16 more than it had the F-15 by increasing its size and adding equipment, most of all the radar.[15] Hillaker, however, was not against some of the changes. Although he said that Boyd and Sprey's frustration was reasonable, he recognized that the mafia's original design was perhaps too limited: "If we had stayed with the original lightweight fighter concept," he explained, "that is, a simple day fighter, we would have produced only 300 F-16s." Hillaker later worked on other models, such as the F-16XL, designed to maintain many of the plane's advantages when carrying a large bomb load.[16]

In the spring of 1975 Boyd at least considered the possibility of designing a new craft, "a fighter vehicle at least equal to and in most cases far better than current and incoming specialized vehicles [the F-15 and F-16] perform their individual design tasks." This "general purpose fighter" could, hypothetically, overcome some performance issues associated with higher weight and fuel through the use of "rocket employment on demand." TAC rejected spending $98,000 on a study to investigate the potential of such a fighter. Boyd's associate, John C. Downey, guessed that the reason might have been that Boyd was making too many assumptions about future war scenarios—that only short-range aircraft were needed. "What is the probability that enemy air will be engaged at the design distance?" Downey asked. "Why that one scenario, and how can we lock ourselves in for seven years in advance plus 10–20 years of inventory life with vehicles having that one exclusive design consideration?" The degree to which Boyd considered the general purpose fighter is unclear, but the concept went nowhere.[17]

Some fighter advocates fought against Slay's modifications. On February 4, 1975, Croteau and Christie wrote to Sullivan, arguing that the changes made to the F-16 were "unacceptable." They believed that the aircraft should have "a minimum of sophistication," that the additional avionics and radar capabilities were too complex and expensive, and that the added weight reduced performance in air combat. They charged that "extensive air-to-ground capability of [the] proposed configuration compromises air-to-air capability."

Croteau's memo did offer some compromises. It depicted an "A" model of the F-16 as true to the ideal lightweight fighter. The "B" model included the changes of which the Fighter Mafia disapproved. Croteau and Christie proposed a "C" model that was a compromise between the two, allowing for some additional avionics and radar and a limited ground-attack capability.[18] This C model was never adopted.

By February 21, 1975, Chuck Myers was infuriated with the direction the development of the F-16 was taking. Myers sent a memo to Schlesinger's special assistant, Martin Hoffman, arguing that the changes made to the plane made it "a far cry from the austere FIGHTER" that the Fighter Mafia had envisioned. Myers insisted that leaders limit the avionics equipment the F-16 carried in order to "restore the character of the airplane."[19] He included a paper (presumably written by himself), explaining the way in which addition of air-to-ground capability destroyed the aircraft. He gave instructions for fixing the plane, titled "F-16 (LWF/ACF) Program Restoration." It excoriated the inclusion of ground-attack and radar capability, then charged that "the expansion of mission spectrum is accomplished with an associated increases [sic] in weight, complexity, support burden and a loss of air combat maneuvering capability, the one mission for which the original design had been optimized." The paper concluded, "This mutilation of the character of the LWF through the ACF missionization process is a management travesty which cannot go unchallenged."[20]

Members of the Fighter Mafia tended to assume that the changes made to the F-16 were retaliation for their challenges to the Air Staff. However, the Air Force had understandable reasons for adding additional capabilities to the F-16 that had little, if anything, to do with plotting revenge. The Air Staff argued that if the F-16 had no ground-attack capability, then it could not truly replace the F-4 Phantom. The point of having a high-low mix of F-15s and F-16s was to be able to phase out older aircraft such as the F-4 while maintaining and enhancing the same capabilities. But if the Fighter Mafia had their way, then 30 percent of the Air Force inventory would be incapable of attacking ground targets. The Air Staff found that unacceptable. Although the F-16 could achieve air superiority, the aircraft would be useless once that superiority had been achieved in a conflict. By adding ground-attack functions, the Air Staff argued, the F-16 could gain air superiority and then be used in a "swing role" to attack ground targets after that superiority had been won.[21]

The Air Staff was also concerned about nuclear delivery. Although the Fighter Mafia considered nuclear bombing to be an irrelevant and unnecessary mission, the Air Force worried that if the F-16 replaced older aircraft as planned, then by the early 1980s only one-third of the Air Force inventory would be capable of delivering nuclear weapons. In general, the Air Force was worried that having the F-16 be so specialized would severely limit the Air Force's capabilities.[22]

An austere F-16 also would have faced severe challenges if it lacked substantial radar capability. The inability to operate at night or in low-visibility conditions would render the aircraft problematic at best. Given that US planners expected a potential Soviet mass attack to occur in Europe, known for its often-cloudy weather, deploying large numbers of such a clear-sky, day-only fighter in that scenario would leave US forces particularly vulnerable. An increase in the F-16's maneuverability by removing the weight of a powerful radar would be useless if the pilot could not see through clouds or in the dark, rendering the plane vulnerable to other aircraft that did have such all-weather and night capability.

It is possible that some Air Force officials could have sought some sort of retaliation against the Fighter Mafia's pet project, but the case for multi-role requirements had logical arguments behind it and came from a wide group. The idea that the F-16 was being purposefully ruined by officials bitter against the Fighter Mafia was simplistic at best, although this attitude reflects how the fighter advocates saw themselves—a minority group oppressed to such a degree that the government, the military, and the Air Force viewed them as an enemy. This perception grew over time.

The F-16 modifications were a breaking point for Boyd, especially the wing area question. During the late 1970s, when the Air Force implemented these changes, Boyd frequently gathered with his acolytes Christie, Sprey, Spinney, Burton, and Boyd's assistant, Raymond Leopold, and ranted that the Air Force's "goldplating" was destroying the "pure" fighter he had designed. Coram's biography of Boyd notes that Boyd's anger about the modifications to the F-16 burned within him for the rest of his life, and they are what finally pushed Boyd to give up his involvement with hardware design for good. After this point, Boyd focused entirely on his intellectual activities.[23] These efforts expanded his movement. The Fighter Mafia was about to go public.

Philosophical Bedrock

In August 1975, five months after Boyd's advice to Slay went unheeded, Boyd retired from the Air Force. In the two years leading up to that, Boyd had begun working not only with Leopold, but also with Captain Franklin "Chuck" Spinney, who had already been working closely with Christie since 1968.[24] When the three were not collaborating on internal reports seeking to improve the procurement process, Boyd spent time attempting to outline what he called his "learning theory." By 1974 he had completed early versions of this project, which eventually coalesced into a short paper called "Destruction and Creation." This was an attempt to outline his own thought process and to explain how systems and societies change through a cyclical process of destruction and creation reminiscent of Thomas Kuhn's concept of paradigms developed in *The Structure of Scientific Revolutions*.

Although not directly related to the reform movement or defense, the paper reveals much about Boyd's thought process. He placed the role of the individual above all else, arguing that individuality and individual action were the primary drivers of human existence. Boyd asserted that systems and organizations that are too inwardly focused can create incorrect assumptions about the world, compromising the decision-making process. The remedy, Boyd argued, was for a bold individual to lead a process of destroying the old system and creating a new one. This process was a cycle to be repeated, resulting in the improvement of humanity's capacity for independent action of individuals.[25] Some analysts have found that "Destruction and Creation" has merit on its own terms. Although that paper has been studied as a philosophical work on its own, it is also evidence of Boyd's frame of mind or a self-defense of a stereotypical fighter pilot's mentality: extreme individualism and questioning authority to the point of destroying systems.[26]

Boyd prided himself on living out these ideas. He had continually accused the Air Force of being too inwardly focused—on its bureaucracy and on chasing technology for its own sake. He thought that the Air Force was stuck in a loop of its own internal inertia and had lost the ability to see the larger picture of winning large-scale wars. He saw himself as a person who could challenge that authority, destroy old systems, and build new ones that emphasized what he thought was important. Specifically, that meant a focus on air-to-air combat. Yet in the mid-1970s, Boyd's thinking drifted to areas outside of just the Air Force. Although he had little regard for the US Air Force as a system, he began to apply his criticisms of the service to the entire military, viewing it as an "inwardly focused" system that needed to be re-created.

Even though Boyd retired from the Air Force in August 1975, by early 1977 he was back in the Pentagon. Christie was still working in OSD/PA&E and offered Boyd a consultant position in the Tactical Air Division. Spinney, who had also retired from the Air Force in 1975, joined the same division in April 1977. Leopold, who had spent some time teaching at the Air Force Academy, joined the others in 1980.[27] In his new position, Boyd could offer briefings to a variety of military and government officials and contractors, as well as work on refining his writings. As Spinney recalled, the job gave Boyd "unfettered access to telephones and Xerox machines . . . the weapons of choice among the small fraternity of reform guerrillas."[28]

As Boyd finalized "Destruction and Creation," his next project took those ideas and combined them with air-to-air combat issues. First, NASA asked him to conduct a study of why pilots fly simulators differently from actual aircraft. Boyd concluded that because simulators did not give the same types of visual and physical cues that pilots experience when conducting vertical maneuvering in the real world, pilots tended to operate mostly in the horizontal plane. While studying this problem, Boyd was also preoccupied with the flyoff between the YF-16 and YF-17. His EMT studies on the two craft had predicted the two planes should perform nearly identically, with the YF-17 superior in some places. However, in the flyoff, the YF-16 proved superior in maneuverability. The YF-16, when in a tight turn, lost energy faster than the YF-17. Spinney explained, "Since the dawn of fighter aviation in 1914, power limitations made this kind of energy-dumping maneuver a desperation tactic. Once the energy was lost, it was difficult, if not impossible, to regain energy quickly enough to continue the dogfight." But the YF-16's thrust-to-weight ratio was able to overcome this: "The pilots learned by trial and error to take advantage of this power by evolving quick energy-dumping as well as quick energy-pumping tactics."[29]

Boyd incorporated these concepts into a new briefing: "New Conception for Air-to-Air Combat," completed in August 1976. Boyd suggested that fighters that succeed in air-to-air combat are capable of a "natural hook" tactic, or a "fast transient maneuver." Boyd applied the idea to a variety of air-to-air matchups, then took the idea further, arguing that the concept of winning air-to-air battles through superior maneuverability could apply to any kind of warfare in general. He concluded that the "idea of *fast transients* suggests that—in order to win or gain superiority—we should operate at a *faster tempo* than our adversaries," because "such activity will make us appear *ambiguous* (non-predictable) [and] thereby generate *confusion* and *disorder* among our adversaries." He offered three historical examples: MiG-15s in dogfights against F-86s in the Korean War, the then-current 1976 Israeli raid on Entebbe airport to rescue hostages in Uganda, and the German invasion of France in 1940. He argued that each of these proved his point, that being quicker than the opponent was the key to victory. As his final slide proclaimed, "He who can handle the quickest rate of change survives."[30]

This idea formed the core component of Boyd's intellectual activities for most of the remainder of his life. The next month, the briefing had become the first draft of "Patterns of Conflict," which is perhaps Boyd's best-known work outside of EMT. Boyd rewrote, edited, and refined this presentation continually. With each version, the briefing grew longer. The original form lasted about forty minutes. By the mid-1980s, "Patterns of Conflict" had grown to encompass other briefings combined into a large presentation titled "A Discourse on Winning and Losing," which, according to Burton, was thirteen hours long.[31]

"Patterns of Conflict" was a survey of military history reaching back to ancient Mesopotamia. For each of his examples Boyd argued that the successful strategy was the result of obscuring one's intent through quick movements designed to draw an enemy out. As he stated, conflicts were won by those who are "more subtle, more indistinct, more irregular, and quicker— yet appear to be otherwise."[32]

Part of Boyd's focus on history was due to Sprey's influence. Although Sprey had much in common with fighter pilot stereotypes and was interested in making effective fighter planes, he later recalled that he saw air-to-air combat as a "pimple on [the] ass of real war," which consists of "men in mud, that's what wins and loses." He urged Boyd to study other aspects of military history, especially the German military of World War II. Boyd took his advice and surmised that the "power in the German Command and Control System" was that the officers had spent so much time together that they developed a similar mind-set and could communicate without speaking, allowing them to "reduce time and gain quickness." This interest in the history of the Wehrmacht included meetings with former German general officers. According to Sprey, his mentor Richard Hallock funded a group including Boyd, Sprey, and Christie to travel to Germany to interview several former Wehrmacht officers and bring them to the US for further discussions. This included Hans-Ulrich Rudel, Hermann Balck, Friedrich von Mellenthin, and Heinrich Gaedcke.[33]

To say that these men were controversial would be an understatement. Rudel, a prominent neo-Nazi activist for the remainder of his life, was vocally unrepentant about his Nazi ideology and had founded an organization to assist the escape of German war criminals including Josef Mengele, the SS doctor responsible for human experiments at Auschwitz. Von Mellenthin was, according to historian Wolfram Wette, one of the authors responsible for spreading the "clean hands" myth—the false notion that the Wehrmacht was not responsible for the atrocities and war crimes of the Nazi regime. Historian Robert Citino noted that Von Mellenthin's work was "at best unreliable and at worst deliberately misleading."[34] Balck had been briefly imprisoned for executing an officer without a trial and was later convicted by a

French court for his participation in a scorched-earth campaign in France in 1944 in which he ordered over ten thousand civilians to concentration camps. However, the US did not extradite him.

Boyd and Sprey were fascinated with these men, who advocated for many of the same ideas that Boyd was promoting in "Patterns of Conflict" about speed and movement. Sprey allegedly used Rudel's insight when designing the A-10 Thunderbolt II, and Boyd borrowed his phrase "fingerspitzenge-fühl" ("fingertip feel"), which became one of Boyd's most-used terms to describe his ideal for flexibility in military actions. Balck, however, was their favorite. Boyd and Sprey called him a "genius," and Boyd was so in awe that he was reduced to self-effacing embarrassment in Balck's presence. Sprey recalled that Boyd and Balck became "great friends." Although it is unclear when the groups' introduction occurred, Boyd met repeatedly with Balck and Mellenthin as late as the summer of 1980.[35] Boyd's interest in the subject apparently deepened with time. According to Coram's interview notes, Boyd's wife, Mary, and their children noted that Boyd spoke of his admiration for Adolf Hitler, because he had risen from humble origins to ruling a country and "swayed the thoughts" of so many people.[36] This is not to imply anything about Boyd's sociopolitical views; he and Sprey were not Nazi sympathizers, but seemed to lack a full understanding of—or were willing to overlook—some of the more troubling aspects of their sources of inspiration. Their admiration for the German military was also not unusual for the time; it was a common view throughout the US military services. Many former Wehrmacht and Luftwaffe officers were frequent guest speakers at a variety of US military events in the post-Vietnam era, and many American officers looked to them for inspiration on military matters.[37]

"Patterns of Conflict" contained another concept that became central to the Military Reform movement: simplicity. The briefing argued that complexity (either technical, organizational, or operational) was harmful to successful operations because it reduced speed. Complex systems could cause personnel to "be captured by their own internal dynamics," rendering them unable to adapt and act quickly.[38] The idea that simpler weapons were more effective because they allowed the user to be faster and thus keep an opponent in a state of confusion and disorder was central to the thinking of Boyd and his associates. Burton described "Patters of Conflict" as "the philosophical bedrock of the Reform Movement."[39]

These ideas were not completely new. They bore a resemblance to Basil Liddell Hart's idea of the "indirect approach," first outlined in his 1929 work, *The Decisive Wars of History*. This was later expanded in *The Strategy of Indirect Approach* in 1941 and republished in 1942 as *The Way to Win Wars*. Liddell

Hart claimed that wars were won by the side that achieved surprise and confused the enemy by taking "the indirect approach." According to Sprey, Boyd hated Liddell Hart, saying that he "doesn't know squat."[40] Despite this, their overall arguments are quite similar, as are their methods of using brief surveys of historical examples to argue their points.[41]

Also introduced in "Patterns of Conflict" was Boyd's most influential idea, the OODA loop of "observe, orient, decide, act." This concept has little to do with aircraft design or the reform movement but is the concept for which Boyd is most famous. It has generated significant debate, much of it emotionally charged to the point where attempts to define what the OODA loop is, or to discuss it in depth, are likely to draw objections from either Boyd's advocates or detractors, claiming that one does not fully understand the loop, or is not using the "real" loop.[42]

Part of the problem stems from the fact that Boyd wrote very little. Apart from the essay "Destruction and Creation," almost the entirety of Boyd's output consists of slide shows meant to accompany his briefings. Examined in isolation, the slides are almost incomprehensible. A few poor-quality video recordings exist of individual briefings, but as Boyd scholar and associate Grant Hammond noted, Boyd's briefings "were meant to be conversations between him and his audiences," and thus "the briefings were always in flux."[43] Combined with Boyd's habit of continuously reediting his own work, it is no wonder that his concepts have generated confusion and debate.

The OODA loop is often defined as a "decision cycle" guiding actions against an adversary who is in a similar loop, and victory will come to those who can work through subsequent loops faster, or, "get inside the decision cycle." Some advocates for the concept, such as defense analyst (and former F-16 pilot) Frans Osinga, argue that the "real" loop is "less a model of decision making than an epistemological model." Osinga continued, "It is a model of individual- and organizational-level learning and adaptation processes . . . a meta-paradigm of mind and universe, a dialectic engine, an inductive-deductive engine of progress, a paradigm for survival and growth, and a theory of intellectual evolution."[44] Hammond said Boyd defined it as "a composite of how we think and learn, the source of who we are, and the potential we possess . . . a shorthand for life itself, a model for how we think, and the means by which we both compete and collaborate."[45] The usefulness of such a broad conception to warfighters, commanders, or fighter pilots in the cockpit (which are Boyd's core examples) is unclear.

The OODA concept first appeared in Boyd's "Patterns of Conflict" in the late 1970s as repeated references in the slides, although it is not clearly defined nor presented hierarchically as an overriding core concept. The loop is only referenced specifically in one other presentation, "Organic Design for Command and Control." Not until 1995 did Boyd finalize a version of the OODA loop with the help of Spinney and Chet Richards.[46] This final loop is anything but shorthand—it is a convoluted flow chart with over twenty arrows pointing in various directions, linking sub-aspects of each element of the cycle (with various shaped borders within borders), requiring a significant amount of interpretation.

To analyze the OODA loop is beyond the scope of this book and has been the subject of other works. Yet three points are often underrepresented in that discussion: First, the OODA loop is vague enough that its defenders and attackers can each see what they want to see in it. For some, the OODA concept's flexibility is its strength, but for others it becomes so generalized as to lose its usefulness. The terms are loosely defined, and because most of Boyd's evidence is presented as historical allegory, his variables are not codified in any measurable way as is customary for the social sciences. His ideas are thus difficult if not impossible to formally test.[47] Some social scientists have competing models for human decision making. The most prominent example is psychologist and economist Daniel Kahneman, who has argued that human decision making has two modes: fast and slow, and that quick decisions are usually done more on instinct and training than by going through complex decision cycles.[48] Others have argued that the OODA loop cannot be practically implemented at the strategic or operational levels as described and is thus "deeply flawed."[49]

Second, while Boyd's advocates claim that the OODA loop is based on a rigorous study of prominent academics across multiple fields, from Heisenberg to Darwin, the connections are tenuous and debatable. Boyd's allegorical evidence consists of selected examples from history as proof of his concepts, often chosen with heavy selection bias, while avoiding counterexamples. Most of his analysis is on the tactical level, but he often applies the concepts to a strategic level while avoiding much of the surrounding context of the examples he chooses.[50] Boyd's ideas were never submitted to the scrutiny of academic peer review by any field.

Third, the OODA loop is not unique. In addition to being similar in concept to the scientific method itself, many other models of decision cycles, learning methods, and behavioral therapy cycles exist, predating the OODA loop. Physicist Walter Shewhart's "plan, do, check, act" cycle (later versions add "observe") dates from 1939; naval analyst Dr. Joel Lawson's model of "sense, process, compose, decide, act" originated in 1979; and Air Force analyst Joseph G. Wohl published his cycle of "stimulus, hypothesis, option, response" in 1981.[51] Furthermore, Alfred Adler, a psychiatrist working in the

1910s, developed his four-stage model of behavioral therapy: engagement, assessment, insight, and reorientation.[52] In 1975, educational theorists David A. Kolb and Ronald E. Fry published their "experiential learning model," a cycle with similar steps: concrete experience; observation of and reflection on that experience; formation of abstract concepts based on the reflection; and testing the new concepts. Their work was derived from similar ideas from psychologist Kurt Lewin in the 1930s and 1940s.[53] Researchers Alan Mumford and Peter Honey proposed another, similar cycle in the 1980s and 1990s: doing, reflecting, concluding, planning.[54]

These are but a few examples of many decision and learning cycle models that existed before or around the same time that Boyd developed his OODA loop. They are not identical but contain many similarly adaptable concepts. There is no evidence that Boyd intentionally borrowed from these ideas or was aware of them (none appear in Boyd's bibliography), but they are indicative of the generic nature of the concept. The OODA loop is merely one way among a myriad of ways of describing intuitive processes of learning and decision making that most people experience daily. It is not incorrect, but neither is it unique or especially profound.

Regardless of this, something about Boyd's expression of the OODA loop resonated with a certain audience in a powerful way, and the concept remained influential in some circles. Many people find the OODA loop useful, just as many others find other similar cycles useful—that is important and should not be minimized. But those who struggle to find its relevance or applicability are not wrong or misguided; they merely have a different opinion. To the point, the debate surrounding the OODA loop speaks to Boyd's tendency to never finalize his work while insisting he was intellectually superior to those who did not agree with him.

Through the remainder of the 1970s, Boyd gave his briefing in military and government circles and to most of the Pentagon press corps. By the early 1980s Boyd delivered his briefings as many as four days a week across a variety of venues. Congressman Richard "Dick" Cheney (R-WY) heard Boyd's briefing, and the two began having regular private meetings. The philosophy of the Fighter Mafia became a cornerstone of Cheney's thinking about defense issues. Three successive Marine Corps commandants—General Robert H. Barrow, General Paul X. Kelley, and General Alfred Gray—each heard Boyd's briefing and also had regular private sessions with Boyd. Freeman Dyson, a renowned physicist at the Institute for Advanced Study at Princeton who was known for his work on quantum electrodynamics, also attended the "Patterns of Conflict" briefing many times. William Lind, then a staffer for Senator Gary Hart (D-CO), was also in the audience for Boyd's briefing in this period. Lind drew a connection between Boyd's group and the Prussian military reformers of the early nineteenth century, and he first began referring to Boyd and his acolytes as "the Reformers" in the late 1970s.[55]

Some listeners were open to Boyd's ideas, and some were not. For example, Dr. John J. Martin, assistant secretary of the Air Force for acquisition, worked with a group of nuclear physicists that advised on national defense issues—most of whom were quite critical of "Patterns of Conflict." Many Air Force personnel also found the ideas distasteful. Some, such as General John C. Toomay, DCS for development plans at AFSC, admired Boyd's work but were unable to translate the broad ideas of the briefing into specific tasks.[56]

Boyd's acolytes, however, needed to balance their image of Boyd as the preeminent sage with the fact that he received much criticism and even resistance from some of his audience. On the one hand, Boyd's followers described him as the smartest person in almost any room, a man whose intellectual prowess, as Burton described, caused his opponents to "become quivering masses of jelly" or to collapse from nervous breakdowns at the shock of Boyd's intellect. These fans of Boyd frequently told stories of Boyd outsmarting or gleefully telling off generals or academics. As with earlier examples, the details of such stories often disagree, change over time, lack specific information such as names and dates, and originate only with Boyd and his friends themselves. To prop up this vision of Boyd's intellectual dominance, his followers explained that those who rejected his ideas were too old, too entrenched, or even brainwashed by the defense establishment.[57] This was a simplistic interpretation, and it was not always true. Some older officers accepted the ideas, and not all younger ones did. Yet Boyd's followers believed that he was an intellectual superhuman and a messiah figure for the emerging reform movement.

Mutually Devastating

As Boyd looked less at air combat, the Air Force studied it in more detail. The service was frustrated with its air-to-air combat performance in the Vietnam War, particularly the poor performance of the two main types of air-to-air missiles. The radar-guided AIM-7 Sparrow was designed in a Cold War context for BVR attacks against enemy bombers, not fast-turning MiGs. The lack of accurate identify-friend-or-foe (IFF) systems during the war prompted a rule forbidding most air-to-air attacks without visual confirmation. Sparrows were thus rarely, if ever, fired in the conditions they were designed for. They also had technical problems: 63 percent did not launch correctly, and 29 percent

missed their targets. The heat-seeking AIM-9 Sidewinder was somewhat better for close fighting but could often be evaded with a hard turn. It sometimes
locked on to heat sources such as clouds, the sun, or the ground, instead of
the enemy engine. The missile had a 15 percent hit rate, while 56 percent of
the missiles experienced technical failure.[58]

The Air Force developed a new dogfighting missile, the heat-seeking
AIM-4D Falcon, which was introduced in combat in Southeast Asia in 1967.
It was not an improvement. Colonel Robin Olds, an ace pilot from World
War II and commander of the Eighth Tactical Fighter Wing in the Vietnam
War, explained, "Whoever thought up that gadget didn't know a damned
thing about air-to-air fighting, and didn't ask anyone who ever had."[59] Only
fifty-four Falcons were fired during Rolling Thunder, producing only five
hits. As with the Sidewinder, many of these firings were done outside the
missile's proper envelope.[60]

The Navy and the Air Force sought to improve their missiles, and jointly
developed a new version of the Sparrow, the AIM-7F, with solid state electronics. The Navy worked on the long-range, radar-guided AIM-54 Phoenix.
In search of a replacement for the Sidewinder, the Air Force worked on the
CLAW missile, while the Navy developed the AIM-95 Agile missile. While
those were in development, both services implemented an upgraded Sidewinder, the AIM-9L.[61]

The multitude of similar missile options frustrated Congress, who sought
to reduce defense costs. The 1975 Congress pressured the services to not
only agree to one short-range air-to-air missile, but also to study the effect of
aircraft quantity on air-to-air combat as a guide in planning force structure.
This second part of the directive asked a complicated question: how many
of the older, lower-performance fighter planes (such as the F-5) would it take
to defeat an F-15? The result was a series of joint tests with the Air Force and
Navy conducted at Nellis Air Force Base in 1976 and 1977. The first part of
the test, the air-intercept missile evaluation (AIMVAL), was the evaluation of
potential Sidewinder replacements, and the second part was the air combat
evaluation (ACEVAL), testing new aircraft against higher numbers of older
planes.[62]

The stakes of these tests were high, potentially influencing budget, force
structure, foreign aircraft sales, and procurement into the 1990s, and they
later became a key talking point for the Fighter Mafia and later reform movement. But the tests were not well suited to answer the proposed questions.
The biggest problem was that the key advantage of the F-15 (and F-14) and,
to some designers, their raison d'être, was their advanced radar. The Eagle's
AN/APG-63 was optimized to detect enemies at 30 miles and up to 160 miles

away. But the AIMVAL/ACEVAL tests had to be flown above a test range with ground receivers—the only existing range at Nellis was only thirty miles across and could measure only above three thousand feet. The test designers thus ruled that the F-15 and F-14 could not make BVR attacks—which in the minds of advocates for those planes was their chief advantage, if not the whole point of their design philosophy. Pilots also squabbled about the rules, the altitude limitations, and whether the scoring system should reward aggressiveness or defensive tactics.[63]

AIMVAL began on January 3, 1977. Against the "Blue Air" team of Air Force F-15 Eagles and Navy F-14 Tomcats, a group of "Aggressor" pilots flew as the "Red Air" team, using F-5s. Various missile designs were tested in many scenarios, but the most successful by far was the Sidewinder AIM-9L. Previous versions required pilots to maneuver behind an enemy, but the L's more sensitive heat-seeker allowed it to be fired from any angle, and it could calculate how to lead a target. The turn-and-burn of stereotypical dogfights was not necessarily required. The idea of maneuvering battles did not go away, but the new missile did prompt changes in tactics. "Some proclaimed that the days of basic fighter maneuvers [BFM] were over," F-15 pilot C. R. Anderegg recalled. "All one had to do was point and shoot. What they discovered was that BFM was not dead; the maneuvers just got bigger and started further away."[64]

The AIMVAL portion of the test might have challenged the Fighter Mafia's stances on maneuvering and guns, but they later claimed that it reinforced one of their core beliefs: that a simple aircraft (the F-5) posed a lethal threat to the more advanced, expensive aircraft like the F-15. This ignored the fact that the main threat—the AIM-9L—was very complex and significantly more expensive than other weapons, and that the F-15s were not using their BVR capability. Yet the group could point to individual encounters as evidence of their views. The most dramatic example was a test scenario that earned the nickname "the Towering Inferno" (after the 1974 film). In that engagement, four F-15s using AIM-7 Sparrows flew against four F-5s using the AIM-9L. By the end of the encounter, six of the aircraft were downed, leaving one F-15 closing in from behind the last remaining F-5. The Eagle launched its Sparrow missile just as the last F-5 turned around and fired its Sidewinder. The computer tracked the F-5 as "killed," but its missile, already launched, killed the final F-15 with a shot from beyond the simulated grave.[65]

That was just one incident. The ACEVAL tests ran from June 2 to November 10, 1977, and consisted of 720 encounters of various sizes, armaments, and access to support. All the conditions were within the thirty-mile size limitation of the test range. The tests did show that in engagements involving one or two planes on each side, the F-15s and F-14s dominated the F-5s.

With more planes in the air, though, the exchange rates tended to become more even.[66]

These results have been interpreted in several ways. Historian and former fighter pilot Steven Fino argued that when the total number of aircraft is lower, advanced technology does translate into increased situational awareness. But a high number of planes in the sky becomes too much for a pilot to keep in a coherent "mental picture," so the technological advantage is canceled out.[67] Anderegg claimed that the win-loss ratio depends much more on the conditions of each specific scenario and access to ground radar information. He also insisted that many of the tactics that capitalized on the F-15s' advantages had yet to be developed at that time—the new missiles represented a transformation in air combat tactics that had not been fully realized. No longer did pilots have to pass each other in a traditional "merge," the moment where two fighters flying head-on against each other pass before attempting to maneuver behind the enemy into a firing position. "In the early 1970s, if an F-4 pilot briefed his adversary that a Sparrow shot from ten miles would be counted as a kill, he would be laughed out of the briefing room," Anderegg recalled. "As the reliability of the missiles improved, the culture of long-range missiles slowly spread throughout the fighter force." After AIMVAL-ACEVAL, he explained, "the fight did not start at 1,000 feet range as in the days of '40-second Boyd.' The struggle was starting while the adversaries were thirty miles apart, and the F-15 pilots were seriously intent on killing every adversary pre-merge."[68]

Some pilots and observers rejected the tests completely as unrealistic, arguing that the rules, the sense of competition, and the "cat and mouse" tactics engendered between aggressive fighter pilots during the test created data that were not representative of warfare conditions. One anonymous pilot made a satirical presentation slide mocking the tests and slipped it onto the desk of General Robert Dixon, commander of TAC:

ACEVAL-AIMVAL

A shootout in an isolated tennis court between giants armed with rifles, pistols, and knives and midgets armed with only pistols and knives.

Chief rule: Have to identify color of eyes before shooting. . . .

ACEVAL

A test to see how the outcome is affected by the number of giants and midgets in the tennis court. . . .

AIMVAL

A test to see which pistol is best for the giants. . . .

Shootout Results

More or less as expected: Mutually devastating.[69]

Some Senate staffers rejected the tests as unhelpful owing to the unrealistic conditions. The Air Force Studies and Analysis branch urged that the results of the tests not be taken as evidence for any particular points. The tests' director, Navy aviator Rear Admiral Ernest Tissot, warned that the tests "should not be treated in terms of specific system absolutes." The Air Force's DCS/R&D's summary to Congress said that, having "theoretically taken a big skyhook and dropped these airplanes into a 30-mile arena," the tests had been "a canned situation."[70]

Boyd visited the AIMVAL-ACEVAL tests in July 1976 and again at their conclusion in December 1977. In his summary report, he noted that the constraining rules of the tests differed so wildly from real combat that the value of the tests was questionable. He argued that the tactics developed there "applied to *specific* AIMVAL/ACEVAL engagements and *in general could not be extrapolated to any real world conflict.*" Boyd warned: *"It appeared that one could find support for any conclusion or point of view depending upon whom you questioned."*[71] Despite this, the Reformers, including Boyd, seized on AIMVAL-ACEVAL as proof for their position that higher numbers of small, cheap, "simple," technology was superior to more advanced options. These arguments formed the basis for the Fighter Mafia's continued efforts, which soon went public.

Chuck the Apostle

If "Patterns of Conflict" was the philosophical bedrock of the reform movement, Spinney's and Sprey's work gave it specific vocabulary and talking points. This began with Spinney's 1978 briefing "Defense Facts of Life." The project originated partly owing to Christie's concerns about readiness and retention problems in the Air Force. Spinney recalled that, as the newest member of the team, he "got [the] dirty work" and served as the "wrecking crew." Spinney collaborated with Boyd and Sprey, bringing the briefing's arguments, evidence, and language in line with their thinking.[72]

Spinney's overall point was that complex, expensive equipment was the root cause of the military's inability to operate successfully. The result was a crisis: "Our nation faces a long-term defense problem of fundamental importance." He defined complexity as "a quality of the whole that relates the number, arrangement, and coordination of the parts to one's ability to comprehend the whole." Put another way, "increasing complexity runs up the number, increases the variety of arrangements, and complicates the coordination of the parts—and, thereby, decreases one's ability to comprehend the whole." Spinney argued that complexity caused rigidity, and he saw the two as nearly synonymous. Thus he presented a spectrum with "complexity" at one end and "flexibility" on the other. As he saw it, "increasing complexity increases our rigidity in a game where survival of the fittest makes flexibility a paramount virtue."[73]

This spectrum was simplistic at best. Sometimes complexity and flexibility could coexist. For example, the F-15's long-range radar met their definition of complex, yet when used as intended, it increased the flexibility available to pilots, allowing them to know enemy locations early, have initiative on the battlefield, and engage enemies in the time and place of their choosing. The "complex" AIM-9L also increased flexibility, allowing pilots to fire the missile from any direction without having to first pass the merge and then maneuver behind an enemy aircraft. "Complexity" and "flexibility" are broad terms that can be interpreted in many ways. Spinney's definitions in "Defense Facts of Life" were the expression of Fighter Mafia ideals, and that definition set the agenda for the future of the reform movement.

Spinney also argued that complex weapons tended to increase costs—not just in the procurement stage, but by causing a cascading effect of higher costs for operation, support, and maintenance. The long development times of complex weapons caused the financial effects of technological decisions to be delayed for many years. This made future capabilities unpredictable and locked the military into certain spending patterns, regardless of future economic conditions. In Spinney's analysis, this created a systemic decrease in long-term flexibility.[74]

As with his spectrum of complexity versus flexibility, Spinney conceived of a spectrum involving people and technology. He thought that technological complexity was directly opposed to a human's ability to use that technology effectively. As weapons became more complex, they diminished the human contribution that he thought was key to combat effectiveness. When ranking the elements that he thought made a "superior military force," Spinney ranked people as the most important factor, followed by ideas, motivation and psychology, and skills. Machines were last on the list, with a presentation slide declaring in bold text: "Machines don't fight wars—people do!" He was not absolutist, though, acknowledging that "a superior military force is a synthesis of man and machines," but only machines fitting his conception of simple.[75]

One area that "Defense Facts of Life" avoided was the way in which technology can be complex in its design but simple in its user experience.

Fly-by-wire technology is a strong example. According to Spinney's definition, fly-by-wire systems are complex. Many inputs from several sensors are processed by computers and translated into a combination of outputs for flight control surfaces. Designing such systems requires an interdisciplinary approach. Yet from the user perspective, the operation is quite simple: pushing the control stick moves the plane where the pilot wants. Spinney's interpretations of "complexity" and human-machine interactions were at least debatable. His view was not the only approach to issues of military hardware but simply one of them—one that some of his audience shared and others did not.

Spinney preemptively defended himself against criticisms. He was adamant that his stance on complexity did not make him antitechnology or opposed to large military budgets. He supported the use of technology when it enhanced his own goals. The issue was not whether to use high technology but how to keep that technology "simple" according to his definition. As he stated, he was concerned with *"how* we should use our superior technology. . . . *Advanced technology and high complexity are not synonymous."*[76]

Regarding budgetary issues, he said the problems in the Department of Defense were so ingrained that procurement policy was eroding combat capability. "We need more money to strengthen our military; however, we believe that unless we change the way we do business, more money could actually make our problems worse."[77] The root problem, as the Reformers perceived it, was the system itself—from Congress to the Defense Department and the individual services—the mode of thinking and operating throughout the entire establishment was flawed. As Boyd might have seen it, the system needed to be destroyed and re-created.

By the end of "Defense Facts of Life," Spinney pushed his ideas to extremes with inflammatory statements. Using allusions to World War II, as Boyd and Sprey were fond of doing, Spinney claimed that the US had a "Maginot Line" mentality similar to the French on the eve of their defeat. Although the French had high-technology solutions in armor and aircraft, their doctrine and force structure were inappropriate for the type of warfare waged against them in May 1940. Spinney warned that the United States was doing the same. Spinney added that a large factor in Germany's defeat was Hitler's misplaced faith in technological solutions. Spinney argued that the United States was making the same mistake as Hitler, warning that "we have evolved a self-reinforcing . . . faith in the military usefulness of ever increasing technological complexity." Spinney referred to this faith as the "New Religion" within the US military, furthering the image of the Reformers as an oppressed minority preaching the truth within a corrupt order. Spinney's conclusion reduced the issues to a binary choice: "Our strategy of pursuing ever increasing technical complexity and sophistication has made high technology solutions and combat readiness *mutually exclusive.*"[78]

"Defense Facts of Life" set the agenda for the reform movement. Although Boyd was the leader, inspiration, and central figure, his own major work, "Patterns of Conflict," was more philosophical. It provided the underlying outlook and many key beliefs of the reform movement, but Spinney defined the terms for arguments that lasted into the next decade. He also outlined the apologetics the movement could use to defend itself. To extend their own religious analogy, if Boyd was the Jesus of the cult of the Reformers, Spinney was its Paul.

Winners and Losers

Adding to Boyd and Spinney's efforts, in 1979 Sprey made an entry into the Reformers' canon with his briefing "The Case for More Effective, Less Expensive Weapons Systems." Like the other briefings, this one was continually updated and refined over several years.[79] Sprey's main goal in this paper was to argue against the idea that expensive weapons were inherently better. To him, the common phrase "you get what you pay for" was wrong. To that end, he conducted a historical analysis matching up pairs of weapons systems, dividing them into "cheap winners" and "expensive losers." For example, he said the cheaper Armalite AR-15 rifle was more effective in Vietnam than the more expensive M-14 it replaced.[80]

He made similar comparisons with ten other combat systems, chosen somewhat arbitrarily. This included comparing the AIM-9D Sidewinder with the AIM-7 Sparrow, arguing that the Sparrow had only one-third the hit rate of the Sidewinder in Vietnam. He also compared the P-51 Mustang to the P-38 Lightning, both World War II–era fighters, arguing that the P-51 was cheaper and more effective. In emphasizing the Reformers' view that men are more important than machines, Sprey argued that air-defense guns using radar-assisted targeting would be inherently ineffective against maneuvering aircraft. He argued that "well-trained or experienced gunners" using only their eyes through optical sights could outperform the radar-assisted systems.[81] This insistence that an individual's eyesight can be more reliable than technologically assisted targeting systems had been a factor in designing the F-16 cockpit, and reflected the values of the Fighter Mafia—that individual people are key.

These examples have some merit, but they can be misleading, since Sprey's analysis discounts much of the context. For example, the AIM-7 Sparrow was designed as a long-range missile, yet the rules of engagement over Vietnam required visual identification of all enemy aircraft before firing—thus, the Sparrow was rarely, if ever, fired in the situation for which it was designed. Criticizing a weapon for not being versatile, when it was designed for a more specific role, was ironic coming from those who demanded their fighter aircraft be specialized for a single task. Similar dualistic thinking permeated Sprey's entire briefing. He presented each of his examples as either/or propositions in a zero-sum game. Yet decision makers are often presented with far more than two specific choices on issues and rarely need to make choices in such absolute terms. P-38s and P-51s can both exist and perform well in different roles. Sidewinders and Sparrows can be specialized for different circumstances and both be part of a larger combination of weapons systems. In each example, Sprey argued that one choice was effective and the other ineffective. One was simple and cheap, the other was expensive and complex. One was right, at least according to Sprey, and one was wrong. As he put it, one was a winner, and one was a loser.

This winner/loser dynamic pushed the reform movement away from more nuanced arguments into more binary thinking. It also created a set of buzzwords that could be easily repeated and understood in public venues. After this point, those terms began appearing with increasing frequency in interviews and publications of the reform movement. Sprey's choices also created a list of specific hardware programs on which the Reformers focused. Sprey identified eleven categories of military capabilities, and for each one he offered a cheap, simple winner and an expensive, complex loser. He did not explain each choice in detail, focusing most of his analysis on two categories: First, for armor, Sprey found the M60A1 "Patton" superior to the newer M1 Abrams battle tank, primarily because the older tank had more "mobility" in terms of a longer range (despite the M1's increased speed due to its more powerful engine). Sprey focused on rate of fire, rather than other factors, and dismissed the superior Chobham armor of the M1, arguing that since the armor was not present on the rear of the M1, the Abrams was just as vulnerable as the M60A1 Patton.[82]

Most of his analysis centered on the Fighter Mafia's pet subject: air-to-air combat. Unsurprisingly, Sprey argued that the F-16 was better than the F-15 Eagle. He evaluated each according to what he considered "the four principal effectiveness characteristics that contribute to victory in air-to-air combat": surprise, superior numbers, agility and maneuverability, and lethality of weapons. The criteria themselves point to the values of the Fighter Mafia and their interpretation of what air-to-air fighter combat should look like: close-turning dogfights that mimicked the constructed memory of World War I. Sprey assumed that the F-16 could achieve surprise simply because it was smaller, discounting enemy detection capabilities. Because the F-16 was cheaper, more of them could be produced to outnumber opponents (assuming opponents did not do the same). Sprey argued that the F-16 was more maneuverable and agile than the F-15; and, as to lethality, since the aircraft had virtually the same armament, the more agile F-16 was, for Sprey, inherently superior.[83]

These criteria ignore other potential factors, such as ground radar, air defense networks, long-range weapons, and the evolving tactics associated with those, and ignored noncombat factors such as logistics, manpower, training, maintenance, and production. Sprey assumed that, in an air-to-air fight, all parties would shut their radars off to avoid detection, and he also assumed that missiles in the future would perform exactly as they did during the specific conditions of the Vietnam War, from which he obtained his data. If air-to-air combat conformed to the Fighter Mafia's vision of close-range gentlemanly duels in a cloudless sky in daytime, then his analysis might have been correct.

These objections do not dismiss Sprey's arguments completely. In many scenarios, the F-16 is a very effective aircraft—perhaps more effective than the F-15 under certain conditions. Rather, Sprey's argument emphasized the ways in which the Fighter Mafia and the emerging reform movement interpreted military history to conform to their preexisting views. They valued men over machines, saw technological complexity (as they defined it) as a threat, and were legitimately worried about rising budgets. They valued speed and maneuverability above almost all other concerns, and they were convinced that greater numbers could overcome greater quality—although Sprey argued that there was no difference between "quantity" and "quality" and that his cheaper, simpler options were thus both quantitatively and qualitatively superior. Most importantly, Sprey's briefing conveyed the reductive idea that every choice is an all-or-nothing between two discrete options: one a "winner," the other a "loser." One is right, one is wrong. And to Sprey, the "complex" option was always wrong.[84]

This paper helped define the agenda for the reform movement by identifying specific programs that members should target. The F-15 and the M1 Abrams main battle tank were the most often referenced examples of undesirable "complex" weapons. The growing reform movement presented these programs as symbols of what they thought was wrong with the Defense Department. Other examples, such as the Bradley Fighting Vehicle and the

AH-64 Apache helicopter, joined that list later. Like the other documents, Sprey's briefing was shared throughout the Pentagon. The nascent reform movement was growing but was still mostly internal to the military.

The YF-16 prototype was a culmination of the Fighter Mafia's ideals, an advanced fighter aircraft using modern technology to maximize characteristics associated with the knights of the air from World War I. But the Fighter Mafia—Boyd especially—perceived the operational F-16 as a corruption, modified from his pure vision. In frustration, the group, joined by new allies such as Leopold, Spinney, and Burton, moved in a much broader direction, both in audience and subject matter. The texts produced by Boyd, Spinney, and Sprey became the canonized scripture of their movement, forming the basis for the writing and advocacy that came afterward. Still, their ideas were motivated by the elements of the knights of the air myth. In their attitudes and personal approaches as well as in the changes they advocated, the main elements of the fighter pilot stereotype were present: aggressiveness, resistance to authority, individualism, valuing only their preferred technologies, protection of their own community, and use of heroic imagery.

In the late 1970s and the 1980s, they began talking about the technology of tanks, artillery, personnel carriers, and other weapons, but they still emphasized the same elements that they had emphasized when talking of fighter planes: agility, maneuverability, the ability to surprise, and the conviction that machines needed to be "simple." They also expanded their audience to include politicians and the general public. Aided by journalists and members of Congress, Boyd and many members of the Fighter Mafia created the "Military Reform" movement and argued for cheaper, simpler weapons. The movement loomed large throughout the 1980s in the public press, popular literature, and on Capitol Hill.

CHAPTER 7

"Zealots of the Classic Variety"

> It is equally fallacious to conclude that criticism from uniformed mavericks represents "outside-the-box" thinking or that these critics are really agents of change. In fact, they often represent the more conservative elements.
>
> —Brian McAllister Linn, *Echo of Battle*

From 1975 to 1991, the United States experienced a second interwar period, between the major wars in Vietnam and the Persian Gulf. Like the first interwar period between the World Wars, this one was a time of exploration of new military technologies and doctrines. But the mood of the country was different this time. Emerging from the Vietnam War, most Americans felt that something had gone very wrong there. Beyond those who had been opposed to the war, many who supported it—and the military itself—thought it had been problematic at best. The US military services came out of Vietnam with a strong desire for change—a sense that drastic reforms were needed to ensure that another Vietnam never happened. But there was wide disagreement on what the real problems were, so prescriptions for change were numerous, varied, and sometimes contradictory. On a larger scale, the late 1970s brought not only economic crisis but a sense that US power and prestige were in decline—the Iranian hostage crisis, and the failed rescue attempt, added to a sense that the US military, if not the US itself, was fundamentally broken.

Into that pervading malaise walked the Reformers. Led by John Boyd, Pierre Sprey, Charles Spinney, and others, the movement had a message that resonated: The military *was* broken. But we know how to fix it. They argued that military technology had gotten too complex, the system too full of corrupt insiders. By looking nostalgically to the past—a time of simpler, cheaper weapons and a military run by warriors instead of bureaucrats—they could restore greatness to the military and maybe, by implication, to America itself. This view was informed by the underlying assumptions and thought patterns of the fighter pilot culture that had informed the Fighter Mafia, and their view of the past was obscured by thick rose-colored glasses, if not wholly imagined. Nonetheless, their message spoke to many Americans both in and out of the military, creating a broad movement calling for massive change.

Muscle-Bound

By the late 1970s, the Military Reform movement had formed around a core group of five individuals, each with specific areas of interest and connections that allowed the group to expand into the public and the halls of government. The linchpin of the group, providing connections into government circles, was William Lind, a staffer for Senator Gary Hart (D-CO). Before joining Hart, Lind had worked for Senator Robert Taft Jr. (R-OH) and authored a white paper calling for a cut in the Army's budget to fund a fleet of large numbers of smaller aircraft carriers and diesel submarines.[1] Lind was familiar with Boyd's "Patterns of Conflict," having been among the many who heard it throughout the late 1970s.

According to Lind, Boyd was the "intellectual patriarch" of the movement. Pierre Sprey focused on hardware reform. Defense consultant Dr. Steven Canby was the group's "tactician," who focused on small-unit infantry tactics and was opposed to the concept of attrition warfare. Norman Polmar, a contributing editor for *Jane's Fighting Ships*, was the group's naval and aerospace analyst.[2] These five men formed the initial core, whose purpose was "to discover the root causes of our military failures, develop the ideas necessary for restoring military effectiveness, and turn those ideas into policy."[3] The group soon grew its sphere of influence by reaching out to journalists, members of Congress, other defense consultants, and active-duty military personnel.

One of the key individuals in popularizing the Reformers was James Fallows, the Washington editor for the *Atlantic* magazine and former speechwriter for President Jimmy Carter. Fallows, concerned about defense spending, contacted Lind in 1979 for a story about military procurement. Having studied economics at Oxford University, Fallows focused on the financial issues of weapons procurement, in line with the Reformers' emphasis on costs. Lind told Fallows that he should talk to John Boyd. Fallows met extensively with Boyd and the other Reformers. The result was "The Muscle-Bound Superpower," published on October 2, 1979, in the *Atlantic*.[4]

James Burton recalled that the publication of Fallows's article was one of the most important events in launching the Military Reform movement.[5] It was also the first full public presentation of the Reformers' views. Fallows argued that American defense was in crisis, because "the United States has become shackled to high technology that may fail when put to the ultimate test." The article presented Boyd and his group as the voice of reason within the Pentagon, an oppressed minority, preaching their message of reform to those who had not ears to listen. As Boyd put it, "The Aerospace industry is out of control. But I will tell you this: There is no smaller lobby in this nation than the lobby for real defense." By "real defense," which became the catch-phrase of the article, Boyd meant "war, waging it, and winning it."[6]

Fallows framed the issue of reform in a slightly new way. He blamed three individuals for eroding American military effectiveness. The first was former secretary of defense Robert McNamara, whose emphasis on management techniques was, to Fallows, the opposite of "real defense." This criticism built on the older idea that leaders deserve respect only if they perform certain acts—similar to how many pilots of earlier eras hesitated (or refused) to show respect for authority figures who were not fighter pilots themselves. Fallows and the Reformers turned this critique against the defense bureaucracy and industry at large. "Almost nobody is trained for combat anymore," Sprey complained. "They're businessmen. Until we change that, nothing else will count." Instead, Fallows argued that "what we need . . . is a different calculus, based not on computer printouts but on the realities of the battlefield."[7]

This stance was ironic for a follower of Boyd, whose most significant contribution to defense was EMT theory—consisting of reams of computer printouts. Boyd himself had often been accused of ignoring the human factor in favor of computer-derived theoretical data based on machine performance. For example, in 1969, Navy fighter pilots and founders of the "Top Gun" school Dan Pedersen, Milburn "Mel" Holmes, and Jerry Sawatzky recalled Boyd giving a lecture on EMT at Tyndall Air Force Base, during which Boyd claimed that no US aircraft should ever dogfight with a MiG because he had mathematically proved that the F-4 had inferior performance to MiG fighters. Exhibiting many of the same fighter pilot stereotypes that Boyd did, Pedersen recalled Holmes arguing, "No algorithm could predict much if it excluded the most important factor of all: the skill, heart, and drive of the pilot in the cockpit. The moment of truth was the Merge. It was then that you had your chance to take the measure of a man." He continued, "Energy-maneuverability theory had little to say about tactics or the people who make them work. The pilot is the key part of the equation, though as a variable it cannot be quantified." After explaining that any of the Top Gun founders (or himself) could beat Boyd in a dogfight, Pedersen rejected Boyd's approach because it "required adherence to fixed ideas, reduced airplanes to numbers, [and] considered its instructors as 'priests.'"[8] The Reformers themselves would likely reject such a characterization, but the critique of being too focused on machines instead of people is one that both the Reformers and their opponents frequently lobbed at each other.

Fallows also targeted Hyman Rickover, the Navy admiral who had directed the development of nuclear-powered vessels, which Fallows derided as "technology run wild." Fallows argued that the Defense Department pursued technology for its own sake: "What can be built, will be built, even at the cost of bad military sense." As evidence, Fallows referred to the AIMVAL-ACEVAL tests. Fallows noted that in the one-on-one matchups, the "fancier and more complex model which costs about five times as much" (the F-15) performed better, and in larger engagements the "cheap and simple plane" (the F-5) brought the exchange rate closer to equal. True to the origins of the fighter pilot myth, Fallows argued that "most of the 'kills' came from visual sighting, as they had in the dogfights in World War I." He did not mention that the reason for the reliance on visual confirmation was the strict rules of the test, taking away the F-15's chief advantage (and the main source of its price tag), the long-range radar. In addition to bashing the "complex" F-15, Fallows borrowed Sprey's other main example, the M1 Abrams tank, to argue that advanced technology was, to him, nothing more than a "Rube Goldberg illustration."[9]

Third, Fallows blamed Paul Nitze, who had a large role in shaping theories regarding potential nuclear war. Fallows called deterrence theory "the modern equivalent of medieval theology" and was of the opinion that the military pursued technology as if it were "the grail." Fallows implied that politicians like Senators Sam Nunn (D-GA) and Henry Jackson (D-WA) used nuclear capability to "blackmail" their constituents and implied that such politicians did more harm to the country than the nation's military adversaries. Fallows also argued that weapons testing required oversight. His prime example was the AIM-4 Falcon missile, which had tested well yet had performed dismally in the Vietnam War. Although weapons-testing procedures were problematic in some ways, the AIM-4 was rarely, if ever, fired under the conditions for which it was designed and successfully tested.[10]

Fallows concluded with six steps to restore "real defense," including canceling the Trident submarine, abandoning ICBMs, and instead of large military actions focus on a "modest policing force" that emphasized "quickness and adaptability." Also, in a point influenced by Lind, Fallows argued that NATO allies were not contributing enough of their budgets and must increase their defense spending.[11]

Fallows's two final points show the heaviest influence from Boyd and his associates. First, he said that the military should eliminate weapons that are too "high-cost, high-technology, high-vulnerability," and which he thought did not make "a fundamental difference" to defense. That included aircraft carriers and Navy aircraft (generally speaking), the Pershing II tactical nuclear missile, and the Aegis missile defense system, all of which he argued could be replaced by a fleet of small diesel submarines. Repeating an argument of Lind's, Fallows argued that blimps could counter the Russian submarine threat. Fallows argued that the use of air power for interdiction and strategic bombing should be abandoned. Chasing after bombing capability, he claimed, led to "expensive" aircraft "with exotic engines, radar, and wings." These planes did not "make a difference," he said. "What does make a difference is numbers of planes."[12]

His last point was that "the Army is no longer made up of, or led by, men who can fight," but that the military was stuffed with careerists and bureaucrats. For a positive example of military organization, Fallows, like Boyd and Sprey earlier, pointed to the Wehrmacht of the Nazi era. Approximately one-third of the 650 German general officers in the Second World War were killed in action. For Fallows and the Fighter Mafia, this indicated aggressiveness—officers who correctly led from the front. Fallows complained that in Vietnam only three American general officers were killed—two of them in noncombat accidents.[13] It is difficult to imagine how one could regard the death of hundreds of general officers as a measure of success, but through the lens of the fighter pilot myth, this claim made sense.

"Muscle-Bound Superpower" took the Fighter Mafia public. Their agenda became a hot topic within the defense community and expanded to multitudes of popular articles and books throughout the 1980s. The movement was shaped by the five characteristics of original fighter pilot culture. The Reformers acted aggressively and sought to increase aggressiveness in the military. Expressing individualism, they emphasized man over machine, implying that authority figures were incompetent or corrupt. They used religious and medieval imagery to portray themselves, seeing themselves as voices in the wilderness, disciples of the messianic Boyd, who had come to redeem the broken defense industry. The Reformers were protective of their members and suspicious of outsiders, nearing the point of paranoia that the establishment was out to get them. They advocated for technology only if it furthered their goals of cheap, simple weapons. The Reformers had a lot in common with the Fighter Mafia. Although they were separate entities, the former was an outgrowth, or perhaps a mutation, of the latter.

A Psychic Wound

"Muscle-Bound Superpower" arrived at a time of national anxiety and self-doubt in the wake of the fall of Saigon in 1975 and the subsequent economic turmoil. Leaders were hesitant to use military force, and many people doubted that such force could achieve victory.[14] This "malaise that has allegedly reduced the United States to a state of impotence in a menacing world," as historian George Herring put it in 1981, had a name: "Vietnam Syndrome."[15] Repeated refrains of the failure of Vietnam and the reluctance to repeat that mistake echoed through the government and news media. In November 1978, *U.S. News & World Report* ran a story headlined "America—Declining Power?" The March 1979 *Business Week* proclaimed "The Decline of U.S. Power," complete with a cover image of the Statue of Liberty weeping. The article claimed that the "shattering experience of Vietnam" had put the US in "decay" and that "there are signs of U.S. weakness everywhere." The Vietnam experience was "threatening the way of life built since World War II," and the entire economic system of the world was "now in crisis."[16]

Similar doubts from some military leaders tended to manifest themselves as a mistrust of civilians and a demand that future wars have clear, obtainable objectives. The worry of "another Vietnam" dominated almost any discussion of foreign policy in the late 1970s and 1980s.[17] For some liberals, Vietnam Syndrome was healthy—a check on military adventurism and high defense spending. Conservatives, particularly the Reagan administration, tended to see Vietnam Syndrome as a disease to be cured by increased militarism.[18] In any case, much of the public was skeptical that the military could be victorious and was reluctant to find out. As late as December 1990, in the build-up to the Gulf War, *Newsweek* noted, "Vietnam hangs in the collective subconscious like a bad dream, a psychic wound that leaves the patient forever neurotic."[19]

That wound reopened with the disaster of Operation Eagle Claw. On April 24, 1980, in an attempt to end the Iranian hostage crisis, eight RH-53D Sea Stallion helicopters flew to a staging base from which they were to launch a raid on Tehran to rescue trapped Americans. Problems began in conception, as planners chose helicopters whose operational capabilities were not suited for the mission. The pilots had no idea that dust storm conditions existed, because weather information was classified, although they were not trained for those conditions anyway. Three of the eight aircraft abandoned the mission early, two from mechanical failures, another because of a dust storm. The commanders of the force decided to abort the mission, and Carter confirmed within twenty minutes. When the US forces began their return from the staging base, one of the helicopters crashed into a transport plane. Eight Americans were killed. As if that were not enough, some of the helicopters were not cleansed of sensitive information, and the Iranian revolutionary government captured classified intelligence material, including the names of several Iranian agents working for the US government.[20] Carter accepted full responsibility for the failure.

This event seemed to confirm the worst fears associated with Vietnam Syndrome. The incident later prompted change and improvement, although some of the Reformers—particularly Spinney—saw the tragedy as evidence of their arguments. As news of the operation broke on television, Spinney's wife happened to go into labor with their child. Allegedly, as she shouted at Spinney to take her to the hospital, he instead watched news reports with a calculator, reviewing data from helicopter reliability studies. He concluded that the military should have sent fourteen helicopters instead of eight— an assessment with which some analysts agreed after the fact, although the number of craft was far from the only problem with the operation.[21]

The malaise continued to grow. One month later, on May 29, 1980, in a meeting of the House Armed Services Committee's Investigations Subcommittee, Army Chief of Staff General Edward C. Meyer testified, "We have a hollow army." It was in answer to a direct question about the number of tanks in a specific armored division at Fort Hood, Texas, but the *Washington Post* overplayed Meyer's comment, giving the impression that the US military was too small and ill-equipped to counter the Soviet threat. A close reading of Meyer's testimony refuted this, demonstrating that enlistment numbers were actually higher than in previous years, and infantry requirements had been met. Nevertheless, the term caught on, and "hollow army" or "hollow force" became catchphrases in the early 1980s to describe low preparedness and a way to attack the Carter administration as soft on defense.[22]

On the same day as Meyer's testimony, Representative Victor Fazio (D-CA) brought the ideas of the Fighter Mafia to the House floor. Current US aircraft were inadequate for a potential conflict, he claimed, because they were too "sophisticated" and difficult to maintain. Fazio cited an article from the *Chicago Sun-Times* criticizing the F-14, F-15, and F-111 as being too complex and lacking in readiness because of a shortage of parts. The article quoted Representative Jack Edwards (R-AL), who claimed that "at some fighter bases, maintenance personnel have actually used their own money to purchase parts at local electronic supply outlets such as Radio Shack."[23] This revelation had come from Edwards's staffer Charlie Murphy, who visited several Air Force bases in 1979 and saw the degree to which some aircraft were being cannibalized for parts to keep others flyable. Some mechanics reported buying parts from Radio Shack.[24]

This swirl of fear about US military capabilities was the context in which Fallows's article debuted. In these churning waters, the reform movement could occupy a unique place that could reach both sides of the political and ideological aisle: They were hawks, but they appealed to those who questioned the military and wanted to reduce the defense budget. They could argue that the armed forces were in crisis or even incapable of victory—but not because America was weak or needed to avoid conflict. To the contrary, the Reformers said the problem was internal. American defense technology was too expensive and too complex. But with the right weapons (cheaper, simpler ones), America could and, by implication, should be an active military force around the world.

The Reformers' efforts soon drew allies from within the military and in Congress. "Muscle-Bound Superpower" had named many of these allies, such as Senators Sam Nunn and Gary Hart, and also Lind, who had first coined the term "the Reformers" and was still a staffer for Hart at the time. In their desire to be set apart from the defense establishment, the Reformers inculcated a reputation for being not just confrontational, but "zany" with a pinch of "kookiness." Lind took this to extremes, such as displaying a portrait of fascist dictator Benito Mussolini in his office. Despite this, Fallows became a convert to the Reformers' new gospel, and he admitted that he had "[come] to respect and value them more than anyone else I met."[25] These men formed the core of a group that was about to explode.

Drinking from a Fire Hose

In the summer of 1980, Boyd, Spinney, and Christie met with Nunn and soon gave more briefings to other senators and staffers. The "Defense Facts of Life" made its way into the press. Boyd was giving his "Patterns of Conflict" briefing to military schools, generals of all services, members of Congress, and reporters—sometimes repeatedly to the same people—several times a week. By mid-1981, Boyd had repeated private meetings with Representative Newt Gingrich (R-GA), Representative Dick Cheney (R-WY), Patrick Oster of the *Chicago-Sun Times*, Marshall Hoyler at the Congressional Budget Office, Winslow Wheeler, a staffer for Senator Nancy Kassebaum (R-KS), and many others. From 1980 to 1981, Spinney's work was cited in press outlets including *Forbes*, *Newsweek*, *U.S. News & World Report*, the *New York*

Times, the *Washington Post,* and the *Boston Globe,* and his ideas were featured in prime-time television news segments on ABC and CBS. Hart authored two articles—with heavy influence from Lind—that also garnered much steam for the movement: "The Case for Military Reform" in January 1981 for the *Wall Street Journal,* followed the next month by "What's Wrong with the Military" for the *New York Times.* In April, Gingrich contributed "Think Now, Buy Later," for the *Washington Post.*[26]

The Reformers gained support from several military leaders. Major General Jack N. Merritt from the Army War College said that Boyd "really is one of the most innovative and original guys I've ever had anything to do with." Marine commandant General Robert H. Barrow and Marine Lieutenant General P. X. Kelley were also Boyd's acolytes by this point. Hart used Boyd's ideas as a standard against which to measure other defense plans, and the Navy was so taken with Boyd's concepts that the *Proceedings of the U.S. Naval Institute* published studies applying Boyd's concepts to naval warfare. Making the connection to the first generation of fighter pilots even more explicit, Sprey was quoted in the *Washington Post* as saying that Boyd's work was "the best work of its kind since that done by Germany's famous 'Red Baron' of World War I, Manfred von Richthofen."[27] Extensive media coverage throughout 1981 tended to feature the same arguments about the necessity of rapid movement, the folly of complex technology, the need for simplicity, the problem of over-bureaucratization, and the notion that US defense was in crisis. Some of these articles exaggerated Boyd's record. For example, in a widely syndicated piece for the *Atlanta Constitution,* Boyd was referred to as an "ace," although he had zero aerial victory credits.[28]

In May 1981, Fallows followed up with two publications that expanded the footprint of the reform movement. The first was another article for the *Atlantic,* "America's High-Tech Weaponry."[29] The second was much more important—his first book, *National Defense.* The work was a distillation of the Reformers' ideas. One of its core arguments was that "more money for defense, without a change in the underlying patterns of spending, will not make us more secure, and may even leave the United States in a more vulnerable position than before."[30] This point was nearly a quotation from Spinney's "Defense Facts of Life."

National Defense was influenced by Sprey's briefing also, particularly his pairings of weapons systems. Fallows focused on Sprey's two prominent examples: the M-16 rifle and the F-16 Falcon, arguing that both had been ruined by bureaucracy. He also argued that the F-15 was not worth the cost, pointing to the AIMVAL/ACEVAL tests as evidence that the expensive radar avionics equipment that raised the cost and size of the F-15 was ineffective. His argument assumed that visual identification of enemy air-craft would always be a requirement and that the enemy could detect radar signals pointed at it, which would give away the F-15's position, costing it the element of surprise. These assumptions—influenced by Sprey's and other Reformers' thinking—were based on the conditions of the Vietnam War, and they would not necessarily hold true in future conflicts. Fallows implied that the F-15's improvements over the F-5 did not justify its cost. Based on data provided by Riccioni, Fallows said that the cost of 250 F-15s was equal to the cost of 1,000 F-5s, and in the time that 250 F-15s could be flown, the F-5s could run twenty-five hundred sorties. He concluded by repeating Spinney's main argument, that complexity in and of itself is a "form of organizational cancer."[31]

National Defense concluded with four recommendations that were directly in line with the Fighter Mafia's ideals. First, the US needed to "restore the military spirit" of the armed forces, echoing the Fighter Mafia's emphasis on aggressiveness and combat spirit. He also shared their frustration with leaders who, they thought, had not earned their place through combat. Fal-lows pointed again to the German General Staff of World War II, arguing that officers must first serve as enlisted men before rising through the ranks. This was meant to "avoid the worst warping effects of the academies," for which the Fighter Mafia often expressed contempt. Second, Fallows repeated the mantra of "stop[ping] the progression toward ever more costly and complex weapons." Nuclear submarines and F-15s should be canceled and replaced with diesel subs and F-16s or F-5s. Third, Fallows repeated his call to abandon the "theology of nuclear weapons." His final point was that debate about defense questions tended to lack nuance, often devolving into simplistic debates over funding totals, rather than how those dollars were spent.[32] There is merit in this argument, although critics argued that it was the Reformers who lacked nuance.

The book was a hit, but its main contribution was to make the Reformers' ideas accessible to the public. Winslow Wheeler, himself a friend of Boyd's and an active member of the movement, noted that the Reformers' presenta-tions were not only a "fire hose" of information, but took an insulting tone toward their audience. Fallows made the movement comprehensible, even attractive to the public.[33]

Although popular, *National Defense* generated resistance from the defense establishment. Lieutenant Colonel Walter Kross, a senior fellow at the National Defense University in Washington and a former fighter pilot himself with one hundred combat missions in the Vietnam War, said that *"National Defense* is part of a plan to reorder the U.S. military fundamentally . . . part of the efforts of a small group of well-placed civilian analysts who want to recast the United States military in their preferred mold."[34] Kross's review of Fallows's book was a rebuke of the whole movement. His main charge was that the Reformers were a small, parochial group whose use of evidence was problematic. "The Reformers mostly quote and footnote themselves, the same one dozen experts" who "see what they want to see in history." Kross said the Reformers "venerate General Heinz Guderian because he put a radio and a radio operator in each German tank in 1940. Yet they oppose modern equivalents of this important action. Had they been on the German General Staff in 1935, they might have accused Guderian of being fixated on overcentralization and high technology."[35]

Attacking the movement's emphasis on air-to-air combat, Kross said the Reformers "would have the public believe that the visual air battle is the decisive activity," even though "historically, 90 percent of all aircraft are lost to ground fire." He reminded readers that the new weapons the reformers opposed were a modest fraction of the inventory—F-15s and F-111s combined totaled only 19 percent of the fighter force. There was no binary choice between only new or old fighters; the reality was a blended Air Force in which complex new aircraft complemented the older types that the Reformers preferred. Kross did agree with the Reformers in some respects, particularly in their charge that an increase in bureaucracy had created apathy in the officer corps. Kross supported reform, but preferred an evolutionary, balanced adjustment rather than the revolution that the Reformers wanted.[36] His review revealed that even critics of the movement were open to some of the Reformers' ideas, although the Reformers themselves felt persecuted.

The Reformers had often claimed that they were a guerrilla movement within the Department of Defense, and the establishment certainly felt the same way as the fight between the groups grew ever fiercer. General Wilbur Creech, commander of TAC, worried that the increasing coverage of the reform movement threatened many programs he considered vital to the Air Force mission, such as night attack capability on aircraft, which the Reformers opposed. "We're winning more of these battles than we are losing," he said, "but it is absolutely open guerilla warfare. Day by day. I mean we just fight, fight, fight, fight, fight. Tooth and claw."[37]

Creech attempted to address the Reformers' criticisms head-on. After Fallows's first article, the Air Force tried to change his mind. Prompted by Fallows's comment that "if the [F-15] was so phenomenal, it would certainly be interesting to ride," Creech invited the journalist to Langley Air Force Base to do exactly that, escorted by Major Richard Anderegg. The Langley DCS for operations, Major General John L. Piotrowski, insisted that Fallows wear the same white scarf with the hat-in-the-ring logo worn by all the pilots of the unit—the 94th Aero Squadron, which had been Eddie Rickenbacker's unit, with more aerial victories than any other US squadron in World War I. Fallows participated in a mock air-to-air combat exercise with two F-15s (call sign SPAD-1 and SPAD-2 after the World War I fighters of the same name) against two F-4 Phantoms playing the role of the Soviets. Once the maneuvering began, Fallows spent most of the flight alternating between taking gulps of oxygen from his flight mask, then ripping it off so he could vomit into the many plastic bags Anderegg had given him.[38]

Despite the firsthand experience of the effectiveness of the F-15's long-range radar and maneuverability in a variety of scenarios, Fallows remained unconvinced. He argued that the Air Force was relying on too many assumptions about Soviet forces, or that a Soviet invasion in Europe was not a likely threat (although he offered no alternatives of a more realistic threat assessment). Fallows was also skeptical that the new technology would continue to work, and repeated that he still thought the plane was too expensive, implying that the Air Force's assumptions about technology and future conflicts were flawed.[39]

Caucus

Senator Gary Hart's January 1981 article "The Case for Military Reform" spurred the interest of Representative William Whitehurst (R-VA). The two agreed to start a caucus. The first meeting, on May 12, 1981, included Hart, Whitehurst, Gingrich, and Senator Paul Trible (R-VA). Within a week, they were joined by Senators Nunn, William Cohen (R-ME), and John Warner (R-VA). This new Military Reform Caucus (MRC) was one of several ad hoc caucuses forming at that time, with no official office or staff. The group was the product of the specific historical moment, the sense of crisis and malaise that hung over every discussion of US defense in the late 1970s and early 1980s. As Reformer Jeffrey Record put it, the MRC was formed out of a "profound dismay over the 30 years of U.S. military defeats and miscarriages, stretching from the rout of MacArthur's forces along the Yalu in 1950 through Vietnam to the bungled attempt to rescue American hostages in Iran in 1980."[40]

The MRC was also motivated by its members' frustrations with the congressional committee system. The group wanted to use "nontraditional methods," rejecting the typical norms of congressional procedure. The group was also not meant to be a disciplined voting bloc but functioned primarily as a discussion forum for defense issues. Lind was at the center of those discussions. Lind sometimes led talks himself and also invited guest speakers such as Sprey or other Reformers to address the group. Lind also served as a linchpin, inviting other members of Congress and serving as a conduit for the movement to spread throughout both houses.[41]

One of the main mechanisms for growing the caucus was a briefing and slide show titled "Reforming the Military: Military Reform—a Winning Military at an Affordable Price," written by Boyd, Sprey, and Lind. Caucus members gave the brief to other members of Congress, defense groups, and constituents in and out of Washington. The briefing was based on the Reformers' earlier writings, especially Spinney's work, set firmly in the context of the failures of Vietnam and Operation Eagle Claw.[42] The presentation's message was clear: US defense was in crisis, but the Reformers—and their caucus—had the answers. It was an attractive notion, particularly in that historical moment.

The caucus's goals were to first focus on people—increasing morale and group cohesion—then on doctrine, tactics, and strategy, and finally on hardware. There was disagreement on this prioritization scheme. Some Reformers, like Record, thought doctrine was the most important piece, and others dismissed it as too academic. Many seemed fixated on particular weapons systems.[43]

The MRC went on the offensive, presenting a series of demands to the newly incoming secretary of defense, Caspar Weinberger. Claiming that costs were too high for what Whitehurst referred to as "space-age contraptions," the caucus asked for many of the changes the Reformers had been preaching, including the cancellation of nuclear submarines in favor of smaller diesel ones, the development of another small and cheap fighter aircraft, as well as the creation of a new think tank and oversight committee to reconsider American military strategy and evaluate President Reagan's defense spending plans. Whitehurst echoed the Reformers' mantra: complex weapons reduced combat readiness, and thus the nation needed to revert to simpler weapons.[44] In December 1981 the MRC released a briefing with a grim message: "We are worried that our military can no longer win. Second, we have doubts as to whether the American people will continue to support high and increasing budgets for a non-winning military."[45]

The list of programs the MRC wanted canceled continued to grow. Next on the chopping block was the Navy's F/A-18 fighter plane—which originated from the YF-17 that had competed against the YF-16. Just as the Air Force had modified Boyd's pet project, the Navy had added weight and extra capabilities to the F/A-18. The MRC argued that the aircraft's costs had risen too far and that the program should be canceled—the money instead used to purchase a larger number of older A-7 Corsair IIs. Sprey called *New York Times* reporter Nicholas Wade, planting an editorial to that effect titled "When Weapons Flunk." In January 1982 the MRC deemed the Bradley Infantry Fighting Vehicle too expensive and complex. Instead, they thought the Army should continue to rely on the main armored personnel carrier used during the Vietnam War, the M113.[46]

The MRC grew at a rapid rate, partly owing to press coverage, as well as the evangelism of its members. By May 1982 it had grown to fifty-five—a bipartisan group of thirteen senators and forty-two representatives. The group's boldness also increased. They demanded an audit of all service academies and war colleges to determine "the extent to which, if at all, military history is taught." By this they meant Boyd's interpretation of history, which they wanted written into field manuals and training programs. The MRC ordered the deadline of January 1, 1983, to rewrite those materials to incorporate Boyd's brand of maneuver warfare.[47]

Policy makers within the military did begin adopting some of the Reformers' ideas. In the fall of 1981, Brigadier General Donald Morelli of the Army Training and Doctrine Command told reporters that Army doctrine was shifting toward Boyd's ideas "of lightly armored, highly agile units capable of pursuing the tactics of speed and deception." In April 1982, the Air National Guard published a study called *Vista 1999*. Contemporary evaluations of the plan summarized, "Many of their recommendations are resounding echoes of Boyd."[48] The study, led by Major General Francis R. Gerard, argued for large numbers of simple, austere weapons and called for "a small, simple, lethal fighter for $3 million a plane," which was much lower than the F-16 Fighting Falcon itself, which cost $13 million each at the time. Although they liked elements of the F-16, the Reformers insisted "that even cheaper, more austere planes should be built."[49]

The Heritage Foundation became aligned with the reform movement through its connections with Lind. The foundation's basement became a regular meeting place for the Reformers, although Boyd was wary of the group's connections to the military-industrial complex.[50] In 1981, the foundation released a collection of essays written by Reformers, including an article on the Marines by William Lind, and one on tactical air power by Pierre Sprey.[51]

The "In" Thing to Do on Capitol Hill

By the summer of 1982, the Reformers had settled on seven major weapons systems as targets, fighting for their reduction, delay, or outright cancellation.

These included the Trident nuclear submarine, Nimitz class carriers, the F/A-18 Hornet, the Apache attack helicopter, the M1 Abrams main battle tank, the Bradley Infantry Fighting Vehicle, and the F-15 Eagle, the aircraft that arguably started the movement. Their arguments against all of these systems amounted to the idea that complexity made them inherently unreliable.[52] Sprey went further when discussing his vision for a lightweight fighter aircraft. In 1982 he argued that the austere F-16 was too bloated and that what the Air Force really needed to succeed at air-to-air combat was a plane one-third the size: "7,000 pounds or less wrapped around a 30 millimeter cannon" and costing no more than $3 million each. The list of programs that some Reformers wanted to cancel grew further. They targeted the B-1 bomber and C-5 Galaxy, arguing that cutting those programs would save almost $200 billion over five years.[53]

Some thought that killing individual programs was not enough—systemic issues required a revolution. They argued that canceling individual programs was just a way to "shoot the cripples," when a better solution would be to change procurement policy from the ground up.[54] Some Reformers, including Boyd, argued that the pursuit of technology for its own sake was part of American culture and heritage, and thus resisting it took active effort. Reporter Bob Adams summarized what he called "the general American fascination with technology." He claimed, "This is a nation of tinkerers. Can any nation that invented everything from the electric lightbulb to the airplane, and put a man on the moon, be incapable of inventing a tank that will outdrive, outshoot, and outfight any other?" The Reformers alleged that few decision makers within the government or military leadership were willing or able to stop these trends, because of rampant careerism. Their views stemmed from fighter pilots' traditional distrust of leadership figures who had not proven themselves in air combat. "There's just a mindset at the Pentagon. They can't stop themselves," asserted Senator Thomas F. Eagleton (D-MO). "It's almost indigenous to the process that you don't buy something that's functional and simple. It has to be supersophisticated—almost ahead of the state of the art."[55]

The reform movement was a big tent and purposefully tried to avoid policy proposals that could become too partisan or ideologically divisive. Earning the nickname "cheap hawks," the movement employed a rhetoric attractive to those on both sides of the ideological aisle. Conservative hawks could continue to claim they were being strong on defense, while showing their more liberal members that they were trying to reduce military spending. Similarly, liberal members of Congress could play both sides of the argument, portraying themselves as holding the military-industrial complex to account while appeasing their hawkish constituents. Essentially, the MRC provided political cover all around, and the popularity of the movement with the public led to a sense that many politicians, as Jeffrey Record noted, "appear to have joined because it seemed to be an 'in' thing to do on Capitol Hill." Nonetheless, the MRC had the appearance of a bipartisan, ideologically diverse group that included people as politically disparate as Gingrich and liberal representative-turned-senator Al Gore (D-TN). This diversity only went so far. Record argued that the MRC has a "markedly conservative bent" and that although some liberals participated, the more prominent liberal leaders in Congress at that time—such as Senators Ted Kennedy (D-MA) and Mark Hatfield (R-OR)—were not among them.[56]

Ideological tension sometimes surfaced. In July 1983, Edwin Feulner, the first president of the Heritage Foundation, attacked liberals in the MRC, accusing them of jumping on the bandwagon of the Reformers just so they could make cuts in defense spending. "What started as an in-earnest effort to strengthen U.S. defenses—get 'more bang for the buck'—is being used by congressional disarmers to indiscriminately chop into the defense budget." He particularly targeted Hart, dismissing him as "one of those who continues to parade around in the dress blues of military reform, as if wearing some holy man's garb."[57] By December 1983 reporters noted, "The caucus has taken on a more conservative look lately." Representative Jim Courter (R-NJ) rose to a leadership role, and more conservatives, such as Senators Charles Grassley (R-IA), Jeremiah Denton (R-AL), William Roth (R-DE), and Nancy Kassebaum (R-KS), joined the movement, although not all the conservatives saw eye to eye.[58]

By the mid-1980s the group had gained significant traction. By 1985, several prominent historians, professors, and researchers furthered the Reformer agenda, including Edward Luttwak, Russell Weigley, Richard Gabriel, Thomas E. Etzold, and Paul Savage. Gingrich became a particularly avid spokesman for the group. He was the keynote speaker at a West Point conference in June 1982, the audience of which included Army Chief of Staff General Edward Meyer. Gingrich toured military bases and lectured soldiers on the tenets of the movement and continually expressed his opinion (and that of the Reformers) that the American military was in the midst of its largest crisis. "I am absolutely convinced," he said, "that we would lose a war on the Eurasian mainland to the Russians either today or under any plans I have seen so far in this administration," he said. "We have a fundamental crisis in grand strategy."[59]

The Reformers did have some concrete successes. In May 1981, Congress passed the Nunn-McCurdy Act, which set certain budget thresholds for weapons procurement. The Department of Defense was required to report to Congress if a program's costs increased by more than 15 percent of its present estimate, or more than 25 percent of its original estimate.[60] In 1983, the MRC had what was most likely its biggest success, an amendment to the 1984 Department of Defense Authorization Act that established a civilian director of operational test and evaluation. This amendment, written by Senator David Pryor (D-AR) with help from journalist and activist Dina Rasor, Sprey, and other Reformers, created specific guidelines for equipment testing that were meant to more adequately reflect combat conditions, and established congressional oversight for those processes. The amendment took significant effort from the MRC and its allies coordinating with press outlets to put pressure on members of Congress.[61]

"Mr. Sprey's Snake Oil"

Any attempt to make significant change to a large system is sure to encounter resistance, and the Reformers were no exception. Some policy makers found the Reformers' ideas less than ideal, even dangerous. Lieutenant General John T. Chain Jr., the Air Force deputy chief of staff for plans and operations, nicknamed them "fuzzy heads," and he claimed that they were "doing a disservice to the country" by pushing for "plain vanilla airplanes."[62] Secretary of Defense Weinberger argued, "The Soviets have very large numbers of very complex, very sophisticated, very survivable weapons." He continued, "And we have to equip our people so that they can compete on equal terms. What we feel we need is not gadgetry, or complexity, or technology, for its own sake. It's simply to keep our weapons at least equal to, and preferably superior to, the Soviets' weapons." Other Air Force leaders noted that many new Soviet weapons featured the very technologies that the Reformers argued against, such as long-range radar and all-weather capacity. Senator John G. Tower (R-TX) went even further, castigating the Reformers: "Are you going to trade blood for money, and put your guys in an M-60 tank that won't stay on the battlefield with a Russian T-72 or T-80? . . . The Russians have 50,000 tanks. What are you going to do—buy 100,000 (cheaper) tanks and put them out there knowing that only some will survive?"[63]

Kross, frequently interviewed as an expert who could counter the Reformers' claims, said that regarding readiness, the Reformers were cherry-picking their data. "We were forced to ask which would be better by 1984: combat-ready wings of F-4s or a new generation of fighters like the F-15," he said. "We decided to go for the planes first and the spare parts later. Spinney measured readiness at its nadir." Meaning, the Air Force could not buy new planes and spare parts at the same time. He also noted that a poorly coded computer program had been the culprit behind the seemingly ridiculous high cost of some spare parts. The lack of spare parts and the trips to Radio Shack that the Reformers cited were not due to bad bureaucracy but were one part miscalculation and one part budget management choice. The defense industry was grateful that the Reformers pointed out the problem but was, in Kross's view, capable of self-regulation.[64]

Kross thought the press had been too kind to the Reformers and not given enough attention to the rebuttals against them. To address that imbalance, he wrote a book about the reform debate, released in 1985. He acknowledged that many of the Reformers' points were helpful, such as the promotion of more rigor in testing and evaluation, but overall he rejected the movement. "The Reformers have created a great deal of misinformation regarding the fighting concepts and weapons that they oppose," Kross said. "But the critical follow-through has always been missing—because their constructs are far too selective and simply cannot withstand second-order scrutiny and evaluation. . . . The Reformers' constructs represent only a partial, easily circumvented set of remedies."[65]

Christie referred to Kross as a "spymaster" who had been placed there as part of a "conspiracy" to undermine the movement. Christie saw it as a badge of honor that the military establishment was taking so much effort to stop the Reformers, recalling that "Kross gave [the Reformers] more credit than they gave themselves."[66]

Kross's tone was measured, but other critics were not. Defense journalist and former Marine Fred Reed argued that many of the critiques of the complex weapons the Reformers decried were simply not true but were caricatures brought about by ignorance. The M1 Abrams tank, for example, was savaged by Rasor as having a seat that could not fit an average-size soldier, but she failed to notice the seat was adjustable. Sprey similarly had argued that an electronics failure would render the tank incapable of firing—yet neglected the manual backup systems that had been designed for just that case. Reed accused the Reformers of having "first, a robust disregard for truth. Second, a taste for parody." He was shocked at their "lack of adherence even to high-school standards of research." He found that their "relentlessly sloppy research and cultivated ignorance" undercut any of their useful ideas, of which they had several, even if they were "intellectually not much beyond childhood." Ultimately, Reed's scathing critique concluded that "the Reformers are zealots of the classic variety, with the usual self-righteousness and the usual hermetically-sealed minds. Having . . . partitioned the world into Themselves and The Enemy, they are perfectly unconscious of the rolling non sequiturs and athletic leaps of logic that constitute their conversation. If the cause is good, the details aren't important."[67]

The F-15 remained a symbolic rallying point for both the Reformers, who criticized it or sought to cancel it, and the Air Force establishment, who sought to protect it. In response to the charge that the F-15 was too complex, Major General Albert G. Rogers, the deputy chief of staff for logistics at TAC, argued, "Imagine the logistical problems when the longbow replaced the spear." He explained, "What happened when the bow got wet? Or when it dried out again? And you lost your arrows a lot? And you had little guys who couldn't pull the bow? But the longbow played hell with the spear-throwers. It killed them before they got close enough to throw their spears."[68]

The ACEVAL tests continued to be a source of contention. The Air Force's spokesman for the F-15 program, Lieutenant Colonel Robert Nicholson, emphasized that the design of those tests eliminated the advantages of the F-15 and that the knights of the air conception was outdated: "The F-15 has the ability to fly out of a dogfight," he said. "You want to avoid a dogfight in the World War I sense, where planes are thick as flies. We train our people to shoot down the enemy before they even know we're around." General Rogers of TAC similarly dismissed the Reformers' idea of using quantity to trump quality, insisting "we're not in a numbers game."[69] Admitting that missiles were not yet the perfect solution, Air Force planners pointed to the then-in-development AMRAAM (advanced medium-range air-to-air missile) as the solution to missile problems.

The Reformers' conceptions of "complex" and "expensive" were also relative to the time. Senator Eagleton inadvertently revealed this by holding up the F-4 Phantom as a model of a simple aircraft that was reasonable in cost.[70] The irony was that when the F-4 was new in the late 1950s, many critics argued that it was complex, expensive, and too advanced for its own good.[71] Yet by the early 1980s, the aging Phantom appeared relatively stable, simple, and affordable by comparison to the newer F-15. Most new weapons platforms, like most new technologies in other contexts, can seem complex and expensive at the moment of their creation; yet continued advancement can make the once complex and expensive seem simple and cheap by comparison.

The assistant secretary of the Air Force for manpower, reserve affairs, and installations, Tidal W. McCoy, disagreed with the Reformers but sought a middle ground. He argued that the choice between complexity and affordability was a false one. High-tech weapons could in fact be cheaper and easier to maintain. His main evidence was the F-16's ground-attack capability—the element of the F-16 that Boyd objected to the most. McCoy argued that the damage done in the Schweinfurt raids of World War II—which required 291 heavy bomber aircraft and 2,910 crew members—could be done with only six F-16s. Yet the F-16 cost only 1.6 times the cost of a B-17. He then turned the Reformers' often-used analogy of France in 1940 against them: "The defense of this nation cannot rest on yesterday's fortifications," he said. "We cannot fall behind a 'Maginot Line' of less sophisticated equipment and expect to win a conflict against a force that is both technologically and numerically superior. The national defense effort must continue to be based on sophisticated technological advantages that make our weapons highly capable—and simpler to operate and maintain."[72]

The Reformers fought back against these critiques, especially sensitive to charges that they were antitechnology. "People say, 'That crazy bunch—they want to use Piper Cubs instead of F-15s,'" Nunn said. "That's a strawman argument. We need high technology. But we don't need to put every new gadget on every new weapon system." Others focused on testing procedures and the connections between industry and the Pentagon as the real problem, rather than any one specific hardware platform. The Reformers also accused the Pentagon of inflating the Soviet threat. Representative Les Aspin (D-WI), a former Pentagon employee and later secretary of defense, alleged that the Pentagon estimated Soviet military spending by stating an amount that the US would have to spend to match. Thus inflation in the United States could make it seem that the Soviets had increased spending when in actuality they had not.[73]

The media tended to favor the Reformers. Many reporters may have been attracted to the movement because it reflected the sense of military crisis, malaise, and apprehension of those years, or because of the "David vs. Goliath" story it seemed to embody, in which the Reformers stood for the brave underdogs fighting against a monolithic machine. On a surface level, the Reformers' arguments seemed to have merit, although many reporters struggled to understand or communicate the intricacies of the technology debates. The Reformers pointed out that defense spending was increasing, but the Air Force had fewer planes than before. They argued that the newer weapons the Pentagon was buying had not been tested in combat.[74] Yet, numbers of aircraft are not necessarily a solid measure of effectiveness, and of course new technologies had not been tested in combat—since the United States had not fought in a major conventional conflict since 1972. But this did not mean that the United States should restrict itself to equipment used in previous wars.

The Reformers got a significant public boost in January 1983, when Spinney completed a new briefing, "The Plans/Reality Mismatch." This document was an expansion of ideas from his previous work, arguing that the entire procurement and budget process was flawed and overoptimistic—and that this was a structural problem within the Defense Department. He recommended that many expensive programs be canceled and the savings put toward production of simpler weapons. Despite the efforts of David Chu, head of PA&E, to stop Spinney, Nunn worked to make an unclassified version of the briefing public. On March 7, 1983, after Boyd had connected Spinney with reporters from *Time*, the magazine featured Spinney as the cover story with the headline, "Are Billions Being Wasted?" The story repeated many of the Reformers' assertions about runaway defense spending on weapons and systems that were ineffective. The piece introduced all of the Reformers as iconoclastic rebels and presented Spinney as a "maverick" and an "unlikely hero."[75]

Not everyone accepted the *Time* story. In a statement in the Senate on March 3, 1983, Barry Goldwater (R-AZ and former Air Force pilot and Air Force Reserve major general) thrashed the story, saying that "little or no effort was made to verify any of the factual assertions made by the authors," that the story made "unsubstantiated assertions," that its implications were "misleading or perhaps downright dishonest," and that ultimately the piece was "shoddy journalism." He claimed that this was because the magazine had been "seduced" by the Reformers, as a result parroting nothing more than "hype" and "sensationalism" that did not stand up to scrutiny.[76]

The Reformers sought press coverage as much as they could. They kept lists of journalists who reported on military matters. Representative Jim Courter (R-NJ), who cochaired the MRC in 1984, wrote several pieces advocating for the reform movement in major media outlets such as the *Wall Street Journal*, the *New York Times*, and the *Christian Science Monitor*, in addition to making regular television appearances on programs such as the *Today Show* and the *MacNeil/Lehrer News Hour*. In addition, the MRC often pressed for the release of documents proving their case, portraying themselves as promoting transparency, while they often already knew the contents of documents, as they were usually written by other Reformers. For example, in 1984, Courter called for the release of a report about mistakes made in the Grenada invasion that proved the Reformers' views correct—a document that happened to have been written by William Lind. However, some Reformers saw Courter as a wolf in sheep's clothing. Wheeler noted that Courter and Tower had actively gutted Senator Pryor's operational testing amendment, accusing them of taking orders from the Pentagon.[77]

The invasion of Grenada and the bombing of a Marine Corps barracks in Beirut in 1983 prompted further discussion of US military effectiveness.

Record, writing in 1984, agreed with other Reformers that technocratic values had replaced "traditional warrior values" since World War II. Record implied that the management and technocratic impulses he criticized were borderline treasonous and deserving of court-martial. Nonetheless, he added that "some of [the Reformers'] proposed reforms would probably create more problems than they solve." He concluded that "if the reformers do not have invariably correct answers, they are nonetheless asking the right questions."[78]

Arguments between the Reformers and their critics sometimes got heated. In 1982, Sprey was invited to speak at the Wilson Institute's annual proceedings at the Smithsonian Castle in Washington, followed by a rebuttal by General Alton Slay—himself a fighter pilot who began flying fighters at the end of World War II and had flown 181 combat missions in the Vietnam War. The general did not mince words: "I haven't heard a slicker pitch since a carnival barker talked me into a ticket to see the two headed lady when I was 12 years old," said Slay, concluding that Sprey's ideas were "absolutely dead wrong in general and in detail." Slay admitted that he understood the fascination with World War I fighters and the desire to chase those performance characteristics. He loved them too: "Spad, Camel, P-12, anything that I could do a roll or a loop in and that had a gun I could fire. What fun!" He added, "But I would hope that someone would commit me to an institution for the criminally insane if I should ever suggest that it could be used in modern air warfare."[79]

Slay then attacked, saying that Sprey was "so much of a history buff that he's completely rewritten the history of fighter aviation from WWII to the present," and asked, "Where does he get data to back up his ridiculous claim? Pulled out of his left ear or other body orifice?" Going point for point, Slay argued that Sprey's statistics on missile accuracy and mission capability rates were all blatantly false. Slay pointed to historical examples such as Richard Bong, the highest-scoring American ace fighter pilot of all time, who got every single one of his forty kills in the P-38 Lightning, the plane Sprey derided for being too complex and ineffective in air-to-air combat. Slay quoted one of Sprey's favorite inspirations, Hans Rudel, to argue that removing all-weather and nighttime radar from airplanes would lead to disasters for US forces like the initial German successes in the Battle of the Bulge. Slay quoted revered German fighter ace Adolf Galland, who said he would rather have one Me-262 jet fighter—expensive and complex by any measure—than five cheaper, simpler Me-109s. Slay's hardest-hitting argument was a moral one:

> Sprey would have you believe that we would be infinitely better off to send hordes of simple inexpensive day fighters against the threat. Does he apply his "simple" criterion to pilots as well? . . . It appears that he wants

us to recruit "simple" pilots to man all these "simple" airplanes. The Japanese did that in the closing days of WWII—they were called Kamikazes. Does he think his simple fighter without sophisticated sensors or sophisticated ECM [electronic countermeasures] and navigation gear could even get to a well defended target without getting shot down? Would he want to send his son out in one of his simple, unsophisticated machines to find and attack a target at night in the midst of the awesome threat arrays we see around the world today? Would he want to go himself?

Slay closed by urging the audience of senators and representatives to not swallow "Mr. Sprey's snake oil" and to refuse to listen to men "who have never been in the cockpit of a fighter or to Korean War vintage pilots [like Boyd] who have never flown modern aircraft and who still think in the red scarf terms of that era."[80]

Losing the Spark

At its height, the MRC had over 150 members, although in the eyes of the core group, most of these were not serious. Wheeler recalled that "its truly active members were never more than 10." By 1985, the MRC was cochaired by Senator Pryor, Representative Dennis Smith (R-OR), and Representative Mel Levine (D-CA). A membership list, most likely from Kassebaum's office, noted that "some members actually opposed Reform Caucus actions[;] most were passive." The passive members included Gore, Representatives John Kasich (R-OH), Harry Reid (R-NV), and many others. Only twelve members were marked as "active," and four members (including Nunn) were marked as being opposed to the group's goals. The list singled out Cheney for his frequent meetings with Boyd; indeed, Sprey remembered him as "one of [the] most serious" members.[81]

Although Gary Hart had been criticized by the more conservative faction of the movement, he still made the reform cause part of his bid to obtain a presidential nomination in the 1988 primary. Released in 1986, Hart's book *America Can Win: The Case for Military Reform* was cowritten with William Lind. The book not only spread the reform gospel further, repeating many core arguments of the Fighter Mafia—including that "the F-16 should be returned to what it originally was: a pure fighter"—it also painted a picture of how many Reformers saw themselves: "a loose band of intellectual and political guerrilla fighters . . . ambushing the defense establishment with unexpected questions, unwelcome facts and innovative alternatives."[82]

The Reformers continued to push for more controversial reforms, including disbanding the Joint Chiefs of Staff. Attacking the F-16, the MRC—at

Courter's insistence—demanded a flyoff competition between the F-16 and the F-20 Tigershark (which had originally been the G-model variant of the F-5), arguing that the simpler, cheaper F-20 could be a potential replacement, especially for National Guard units.[83] This issue mirrored a similar debate about canceling the F-15 program to spend the money on F-5s instead—the specifics of which have been a point of contention.

General Creech recalled that Boyd and Riccioni, as well as Northrop, pushed for the cancellation of the F-15, to be replaced by larger numbers of F-5s, and that this debate raged for several years. Spinney said of the idea, "This is complete crap. I never did anything of the kind. . . . Neither did John Boyd. I was with him for the entire period and I never saw him propose such a stupid thing." He claimed to have no memory of Riccioni advocating it, either. Spinney recalled that the idea had come from "bean counters" in the Defense Department who added F-5s to a budget proposal that was likely to be canceled. Spinney claimed, "I went ballistic when I saw this F-5 proposal, and recommended to my boss that it be dropped, because it was stupid and would only serve to piss off the AF." Creech did not recall which individuals were responsible but maintained that the idea was actively promoted by Spinney's and Christie's office. "I have no 'smoking gun' evidence to prove that John Boyd led a charge to stop the F-15 production," he said. "I do, however, know that OSD/PA&E (in its official position—the competing views within PA&E aside) did lead such a charge. And that was a charge which the DRM [defense reform movement] warmly welcomed, and exploited to every extent possible."[84]

To deny that the Reformers advocated replacing F-15s with F-5s is splitting hairs. They might not have specifically said the exact words, but they made frequent comparisons of the two planes, heavily implying that the F-5 was a better use of funds and that they strongly preferred it to the F-15. Fallows had referenced the two aircraft extensively in his writing, citing Riccioni as his main source, claiming that the F-5 was the superior airplane for the money. Many journalists and members of the MRC did advocate for canceling the F-15. If the Reformers did not outright advocate the F-5 over the F-15 through official Defense Department channels, they strongly implied that position in many writings.[85]

By 1987 the reform movement had lost most of its steam. Boyd and Sprey were no longer sought-after around Washington, DC. Sprey became so frustrated that he quit his position as a consultant at the Pentagon to open a music recording studio. As for Boyd, as members of the media and popular press became less interested in him, he tried to focus on making new briefings that rehashed his philosophical ideas from "Destruction and Creation," but he became increasingly withdrawn. After suffering some health problems, he moved to Florida.[86]

Wheeler blamed the dissolution of the movement on several issues: the press losing interest in similar-sounding stories of overspending, the Reformers themselves failing to shift the debate to new topics or perspectives, and the congressional members and allies of the MRC using the movement as a stepping-stone for their careers, while refusing to follow through on the reforms the core group was willing to fight for.[87]

Burton pronounced the death of the reform movement around 1987, arguing that it had begun to decay as soon as it shifted its focus to Washington, DC. He charged that the members of the MRC had "abandoned their troops under fire." By 1987, the "spark and fire" of the movement was, in his eyes, gone.[88] This was a slight exaggeration, as the media continued to discuss the issues, and the MRC still functioned. But by 1989, the pace of deterioration increased. The caucus decreased to ninety-one members. Despite its lean toward conservatism, some liberals were still active in the group, including Representative Barbara Boxer (D-CA), who cochaired the caucus with a conservative colleague, Representative William Roth (R-DE). Other ideologically opposed members included liberals such as Representative Joseph P. Kennedy II (D-MA) and Senator Alan Cranston (D-CA) and conservatives like Senator Lloyd Bentsen (D-TX) and Representative Cheney, who remained a member of the caucus until he was tapped to be secretary of defense in March of that year.[89]

What kept this diverse group together, in addition to the goals of the reform movement itself, was a sentiment of resistance to established authority. One analyst from the General Accounting Office noted, "It's made up of the people who are not in the establishment, in the sense of who is in the managing hierarchy." The sense of being an outsider David fighting against a corrupt Goliath was a powerful motivating force, and it explains much of the group's appeal. However, in some ways the movement was a victim of its own success. To remain in the spotlight, an anti-authority cause needs continued anger and resistance. As the reform movement began to achieve some of its goals, the sense of crisis decreased. As one reporter argued, "the urgency for the caucus has declined in recent years, as the House and Senate Armed Services Committees have become more receptive to reform issues."[90]

"Ultimately, the Congressional Military Reform Caucus lost almost every battle it fought," recalled Wheeler.[91] The military establishment saw the Reformers as a thorn in their side, and although many politicians joined the movement, most were not especially active, likely using it as a way to earn political points with both hawks and doves. But the Reformers' message resonated powerfully with some people. In a time of crisis, of reflection on military and societal failures, and of declining confidence in American power, the Reformers offered easy-to-understand explanations for what caused the problem and provided simple solutions to restore military greatness. That those answers promised better defense for less money made the movement that much more attractive.

Despite the criticisms of their proposed solutions as simplistic or flawed, the Reformers played an important role. By acting as a foil for the mainstream defense establishment, the Reformers forced US leaders to both ask and answer difficult, uncomfortable questions about their procurement processes and doctrinal assumptions. Weapons testing practices did benefit from the Reformers' legislative efforts, and the connections between the military and the defense industry did need the additional scrutiny that the Reformers called for. Many critics may have dismissed the Reformers' specific policy proposals (and the manner in which they delivered them), but the movement prompted introspection and improvement across the defense establishment.

The Reformers' analysis, like the fighter pilot culture that informed their core leaders, was rooted in nostalgia, constantly looking backward to the past—or rather their particular interpretation of the past, which imagined a time of simple weapons and warrior virtues while ignoring much of the complicated context. Although the Reformers had chosen their name as a reference to the Prussian reforms of the early nineteenth century, Boyd and his followers were not nearly as progressive as their role models. They assumed that the circumstances and challenges of previous wars such as Vietnam would continue to define future conflicts. They assumed that new technologies could not be effective. But the technological breakthroughs of the 1970s and 1980s represented a significantly larger shift in military capability than the Reformers foresaw. More effective guided weapons, integrated command and control, the suppression of enemy air defenses, major improvements in the types, cost, and reliability of electronics all worked together, demanding more than piecemeal change to individual capabilities. The military attempted to incorporate these emerging technologies in a holistic way. While the Reformers mostly considered maneuver on a tactical level, these new technologies, if integrated synergistically, could increase quickness and maneuverability on an operational and strategic level.

One of the Reformers' complaints was that these new complex, expensive weapons had not been tested in the crucible of combat. That was about to change. On August 2, 1990, the Iraqi army invaded Kuwait. The United

States was about to find itself in a large-scale conventional war against a major military power for the first time since the Vietnam War. Within days, some observers hailed the Iraq crisis as "a test case" for the contrasting ideas of the defense establishment versus the Reformers. The latter began preaching that the end was near—the US military was about to realize that it should have listened to the Reformers all along. Gary Hart, parroting the words of James Fallows from ten years earlier, argued that the United States was "virtually muscle-bound in dealing with regional conflict" and that "the vaunted military buildup of the 1980s fails us. . . . We are prepared for a nuclear war with a disintegrating Soviet Union and unprepared for military action in Kuwait."[92] Iraq did indeed serve as a test case for the debates of the previous ten years. But it would not be the vindication the Reformers sought.

CHAPTER 8

Kicking Vietnam Syndrome

> Airpower won this war, and every one of you in the
> F-16 community should be proud of what you accomplished. . . . [You] dropped more bombs than any
> other aircraft.
>
> —Brigadier General Buster Glosson, director of
> campaign plans for Operation Desert Storm

The new doctrines and technologies developed
after Vietnam were put to the test in Iraq in 1991. Most observers interpreted
the war as a refutation of the Reformers' ideas: advanced, expensive technologies were devastatingly effective. The Reformers themselves saw the war
as a validation of their ideas, seizing on particular examples and interpretive lenses while giving John Boyd credit for the US victory. The Gulf War
was also a very different type of conflict from the one the Reformers had
envisioned. They had advocated measures intended to be used in a kind of
war that never actually happened. In that sense, their ideas were never truly
tested, but what did happen made clear that the Reformers' ideas did not
have universal application. If the Reformers were right, they were right in a
specific, purely hypothetical scenario.

Regardless of which side of these debates was more correct, the Reformers asked important questions about doctrine, the efficacy of weapons, and
the procurement process, even if most observers and participants in the Gulf
War rejected the movement's answers. Nonetheless, the Reformers' interpretations, and the steadfast adherence to them, were an outgrowth of the
fighter pilot culture that lay at the root of their movement. The Reformers
displayed the same vulnerabilities inherent in any continuous organizational
culture, which sociologist Barry Turner classified as vicious, self-reinforcing
cycles, limited perspectives, and "the danger of a collective blindness."[1]

All That You Can Be

Not only were the Reformers attempting to change military hardware and procurement policy during the second interwar period between Vietnam and the Gulf War, but they also exerted influence on changing service doctrines, beginning with the Army. In July 1976, the Army released a revised Army Field Manual 100–5, *Operations*, under the direction of Army Training and Doctrine Command (TRADOC) commander General William E. DePuy. Influenced by the recent Arab-Israeli War of 1973, DePuy thought that the tempo of future wars would be faster than previous conflicts, and thus the US Army needed to emphasize training, suppression, use of their terrain, and the use of combined arms to increase lethality.[2]

Boyd and the Reformers dismissed the new manual, arguing that it merely restated earlier doctrines based on firepower and frontal assaults and did not embrace Boyd's ideas of agility, speed, and movement. Some of their critiques referenced knights of the air tropes. The manual called for maneuver in order to gain an advantageous firing position, seemingly in line with a fighter pilot approach, but Burton said, "Boyd preached the opposite—shoot in order to create opportunities to maneuver—and maneuver in order to create chaos, panic, and collapse and get behind the enemy to capture its forces. 'Fighter pilots always come in the back door, not the front,' he stated over and over."[3] William Lind, when lecturing at institutions in all four services, called the new Army doctrine a "piece of garbage." Boyd himself ridiculed the Army for spending months to come up with a new doctrine that he considered essentially the same as the old one. Allegedly, in the late 1970s, whenever Boyd noticed Army generals in the audience of his briefings, he held a copy of the manual over his head, proclaiming, "It's a piece of shit."[4]

In 1977, General Donn A. Starry replaced DePuy as head of TRADOC and worked on further changes to Army doctrine. Through a series of studies in 1978 and 1979, Starry and Army chief of staff General Edward C. Meyer developed the idea of the "extended battlefield." They thought of the battlefield as multidimensional, not just involving air and land dimensions, but incorporating time, space, and potential chemical or nuclear dimensions. All of these had to be juggled in different ways at various levels of command. Time, and predicting the state of a battle at twelve, twenty-four, and seventy-two hours in the future, were crucial factors. Starry and Meyer also called for US forces to be more aggressive to predict and prevent Soviet rear-echelon forces from being active in the front line. This kind of planning called for careful coordination with ground and air assets, which is why the doctrine earned the name "AirLand Battle."[5]

The new Field Manual 100–5 describing AirLand Battle, publicly released in March 1981, bore a striking similarity to Boyd's "Patterns of Conflict." Burton asserted it was a "flagrant rip off of Boyd's ideas."[6] Like "Patterns," the new manual emphasized movement, aggressiveness, agility, increased tempo, and the comparison to doctrine of the German Wehrmacht in World War II. Major General Donald Morelli, deputy chief of staff at TRADOC and an influential voice in creating the new doctrine, described AirLand Battle in many of the same terms that Boyd used, saying it would "stress the use of lightly armored, highly agile units capable of pursuing the tactics of speed and deception." The press, seeing these similarities, interpreted the new doctrine as linked with the reform movement.[7] The *New York Times* also described AirLand Battle using almost the exact same language that Boyd had used: "The new doctrine . . . departs from the traditional emphasis on a war of attrition with massed firepower on a well-defined front. AirLand Battle . . . calls for deep counterattacks behind enemy lines coupled with a tactical use of agility, deception and surprise."[8]

Whether or not Boyd and the Reformers had any direct influence on DePuy, Starry, or Morelli is unclear, and Boyd is hardly the only person to ever advocate for maneuver warfare. At a time when all services were looking for new models of warfighting in the wake of Vietnam, independent, parallel thinking was plausible. But the press tended to conflate the Army efforts with the Reformers, who themselves noted the similarities in language. And they were not happy.

During a 1981 briefing by Morelli, Burton recalled commenting that Morelli's presentation was similar to Boyd's. Morelli denied the charge by, as Burton claimed, "exploding into a tirade. His reaction was so emotional and defensive that I [Burton] presumed he had run into this same criticism before." Burton insisted "there can be no question" that the Army's ideas were directly influenced, if not copied wholesale, from Boyd's ideas. According to him, Boyd had met with DePuy and briefed him on his ideas, and Burton asserted that TRADOC had kept copies of Boyd's briefings on hand throughout the 1970s.[9]

If Morelli denied Boyd's influence on TRADOC, other Army institutions welcomed Boyd and his ideas. General Jack N. Merritt, the commandant of the Army War College, sought to incorporate Boyd's ideas into the school's curriculum.[10] In 1982, West Point hosted a symposium on the Military Reform movement. Another contributor to the composition of AirLand Battle doctrine, Lieutenant Colonel Huba Wass de Czege, was an instructor at the Army Command and General Staff College at Fort Leavenworth, Kansas. He invited Boyd and Lind to give guest lectures there. Wass de Czege later founded and was the first director of the School of Advanced Military Studies. Boyd's "Patterns of Conflict" briefing was an official part of the school's curriculum throughout the mid-1980s.[11]

Despite accusations of plagiarism, some of the Reformers criticized the Army for adopting only some of Boyd's ideas and not all of them. Specifically, AirLand Battle called for forces to be "synchronized," while Boyd favored groups acting independently, arguing that this would increase the enemy's confusion. His often-repeated mantra was "You synchronize watches, not people." Boyd remained highly critical of the Army and did not realize the degree to which it had reformed. As he told Wass de Czege during a discussion about Army strategy, "They still believe in high diddle diddle, straight up the middle."[12] This was an oversimplification of the Army's actual approach.

Reforming the Services

The Reformers had greater success with the Marine Corps. In the late 1970s, Lieutenant Colonel Michael Wyly was an instructor at the Marines' Amphibious Warfare School at Quantico, Virginia. While updating the school's curriculum, Wyly asked Lind to recommend someone who could help him theorize new strategic approaches; Lind recommended Boyd. In January 1980, Wyly brought Boyd to Quantico. After more than eight hours of Boyd's "Patterns" briefing, Wyly was captivated; he became a full-fledged member of the reform movement and Boyd's devoted acolyte. Wyly assembled a collected volume of Boyd's briefings, which became colloquially known as "the Green Book" and was required reading for Marine Corps officers at Quantico. Boyd became a frequent lecturer at the Amphibious Warfare School through 1982, and he and Wyly assigned works written by former Wehrmacht and Luftwaffe officers, emphasizing maneuver warfare tactics.[13]

Wyly published the ideas of the Reformers in the Marine Corps *Gazette*, the service's journal, edited by Colonel John Greenwood, a retired Marine officer who also supported the Reformers' ideas. The Marines got another dose of maneuver warfare from General Alfred Gray, who, as commander of the Second Marine Division by 1981, designed Marine training exercises at Camp Lejeune based on the concept. Gray had studied operational history and arrived at many of the same maneuver warfare concepts as Boyd long before he had known about Boyd. By 1987, Gray had become commandant of the Marine Corps and wanted to spur institutional change. He founded the Marine Corps University and ordered the creation of a new doctrine manual. To write it, Gray turned to Captain John Schmitt, who had previously attempted to write a new ground assault doctrine manual incorporating

Boyd's maneuver warfare concepts. The new manual, *FMFM-1: Warfighting*, was completed in March 1989 and incorporated many of Boyd's ideas about maneuver, tempo, and the decision cycle, as well as the ideas of other historical military thinkers. Although Schmitt had several phone conversations with Boyd during the writing process, Boyd did not write the manual himself.[14] Despite the debate that occurred within the Marine Corps about the extent to which maneuver warfare should be implemented, it is undeniable that the Marines accepted Boyd's ideas to a larger degree than the other services did.

The Reformers were frustrated with the Army and cautiously optimistic about the Marines, but they were particularly frustrated with the Navy and Air Force. Coram claimed that Boyd had no effect on the Navy, and, as for the Air Force, Coram asserted, "The Air Force did not change at all. Even today, retired senior generals take pride in the fact that Boyd's ideas had no influence whatsoever on the Air Force."[15] Burton pointed out that CSAF General Lew Allen did initiate "Project Warrior" in 1982, which encouraged Air Force officers to study strategy and warfighting theory by reading books that Boyd personally recommended. Burton claimed that this was merely a token effort and insisted that "the Air Force did the least to change its thinking."[16]

That view is incorrect. Both the Air Force and the Navy made large changes in their doctrine, and they incorporated many of Boyd's ideas as well as some concepts from the broader reform movement. Yet, because they adopted Boyd's ideas only partially rather than completely, Boyd and his followers became frustrated and accusatory. Just as earlier fighter pilots were protective of their community, by the 1980s the Reformers had grown so self-protective, inward looking, and wary of potential threats that they saw the Air Force not as an ally that adopted some of their ideas but rather as an enemy conspiring to take them down.

The Navy's internal reforms came in the context of the perceived problems in Vietnam. The Navy recognized the major problems with missile accuracy in that war, and, after a thorough review resulting in the "Ault Report," the Navy changed its maintenance and transportation procedures to improve handling of the sensitive warheads. The Navy also realized that the training of fighter pilots, especially in the realm of air-to-air combat, was deficient, and it had taken steps during the Vietnam War to change that, such as creating the Navy Fighter Weapons School, known colloquially as "Top Gun." The Navy also decided to procure the lightweight fighter that had competed against the YF-16 that Boyd had codesigned—and thus the YF-17 became the basis for the F/A-18 Hornet. In December 1980, the US Naval Institute *Proceedings* published a study of how to apply Boyd's strategic theories of maneuver warfare to naval doctrine.[17] The Navy did not completely overhaul its doctrine from the ground up to be in line with the Fighter Mafia's ideas about maneuver warfare and its focus on small, lightweight fighters. Still, it did incorporate parts of these ideas into its reform efforts in the 1970s and 1980s.

The Air Force also instituted many changes in these years, although its changes were less sweeping than those instituted by the other services. George Herring has argued that in the post-Vietnam years, "the Air Force was not inclined toward self-criticism or disposed to look searchingly at the Vietnam experience."[18] There is some truth to this, as the war and its possible lessons were not discussed in Air Force service journals to a large degree. Yet to characterize the Air Force as unchanging is misleading.

The Air Force went through a myriad of changes in this period, not only in the procurement of technology but in its approach to warfighting. The Air Force exchanged much of its inventory in the 1970s and 1980s, replacing older planes with new fleets of aircraft that Boyd had had a hand in developing, such as the F-15 and F-16. It also included guns on its aircraft, developed new air-to-air missiles, and, much like the Navy, created entirely new training systems that emphasized air-to-air combat and maneuverability. The result came in the Red Flag exercises, which were accurately described as a revolution in training procedures so significant that the National Aeronautic Association awarded TAC and its commander, General Robert Dixon, the 1977 Collier Trophy "for the greatest achievement in aeronautics or astronautics in America."[19] Once again, Boyd, the Fighter Mafia, and the Reformers might have been upset that the institution did not follow every single one of their recommendations to the letter, but many of their ideas did influence the post-Vietnam Air Force.

The Air Campaign

One individual who did much to shape the Air Force before the Gulf War was not John Boyd but Colonel John Warden—a man who was a sort of altered reflection of Boyd, with so much in common yet still drastically different. Warden, like Boyd, was a former fighter pilot who turned into a firebrand strategic thinker who enjoyed pushing against authority. Warden had flown F-4 Phantoms but not in air-to-air combat. His time in Vietnam was spent mostly as a forward air controller in an OV-10 Bronco. Later, Warden transitioned to flying the F-15 Eagle.

Warden was not the "typical" fighter pilot. He showed some stereotypical fighter traits and rejected others. Certainly, Warden, like Boyd, was an

individualistic and independent thinker whose ideas pushed against the established doctrine of his day. Both men also tended to alienate many of those
around them, although Boyd did that through his bombastic, aggressive, and
offensive personality, whereas Warden was withdrawn and overly formal.
Major (and later four-star general) Gregory S. Martin observed, "Warden was
not your typical sloppy pilot type who would hang around in the bar and talk
about air maneuvers."[20]

In 1988, Warden released his influential book *The Air Campaign*. It was an
ambitious work that examined the theory and philosophy of air power with
a focus on the operational art. Whereas Boyd focused on creating confusion
through getting inside the enemy's decision cycle, using "fingertip feel," agility, and surprise, Warden emphasized identifying the correct center of gravity for the given objective and applying decisive force against it while aligning
a campaign's ends, ways, and means. More notably, while the Reformers saw
AirLand Battle as a rip-off (if an incomplete one) of Boyd's ideas, Warden
rejected the doctrine wholesale, arguing that it relegated air power to being a
servant of the Army rather than maintaining its strength as an independent,
flexible force.[21] While Boyd and his acolytes seemed to pursue air combat
as an end unto itself, Warden was more concerned with using air power in
operational and strategic ways that looked beyond the battlefield. Gaining
air superiority was crucial, but Warden believed air power had enormous
potential if it was carefully applied at the operational level.

Warden's work was controversial, but endorsed by some key leaders. The
commandant of the National War College, Air Force Major General Perry
M. Smith, noted, "this is the most important book on air power written in
the past decade. Must reading for everyone interested in future combat. This
is the book I wish I had written." Smith distributed the book to several Air
Force generals, including Charles L. Donnelly, the commander of USAFE.
General Donnelly later wrote the introduction for the published version of
The Air Campaign, noting, "This book is the start of something very impor-
tant. . . . A book of this type has been needed for a long time."[22]

Warden later took command of the 36th Tactical Fighter Wing, the main
F-15 Eagle unit in Europe at Bitburg, Germany. He recognized the presence of fighter pilot stereotypes among his pilots but did not encourage
them. "The guys flying the F-15s are like the knights on the horse," Warden recalled. "But somebody first has to put the horseshoes on the horse."[23]
Members of the wing coincidentally gave Warden the call sign "Genghis,"
similar to Boyd's unofficial nickname "Genghis John." Yet that is where the
similarities between the two ended. Warden's command worked against typical fighter pilot values. He insisted on air-to-air combat training using "big

wing" formations of up to twenty-four F-15s. The numerical superiority usually equated to success in mock combat, even if pilots who valued individual, uncoordinated, unsupervised action were initially skeptical. Other measures included smaller, symbolic matters that rubbed fighter pilots the wrong way, such as insisting on proper dress code in the officers' club (coat and tie after 4 p.m.), following full formal ceremonies for promotions of officers even at lower-level positions down to flight commander, and—the decision that generated the most enmity among his subordinates—the elimination of reserved parking spaces.[24]

Warden was not a member of the Reformers nor a follower of Boyd. Boyd and the Reformers were more concerned with technology, training, bureaucracy, and the procurement process, whereas Warden focused instead on the operational and strategic employment of air power. If Boyd recalled the romanticized ideal of ace fighter pilots and knights of the air from the First World War, Warden had more in common with the air power prophets and theorists of the 1920s and 1930s, such as Giulio Douhet and Billy Mitchell.[25] The upcoming Gulf War became a test of the ideas of both thinkers.

The Box Score

On August 2, 1990, Saddam Hussein invaded Kuwait, prompting a quick response from Western planners. General Norman Schwarzkopf was then the commander of US Central Command (CENTCOM, responsible for security issues in the Middle East, Egypt, and parts of Central and South Asia). In the early planning stages, he sought an option for a large-scale air attack before ground troops could arrive. Schwarzkopf's request to the Air Staff for such a plan eventually went to Warden.[26] Warden applied his concepts of air power to an air campaign plan he named "Instant Thunder," in contrast to the gradual bombing campaigns of "Rolling Thunder" during the Vietnam War. The plan called for attacks against specific centers of gravity to paralyze the enemy. Lieutenant General Charles Horner, commander of Central Command Air Forces, regarded Warden's plan as too "embryonic" and essentially removed him from the project. Other elements of Warden's team, led by former fighter pilots Brigadier General Buster Glosson and Lieutenant Colonel David Deptula, remained to modify Instant Thunder into an executable plan. They retained its conceptual philosophy but emphasized the role of stealth technology and the idea of "simultaneity"—hitting related targets in close succession to shock the enemy.[27]

The entire air plan for Desert Storm was based on extensive use of the technologies and strategies that the Fighter Mafia and the Reformers had railed against. Boyd, the Fighter Mafia, and the Reformers had predicted a future war in which large fleets of aircraft battled for air superiority in ferocious dogfights. That hypothetical scenario demanded, they argued, smaller, simpler aircraft, relying on the flying skill of the individual pilot. Planes like the F-16 would be far more useful than the cumbersome F-15 Eagle, but even the F-16 was perhaps too complex in their evaluation. They assumed that the large all-weather radar of the F-15 was unnecessary and made the Eagle vulnerable. They also assumed that missiles would be useless. The ranges would be too small, the planes too agile, and achieving a lock would give away an attacking pilot's position. Instead, the pilots would become knights of the air, using their skills to outmaneuver enemies before blasting them out of the sky with guns at close range. Key to that dogfighting ideal were the assumptions that an enemy air force would be highly trained and disciplined, would operate in large numbers, and would have a deep familiarity with their systems.

In the skies over Iraq in 1991, almost none of these assumptions were true.

First, radar played a key role in gaining and maintaining air superiority. The E-3 Airborne Warning and Control System (AWACS), E-2 Hawkeye, and RC-135 aircraft could alert coalition pilots to approaching enemies long before battles began. That added to Eagle pilots' disciplined target-sorting tactics and enemy-identification methods, meaning that air-to-air engagements only rarely went to the merge. Most kills happened from several miles away, many from beyond visual range (BVR). EF-111s and EA-6s aided this effort through electronic jamming of enemy communications. The coalition flew decoy drones both to distract enemy radar away from strike aircraft and to keep enemy radar sources active so they could be targeted. Those Iraqi radar sources were then slammed with high-speed anti-radiation missiles (HARMs), most often fired from F-4Gs, although other aircraft carried them as well.[28] Air-to-air missions were no longer about heroic individuals, if they ever were. By 1991, air-to-air combat was an integrated system of many trained specialists interacting with various advanced technologies in a coordinated whole that utterly demolished Iraqi defenses.

Second, air-to-air combat did not involve the types of aircraft that the Reformers thought it should. Air-to-air sorties consisted almost exclusively of F-15Cs (for the Air Force, while the Navy primarily flew its F-14 Tomcats in that role). The F-16, which Boyd had wanted to be the platonic ideal of an air-to-air fighter, was not used in air-to-air combat in Iraq at all but as a fighter bomber almost exclusively to attack ground targets. F-16s achieved zero aerial victories in the Gulf War. The only time that F-16s flew in an air combat capacity (a CAP—combat air patrol—sortie) was the day before Operation Desert Storm launched, specifically to deceive or confuse Iraqi ground controllers, as they expected to see F-15s in that role.[29] Boyd's associates have argued that this was due to the Air Force establishment's preference for the F-15. Allegedly, Horner ordered that any F-16 pilots who attempted an air-to-air engagement would be "sent home." Some Reformers have implied that the F-16 would have performed well in the air-to-air role had it been permitted to do so. That is very likely true, but it was not tested in 1991.[30]

Examining air-to-air combat statistics, the conflict was one-sided, to say the least. From January 17 to March 22, 1991, coalition pilots destroyed forty-two Iraqi aircraft in the air. Although Iraqi ground defenses shot down thirty-two coalition planes, only one was lost to air-to-air combat: a Navy F/A-18 Hornet piloted by Lieutenant Commander Michael Scott Speicher was shot down by an air-to-air missile. Of the forty-two victories, thirty-seven of them (88 percent) were by an F-15 Eagle. The Navy claimed three kills, one from a pair of F-14s and two from F/A-18 Hornets. The remaining two kills were from A-10 Thunderbolts destroying helicopters.[31]

The third inaccurate assumption from the Reformers was that enemy air forces would consist of highly trained, capable pilots. This could hardly have been further from the truth. Many of the coalition pilots had participated in extensive training in air-to-air combat against a variety of simulated threat types and force structures, either through the Air Force's Red Flag exercises or the Navy's Top Gun program. The Iraqi Air Force had no equivalent. Western intelligence sources noted that Iraqi fighter pilots were poorly trained and inexperienced. Iraqi pilots trained in a rigid, almost rote pattern, taught to execute specific maneuvers based mostly on instruments, and rarely, if ever, looking outside the cockpit. Efforts to upgrade Iraqi pilot training were hamstrung by financial problems. One US Navy Intelligence report stated, "Intercept tactics and training [were] still predominantly conservative, elementary, and generally not up to western standards." Also, the culture of the Iraqi Air Force favored ground attack as the more desirable role. The most skilled pilots gravitated to CAS assignments, leaving air-to-air to the least competent and least-trained pilots. Although the Iraqi Air Force consisted of state-of-the art Soviet aircraft, the Iraqi pilots, as historian Williamson Murray put it, "did not possess the basic flying skills to exploit fully the capabilities of their aircraft."[32]

Iraqi air-to-air weakness also stemmed from doctrine. Adhering to the Soviet doctrinal model, Iraqi pilots relied on ground-controlled intercept (GCI) operators who monitored aircraft via radar and gave orders to pilots. But the tightly organized Iraqi system focused more on aiding SAM missile launch sites and antiaircraft artillery gunners and was less oriented toward air-to-air encounters. Each of four sectors possessed operations centers to gather radar and visual tracking information that was then coordinated at air defense operations centers in Baghdad, relying on the French-built computer system called KARI (the French spelling for "Iraq" written backward). This system had several redundancies, with key nodes in hardened shelters to ensure that it remained operational during an attack.[33]

The US military's changes in training, equipment, and doctrine, as well as Warden's targeting plan, had been geared to combat the Soviet GCI model. Coalition aircraft conducted near-simultaneous attacks against headquarters in Baghdad as well as the operations centers in various sectors. Although KARI was still partially functional, the Iraqi Integrated Air Defense system was no longer integrated. Radars and SAM sites had trouble communicating, and many were completely inoperable. For the SEAD (suppression of enemy air defenses) mission, coalition planners had estimated to lose as many as twenty to twenty-five aircraft on the first night of the war. In fact, they only lost one—Speicher's F/A-18.[34]

Iraqi command and control took heavy damage, but Iraqi pilots performed poorly even before the effects of the bombing had set in. As F-15s flew CAP missions during the opening strikes, searching for possible MiG threats, infrared cameras revealed one MiG-29 crashing into the ground, while another launched a missile that destroyed a friendly MiG-23 crossing ahead of it. In some cases, when coalition pilots obtained radar locks, Iraqi pilots made little to no attempt to maneuver before missiles destroyed their planes. Some of the engagements did involve close maneuvering against skilled Iraqi pilots, but those were rare exceptions.[35]

After the third day of the war, air-to-air encounters decreased significantly. Iraqi pilots avoided combat, although much of their force remained intact. When coalition planners began targeting the hardened shelters protecting Iraqi aircraft, many pilots attempted to flee to Iran. Many of them did not have enough fuel for the trip and crashed—again indicative of the lack of competence in the Iraqi fighter pilot force. Coalition pilots seized the opportunity to destroy the enemy in the air as they fled. These encounters mattered little to the outcome of the war, but Murray saw them as "opportunities to add to the box score."[36] Whereas the Fighter Mafia had argued that USAF fighters—particularly the F-15—were not specialized enough for the air-to-air role, political scientist Karl Mueller argued that the war revealed that the F-15 might have been too specialized, noting that "hundreds of single-role F-15C fighters had little to contribute to the war after air supremacy had been established."[37]

The Reformers were probably the most incorrect about missile performance. Their assumption that missiles would be useless, especially long-range radar-homing missiles, was proven false. Of the forty-two official coalition aerial victories, three were due to ground impact, and two were A-10s that shredded Iraqi helicopters with the Thunderbolt's infamous GAU-8 cannon. In one case, an F-15E Strike Eagle dropped a laser-guided GBU-10 bomb onto a helicopter and was given an aerial victory credit. The remaining thirty-six—almost 86 percent—were the result of a guided missile. The heat-seeking AIM-9M (an upgraded version of the "L" model) accounted for twelve—exactly one-third—of the missile kills. The remaining two-thirds of them were due to the AIM-7M Sparrow—an upgraded model of the radar-guided missile against which the Fighter Mafia had argued so vehemently. Their assumption had been that the rules of engagement present in Vietnam, which prohibited missile firings from beyond visual range, would be present in any future war such as this one. However, the integration of AWACS with the F-15's AN/APG-63 radar and pilots' target-sorting tactics allowed for frequent BVR attacks. In fact, sixteen of the AIM-7 kills (44 percent of the total number of missile kills) were BVR attacks.[38]

One of the most surprising encounters of the war took place during the first night, January 17, in which an unarmed EF-111 achieved an unofficial aerial victory against an Iraqi Mirage F1. The EF-111 was a modified version of the aircraft so hated by Boyd and the Fighter Mafia. Equipped for electronic warfare (radar tracking and jamming), the plane had no weapons, yet it found itself in the sights of an Iraqi fighter pilot, who launched two heat-seeking R.550 "Magic" air-to-air missiles. After a combination of gut-wrenching evasive maneuvers and flares, the EF-111 dodged the missiles, and the Iraqi pilot closed in for a gun kill. The EF-111 crew, Captains James Denton and Brent Brandon, used their aircraft's technological advantages. In the dark desert night, they got as low to the ground as possible, relying on their complex, expensive, ground-looking radar to map the terrain as they flew. After ensuring the Iraqi pilot was committed to pursuit, Denton pulled up hard. The Iraqi pilot, unable to see into the darkness, crashed in a giant fireball almost immediately as the EF-111 escaped.[39] The Fighter Mafia and the Reformers had argued vehemently against the F-111 itself, against the concept of having a two-seat aircraft, and against the type of complex radar it carried. Yet not only did all those components make a substantial contribution to the overall effort in the Gulf; those exact components also proved able to score air-to-air victories, even without the use of offensive weapons.

This is not to imply that these systems were perfect. Problems did exist. Intelligence data were at times flawed, the large number of aircraft tended to overwhelm air traffic controllers, and tensions between services—particularly between air and ground commanders—created friction, just to name some of the hurdles that the coalition air effort struggled with.[40] Yet the major problems that the Reformers predicted were not among them.

Fathers of Victory

For many observers, the Gulf War proved the Reformers wrong. Air power historian John Correll said that the war "really took the ginger out of the Reform movement. . . . High technology undeniably worked. Its star performers included the much-maligned F-15 and all of the other systems that had been attacked by the Reformers."[41] Complex, advanced weaponry performed so well that many participants and analysts argued that not only were the Reformers wrong, but the Gulf War signified a "Revolution in Military Affairs" (RMA), by which they mean that new technologies such as stealth, precision weapons, and information systems fundamentally altered the nature of warfare, and that countries that lacked those capabilities would be the quick losers in any future war.[42] Although the idea of RMA captured the imagination of many analysts at the time, the events of 9/11 and the subsequent wars in Afghanistan and Iraq in the twenty-first century have revealed that just as the Reformers based their arguments on sweeping assumptions, RMA advocates did also.

Nonetheless, if the concept of RMA was correct, then the days of dogfighting knights of the air were truly over. But to say that the Gulf War proved the Reformers wrong is an oversimplification. Although the complex, expensive weapons that the Reformers opposed did prove effective in 1991, the war was different from what the Reformers had predicted. They had been worried about a large-scale conventional conflict, most likely against the Soviet Union, involving large numbers of well-trained military units of all types that would engage in large-scale battles of maneuver, including dogfights with high-quality fighter pilots dueling in clear skies. Instead, in the Gulf War, weather conditions, including heavy fog, low clouds, and frequent rain, required the all-weather capabilities that the Reformers had decried. And the Iraqi forces were not the high-quality opponent that the Reformers envisioned fighting, even though, before the war began, it appeared that they might be. On paper, Iraq had the world's fourth-largest army and its sixth-largest air force. Certainly, Iraq in 1990 did not seem like a paper tiger.[43]

But once the war began, the bulk of the Iraqi military, and especially its air arm, proved to be a mostly hollow force. The combination of terrain, environment, and the composition and quality of the enemy rendered Iraqi forces vulnerable to just the type of attack that Warden had envisioned. Some fierce fighting did occur in some places against highly trained Iraqi troops, especially Republican Guard units and a few intense dogfights. But for the most part, most of the Reformers' ideas went untested. What is clear is that the Reformers' vision was not applicable to all wars.

In an example of all parties seeing what they wanted to see, just as some interpreted the Gulf War as a refutation of the reform movement, the Reformers themselves took it as a validation. The Reformers could not point to the F-16 or to air-to-air combat in general as evidence for their views and looked elsewhere. Burton held up the A-10 Thunderbolt II, whose design was influenced by Pierre Sprey. Burton claimed the A-10, the "inexpensive, simple, slow-flying, ugly but lethal symbol of the Reform Movement," was responsible for over half of the bomb damage in the war.[44] This was an exaggeration. First, the A-10 is hardly "simple." Its focus on close air support and survivability may be conceptually simple, but it incorporated new technologies that were relatively complex for the period, including the AAS-35 Pave Penny laser identifier, the AGM-65 Maverick missile, and the unique GAU-8 Avenger 30 mm cannon.[45] Second, although the A-10 was very successful in the ground-attack role in Desert Storm, it performed fewer than 17 percent of the ground-attack strikes. After three A-10 pilots were shot down in rapid succession, Horner scaled back the number of Thunderbolt II sorties, instead sending in F-16s. The latter's agility and speed rendered it effective on ground-attack missions in high-threat areas, and the F-16 performed almost double the number of ground strikes as the A-10. Undoubtedly, despite sortie counts, the A-10 delivered significant damage, but was unlikely to have delivered over half the bomb damage. B-52s and F-16s alone delivered 70 percent of unguided bomb tonnage, and although A-10s delivered the vast majority of guided Maverick missile strikes, the total tonnage of guided weapons dropped in the war by all aircraft was only 8 percent. Furthermore, bomb damage assessment was, according to the government's Gulf War Air Power Survey, "one of the most controversial issues of the war." A General Accounting Office (GAO) report concluded that "data on a large number of A-10 strike events were unclear or contradictory," and it was "impossible to reliably analyze and include A-10 strike data."[46]

Besides searching for positive examples, some Reformers also criticized complex weapons. In June 1997, the GAO produced an evaluation of the air campaign with contributions from some Reformers, including Boyd's associate Winslow Wheeler, aide to Senator Kassebaum. The report argued that many of the high-technology systems—particularly the F-117 Nighthawk stealth fighter and laser-guided bombs (LGBs)—were not as effective as had been reported, and that the F-117 bombing accuracy rate was between 41 and 60 percent, far less than the reported rate of 80 percent. However, the lower rates included sorties that were aborted because of bad weather or mechanical problems and thus did not launch a weapon on their targets. The report judged the actual hit rate of F-117 strikes could have reached the reported 80 percent, but could have been as low as 55 percent. Although Wheeler commented that the lower rate rendered the F-117 an "abject failure," the report itself acknowledged that even the lower rate "is considered highly effective."[47]

The report also argued that LGBs did not achieve the "one target, one bomb" claims of the manufacturer—that multiple bombs were needed to destroy a single target. This was often because thick enemy defenses required multiple bomb hits to penetrate. The report did not acknowledge the unprecedented (for the time) precision required to hit the same target with subsequent bombs in order to degrade those defenses. However, weather conditions did limit the effectiveness of many precision weapons. The report concluded that there was little difference between guided and unguided bombs and questioned if precision weapons were worth their cost. The report did note one major advantage of precision guided munitions: that accurately delivering unguided weapons placed pilots at great risk and resulted in high casualty rates.[48]

The GAO report questioned the role of expensive, complex weapons but admitted that the air-to-air role had not been thoroughly tested, as "the Iraqi air force essentially chose not to challenge the coalition." Despite casting doubt on the effectiveness of complex weapons, the report could not deny the outcome. It concluded, "Although some initial claims of accuracy and effectiveness of these weapon systems were exaggerated, their performance led, in part, to perhaps the most successful war fought by the United States in the 20th century. . . . Their performance in combat may well have been unprecedented."[49]

Since the air war did not reflect the Reformers' vision, they instead claimed credit for the success of the ground campaign. Robert Coram cited then–Secretary of Defense Cheney's prior meetings with Boyd as part of the reason that Cheney "knew more about warfare than did many of his generals," and that the entire plan for the war—including beginning with an air strike, then having a feint in the east by the Marines as the main ground force performed a "left hook" maneuver—was all Boyd's. Coram claims that Cheney rejected Schwarzkopf's initial plan for a frontal assault, then invited Boyd to Washington to develop a new plan, concluding with the unsupportable claim, "Everything successful about the Gulf War is a direct reflection of Boyd's 'Patterns of Conflict.'"[50] According to Coram's interview notes, Cheney did not go quite that far, instead noting that the air campaign was already planned and approved. Cheney recalled that "nobody liked" the plan for a ground assault straight at the enemy, and that General Colin Powell then traveled to the theater for planning sessions with Schwarzkopf, after which the new plan emerged, but only the broad concept of adding more troops for a flanking maneuver—Cheney did not see it as his job to "figure out [the] nitty gritty" and had little influence on the plan himself. Regarding Boyd's involvement, Cheney did bring him to the Pentagon to discuss planning and said, "He clearly was a factor in my thinking."[51]

Other sources have painted a different picture. Cheney's assertion that "nobody liked" the assault plan was very true—Schwarzkopf himself hated it and insisted it was not his recommendation. Army planners originally considered three scenarios, including two that involved actions farther to the west. Schwarzkopf put forward the "up the middle" plan but warned that he did not approve of it—it was a political maneuver that allowed him to make a case for additional troops. Cheney became enamored of a "Western Excursion" plan, thought up mostly by Henry Rowen from the Stanford University Graduate School of Business. Rowen's plan was further developed by a group of active-duty and retired officers organized by the undersecretary of defense for policy, Paul Wolfowitz, and led by Lieutenant General Dale Vesser. Boyd's summons to Washington for planning meetings might have been as a part of this group. Schwarzkopf judged that the logistical problems of operating as far west as that plan called for rendered the idea as "bad as it could possibly be." Simultaneously, General Colin Powell formed his own planning group led by Lieutenant General Thomas Kelly and Lieutenant General Martin Brandtner. Powell's group also rejected Cheney's Western Excursion as "logistically difficult, and of dubious strategic benefit." They instead developed the "left hook" action, which was not as far to the west.[52]

Aside from arguments about who should be credited with the "left hook" idea, the other core argument of the Reformers was about how that hook was executed and with what technologies, claiming that if Boyd's concepts were properly adhered to, the war would have been more successful than it already was. Burton in particular led that cause, arguing that the M1 Abrams tank was a technological failure, and that the corps commanders charged with executing the hook, particularly VII Corps commander Lieutenant General Frederick Franks, failed to rely on Boyd's maneuver concepts, letting the Republican Guard escape.[53]

Assigning blame for the escape of the Republican Guard and whether Franks moved too slowly have been discussed in many books and articles—

many influenced by Schwarzkopf's sustained fury at Franks. Historians have differing interpretations. The most prominent, from General Bernard Trainor and journalist Michael Gordon, was that the escape of the Republican Guard had little to do with Franks and was mostly because the Marine Corps action in the east—intended to be a feint and a fixing action—was so successful that it became a piston, driving the Republican Guard north far earlier than expected. As for Franks, he was certain that the enemy forces in front of him were formidable and required massive consolidation of firepower; he was reluctant to split up his forces. Schwarzkopf had decided to speed up the timetable significantly, forcing Franks to move his corps before preparations were complete, requiring movement at night. Lacking the necessary number of thermal sights for night operations, those movements were dangerous and produced many incidents of fratricide, forcing Franks to stop to protect those under his command. Minefields in the way also forced a slowdown.[54]

Almost no other analysts have blamed the M1, which proved itself very capable. Although there were logistical problems involving getting enough fuel to Franks's VII Corps, this was not solely due to the M1, and furthermore, the M1's capabilities allowed US units to devastate Iraqi forces. The M1 was able to fire from safely outside the range of Iraqi T-72 tanks, and its depleted-uranium shells frequently blew enemy turrets off their base or blasted straight through a whole Iraqi tank while retaining enough velocity to destroy a second one behind it. The few direct hits sustained by M1s glanced off the upgraded ceramic armor. Not a single M1 Abrams was destroyed or even had its armor penetrated during the whole war.[55]

The escape of the Republican Guard is one of the most debated aspects of the Gulf War, but there are many sides to that story. The Reformers raised some important points, but to insist that the failure was the result of planners not listening to them enough is simplistic at best. One of the most persistent axioms in military history is that "victory has a thousand fathers." It is not surprising that the Reformers tried to be one of them.

The Gulf War, which became colloquially known as the "hundred-hour war," brought a wave of triumphalism and a resurgence of confidence in the American military that had not been present since before 1964. As President George H. W. Bush proclaimed on March 1, 1991, "by God, we've kicked the Vietnam syndrome once and for all."[56] This triumphalism seemed to push the Reformers out of the spotlight completely, as observers praised the role of "complex" technologies, especially aircraft such as the F-15 Eagle that the Reformers had resented. However, Boyd, Spinney, Burton, and their allies insisted that the war had proved them correct. Some agreed. Business writer Tom Peters, a Boyd devotee who had worked in the Pentagon and in the Nixon administration, argued that the Gulf War was not actually a fair test of the Reformers' ideas. He insisted that the enemy faced in Iraq was incompetent and ill-equipped. In a contest against the Soviets, he said, American "high-tech" weapons would not be as effective. As he surmised, the only thing the Gulf War proved was this: "That heavyweight boxing champ Evander Holyfield could beat the tar out of me—and it wouldn't take him 100 hours."[57]

If the Gulf War killed the Military Reform movement, it was at least in part because the movement had been on its last legs for some time, with less and less media coverage and a shrinking caucus membership. However, the war did serve as a powerful piece of evidence that the technology the Reformers had fought against was in fact very effective, at least against a particular type of enemy. The Gulf War and its high-technology approach also accomplished what the "cheap hawks" could not: restoring a sense of US military greatness. The Vietnam War continued to be a social and political grievance for many, but for the moment, the reform movement's answer to the military malaise of the late 1970s and 1980s was undercut by the success of US technology in kicking the Vietnam Syndrome. Of course, later conflicts, especially in Afghanistan and Iraq, proved just how fleeting that sense of success was.

But the Gulf War represented much more than a referendum on the Military Reform movement. It seemed to indicate that the entire fighter pilot mythos might be somewhat outdated—at least in the form that the Fighter Mafia had assumed it would retain. Air-to-air combat was a very small part of the war. Air superiority had been achieved not with close-turning gun battles with fantasized scarves waving in the breeze but mostly with the large, heavy F-15, using a complex radar, sorting targets, and firing missiles from longer ranges, ending most fights long before they could become gentlemanly duels. This did not mean that fighter-pilot culture or the "knights of the air" mythology had died—as Steven Fino has argued, this culture merely translated itself to a different tactical and technological environment.[58] However, those who had claimed in the 1950s that the era of dogfighting was a relic of the past in the missile age had not been wrong; they had just been early. The vision that the Fighter Mafia had championed of acrobatic gun duels in the sky was only barely relevant by 1991. Although pilots did still prudently train for the possibility of dogfighting, it was not the cornerstone of air power strategy that the Fighter Mafia had envisioned—nor had it ever been.

Conclusion

With these guys, there is an agenda at work here. And
that agenda is to recast the past so as to influence the
future of military affairs.

—General Wilbur Creech

After 1991, the Military Reform debate was
confined to ever smaller sectors, and the movement declined. The flurry
of newspaper coverage virtually ceased, and key caucus members either
abandoned it or lost enthusiasm. About seven months after the war, Senator Nunn argued for ceasing funding for F-16s: "We used 250 [F-16s in Gulf
War operations]," he said. "We have a total of 1,600. How many more do we
need?" Secretary of Defense Cheney argued for canceling the F-16 program
after 1993. Harry Hillaker himself, who had codesigned the Fighting Falcon
with Boyd, acquiesced: "At some point, you've got to recognize that you've
got to shoot that horse. . . . It's time to get on with things."[1] As if to signify
the death of the lightweight fighter program, a matter of months after the
Gulf War ended, the first delivered production F-16 airframe was mounted
in Memorial Park at Langley Air Force Base.[2]

By the mid-1990s, the Military Reform Caucus had disbanded, although it
had largely run out of steam before then.[3] Some members of the movement,
especially Chuck Spinney, tried to keep it going. Remaining in the Pentagon,
he saw himself in a one-man war to eliminate high spending on defense technology, attacking programs like the Navy's F/A-18E/F Super Hornet. He
went as far as to say that Pentagon procurement policy in the 1990s "undermines our form of government." Even his ally and former boss Tom Christie thought such statements were counterproductive. Once a prophet in the

wilderness, by this point Spinney was portrayed by the press as "a solitary voice at the bottom of a well."[4]

Pierre Sprey also moved on. Frustrated, he quit the defense business in 1986, stating that "it would be impossible to build another honest aircraft." Instead, he became a recording engineer and music producer with enough success that Kanye West sampled some of his work. Sprey insisted that the Reformers' ideology of simplicity informed how he recorded and arranged music.[5]

Remnants of the Reformers continued to produce a stream of literature. Winslow Wheeler, a friend of Boyd's and a Senate staffer, released *The Wastrels of Defense: How Congress Sabotages U.S. Security* in 2004, making many of the same arguments that Reformers made. Reform supporters such as Jeffrey Record and James Fallows promoted the book.[6] In 2011, Wheeler collaborated with Sprey, Spinney, Christie, and other Reformers on *The Pentagon Labyrinth*, dedicated to Boyd, which argued many of the same reform movement issues.[7]

Some of the Reformers remained active in government and increasingly associated with the radical wing of conservative US politics. For some of these activists and politicians, reform movement concepts such as suspicion of the federal government and vilification of the media shifted to extremes, and the wariness of technological complexity grew to a distrust of other forms of complexity, including regulatory policy and tax codes. Newt Gingrich often epitomized this approach, but William Lind represented the most striking degree of radicalization extending from the Military Reform movement. Lind's views had been extremist for many years; his colleagues had noted it in the 1970s, not only from the portrait of fascist dictator Benito Mussolini hung in his office.[8] But Lind grew more extreme over the years. He became invested in his concept of "paleoconservatism," identified himself as a monarchist, and promoted unfounded conspiracy theories (such as "cultural Marxism"). His 2014 novel *Victoria* depicted a militia movement violently overthrowing the US government and creating a theocratic fascist state that executes political, religious, and cultural undesirables. His views on warfare evolved from a focus on maneuver warfare, as he advocated with Boyd, to arguing instead that the largest threat facing the state is "fourth generation warfare," in which decentralized, non-state actors attack a state not only in a military sense but also in a cultural and ideological sense.[9]

The ideals of the Military Reform movement and the Fighter Mafia did not disappear. They still influenced debates on defense technology forty years after the height of their influence. For example, President Donald

Trump, early in his administration, espoused similar concepts and policies. In 2017, Trump criticized the F-35 Lightning II, instead preferring the 40 percent cheaper, and technologically simpler, F/A-18E/F Super Hornet—which itself had its origins in the lightweight fighter program that produced the F-16. Trump's earliest budget plan called for the purchase of eighty Hornets, although his views on the plane were inconsistent and contradictory.[10] Trump also argued against the use of electromagnetic catapults on Navy aircraft carriers because of his perception of their being complex and expensive: "It sounded bad to me. Digital. They have digital. What is digital?" he said. "And it's very complicated, you have to be Albert Einstein to figure it out. And I said—and now they want to buy more aircraft carriers. I said, 'What system are you going to be'—'Sir, we're staying with digital.' I said, 'No you're not. You going to goddamned steam, the digital costs hundreds of millions of dollars more money and it's no good.'"[11]

Trapped by Nostalgia

The Military Reform movement has had a strong legacy but was rejected by most of the defense community. "Look, the whole defense reform movement . . . they were focused on the wrong thing. They were focused on equipment," said former CSAF General Merrill McPeak in 2017. "Their real paradigm was the F-86. And the F-16. The minute that the Air Force got its hands on it, they wrecked the F-16, according to these guys, by making it a jack of all trades," he said. "But they forget that the F-86 was the most complicated aircraft in the Korean War. If you want a simple aircraft you should've looked at the MiG-15, right? So they got the argument a little bit wrong." As commander of PACAF, McPeak had overseen a wing of F-16s. He recalled that "they did everything. There wasn't anything the F-16 couldn't do. And the defense reform movement would've said, 'You bastardized it. You should've kept it as a light fighter forever, as a gun fighter. Don't ruin it by putting some of the missiles on it.'" Echoing General Alton Slay's arguments against Sprey, McPeak asserted that the Reformers' policies of cheaper, simpler weapons in more numbers would have led to high casualty rates. Of the A-10 specifically, he said, "Yeah, it was cheap because they were all going to die. Let's be honest here." Ironically, McPeak criticized the Reformers for overemphasizing technology: "The real payoff is when you've got a warrior spirit and your guys just won't quit. They'll fight for you. That they never stumbled onto—the human being element is what we need to reform." Regarding the movement's inspirational figure, McPeak said, "Boyd is highly overrated. . . . People said, 'Wow, a fighter pilot with a brain!' They tended to listen to him when in many respects he was a failed officer and even a failed human being in some ways."[12]

The Reformers, and Boyd in particular, were polarizing. Few people within the defense community had lukewarm thoughts about them. They were lionized, or hated; Boyd was either a heroic messiah, or a terrible influence that needed to be stopped. Both viewpoints do a disservice to Boyd and the movement he spearheaded, and such a binary mode of thinking obscures an understanding of their contributions and why they gained such a strong foothold and devoted following. Boyd, the Fighter Mafia, and the Military Reform movement are best understood as complex and nuanced. They were not saviors, but neither were they villainous, and they did make important contributions to American defense.

Furthermore, their ability to speak to the frustrations felt in the wake of the Vietnam War and provide attractive answers to the perceived problems with US defense resonated powerfully with some people. The level of devotion some expressed toward the Reformers and to Boyd in particular reveals how dissatisfied, restless, and disconnected many people both in and out of the military were with the state of US power in the 1970s and 1980s. In that post-Vietnam moment of crisis, some people needed heroes; Boyd and the Reformers—with the added mystique of their "underdog" nature—appeared heroic.

Boyd's largest contribution was the energy maneuverability theory that he developed and later expanded through his work with Christie, Robert Drabrant, Robert Titus, and many others. EMT shaped aircraft design, evaluation, testing, pilot training, and tactical development for decades. Boyd's "Fast Transients Brief," which focused on methods for fighter pilots to constantly maneuver in ways that created problems for their opponents, continued to be an influential tool for the training of fighter pilots for many years. Boyd also influenced the design of the F-15 and F-16 fighters, although the degree to which he did so is often exaggerated.

Boyd did not work alone, especially in his aircraft design efforts. Sprey, Christie, Everest Riccioni, Chuck Myers, William Ritchie, and others worked to make the F-15 into their ideal fighter design. They received significant help from other, similar independent efforts from higher up the command chain, including Generals Glenn Kent and Otto Glasser. Disappointed by the F-15, fighter advocates worked toward a lightweight fighter that would fit their vision, ultimately resulting in the F-16, with extensive design work from Harry Hillaker. Again, the group received significant help from others such as Kent, Glasser, and Secretary of Defense James Schlesinger. Kent and Glasser's work sometimes involved damage control, as the aggressive advocacy of some fighter advocates like Riccioni were harmful to their cause. The group also stood on the shoulders of years of work by engineers at FDL and NASA on the advanced technologies that made the F-16 possible. The many engineers who worked on these aircraft at contractors such as McDonnell Douglas and General Dynamics also played a key role in both aircraft.

Much mythology has built up surrounding Boyd and the Fighter Mafia's involvement in these projects. They played a role in the creation of both planes—and on the F-16 they played a fundamental role. Works praising Boyd tend to either claim he was responsible for both planes, or that he made the F-15 effective and was responsible for the F-16.[13] This mythology also tends to play up the dramatic elements regarding the secretive nature of meetings, the guerrilla-style efforts against the establishment, the degree to which the Air Staff and others resisted the Fighter Mafia, and the alleged genius of Boyd. Like other hyperbolic claims surrounding him, these tend to originate from Boyd, his friends, or their fans. The stories are often vague and contradictory, depending on the source. There are likely kernels of truth behind many of these tales, but their veracity is unclear. Such legends also do a disservice to the myriad of people from elsewhere in the military and aerospace industry who contributed to both airplanes.

Others within the Air Force, such as Kent, Glasser, and General John Burns, to name a few, argued for aircraft similar to those championed by Boyd, and likely would have done so if he were present or not. Companies like Northrop had been studying lightweight fighter design concepts since before Boyd got involved. The F-15 and F-16 as they existed might not have occurred without Boyd, but something very similar to them likely would have emerged as a result of the efforts of other like-minded groups. Boyd's major contribution, then, was his EMT work that formulated a new methodology for evaluating, designing, and simulating aircraft performance. Just because he was not the first to come up with the concept, or to use the technique of charts to visually depict the results, does not diminish the importance of the EMT project he started. The Air Force would not have seized on EMT in the way it did without Boyd's effort.

The importance of Boyd's later work, such as "Patterns of Conflict," "A Discourse on Winning and Losing," or the OODA loop, is less clear. Some have found them enlightening, and that is important. Many fighter pilots, among others, continue to use the OODA loop as a useful tool. But the lack of original insight, clarity, and applicability of these works will likely limit their staying power. Despite the claims of many Boyd fans that he is the equivalent of Sun Tzu, Clausewitz, or Moses, it is not likely that Boyd's work will still be found useful seven centuries after him. Defenders of Boyd's genius and continuing relevance have yet to make a convincing case beyond saying that Boyd's critics simply do not understand him or that he can only be understood by hearing his lectures in person—that Boyd must be judged not by what he wrote, but what he did not write—by what happens to be preserved on a few poor-quality video recordings.[14] Some of those defenders seem to want to hold to two opposite ideas: that Boyd is an iconoclast who has not gotten the credit he deserves, yet also has been enshrined as one of the most influential thinkers of all time—that he is a great leader and a great rebel. Some contend that the successes of the F-15, F-16, and AirLand Battle are all validations of Boyd's brilliance, despite the fact that he railed against all three.[15]

It should be enough to credit Boyd for his important contributions, especially EMT. Hyperbolic claims that Boyd was a genius, that his intellect shocked and incapacitated those who heard him, that he was the greatest fighter pilot who ever lived (despite relatively little combat time and zero aerial victories), that he is the greatest strategic thinker since Clausewitz—these claims only serve to muddy the waters of history. In addition, too little attention has been paid to Boyd's personality flaws and failure of leadership. The "fighter jock" traits that he took to such an extreme alienated many of the very people he was trying to reach. These traits were far too often celebrated. Boyd's life demonstrates that radical hypermasculinity is not a substitute for leadership; it is a self-destructive, toxic force that undermines one's goals.

Regarding the Military Reform movement broadly, it also made important contributions, the most significant being the creation of the Directorate of Operational Test and Evaluation in 1983 as part of the 1984 Department of Defense Authorization Act. The movement also helped shape the debate of the second interwar period in the 1970s and 1980s. As a foil to the Pentagon, the Reformers asked many important questions that forced the defense establishment to conduct much-needed self-evaluation and justification. That the Reformers did not achieve all their goals is not a mark of failure.

Ultimately the Reformers became trapped by nostalgia. Constantly looking backward, they sought to re-create earlier forms of combat, especially the gun-battle aerial dogfights of the World Wars, or at least a romanticized image of them. Learning from history is wise. But the movement tended to assume that the problems of the past would remain the problems of the future. Since missiles were less effective in Vietnam, they would never be effective in the future. Since past air-to-air combat tactics relied on maneuverability after the merge to get in position for a gun kill, that paradigm would not change. This was not the case.

Air combat did change. The Air Force adapted to the evolving nature of aerial warfare. For example, in June 2017, two USAF F-15Es shot down Iranian Shahed 129 drones, and F/A-18 pilot Lieutenant Commander Michael Tremel shot down a piloted Syrian Su-22, sparking a flurry of debate about whether air-to-air combat was "back" and what that meant for pilots.[16] But these were isolated events, and the very fact that the discussion centered on whether air combat had truly "returned" showed that it had already left in the twenty-first century. Indeed, from 1973 to 2021, no individual US pilot has earned more than three victory credits—and only four US pilots have done that, the last in 1999. Similarly, these few victories were accomplished with missiles; no US fighter plane shot down an enemy plane with a gun in those years.[17]

Speaking to the nature of twenty-first-century aerial battle, Lieutenant Colonel John Anderson, commander of the 353rd Combat Training Squadron, said in 2019, "The dogfight in modern air warfare takes place at what we call BVR, beyond visible range. So generally, you're killing them off, or they're killing you, and you'll never even know that they're there." He clarified, "The dogfight hasn't gone away, but it is a bit of a contingency at this point. If you find yourself that close to an enemy, with today's technology, something's probably gone wrong." Although Boyd might disapprove of fighting completely pre-merge, with long-range radar-guided missiles, pilots in 2021 do still rely on his energy maneuverability theories and other concepts to guide their decision making.[18]

Fighter pilots have retained a privileged place within the Air Force, despite the realities that the service supports many missions, most of its personnel are not pilots, and most of its pilots do not engage in air-to-air combat training. A common joke heard around the service is that one cannot make a leadership position in the Air Force without "flying a pointy-nose." This is exaggerated, as many officers make the rank of general from a variety of backgrounds. However, from 1982 to 2021, all the chiefs of staff of the Air Force have been fighter pilots, with only one exception: General Norton A. Schwartz, whose background was in airlift and special operations.[19]

Memorial displays in key locations show a similar preference for fighters. Most Air Force bases have displays of aircraft associated with the history of the particular base, but the two main educational institutions of the Air Force stand apart. The Air Force Academy grounds in Colorado Springs has ten outdoor aircraft on display, and seven of them are related to air-to-air combat: an F-15, an F-16, an F-105, the F-100 Super Sabre flown by fighter ace Brigadier General James "Robbie" Risner, a T-38 Talon honoring the Thunderbirds demonstration team, and the F-4 Phantom in which Brigadier

General Richard Ritchie became the first US Air Force ace of the Vietnam War. Also included is one of the A-10 aircraft that scored an aerial victory against a helicopter in the Gulf War in 1991. Even when displaying a ground-attack plane, the displays emphasize the air-to-air role.

Maxwell Air Force Base, billed as "the intellectual and leadership center of the Air Force" and home of most of the service's education institutions such as the Air Command and Staff College and Air War College (among others), shows a similar pattern. Although there is a B-52 bomber on display (ironically on a street named "OODA Loop" after Boyd's concept), along with a World War II–era B-25 Mitchell, the first plane display greeting entering visitors is a T-38. The display at the main entrance to the academic area consists of an F-86 Sabre, an F-100 Super Sabre, an F-101 Voodoo, an F-105 Thunderchief, and an F-4 Phantom II. Of course, there are practical reasons to display smaller aircraft that take up less space and are easier and cheaper to install and maintain. But the impression that fighters are perhaps more important to the service is clear.

This emphasis is not necessarily misplaced, as tactical fighters play a large role in the Air Force. But the prominence placed on fighter roles and experiences reflects the degree of influence the culture and beliefs of the relatively small fighter pilot community had on technological decision making in the Air Force. Williamson Murray and Mark Grimsley have stated, "Many, if not most, case studies of the making of strategy would make no sense without consideration of the role of belief systems."[20] What they argue of strategy is also true for technology. Military technology does not develop along a predetermined linear path of advancement, nor does it have a mind of its own. The notion that defense technologies stem solely from operational requirements can put limits on design options, even unconsciously. When designing new technologies, institutions, including militaries, should be aware that their technological decisions are influenced by cultural prejudices. Technology is an outgrowth of culture. Its development is shaped by belief systems. Humans build things, including weapons, at least in part because their culture has led them to think that certain weapons are cool.

The Fighter Mafia and the Reformers thought air-to-air combat was cool, and they wanted to build airplanes that excelled at that role. In their nostalgia, these groups were true to their roots, the culture of fighter pilots that looked to the past—a constructed, largely unreal past of knightly duels in the sky between maneuverable planes, pitting one man against another in a chivalrous battle of honor with white scarves blowing in the wind. This culture revolved around the elements of aggressiveness, individualism, specific fighter technologies, heroic imagery, and a protective community—all of these intertwined with hypermasculinity. Although fighter pilots embodied many of these elements to varying degrees, the Fighter Mafia and the Reformers were at a far extreme end of a spectrum, exhibiting those elements whether they were active fighter pilots or not, even if they were flying a desk in a Pentagon office.

The YF-16 prototype was the closest this group got to achieving their goal of a lightweight, clear-skies, day fighter that emphasized maneuverability to the exclusion of other capabilities. Phillip Oestricher, the first man to fly the YF-16, said the plane was "a pure air-to-air fighter airplane. . . . It's not complicated with all kinds of look through the floorboard sensors and all of this. It was a pure airframe." Recalling the medieval imagery from the earliest days of fighter pilot culture, Oestricher said that the YF-16 "was the Camelot of aeronautical engineering."[21] It was not adopted by the Air Force in its original form, but was modified in a way that, to the Fighter Mafia, compromised its purpose and undermined their vision.

With the YF-16, the knights of the air had built their Camelot. Just as King Arthur was—as one version of the legend goes—lost to the mists of Avalon, so the dream of recapturing the romanticized vision of the knights of the air faded away.

NOTES

Introduction

1. Craig Brown, *Debrief: A Complete History of U.S. Aerial Engagements, 1981 to the Present* (Atglen, PA: Schiffer Military History, 2007), 102–108.

2. Dan Hampton, *Viper Pilot: A Memoir of Air Combat* (New York: William Morrow, 2012), 23, emphasis in original.

3. John Darrell Sherwood, *Officers in Flight Suits: The Story of American Air Force Fighter Pilots in the Korean War* (New York: NYU Press, 1996), 6; Steven A. Fino, *Tiger Check: Automating the US Air Force Fighter Pilot in Air-to-Air Combat, 1950–1980* (Baltimore: Johns Hopkins University Press, 2017), 18–19.

4. For example, see complaints about pilot culture being "under attack" owing to officers being held legally accountable for their actions, in Rob Burgon, *Piano Burning and Other Fighter Pilot Traditions* (Salt Lake City: Slipstream, 2016), 20–21.

5. Brian McAllister Linn, *Echo of Battle: The Army's Way of War* (Cambridge. MA: Harvard University Press, 2007), 6–7.

6. Wade A. Scrogham, *Combat Relevant Task: The Test and Evaluation of the Lightweight Fighter Prototypes* (Edwards Air Force Base, CA: Air Force Test Center History Office, 2014), 67.

7. David Nye, *Technology Matters: Questions to Live With* (Cambridge, MA: MIT Press, 2007), 19–21, 47.

8. David Nye, *America as Second Creation: Technology and Narratives of New Beginnings* (Cambridge, MA: MIT Press, 2004), 1–7.

9. Thomas P. Hughes, "Technological Momentum," in *Does Technology Drive History? The Dilemma of Technological Determinism*, ed. Merritt Roe Smith and Leo Marx (Cambridge, MA: MIT Press, 1994); See also Hughes, *Networks of Power: Electrification in Western Society, 1880–1930* (Baltimore: Johns Hopkins University Press, 1983).

10. Wayne Lee, *Barbarians and Brothers: Anglo-American Warfare, 1500–1865* (Oxford: Oxford University Press, 2011); and Lee, "Mind and Matter—Cultural Analysis in American Military History: A Look at the State of the Field," *Journal of American History* 93 (March 2007): 1116–1142; Isabel V. Hull, *Absolute Destruction: Military Culture and the Practices of War in Imperial Germany* (Ithaca, NY: Cornell University Press, 2005).

11. J. E. Lendon, *Soldiers and Ghosts: A History of Battle in Classical Antiquity* (New Haven, CT: Yale University Press, 2005); Antulio Echevarria, *After Clausewitz: German Military Thinkers before the Great War* (Lawrence: University Press of Kansas, 2000). The cultural approach I am taking to understanding US fighter pilots is related to, but distinct from, the "ways of war" school of military history that attempts to link

battlefield actions to specific cultures. For a brief summary and critique of the "ways of war" school see Antulio Echevarria, *Reconsidering the American Way of War: US Military Practice from the Revolution to Afghanistan* (Washington, DC: Georgetown University Press, 2014). The seminal work on the American way of war is Russell Weigley, *The American Way of War: A History of United States Military Strategy and Policy* (New York: Macmillan, 1973). That work's argument has been widely critiqued, not least of all by the author himself, in Weigley, "Response to Brian McAllister Linn," *Journal of Military History* 66, no. 2 (April 2002), 531–533. Other scholars have attempted to draw direct lines between their interpretation of national or regional cultures with specific tactics and strategies, although the level of abstraction required of such a broad view can sometimes problematize those arguments; see, for example, Adrian Lewis, *The American Culture of War* (New York: Routledge, 2012).

12. Fino, *Tiger Check*; Timothy Schultz, *The Problem with Pilots: How Physicians, Engineers, and Airpower Enthusiasts Redefined Flight* (Baltimore: Johns Hopkins University Press, 2018).

13. Carl H. Builder, *The Masks of War: American Military Styles in Strategy and Analysis* (Baltimore: Johns Hopkins University Press, 1989); Builder, *The Icarus Syndrome: The Role of Air Power Theory in the Evolution and Fate of the U.S. Air Force* (New York: Routledge, 2002); Mike Worden, *Rise of the Fighter Generals: The Problem of Air Force Leadership, 1945–1982* (Maxwell Air Force Base, AL: Air University Press, 1998); Sherwood, *Officers in Flight Suits*; Sherwood, *Fast Movers: Jet Pilots and the Vietnam Experience* (New York: Free Press, 1999).

14. Linda R. Robertson, *The Dream of Civilized Warfare: World War I Flying Aces and the American Imagination* (Minneapolis: University of Minnesota Press, 2003).

15. By enthusiast literature, I refer to books that focus on operational or technical details of military aircraft, are aimed a variety of audiences from veterans to scale modelers, but are not subjected to peer review. Some of these works are unreliable, but many are thoroughly researched. The most useful for this book were Jay Miller, *The General Dynamics F-16 Fighting Falcon* (Austin, TX: Aerofax, 1982), and James Stevenson, *McDonnell Douglas F-15 Eagle* (Fallbrook, CA: Aero, 1978).

16. Kenneth P. Werrell, *Chasing the Silver Bullet: U.S. Air Force Weapons Development from Vietnam to Desert Storm* (Washington, DC: Smithsonian Books, 2003); Brian Laslie, *The Air Force Way of War: U.S. Tactics and Training after Vietnam* (Lexington: University Press of Kentucky, 2015). See also Craig C. Hannah, *Striving for Air Superiority: The Tactical Air Command in Vietnam* (College Station: Texas A&M University Press, 2002).

17. Robert Coram, *Boyd: The Fighter Pilot Who Changed the Art of War* (New York: Little, Brown, 2002); Grant Hammond, *The Mind of War: John Boyd and American Security* (Washington, DC: Smithsonian Books, 2001). Other authors who have examined specific aspects of Boyd's career but retain the reverent tone include James Burton, *The Pentagon Wars: Reformers Challenge the Old Guard* (Annapolis, MD: Naval Institute Press, 1993); Ian T. Brown, *A New Conception of War: John Boyd, the U.S. Marines, and Maneuver Warfare* (Quantico, VA: Marine Corps University Press, 2018); Frans P. B. Osinga, *Science, Strategy and War: The Strategic Theory of John Boyd* (London: Routledge, 2007); and Osinga, "The Enemy as a Complex Adaptive System: John Boyd and Airpower in the Postmodern Era," in *Airpower Reborn: The Strategic Concepts of John Warden and John Boyd*, ed. John Andreas Olsen (Annapolis, MD: Naval Institute

Press, 2015); David S. Fadok, "John Boyd and John Warden: Air Power's Quest for Strategic Paralysis" (thesis, School of Advanced Airpower Studies, Maxwell AFB; Air University Press, 1995).

18. John Andreas Olsen, "Boyd Revisited: A Great Mind with a Touch of Madness," *Air Power History*, Winter 2016, 7–16; David Metz, "Boydmania," *Air and Space Power Journal* 18 (Fall 2004): 98–108; James Hasík, "Beyond the Briefing: Theoretical and Practical Problems in the Works and Legacy of John Boyd," *Contemporary Security Policy* 34, no. 3 (2013): 583–599.

19. Boyd himself wrote very little, but the slide shows meant to accompany his presentations have become somewhat famous. A collection of the bulk of Boyd's public work is John R. Boyd, *A Discourse on Winning and Losing*, ed. Grant T. Hammond (Maxwell Air Force Base, AL: Air University Press, 2018).

20. The most prominent of these include James Fallows, *National Defense* (New York: Random House, 1981); Burton, *Pentagon Wars*; Winslow Wheeler and Lawrence J. Korb, *Military Reform: An Uneven History and an Uncertain Future* (Stanford, CA: Stanford University Press, 2007); Gary Hart and William S. Lind, *America Can Win: The Case for Military Reform* (Bethesda, MD: Adler & Adler, 1986).

21. Walter Kross, *Military Reform: The High-Tech Debate in Tactical Air Forces* (Fort McNair, Washington, DC: National Defense University Press, 1985). Critiques of the movement were common in contemporary popular newspapers, magazines, and service journals. For a brief noncontemporary analysis not written by the Reformers see John T. Correll, "The Reformers," *Air Force Magazine*, February 2008, 40–44.

22. Lendon, *Soldiers and Ghosts*.

1. The Fighter Pilot with a Thousand Faces

1. Burgon, *Piano Burning*, 2–4.

2. Lee, *Barbarians and Brothers*, 6; see also Lee, "Mind and Matter," 1116–1142.

3. Hull, *Absolute Destruction*, 2.

4. Hull, 94–97.

5. Edgar H. Schein, "How Culture Forms, Develops, and Changes," in *Gaining Control of the Corporate Culture*, ed. Ralph H. Kilmann et al. (San Francisco: Jossey-Bass, 1985), 19–20.

6. Alan L. Wilkins and Kerry J. Patterson, "You Can't Get There from Here: What Will Make Culture-Change Projects Fail," in Killman et al., *Gaining Control*, 268.

7. Hull, *Absolute Destruction*, 96.

8. Schein, "How Culture Forms," 19.

9. Mary Jo Hatch and Majken Schultz, "The Dynamics of Organizational Identity," *Human Relations* 55 (August 2002): 1000. See also Jonathan Riley, *At the Fulcrum of Air Force Identity: Balancing the Internal and External Pressures of Image and Culture*, Drew Paper No. 11 (Maxwell Air Force Base, AL: Air University Press, 2014), 12–13.

10. Builder, *Masks*, 19, 22.

11. Builder, *Icarus Syndrome*, 35.

12. Builder, *Masks*, 23.

13. Hull, *Absolute Destruction*, 96; Schein, "How Culture Forms," 24–27.

14. For the role of Strategic Air Command and bomber culture broadly see Caroline F. Ziemke, "In the Shadow of the Giant: USAF Tactical Air Command in the Era of Strategic Bombing, 1945–1955" (PhD diss., Ohio State University, 1989); Benjamin Lambeth, *The Transformation of American Air Power* (Ithaca, NY: Cornell University Press, 2000); Hannah, *Striving for Air Superiority*; Marshall Michel, "The Revolt of the Majors: How the Air Force Changed after Vietnam" (PhD diss., Auburn University, 2006); Earl H. Tilford, *Crosswinds: The Air Force's Setup in Vietnam* (College Station: Texas A&M University Press, 1993); Perry McCoy Smith, *The Air Force Plans for Peace, 1943–1945* (Baltimore: Johns Hopkins University Press, 1970).

15. Ioannis Koskinas, *Black Hats and White Hats: The Effect of Organizational Culture and Institutional Identity on the Twenty-Third Air Force*, CADRE Paper No. 24 (Maxwell Air Force Base, AL: Air University Press, 2006), 18, 20.

16. Quoted in Worden, *Rise of the Fighter Generals*, 55.

17. Koskinas, *Black Hats*, 19.

18. Schein, "How Culture Forms," 21–27.

19. I say allegedly because kill claims and victory credits are notoriously unreliable owing to the problems of verification, the desire of all sides to increase numbers, and the emotional nature of such claims. Douglas C. Dildy and Warren E. Thompson, in their discussion of victory credits during the Korean War, conclude that using kill claims to establish a kill ratio is "grossly fallacious arithmetic" and that aerial victory credits "are more closely related to political ends, propaganda grist, and individual pilot glory" than to actual combat results. See Dildy and Thompson, *F-86 Sabre vs MiG-15: Korea 1950–1953* (Long Island City, NY: Osprey, 2013), 71–74.

20. Marshall L. Michel III, *Clashes: Air Combat over North Vietnam, 1965–1972* (Annapolis, MD: Naval Institute Press, 1997), 166–167; see also Fino, *Tiger Check*, 158–159; C. R. Anderegg, *Sierra Hotel: Flying Air Force Fighters in the Decade after Vietnam* (Washington, DC: Air Force History and Museums Program, 2001), 40.

21. Quoted in Joseph Tuso, *Singing the Vietnam Blues: Songs of the Air Force in Southeast Asia* (College Station: Texas A&M University Press, 1990), 112.

22. Sherwood, *Fast Movers*, 190–191.

23. Hampton, *Viper Pilot*, 48–51; Anderegg, *Sierra Hotel*, 40, examples of WSOs participating in fighter pilot recreational culture on 49.

24. Quote in Robin Olds, with Christina Olds and Ed Rasimus, *Fighter Pilot: The Memoirs of Legendary Ace Robin Olds* (New York: St. Martin's, 2010), 78.

25. Major General John Alison Corona Ace interview, January 27, 1977, Air Force Historical Research Agency, K239.0512–1065 (hereafter cited as Alison OHI), 43.

26. Merrill A. McPeak, *Hangar Flying* (Lake Oswego, OR: Lost Wingman, 2012), 281–282.

27. Sherwood, *Fast Movers*, 33.

28. Kenneth P. Werrell, *Sabres over MiG Alley: The F-86 and the Battle for Air Superiority in Korea* (Annapolis, MD: Naval Institute Press, 2005), 183–185.

29. David R. "Buff" Honodel, *The Phantom Vietnam War: An F-4 Pilot's Combat over Laos* (Denton: University of North Texas Press, 2018), 7–8. For an exploration of the differences in status between ground-attack pilots and air-to-air pilots particular to the Korean War see also Sherwood, *Officers in Flight Suits*, 98–115.

30. Rick Newman and Don Shepperd, *Bury Us Upside Down: The Misty Pilots and the Secret Battle for the Ho Chi Minh Trail* (New York: Ballantine Books, 2006), xx.

31. McPeak, *Hangar Flying*, 278.

32. Don Shepperd, ed., *Misty: First Person Stories of the F-100 Mist Fast FACs in the Vietnam War* (Don Shepperd, 2002), 4.

33. Quoted in "Knights of the Air," *Literary Digest* 49, no. 18 (October 31, 1914): 841.

34. Bennett Molter, *Knights of the Air* (New York: D. Appleton, 1918), 11–12.

35. Fino, *Tiger Check*, 18.

36. Robertson, *Dream of Civilized Warfare*, xiii–xv. This theme is common in many works of World War I aviation; for some examples see also Peter Fritzsche, *A Nation of Fliers: German Aviation and the Popular Imagination* (Cambridge, MA: Harvard University Press, 1992), 82–83; Lee Kennett, *The First Air War: 1914–1918* (New York: Free Press, 1991); John Murrow, "The First World War, 1914–1919," in *A History of Air Warfare*, ed. John Andreas Olsen (Dulles, VA: Potomac Books, 2010). The idea is explored and somewhat critiqued in James Hamilton-Patterson, *Marked for Death: The First War in the Air* (New York: Pegasus Books, 2016).

37. Hamilton-Patterson, *Marked for Death*, 154.

38. For a full exploration of the development of military theory leading up to World War I see Echevarria, *After Clausewitz*.

39. Quoted in Echevarria, *After Clausewitz*, 80.

40. This concept is explored more fully in Robertson, *Dream of Civilized Warfare*, Wilson quoted on xv.

41. Kennett, *First Air War*, 159.

42. Kennett, 152–157.

43. Fritzsche, *Nation of Fliers*, 76.

44. Fritzsche, 86.

45. Echevarria, *After Clausewitz*, 166–174, quote on 167. The most influential work on the public fascination with aircraft in the early twentieth century is Joseph Corn, *The Winged Gospel: America's Romance with Aviation, 1900–1950* (Oxford: Oxford University Press, 1983); see also Michael Sherry, *The Rise of American Air Power: The Creation of Armageddon* (New Haven, CT: Yale University Press, 1987).

46. Fritzsche, *Nation of Fliers*, 86–87.

47. Quoted in Sherry, *Rise of American Air Power*, 39.

48. Hamilton-Patterson, *Marked for Death*, 191; Fritzsche, *Nation of Fliers*, 93.

49. Mike Spick, *The Ace Factor: Air Combat and the Role of Situational Awareness* (Shrewsbury, UK: Airlife, 1988), 6.

50. Robertson, *Dream of Civilized Warfare*, 264.

51. Robertson, quote on 113; the argument is explored throughout the work, particularly in 87–301.

52. Quoted in Hamilton-Patterson, *Marked for Death*, 118.

53. Fritzsche, *Nation of Fliers*, 65; Kennett, *First Air War*, 75.

54. Pierre de Cazenove de Pradines, "Triumphs and Tribulations," interview conducted and edited by Jon Guttman, no date (c. 1978), University of Texas at Dallas (hereafter UTD), James Kerr Papers, box 30, folder 3, 68–69.

55. Floyd Gibbons, "The Red Knight of Germany," *Liberty*, November 5, 1927, 61, 65.

56. Hamilton-Patterson, *Marked for Death*, 168.

57. Michael D. Collins, "A Fear of Flying: Diagnosing Traumatic Neurosis among British Aviators of the Great War," *First World War Studies* 6 (July 2015): 190.

58. Diary of Walter L. Avery, print edition, 1980, UTD George Williams Collection, box 27, folder 4 (hereafter cited as Avery Diary), 38, 63–66, 68, 71, 21, 83.

59. Henry Clay to James Ashton Clay, December 22, 1917, and February 22, 1918; Henry Clay to Jas A. Clay, February 6, 1918, UTD, Henry Clay Papers, box 1, folder 10.

60. Hamilton-Patterson, *Marked for Death*, 2.

61. Burgon, *Piano Burning*, 19, 16, emphasis in original.

62. Burgon, 16–20. Roll calls originate from World War I post-battle roll calls of pilots to determine any casualties. Piano burnings are literal: pilots obtain a piano, destroy it, then burn it as a bonding exercise. The origin of this practice is unknown and debated. See Burgon, 35–45, 125–127; and Roy Heidicker, "Battle of Britain: RAF Piano Burning Tradition," 4th Fighter Wing, Seymour Johnson Air Force Base, August 18, 2017, https://www.seymourjohnson.af.mil/News/Commentaries/Display/Article/1282899/battle-of-britain-raf-piano-burning-tradition/.

63. Werrell, *Sabres over MiG Alley*, 145.

64. Olds, *Fighter Pilot*, 254, 324–325.

65. Quoted in Fino, *Tiger Check*, 18.

66. Olds, *Fighter Pilot*, 6. Although quite plausible, this story must be taken with some skepticism, as the list of World War I pilots that Olds claims to have met as a child includes Major Edward Mannock, who died four years before Olds's birth.

67. Thomas Gladysz, "Now We're in the Air: The Silent Cinema and Aviation," SFGate, February 23, 2012; Shawna Kelly, *Aviators in Early Hollywood* (Charleston, SC: Arcadia, 2008), 9; Stephen Pendo, *Aviation in the Cinema* (Metuchen, NJ: Scarecrow, 1985), 3; Barbara Tepa Lupack, *Richard E. Norman and Race Filmmaking* (Bloomington: Indiana University Press, 2014), 162–179.

68. Many of these works have been archived, remastered, and rereleased via Age of Aces Books: http://www.ageofaces.net/, accessed October 7, 2020.

69. James J. Hudson, *Hostile Skies: A Combat History of the American Air Service in World War I* (Syracuse, NY: Syracuse University Press, 1968), 33

70. For a detailed examination of aviation in US films see Pendo, *Aviation in the Cinema*.

71. John T. Correll, "A Brush with the Air Force," *Air Force Magazine*, July 2007, 42–49; and "Up in the Air with Milton Caniff," *Air Force Magazine*, April 2013, 66–73; see also Steve Call, *Selling Air Power: Military Aviation and American Popular Culture after World War II* (College Station: Texas A&M University Press, 2009), 90.

72. Ed Rasimus, *Palace Cobra: A Fighter Pilot in the Vietnam Air War* (New York: St. Martin's, 2006), 119.

73. Olds, *Fighter Pilot*, 314.

74. Olds, 6, 83.

75. Quoted in Fino, *Tiger Check*, 18.

76. Hamilton-Patterson, *Marked for Death*, 3–6.

77. Jim Beard, "WonderCon 2012: Captain Marvel," Marvel.com, accessed December 10, 2018, https://www.webcitation.org/6BjZkxz9A?url=http://marvel.com/news/story/18290/wondercon_2012_captain_marvel#.

78. Worden, *Rise of the Fighter Generals*, 7, 12–13.

79. *Weapons System Evaluation Group Report 116: Air-to-Air Encounters in Southeast Asia* (hereafter cited as Red Baron Report), vol. 1 (Arlington, VA: Institute for Defense Analyses Systems Evaluation Division, 1967), 1, 7, 13.

80. John Boyd Corona Ace oral history interview, January 22, 1977, K239.0512–1066. The same introduction precedes each Corona Ace interview.

81. Alison OHI, 107–110.

82. General Frank F. Everest, oral history interview, August 23–25, 1977, USAF Historical Research Agency, K239.0512–957 (hereafter cited as Everest OHI), 365–366.

83. Fino, *Tiger Check*, 19.

2. "You Can Tell a Fighter Pilot (But You Can't Tell Him Much)"

1. Brigadier General Frank L. Gailer, Corona Ace interview, January 19, 1977, USAF Oral History Program, USAF Historical Research Agency, K239.0512–1061 (hereafter cited as Gailer CA interview), 21, 32, 17–18.

2. T. B. Murphy, *Kiffin Rockwell, the Lafayette Escadrille and the Birth of the United States Air Force* (Jefferson, NC: McFarland, 2016), 122.

3. Kenneth W. Clendenin, "Who Said Rats," 147th Aero Squadron, UTD, Ola Sater Collection, box 17, folder 10, 20. Emphasis in original.

4. Quoted in Murphy, *Kiffin Rockwell*, 119.

5. "Ceremony of Unveiling the Tablet to the Fallen of the 22nd Pursuit Squadron, American Expeditionary Force, American Flying Club, February 28, 1920," UTD, Ola Sater Collection, box 17, folder 9.

6. John T. Correll, "The Legend of Frank Luke," *Air Force Magazine*, August 1, 2009, https://www.airforcemag.com/article/0809luke/; Hudson, *Hostile Skies*, 123, 167–168, 182–183, 281; Robertson, *Dream of Civilized Warfare*, 372–373; W. David Lewis, *Eddie Rickenbacker: An American Hero in the Twentieth Century* (Baltimore: Johns Hopkins University Press, 2005), 190–191.

7. Alison OHI, 6, 15.

8. Gailer CA interview, 6.

9. Adolf Galland, *The First and the Last: The Rise and Fall of the German Fighter Forces, 1938–1945*, trans. Mervyn Savill (New York: Bantam, 1978, originally published New York: Henry Holt, 1954), 15, 30, 53–54.

10. Gailer CA interview, 54.

11. Chuck Yeager and Leo Janos, *Yeager: An Autobiography* (Toronto: Bantam Books, 1986), 15, 83–85.

12. Colonel David Lee "Tex" Hill, Corona Ace interview, January 20, 1977, USAF Historical Research Agency, K239.0512–1063 (hereafter cited as Hill CA interview), 28, 39, 190, 54, 58, 60.

13. Sherwood, *Officers in Flight Suits*, 34–35.

14. Quoted in Fino, *Tiger Check*, 3.

15. Sherwood, *Officers in Flight Suits*, 85.

16. Werrell, *Sabres*, 146–149.

17. Werrell, 153–155. Research into Soviet records has called Jabara's status as the first US jet ace into question. See Xiaoming Zhang, *Red Wings over the Yalu: China, the Soviet Union, and the Air War in Korea* (College Station: Texas A&M University Press, 2003), 129 and n21.

18. Everest OHI, 182.

19. Anderegg, *Sierra Hotel*, xii, 47, 51–52.

20. Interview of Robin Olds, July 12, 1967, USAF Oral History Program, K239.0512–160, 45–46.

21. Anderegg, *Sierra Hotel*, 49.

22. Hampton, *Viper Pilot*, 48–49.

23. Fino, *Tiger Check*, 20.

24. Quoted in Fino, 20.

25. Livingston Irving interview, October 23, 1964, Cross and Cockade Bay Area Chapter, UTD, Ola Sater Collection, box 18, folder 14, 5.

26. *Fighting in the Air*, S.S. 591, April 1918, UTD, Henry Clay Papers, box 1, folder 18, 7, 14, 17.

27. Henry Clay to Jas A. Clay, February 6, 1918, UTD, Henry Clay Papers, box 1, folder 10.

28. Avery Diary, 8.

29. Avery Diary, 10. Originally published in *McClure's Magazine*, September 1917, 34. Avery's quoted version of the poem isn't perfectly accurate.

30. Gailer CA interview, 15.

31. Everest OHI, 365–366.

32. Quoted in Sherwood, *Officers in Flight Suits*, 36, 71.

33. Quoted in Fino, *Tiger Check*, 88.

34. Call, *Selling Air Power*, 139.

35. James Salter, *The Hunters* (Berkeley: Counterpoint, 1997; originally published 1956), 193.

36. Call, *Selling Air Power*, 142.

37. Tuso, *Singing*, 22–24. Line break indications added.

38. Sherwood, *Fast Movers*, 18.

39. Fino, *Tiger Check*, 158–159; Anderegg, *Sierra Hotel*, 40.

40. Tuso, *Singing*, 82–83. Line break indications added.

41. Rasimus, *Palace Cobra*, 26.

42. Tuso, *Singing*, 12–14, emphasis in original.

43. Hampton, *Viper Pilot*, 48, 51.

44. Billy Mitchell, introduction to "No Parachutes" by Alan Winslow, *Liberty Magazine*, February 25, 1933, 6, UTD, Ola Sater Collection, box 18, folder 17.

45. Gailer CA interview, 18.

46. Shown in Fino, *Tiger Check*, 10.

47. Sherwood, *Fast Movers*, 13.

48. Hamilton-Patterson, *Marked for Death*, 49, 64.

49. Clendenin, "Who Said Rats," 8.

50. Livingston Irving interview, 3, 6–7.

51. Avery Diary, 38, 49.

52. Alison OHI, 9, 96.

53. Gailer CA interview, 42.

54. Both quoted in John C. McManus, *Deadly Sky: The American Combat Airman in World War II* (New York: NAL Caliber, 2000), 50–51.

55. Robert F. Dorr, "Why the P-38 Flunked in Europe," *Aviation History* 24 (May 2014): 22.

56. Olds, *Fighter Pilot*, 96–97.

57. Quoted in McManus, *Deadly Sky*, 57.

58. Gailer CA interview, 55–56.

59. Quoted in Fino, *Tiger Check*, 77, 79.

60. Quoted in Sherwood, *Officers in Flight Suits*, 64.

61. Olds, *Fighter Pilot*, 294.

62. Olds, 313–314.

63. Olds, 292–293.

64. Burgon, *Piano Burning*, 4, 16, 37.

65. Gailer CA interview, 34, 28, 31, 74.

66. Quoted in McManus, *Deadly Sky*, 396–397.

67. Quoted in Anderegg, *Sierra Hotel*, 47.

68. Sherwood, *Fast Movers*, 61.

69. Clendenin, "Who Said Rats," 7.

70. William E. Barrett, "Squadron Parade: 90th Squadron," *Warbirds*, September 1934, 111.

71. Gailer CA interview, 24–26, 31.

72. Alison CA interview, 11.

73. Anderegg, *Sierra Hotel*, 48–49.

74. Robertson, *Dream of Civilized Warfare*, 170, xviii.

75. Jeanne Holm, *Women in the Military: An Unfinished Revolution*, rev. ed. (Novato, CA: Presidio, 1993), 64–65, 126, 314–323.

76. Barrett, "Squadron Parade," 109.

77. Winslow, "No Parachutes," 22.

78. Margaret Minis, "High Flying: A World War I Flying Ace Remembers His Exploits with War and the Ladies," *Georgia Gazette and Journal Record* (Savannah), May 28, 1979.

79. Hill CA interview, 54.

80. Sherwood, *Officers in Flight Suits*, 72, 79.

81. Sherwood, 64.

82. Rasimus, Palace Cobra, xiii.

83. Rasimus, *Palace Cobra*, 4, 10, 24.

3. What We Mean When We Say "Fighter"

1. Quoted in Frederick A. Johnsen, "Astronaut Armstrong Recalls the Origins of Test Pilot Society," NASA Public Affairs Office, October 1, 2005, https://www.nasa.gov/missions/research/armstrong_speech.html.

2. Charles E. Myers oral history interview, by Jacob Neufeld, USAF Historical Research Agency, K239.0512–971, July 18, 1973 (hereafter cited as Myers OHI), 2.

3. "The History of SETP," accessed June 14, 2017, http://www.setp.org/about-setp/history.html.

4. Myers OHI, 3–4.

5. Myers OHI, 5–6.

6. Steven A. Fino, "'All the Missiles Work': Technological Dislocations and Military Innovation," Drew Paper No. 12 (Maxwell Air Force Base, AL: Air University Press, 2015), 51–73; Michael H. Gorn, *Harnessing the Genie: Science and Technology*

Forecasting for the Air Force, 1944–1986 (Washington, DC: Office of Air Force History, US Air Force, 1989), 5–7; Major General John J. Burns oral history interview, March 22, 1973, USAF Historical Research Agency, K239.0512–961 (hereafter cited as Burns OHI), 14.

7. Myers OHI, 6–8.

8. Myers OHI, 8–11.

9. Daniel Mark Gillespie, "Mission Emphasis and the Determination of Needs for New Weapon Systems" (PhD diss., Massachusetts Institute of Technology, 2009), 211.

10. Myers OHI, 12–15, emphasis in original.

11. Lieutenant General Arthur C. Agan oral history interview, April 19–22, 1976, USAF Historical Research Agency, K239.0512–900 (hereafter cited as Agan OHI), 84, 95–96, 398, 446.

12. Grant Hammond, introduction to Boyd, *Discourse*, 2–3; and Hammond, *Mind of War*, 200–201.

13. Coram, *Boyd*, 89, 7.

14. Carl Prine, "Q & A with Merrill 'Tony' McPeak," *San Diego Union Tribune*, November 23, 2017.

15. Email, Wilbur Creech, forwarded to Robert Coram via John C. Jones, March 19, 2000, Marine Corps Archives and Records Division, Quantico, VA: Robert Coram Personal Papers (hereafter cited as Coram Papers), box 3, folder 12.

16. John Boyd Corona Ace oral history interview, January 22, 1977, K239.0512–1066 (hereafter cited as Boyd CA interview), 6.

17. Boyd Soldier Qualification Card, Coram Papers, box 9, folder 6.

18. Coram, *Boyd*, 31–32.

19. Boyd CA interview, 7–10, 12.

20. Boyd CA interview, 17–21; email, Jock Maitland to Robert Coram, "John Boyd," June 8, 2000, Coram Papers, box 9, folder 6; Boyd Individual Flight Records, April–July 1953, Coram Papers, box 23, folder 11.

21. Boyd CA interview, 22, 27–29.

22. Boyd CA interview, 55, 58.

23. Boyd CA interview, 58–61.

24. Coram, *Boyd*, 5, 89.

25. Email from Hal Vincent to Robert Coram, "Boyd, from the Naval-Marine side," April 18, 2000, Coram Papers, box 8, folder 5.

26. Hammond, *Mind of War*, 7, n6.

27. Email from Wilbur Creech to Robert Coram, "RE:" May 4, 2000, Coram Papers, box 8, folder 5.

28. Email from Wilbur Creech, forwarded to Thomas Christie, "Forthcoming books on Boyd and his discourse . . .," March 24, 2001, Coram Papers, box 8, folder 4.

29. Gillespie, "Mission Emphasis," 206.

30. Boyd CA interview, 34.

31. For example, John Boyd, "A Proposed Plan for Ftr. vs. Ftr. Training," *Fighter Weapons Newsletter*, February 1956, 67–72, Coram Papers, box 2, folder 13; and John Boyd, "Fire Control Problems in the Pursuit Curve Attack," *Fighter Weapons Newsletter*, March 1959, 18–24, Coram Papers, box 5, folder 10; Boyd CA interview, 36

(note that Boyd misremembers the date of the newsletter); John Boyd, *Aerial Attack Study*, accessed December 26, 2017, http://www.ausairpower.net/JRB/boydaerial attack.pdf.

32. Email from Wilbur Creech to Robert Coram, "RE:" May 4, 2000, Coram Papers, box 8, folder 5; email from Wilbur Creech, forwarded to Thomas Christie, "Forthcoming books on Boyd and his discourse . . ." March 24, 2001, Coram Papers, box 8, folder 4.

33. Boyd CA interview, 45–52.

34. Boyd Officer Military Record, April 5, 1974, Coram Papers, box 9, folder 6; Boyd CA interview, 93–96.

35. Boyd Officer Effectiveness Report (OER), September 7, 1963, Coram Papers, box 4, folder 8.

36. Boyd CA interview, 100.

37. Tom Christie interview notes, 1999, Coram Papers, box 5, folder 7; Boyd CA interview, 101; Thomas Christie oral history interview, October 3, 1973, USAF Historical Research Agency, K239.0512–962 (hereafter cited as Christie OHI), 7.

38. Christie OHI, 2–3.

39. Jacob Neufeld, "The F-15 Eagle: Origins and Development, 1964–1972," Washington, DC: Office of Air Force History, November 1974, 19.

40. Boyd OERs September 1964 and 1965, Coram Papers, box 4, folder 8; John Boyd, "Energy Maneuverability Theory," APGC TDR 64–35, May 1964; Neufeld, "F-15," 18.

41. John R. Boyd, Thomas P. Christie, and James E. Gibson, "Energy Maneuverability," Air Proving Ground Center, Eglin Air Force Base, March 1966.

42. Christie OHI, 3.

43. Edward S. Rutowski, "Energy Approach to the General Aircraft Performance Problem," *Journal of the Aeronautical Sciences* 21 (March 1954): 187–195; Boyd CA interview, 87–90.

44. Henry J. Kelley, "Gradient Theory of Optimal Flight Paths," *American Rocket Society Journal* (October 1960): 947–954; A. E. Bryson and W. F. Denham, "A Steepest-Ascent Method for Solving Optimum Programming Problems," *Journal of Applied Mechanics* 29 (June 1962): 247–257.

45. Christie OHI, 3–4.

46. Boyd CA interview, 89.

47. Boyd, Christie, and Gibson, "Energy Maneuverability," 78.

48. Boyd CA interview, 102, 103.

49. Coram, *Boyd*, 160–161.

50. Myers OHI, 22–23; email, Robert Titus to Robert Coram, March 18, 2000, Coram Papers, box 9, folder 3.

51. Myers OHI, 31–32; Neufeld, "F-15," 7.

52. Burns OHI, 1–2.

53. Neufeld, "F-15," 8–9.

54. Neufeld, 9.

55. Neufeld, 9–10; See also Jacob Van Staaveren, *Gradual Failure: The Air War over North Vietnam* (Washington, DC: Air Force History and Museums Program, 2002), 83–84

56. Neufeld, 11.

57. Burns OHI, 27–29.

58. General James Ferguson oral history program interview #672, May 8–9, 1973, USAF Historical Research Agency, K239.0512–672 (hereafter cited as Ferguson OHI), 37, 47, 50.

59. Mr. Heinrich J. Weigand oral history program interview #862, March 27, 1973, USAF Historical Research Agency, K239.0512–862 (hereafter cited as Weigand OHI), 1–6.

60. Burns OHI, 17.

61. "Weapons System Evaluation Group Report 116: Air-to-Air Encounters in Southeast Asia" (hereafter cited as Red Baron Report 1), vol. 2, "F-105 Events Prior to March 1967, September 1968," 35–38; Red Baron Report 1, vol. 3, "Events from 1 March 1967 to 1 August 1967 and Miscellaneous Events, February 1969," 37–43. See also Van Staaveren, *Gradual Failure*, 106–108; Chris Hobson, *Vietnam Air Losses: United States Air Force, Navy, and Marine Corps Fixed-Wing Aircraft Losses in Southeast Asia, 1961–1973* (Hinkley, UK: Midland, 2001), 17–18.

62. Red Baron Report 1, 3:38, 41.

63. Myers OHI, 36, 25–26, 36.

64. Burns OHI, 5; Ferguson OHI, 41–43; Neufeld, "F-15," 12.

65. Burns OHI, 6.

66. Neufeld, "F-15," 12.

67. Chuck Myers, "FX Review," February 1968, 1, Coram Papers, box 9. folder 3, emphasis in original.

68. Neufeld, "F-15," 10.

69. Burns OHI, 32–33.

70. Neufeld, "F-15," 13.

71. Pierre Sprey oral history interview, June 12, 1973, USAF Historical Research Agency, K239.0512–969 (hereafter cited as Sprey OHI), 35.

72. Neufeld, "F-15," 13.

73. Burns OHI, 29–30, emphasis in original.

74. General Gabriel P. Disosway oral history interview, October 4–6, 1977, USAF Historical Research Agency, K239.0512–974 (hereafter cited as Disosway OHI), 274–275.

75. Lieutenant General Glenn A. Kent oral history interview, August 6, 1974, USAF Historical Research Agency, K239.0512–970 (hereafter cited as Kent OHI), 3.

76. Burns OHI, 31.

77. Neufeld, "F-15," 13.

78. Kent OHI, 3.

79. Neufeld, "F-15," 17; James Stevenson, *McDonnell Douglas F-15 Eagle* (Fallbrook, CA: Aero, 1978), 10.

80. Quoted in Neufeld, "F-15," 14.

81. Coram, *Boyd*, 178.

82. Disosway OHI, 271.

83. Coram, *Boyd*, 179–180.

84. Boyd OER, September 1966, Boyd Papers, box 24, folder 2.

85. Zalin Grant, *Over the Beach: The Air War in Vietnam* (New York: Simon & Schuster, 1986), 38–39.

86. Neufeld, "F-15," 15, Burns OHI, 33.

87. PACAF Tactics and Techniques Bulletin: Counter-Air Tactics Bulletin #45, July 26, 1966, 1, 5.

88. Sprey OHI, 28.

89. Neufeld, "F-15," 17; Stevenson, *McDonnell*, 10.

90. Kent OHI, 7–9.

91. Myers, "FX Review," 1.

92. Email, Chuck Myers, forwarded to Robert Coram, "RE: Meeting and talking to Robin Olds and Bob Titus," November 11, 2000, Coram Papers, box 9, folder 3.

93. High-bypass engines have better mileage for increased range but less acceleration and speed. Most combat planes usually have lower engine bypass ratios of around 1.5:1 or less.

94. Neufeld, "F-15," 17–18.

95. Neufeld, 18.

4. "The Right Fighter"

1. Myers, "FX Review," February 1968, 2, Coram Papers, box 9, folder 3, emphasis in original.

2. Email, Chuck Myers, forwarded to Robert Coram, "RE: Meeting and talking to Robin Olds and Bob Titus," November 11, 2000, Coram Papers, box 9, folder 3; Myers OHI, 30.

3. Coram, *Boyd*, 186–187.

4. John Boyd oral history interview, May 23, 1973, USAF Historical Research Agency, #859: K239.0512–859 (hereafter cited as Boyd '73 interview), 15.

5. Boyd OER, June 1967, Boyd Papers, box 24, folder 2; Coram, *Boyd*, 194–195. The quote is possibly apocryphal, told in other sources sometimes with different wording. See Burton, *Pentagon Wars*, 14; Hammond, *Mind of War*, 77; and Sprey OHI, 8. Ritchie's name is misspelled as "Ricci" in some sources, and Coram does not name him.

6. Sprey OHI, 9–12.

7. Email, Thomas Christie to Robert Coram, May 19, 1999, Coram Papers, box 4, folder 4; Pierre Sprey interview notes, August 2000, Coram Papers, 2–4, box 5, folder 1.

8. Sprey OHI, 8.

9. Sprey OHI, 6.

10. Email, Robert Titus to Robert Coram, March 18, 2000, Coram Papers, box 9, folder 3; Bob Titus interview notes, August 25, 2000, Coram Papers, box 9, folder 3.

11. Boyd OER, June 1967, Coram Papers, box 9, folder 3.

12. Coram, *Boyd*, 205.

13. Glenn A. Kent, *Thinking about America's Defense: An Analytical Memoir* (Arlington, VA: RAND Corp., 2008), 169; Kent OHI, 7.

14. Lieutenant General F. M. Rogers USAF oral history interview, July 17–18, 1974, USAF Historical Research Agency, K239.0512–965 (hereafter cited as Rogers OHI), 5.

15. Kent OHI, 7–9.

16. Kent, *Thinking*, 169.

17. Rogers OHI, 5–7; Kent OHI, 8–10.

18. Rogers OHI, 13–14.

19. Mark A. Lorell and Hugh P. Levaux, *The Cutting Edge: A Half Century of U.S. Fighter Aircraft R&D* (Washington, DC: RAND Corp., 1998), 105; Neufeld, "F-15," 20; Boyd '73 interview, 16–18; Rogers OHI, 11.

20. G. A. Spangenberg, Memorandum for the Record, "The Fighter Study Dilemmas," September 16, 1973, https://web.archive.org/web/20120204215346/http://www.georgespangenberg.com/vf15.htm; see also George A. Spangenberg, Oral History, August 19–22, 1990, tape 14 of 16, side A, accessed December 13, 2019, http://www.f-111.net/articles/George%20A_%20Spangenberg%20Oral%20History.htm; Department of the Navy, "U.S. General Accounting Office Staff Study on the F-14/Phoenix Aircraft Program," April 1973, p. 4, https://www.gao.gov/assets/80/78778.pdf; Michael Ciminera, *The Aircraft Designers: A Grumman Historical Perspective* (American Institute of Aeronautics and Astronautics Inc., 2013), 117.

21. Neufeld, "F-15," 23–24; Boyd '73 interview, 16–19.

22. Cecil Brownlow, "Soviet Air Force Unveils Advanced Designs for Expanded Limited War Capability," *Aviation Week & Space Technology*, July 17, 1967, 21, 26–39; Werrell, *Chasing the Silver Bullet*, 65.

23. Neufeld, "F-15," 25; Michel, *Clashes*, 133, 140, 150.

24. Brereton Greenhous, "The Israeli Experience," in *Case Studies in the Achievement of Air Superiority*, ed. Benjamin Franklin Cooling (Washington, DC: Air Force History and Museums Program, 1994).

25. Quoted in Greenhous, "Israeli Experience," 580.

26. Bob Titus interview notes, August 25, 2000, Coram Papers, box 9, folder 3.

27. Neufeld, "F-15," 21–22.

28. Boyd OER, June 1967, Coram Papers, box 9, folder 3; CFP (S/NOFORN), Advanced Tactical Fighter (F-X), AFRDQ/ANSER, Rev 1, 1 Aug 67, pp. 1–56, quoted in Neufeld, "F-15," 22.

29. Jack Abercrombie and Mike de Garcia, "F-15 Aircraft Development," July 29, 2005, Greater St. Louis Air and Space Museum Collections, 1; Stevenson, *McDonnell*, 10; Neufeld, "F-15," 28.

30. Myers, "F-X Review," Coram Papers, box 9, folder 3, 4–5, emphasis in original.

31. Neufeld, "F-15," 25.

32. Hearings before the Committee on Armed Services United States Senate, 90th Congress, Second Session, on S. 3293, February 29, 1968, 1015, April 30, 1968, 9593.

33. Email, Robert Titus to Robert Coram, "RE: Boyd," March 18, 2000, Coram Papers, box 9, folder 3.

34. Email from Chuck Myers, forwarded to Robert Coram, "Re: Meeting with and talking to Robin Olds and Bob Titus," November 11, 2000, Coram Papers, box 9, folder 3.

35. Abercrombie and de Garcia, "F-15 Aircraft," 1; Stevenson, *McDonnell*, 10–11.

36. Neufeld, "F-15," 28.

37. Neufeld, 25–26.

38. Disosway OHI, 295–296.

39. Quoted in Neufeld, "F-15," 26.

40. Pierre Sprey, "The Impact of Avionics on the Effectiveness of Tactical Air," Staff Study, Office of the Assistant Secretary of Defense, Systems Analysis, June 1968, Boyd Papers, box 9, folder 3.

41. Major General Roger K. Rhodarmer oral history interview, USAF Historical Research Agency, March 29, 1973, K239.0512–972 (hereafter cited as Rhodarmer OHI), 1–5.

42. Neufeld, "F-15," 27–28.

43. Letter, Pierre Sprey to General James Ferguson, July 18, 1968, Coram Papers, box 10, folder 4.

44. Sprey interview notes, August 2000, 10, and Tom Christie interview notes, August 2000, 3, Coram Papers, box 5, folder 1. Sprey says this was in late 1969 but is likely mistaken; Christie indicates it was 1968.

45. Kent, *Thinking*, 169–172; Kent OHI, 11–15.

46. Rhodarmer OHI, 10.

47. Hammond, *Mind of War*, 78.

48. "F-15 DSARC III," Assistant Secretary of Defense, Systems Analysis, February 14, 1973, National Archives and Records Administration.

49. Neufeld, "F-15," 30–31.

50. Stevenson, *McDonnell*, 11; Neufeld, "F-15," 28–33; email from Bob Titus to Robert Coram, "RE: Boyd," March 18, 2000, Coram Papers, box 9, folder 3.

51. "Hearings on Military Posture and Legislation to Authorize Appropriations during the Fiscal Year 1970," House of Representatives Committee on Armed Services, HASC No. 91–14, March 27, 1969, and May 20, 1969, 2633, 3273–3274.

52. Stuart Levin, "F-15: The Teething of a Dogfighter," *Space/Aeronautics* 52 (December 1969): 36.

53. Levin, "F-15," 36–43; "The F-15 Competition," *Armed Forces Journal* 107 (September 13, 1969): 14–24; "Fairchild F-15: New Thunder for the 70's," "Who's Who in Electronics," *Electronics*, March 17, 1969, Smithsonian National Air and Space Museum (hereafter NASM) Archives, Fairchild Industries Collection, box 396, folders 1–4.

54. Abercrombie, "F-15 Concept," Greater St. Louis Air and Space Museum Collections, 1–4; Levin, "F-15," 36–43; "The F-15 Competition," *Armed Forces Journal* 107 (September 13, 1969): 14–24;

55. Neufeld, "F-15," 40–41.

56. Boyd OER, May 1969, Boyd Papers, box 24, folder 2; email from Benjamin Bellis to Robert Coram, May 6, 2001, Coram Papers, box 8, folder 1.

57. Coram, *Boyd*, 244–246.

58. Email, Benjamin Bellis to Robert Coram, May 6, 2001, Coram Papers, box 8, folder 1.

59. C. E. Myers to Allan Simon, October 29, 1969, FX Review, October 1969 addendum, Coram Papers, box 9, folder 3.

60. Press Conference, Air Force Secretary Seamans, December 12, 1969, 7–8, NASM Archives, Fairchild Industries Collection, box 396, folder 6. This date must be an error, as other sources in this folder confirm the 23rd, as well as Abercrombie and de Garcia, "F-15 Aircraft," 1.

61. For a full explanation of Total Package Procurement see *Code of Federal Regulations*, Washington, DC: Government Printing Office, January 1, 1969, 63, https://books.google.com/books?id=POY6AAAAIAAJ&dq=%22Total%20Package%20Procurement%22&pg=PA63.

62. For the C-5 see Jerry V. Poncar and James R. Johnston III, "History and Analysis of the C-5A Program: An Application of the Total Package Procurement

Concept" (thesis, Air Force Institute of Technology, October 1970); for Total Package see Joseph R. Busek, "A Historical Analysis of Total Package Procurement, Life Cycle Costing, and Design to Cost" (master's thesis, Air Force Institute of Technology, June 1976).

63. Quoted in Shannon A. Brown, *Providing the Means of War: Historical Perspectives on Defense Acquisition, 1945–2000* (Washington, DC: Government Printing Office, 2005), 145; Neufeld, "F-15," 34–35.

64. Neufeld, "F-15," 34–36.

65. See Michel, "Revolt of the Majors."

66. Worden, *Rise of the Fighter Generals*, 89.

67. Worden, 168–173.

68. Worden, 187–192, 223–226.

69. Laslie, *Air Force Way of War*; see also Michel, "Revolt of the Majors."

5. "The Lord's Work"

Chapter epigraph quote in Daniel Mark Gillespie, "Mission Emphasis and the Determination of Needs for New Weapon Systems" (PhD diss., Massachusetts Institute of Technology, 2009).

1. Myers OHI, 38, emphasis in original.

2. Email from Charles Myers forwarded to Robert Coram, November 11, 2000, Coram Papers, box 9, folder 3.

3. Pierre Sprey oral history interview, June 12, 1973, USAF Historical Research Agency, K239.0512–969 (hereafter cited as Sprey OHI), 39; memo, Pierre Sprey to James Ferguson, July 18, 1968, Coram Papers, box 10, folder 4.

4. Harry J. Hillaker, "YF-16 Design Concept and Philosophy," Presentation to 23rd Israel Annual Conference on Aviation and Astronautics, February 11–12, 1981, 1, Coram Papers, box 9, folder 4.

5. Miller, *General Dynamics F-16*, 7–8; J. K. Buckner, D. B. Benepe, and P. W. Hill, "Aerodynamic Design Evolution of the YF-16," American Institute of Aeronautics and Astronautics 6th Aircraft Design, Flight Test and Operations Meeting, August 12–14, 1974, 1, https://doi.org/10.2514/6.1974-935; Werrell, *Chasing the Silver Bullet*, 81.

6. Sprey OHI, 39–40; Neufeld, "F-15," 64.

7. Miller, *General Dynamics F-16*, 10.

8. Pierre M. Sprey, "F-XX and VF-XX—Feasible High Performance, Low Cost Fighter Alternatives," Staff Study, Office of the Assistant Secretary of Defense (Systems Analysis), June 9, 1969, Coram Papers, box 7, folder 4, 1, 8, emphasis in original.

9. Sprey, "F-XX," 1–17.

10. Memorandum from AIR-503 and AIR-506, "OASD(SA) Staff Study—F-XX and VF-XX Critique," June 26, 1969, Naval Air Systems Command, Coram Papers, box 7, folder 4.

11. George Spangenberg Oral History, February 21, 1990, transcript, p. 263, https://www.docdroid.net/x9czNLE/george-spangenberg-oral-history.pdf.

12. Hammond, *Mind of War*, 84–85; Sprey interview notes, July 29, August 2000, Coram Papers, box 5, folder 1.

13. Neufeld, "F-15," 65.

14. "Extended Interview: Pierre Sprey," September 28, 2012, Fifth Estate, http://www.cbc.ca/fifth/blog/extended-interview-pierre-sprey.

15. Bill Minutaglio, "Tales of the Fighter Mafia," *Dallas Life Magazine*, May 3, 1987, 12–13.

16. Coram, *Boyd*, 238.

17. Email, Everest Riccioni to Robert Coram, April 3, 2000, Coram Papers, box 5, folder 1.

18. Everest E. Riccioni, "The Air Superiority Fighter, a Modern Analysis," FR 39919, Research Report, Air War College, Air University, Maxwell Air Force Base, AL, April 1968, 3, 13.

19. Riccioni, "Air Superiority Fighter," 19, 32–39, 63.

20. Riccioni, 53–56, 43, 104, 124–125, 150–155.

21. Email, Robert Titus to Robert Coram, March 18, 2000, Coram Papers, box 6, folder 8; email, Everest Riccioni to Robert Coram, April 3, 2000, Coram Papers, box 5, folder 1; Sprey interview notes, August 2000, Coram Papers, box 5, folder 1, 11; Hammond, *Mind of War*, 85.

22. Eileen Bjorkman, "The Outrageous Adolescence of the F-16," *Air & Space Magazine*, March 2014, https://www.airspacemag.com/military-aviation/outrageous-adolescence-f-16-180949491.

23. Bjorkman.

24. Kent, *Thinking*, 173.

25. Kent, 174–175.

26. Hammond, *Mind of War*, 88.

27. Some sources attributed Riccioni's transfer to an incident at a party in December 1970 in which he disparaged the F-15 to Meyer, who then ordered his transfer as a personal punishment. Some of these sources interpreted the move as a purge of dissenting views. For example, see Burton, *Pentagon Wars*, 17–18; and Hammond, *Mind of War*, 88.

28. Drabrant interview notes, Coram Papers, box 3, folder 13.

29. Miller, *General Dynamics F-16*, 12; Herbert Hutchinson, *Inside History of the USAF Lightweight Fighters, 1900 to 1975* (Paso Robles, CA: Xlibris, 2018), 330; Sprey interview notes, August 2000, Coram Papers, box 5, folder 1, 11.

30. Email, Robert Drabrant to Robert Coram, November 8, 2000, Coram Papers, box 9, folder 3; Minutaglio, "Tales," 10.

31. Coram, *Boyd*, 240.

32. Burns OHI, 19.

33. Hammond, *Mind of War*, 88.

34. Quoted in Kelley Beaucar Vlahos, "40 Years of the 'Fighter Mafia,'" *American Conservative*, September 20, 2013, http://www.theamericanconservative.com/articles/40-years-of-the-fighter-mafia/.

35. Burton, *Pentagon Wars*, 17.

36. Coram, *Boyd*, 249–250.

37. Sprey interview notes, June 29, Coram Papers, box 5, folder 1; Sprey interview notes, August 2000, Coram Papers, box 5, folder 1, 11.

38. *Foreign Relations of the United States, 1969–1976*, vol. 1, *Foundations of Foreign Policy, 1969–1972*, Document 29, https://history.state.gov/historicaldocuments/frus1969-76v01/d29.

39. Hammond, *Mind of War*, 90–91.

40. Quoted in G. K. Smith et al., *The Use of Prototypes in Weapon Systems Development*, RAND Project Air Force Report, number R-2345-AF, March 1981, 85.

41. Michel, "Revolt of the Majors," 133.

42. Richard A. Haggren, Memorandum for Dr. Ahearne, "Skunk Works Proposals," March 8, 1971, Coram Papers, box 3, folder 13; Miller, *General Dynamics F-16*, 14; Michel, "Revolt of the Majors," 133–34; G. K. Smith et al., *Use of Prototypes*, 85.

43. Haggren, Memorandum for Dr. Ahearne; Hutchinson, *Inside History*, 333–334.

44. Hutchinson, *Inside History*, 340. Hutchinson misremembers Cameron's combat record as being in the Vietnam War.

45. Kent, *Thinking*, 176–177.

46. Hutchinson, *Inside History*, 340–352.

47. Program Memorandum, Lightweight Fighter Prototype, late 1971, Coram Papers, box 5, folder 2, 1; Hutchinson, *Inside History*, 357–358.

48. Boyd OER, April 12, 1972, Coram Papers, box 9, folder 3; Hutchinson, *Inside History*, 356–369, 380; David C. Aronstein and Albert C. Piccirillo, *The Lightweight Fighter Program: A Successful Approach to Fighter Technology Transition* (Reston, VA: American Institute of Aeronautics and Astronautics, 1997), 7, 11.

49. Scrogham, *Combat Relevant Task*, 9–10; Hutchinson, *Inside History*, 353, 380; Aronstein and Piccirillo, *Lightweight Fighter*, 8, 11.

50. Miller, *General Dynamics F-16*, 19.

51. Hutchinson, *Inside History*, 373–374.

52. George Spangenberg Oral History, 264–265.

53. Tom Christie interview notes, August 2000, Coram Papers, box 5, folder 1; Tom Christie interview notes, Coram Papers, box 5, folder 7.

54. Email, Robert Drabrant to Robert Coram, November 9, 2000, Coram Papers, box 2, folder 31; Tom Christie interview notes, Coram Papers, box 5, folder 7.

55. Email, Robert Drabrant to Robert Coram, November 9, 2000, Coram Papers, box 2, folder 31.

56. Hutchinson, *Inside History*, 375–376, 395.

57. John Boyd, Thomas Christie, and Robert Drabrant, "Maximum Maneuver Concept," June 1972, Weapons Systems Analysis Division, Technical Report AFATL-TR-72-116, Boyd Papers, box 14, folder 8.

58. Melvin Laird, Memorandum for the Secretary of the Air Force, "Lightweight Fighter Program," April 13, 1972, Coram Papers, box 3, folder 13.

59. Development Concept Paper, "Lightweight Fighter Prototype," DCP #120, November 1, 1972, Coram Papers, box 3, folder 13.

60. Boyd OER, October 31, 1972, Boyd Papers, box 24, folder 2.

61. Aronstein and Picirillo, *Lightweight Fighter*, 12, 17. Quote on 12.

62. Hillaker, "Design Concept," 2.

63. Hillaker, 3–8.

64. Hutchinson, *Inside History*, 425–428.

65. See Schultz, *Problem with Pilots*.

66. Aronstein and Piccirillo, *Lightweight Fighter*, 4.

67. Aronstein and Picirillo, 20.

68. Hillaker, "Design Rationale," 11.

69. John T. Correll, *The Air Force in the Vietnam War* (Arlington, VA: Air Force Association, 2004), 25–26; Hannah, *Striving for Air Superiority*, 52, 70–73; "A Comparative Analysis of USAF Fixed-Wing Aircraft Losses in Southeast Asia Combat," Air Force Flight Dynamics Laboratory, Technical Report AFFDL-TR-77–115, December 1977, 14–24; Chris Hobson, *Vietnam Air Losses, USAF, USN, USMC, Fixed-Wing Aircraft Losses in Southeast Asia 1961–1973* (North Branch, MN: Specialty Press, 2001); Werrell, *Chasing the Silver Bullet*, 87.

70. James E. Tomayko, "Blind Faith: The United States Air Force and the Development of Fly-by-Wire Technology," in *Technology and the Air Force: A Retrospective Assessment*, ed. Jacob Neufeld, George M. Watson Jr., and David Chenoweth (Washington, DC: Air Force History and Museums Program, 1997); Werrell, *Chasing the Silver Bullet*, 87–88; William Elliot, "The Development of Fly-by-Wire Control," AFMC Historical Study 7, December 1996.

71. J. P. Sutherland, "Fly-by-Wire Control Systems," Air Force Flight Dynamics Laboratory, Wright-Patterson Air Force Base, OH, AD 679 158, September 3, 1968, 2, 35–36; Tomayko, "Blind Faith," 173.

72. James E. Hunter, "Survivable Flight Control System Fly-by-Wire Development and Flight Test," Air Force Flight Dynamics Laboratory, 55.

73. Tomayko, "Blind Faith," 176–78, 180.

74. Aronstein and Picirillo, *Lightweight Fighter*, 21–22.

75. Tomayko, "Blind Faith," 164; Werrell, *Chasing the Silver Bullet*, 88.

76. Hillaker, "Design Concept," 4.

77. Aronstein and Picirillo, *Lightweight Fighter*, 23–24.

78. Hutchinson, *Inside History*, 409–411; Aronstein and Picirillo, *Lightweight Fighter*, 23–24.

79. Aronstein and Picirillo, *Lightweight Fighter*, 15.

80. Hutchinson, *Inside History*, 395–396.

81. Malcolm R. Currie, Memorandum for the Assistant Secretary of the Air Force (R&D), "Air Force Lightweight Fighter Program," October 23, 1973, Coram Papers, box 3, folder 13.

82. John L. McLucas, Memorandum for Director of Defense Research and Engineering, "Air Force Lightweight Fighter Program," November 23, 1973, Coram Papers, box 3, folder 13.

83. Greenhous, "Israeli Experience," 587–601.

84. Werrell, *Chasing the Silver Bullet*, 90.

85. Gillespie, "Mission Emphasis," 248.

86. Leonard Sullivan Jr., Memorandum for Assistant Secretary of Defense (Comptroller), "USAF R&D PBD," December 6, 1973, Coram Papers, box 5, folder 2.

87. Scrogham, *Combat Relevant Task*, 13–19.

88. Phillip Oestricher, "General Dynamics Flight Report," January 20, 1974, National Air and Space Museum Collection, General Dynamics F-16 Fighting Falcon, AG-033110–01. Footage of this flight is online: https://www.youtube.com/watch?v=UR-48Kri0Tw, accessed September 23, 2017.

89. Aronstein and Picirillo, *Lightweight Fighter*, 28; Scrogham, *Combat Relevant Task*, 50; James G. Rider, "YF-16 Pilot Report," *Air Force Magazine*, October 1976, 32.

90. Aronstein and Picirillo, *Lightweight Fighter*, 29.

91. Werrell, *Chasing the Silver Bullet*, 89; Hutchinson, *Inside History*, 425.

92. Gillespie, "Mission Emphasis," 263–268.

93. Scrogham, *Combat Relevant Task*, 24.

94. Christie interview notes, Coram Papers, box 5, folder 7; Christie email to Robert Coram, July 7, 1999, Coram Papers, box 9, folder 2; Minutaglio, "Tales," 26.

95. Sprey interview notes, August 2000, Coram Papers, box 5, folder 1.

96. Werrell, *Chasing the Silver Bullet*, 91.

97. Gillespie, "Mission Emphasis," 268.

98. "Colonel Richard Hallock Papers (MC284): Biographical Note," Columbia State University, accessed September 24, 2017, https://archives.columbusstate.edu/findingaids/mc284.php.

99. Sprey interview notes, August 2000, Coram Papers, box 5, folder 1.

100. Email, Christie to Robert Coram, July 7, 1999, Coram Papers, box 9, folder 2.

101. Hammond, *Mind of War*, 95–96; Burton, *Pentagon Wars*, 19; Coram, *Boyd*, 294–295.

102. "U.S. Decision in 'Fighter-Plane Sweepstakes' Is Due Jan. 15," *New York Times*, December 26, 1974.

103. "Air Combat Fighter Design Decision Status and Situation," December 30, 1974, box 1, folder "ND 1 Aircraft 3/1/75–6/30/75" of the White House Central Files Subject Files (Ford administration), 8/9/1974–1/20/1977, Gerald R. Ford Presidential Library.

104. Scrogham, *Combat Relevant Task*, 84–85.

105. Scrogham, 33–34.

106. Gillespie, "Mission Emphasis," 271.

107. News Briefing by Secretary of the Air Force John L. McLucas at the Pentagon, January 13, 1975, box 21, folder "Lightweight Fighters (Navy & Air Force), 1974–75 (4)," Martin R. Hoffmann Papers, Gerald R. Ford Presidential Library.

108. "Interview Part I: Harry Hillaker: Father of the F-16," Code One, April 1991, 22.

6. Writing Heresy

Chapter epigraph from Mark Hamilton, "Maneuver Warfare Revisited: A Plea for Balance," April 1986, Army War College Study Project, AD-A170 250, 3.

1. Hammond, *Mind of War*, 104.

2. Fallows, *National Defense*, 105; Hammond, *Mind of War*, 97.

3. Robert J. Croteau, Memorandum for Mr. Sullivan, through Mr. Christie, "F-16 Air Combat Fighter DSARC II," January 27, 1975, Coram Papers, box 3, folder 13.

4. General Dynamics, "F-16 Program Summary," August 15, 1977, ASD 771456, NASM Archives, General Dynamics F-16 Fighting Falcon Series, Briefing Packets, AG-033100-03.

5. Westinghouse, "AN/APG-68, the New Standard for Fighter Radar," pamphlet, no date, NASM Archives; Westinghouse, "Westinghouse Starts Full-Scale Development of the F-16 Radar," public relations release, no date, NASM Archives, both in General Dynamics F-16 Fighting Falcon Series, Avionics Systems, AG-033100-02.

---

6. General Dynamics, "F-16 Energy Management Displays," pamphlet, no date, NASM Archives, General Dynamics F-16 Fighting Falcon Series, Briefing Packets, AG-033100-02.

7. Werrell, *Chasing the Silver Bullet*, 93.

8. Hearings before the Committee on Armed Services, United States Senate, 94th Congress, 2nd Session, S.2965, Part 6: Research and Development, February 25–26, March 2, 4, 9, 1976, 3739–3740.

9. Hearings before the Committee on Armed Services, United States Senate, 94th Congress, 2nd Session, S.2965, Part 9: Tactical Airpower, March 8–12, 1976, 4896.

10. "General Dynamics' F-16 Selected as Air Force's New Jet Fighter," *St. Louis Post-Dispatch*, January 14, 1975.

11. Clyde H. Farnsworth, "Gen. Dynamics' 'Contract of the Century,'" insert, "David S. Lewis Comments on Winning F-16 Contract," *St. Louis Post-Dispatch*, July 29, 1975.

12. See collection of General Dynamics press releases, NASM archival collection, General Dynamics F-16 Fighting Falcon Series, Brochures, AG-033100-04; and press kits, AG-33100-09.

13. Stephen Good, "F-16 Fighters Beginning to Roll Off Production Line," *Morning News—Sunday News Journal* (Wilmington, DE), original article in *Dallas Times Herald*, October 15, 1978.

14. John Boyd, Memorandum for General Slay, "F-16 Wing Area Selection," March 31, 1975; John Boyd, Memorandum for Maj Gen Slay, "F-16 Wing Area," March 4, 1975; John Boyd, Memo to Major General Slay, "ACF Wing Area," January 23, 1975; all in Boyd Papers, box 13, folder 1.

15. Email, Thomas Christie to Robert Coram, February 5, 2001, and email, Ray Leopold to Robert Coram, January 31, 2001, both in Coram Papers, box 6, folder 7; Sprey interview notes, August 2000, Coram Papers, box 5, folder 1.

16. "Interview Part II: Harry Hillaker: Father of the F-16," Code One, July 1991, 9.

17. Letter, John C. Downey to John Boyd, April 30, 1975; mailgram, John C. Downey, March 29 (probably 1975), Boyd Papers, box 21, folder 1.

18. Memo, Robert J. Croteau to Mr. Sullivan, through Mr. Christie, "F-16 DSARC II Position Recommendation," February 4, 1975, box 21, folder "Lightweight Fighters (Navy & Air Force), 1974–75 (5)," 1, 3, Martin R. Hoffmann Papers, Gerald R. Ford Presidential Library.

19. Memo, Chuck Myers to Hoffman, February 21, 1975, box 21, folder "Lightweight Fighters (Navy & Air Force), 1974–75 (4)," Hoffman Papers.

20. Memo, Myers to Hoffman, "F-16 (LWF/ACF) Program Restoration," box 21, folder "Lightweight Fighters (Navy & Air Force), 1974–75 (4)," Hoffman Papers, 2–3.

21. "Air Combat Fighter DSARC-II, General Counsel," March 11, 1975, "Air Force Response to the OSD List of Questions on ACF (F-16)," box 21, folder "Lightweight Fighters (Navy & Air Force), 1974–75 (5)," Hoffman Papers.

22. "Air Combat Fighter," March 7, 1975, box 21, folder "Lightweight Fighters (Navy & Air Force), 1974–75 (5)," Hoffman Papers.

23. Coram, *Boyd*, 308.

24. Franklin C. Spinney, "Genghis John," *Proceedings of the U.S. Naval Institute*, July 1997, 42–47; Spinney interview notes, November 1999, Coram Papers, box 6, folder 7.

25. John R. Boyd, "Destruction and Creation," in *Discourse*, 315–325.

26. Studies of "Destruction and Creation" include Osinga, *Science, Strategy and War*, and Osinga, "Enemy as a Complex Adaptive System."

27. Tom Christie interview notes, February 23, 2001, Coram Papers, box 8, folder 3.

28. Spinney, "Genghis John."

29. James Burton interview notes, February 26, 2001, Coram Papers, box 8, folder 1; Spinney, "Genghis John."

30. John Boyd, "New Conception for Air-to-Air Combat," August 1976, http://www.ausairpower.net/JRB/fast_transients.pdf.

31. Burton interview notes, February 26, 2001, Coram Papers, box 8, folder 1; Boyd, *Discourse*. For a nearly seven-hour long recording of the "Patterns of Conflict" briefing see https://www.youtube.com/playlist?list=PL4pmLxkc7CTcukIlpD0UTh T7Y_K09oxXe, accessed October 7, 2017.

32. Boyd, *Discourse*, 197.

33. Sprey interview notes, June 12, 1999, Coram Papers, box 5, folder 1; Boyd handwritten comments on Guenther Blumentritt, "Experience Gained from the History of War on the Subject of Command Technique," January 1947, Boyd Papers, box 9, folder 3. Hammond, *Mind of War*, 121.

34. Wolfram Wette, *The Wehrmacht: History, Myth, Reality* (Cambridge, MA: Harvard University Press, 2007); Robert Citino, *The Wehrmacht Retreats: Fighting a Lost War, 1943* (Lawrence: University Press of Kansas, 2012), 204–208.

35. Sprey interview notes, June 12, 1999, Coram Papers, box 5, folder 1; Coram, *Boyd*, 235; Boyd 1980 Date Keeper, Boyd Papers, box 22.

36. Interview notes, Mary Boyd, December 9, 2000, and interview notes, Mary, Mary Ellen, Jeff, and Kathy Boyd, Del Ray 2, both in Coram Papers, box 5, folder 1.

37. For example, from 1982 forward, the Air Force held regular conferences called "Gathering of Eagles," featuring prominent aviator veterans as guest speakers. In the 1980s, German Luftwaffe fighter pilots such as Günther Rall, Adolf Galland, and Wolfgang Späte were featured at several of these events. A full list of speakers is available at https://goefoundation.org/, accessed October 7, 2020. For more on German influence in the US military see Roger A. Beaumont, "On the Wehrmacht Mystique," *Military Review* 66 (July 1986): 44–56; Robert W. Hutchinson, "The Weight of History: Wehrmacht Officers, the U.S. Army Historical Division, and U.S. Military Doctrine, 1945–1956," *Journal of Military History* 78 (October 2014): 1321–1348; Ronald Smelser and Edward J. Davies II, *The Myth of the Eastern Front: The Nazi-Soviet War in American Popular Culture* (Cambridge: Cambridge University Press, 2008); and William Astore, "The US Military's German Fetish," *Mother Jones*, February 18, 2010, https://www.motherjones.com/politics/2010/02/us-militarys-german-fetish/.

38. Boyd, *Discourse*, 198

39. Burton interview notes, "76 Plus," Coram Papers, box 8, folder 1.

40. Sprey interview notes, February 24, 2001, Coram Papers, box 8, folder 3.

41. For a fuller discussion comparing Liddell Hart and Boyd see Osinga, *Science, Strategy, and War*, 52–56.

42. The strongest defense and most in-depth analysis of the OODA loop is the work of Frans Osinga: see *Science, Strategy and War* and "Enemy as a Complex Adaptive System." See also Colin Gray, *Modern Strategy* (Oxford: Oxford University

Press, 1999), 90–91; Brown, *New Conception of War*; Fadok, "John Boyd and John Warden"; Olsen, "Boyd Revisited"; and Hammond's introduction and afterword to Boyd, *Discourse*, 1–12, 381–385.

43. Hammond, introduction to Boyd, *Discourse*, 1; for one recorded version of the briefing see https://www.youtube.com/playlist?list=PL4pmLxkc7CTcukIlp D0UThT7Y_K09oxXe, accessed October 7, 2017.

44. Gray, *Modern Strategy*, 90–91; Osinga, "Enemy as a Complex Adaptive System," 50, 74.

45. Hammond, "Appendix: The OODA Loop," in Boyd, *Discourse*, 383.

46. Boyd, *Discourse*; Hammond, "Appendix: The OODA Loop," 383–385; Coram, *Boyd*, 334–344.

47. See Hasík, "Beyond the Briefing," 583–599.

48. See Daniel Kahneman, *Thinking, Fast and Slow* (New York: Farrar, Straus and Giroux, 2011).

49. Jim Storr, "Neither Art nor Science—towards a Discipline of Warfare," *RUSI Journal* 146 (April 2001): 39–45; note that Stoor incorrectly ascribed the loop to Lind and not Boyd.

50. Hasík, "Beyond the Briefing," 583–599.

51. Hasík, 591; For comparisons of these systems to Boyd's see Carl Allard, *Command, Control, and the Common Defense* (New Haven, CT: Yale University Press, 1990); George Orr, *Combat Operations C3I: Fundamentals and Interactions* (Maxwell Air Force Base, AL: Air University Press, 1983); Tim Grant and Bas Kooter, "Comparing OODA and Other Models as Operational View C2 Architecture," 10th International Command and Control Research and Technology Symposium, 2005.

52. See "Adlerian Therapy," *Psychology Today*, accessed October 10, 2020, https://www.psychologytoday.com/us/therapy-types/adlerian-therapy.

53. David A. Kolb and Ronald E. Fry, "Towards an Applied Theory of Experiential Learning," in *Theories of Group Processes*, ed. Cary L. Cooper (New York: Wiley, 1975).

54. See Alan Mumford, ed., *Action Learning at Work* (Brookfield, VT: Gower, 1997).

55. Boyd Date Keepers, 1980–1986, Boyd Papers, box 22; Burton, *Pentagon Wars*, 47–49; Coram, *Boyd*, 330–331.

56. Burton, *Pentagon Wars*, 45–47.

57. Burton, 47–48.

58. Michel, *Clashes*, 151–155; Robert K. Wilcox, *Scream of Eagles: The Dramatic Account of the U.S. Navy's Top Gun Fighter Pilots and How They Took Back the Skies over Vietnam* (New York: Pocket Star Books, 1990), 106. See also Ron Westrum, *Sidewinder: Creative Missile Development at China Lake* (Annapolis, MD: Naval Institute Press, 2013).

59. Olds, *Fighter Pilot*, 305; Michel, *Clashes*, 108–109.

60. Michel, *Clashes*, 156.

61. Steven Fino, "Doubling Down: AIMVAL-ACEVAL and US Air Force Investment in TacAir Post-Vietnam," *Vulcan* 2 (2014): 129–130.

62. Fino, "Doubling Down," 130–132; Anderegg, *Sierra Hotel*, 158–159.

63. Stevenson, *McDonnell*, 75; Fino, "Doubling Down," 132–137.

64. Anderegg, *Sierra Hotel*, 158–159.

65. Anderegg, 159; Fino, "Doubling Down," 139.

66. Fino, "Doubling Down," 140.
67. Fino, 140–141.
68. Anderegg, *Sierra Hotel*, 160–163.
69. Quoted in Fino, "Doubling Down," 141–142.
70. Fino, 136–137.
71. John Boyd and George Burkley, Memorandum for Mr. [Russell] Murray, "Trip Report of John Boyd and LtCol Burkley to Nellis AFB," December 29, 1977, Boyd Papers, box 27, emphasis in original.
72. Christie interview notes, February 23, 2001, Coram Papers, box 8, folder 3; Spinney interview notes, 1601, Coram Papers, box 8, folder 1.
73. Franklin Spinney, "Defense Facts of Life," December 5, 1980, Office of Secretary of Defense, 3, 8, http://pogoarchives.org/labyrinth/defense-facts-of-life-1980.pdf.
74. Spinney, "Defense Facts of Life," 14.
75. Spinney, 6.
76. Spinney, 3, emphasis in original.
77. Spinney, 3.
78. Spinney, 3, 117, 128–129, 133.
79. Correll, "Reformers," 40–44.
80. Pierre Sprey, "The Case for More Effective, Less Expensive Weapons Systems." A June 1982 version of this talk was given at United States Military Academy Senior Conference XX: "The Military Reform Debate: Directions for the Defense Establishment for the Remainder of the Century," 184–185, accessed November 27, 2016, http://pogoarchives.org/labyrinth/11/12.pdf.
81. Sprey, "Case for More Effective," 185–189.
82. Sprey, 192–200.
83. Sprey, 188–192.
84. Sprey, 181–203.

7. "Zealots of the Classic Variety"

1. Peter W. Chiarelli and Raymond C. Gagnon Jr., "The Politics of Military Reform," Center for Naval Warfare Studies Report 84–88, June 1985, 8–9.
2. Michael J. Leahey, "A History of Defense Reform since 1970" (master's thesis, Naval Postgraduate School, December 1989), 43–45.
3. Hart and Lind, *America Can Win*, 4.
4. James Fallows interview notes, March 8, 2001, Coram Papers, box 8, folder 3; James Fallows, "Muscle-Bound Superpower: The State of America's Defense," *Atlantic*, October 1979, 59–78.
5. Burton interview notes, "76 Plus," Coram Papers, box 8, folder 1.
6. Fallows, "Muscle-Bound," 59.
7. Fallows, 62–63.
8. Dan Pedersen, *Top Gun: An American Story* (New York: Hachette Books, 2019), 144–146.
9. Fallows, "Muscle-Bound," 63–65.
10. Fallows, 66–67, 72; Michel, *Clashes*, 156.
11. Fallows, "Muscle-Bound," 72–76.
12. Fallows, 77–78

13. Fallows, 78.

14. Patrick Hagopian, *The Vietnam War in American Memory: Veterans, Memorials, and the Politics of Healing* (Amherst: University of Massachusetts Press, 2012), 408.

15. George C. Herring, "The 'Vietnam Syndrome' and American Foreign Policy," *Virginia Quarterly Review* 57 (Autumn 1981).

16. Quoted in Christian G. Appy, *American Reckoning: The Vietnam War and Our National Identity* (New York: Viking, 2015), 284–285.

17. George Herring, "Preparing Not to Refight the Last War: The Impact of the Vietnam War on the U.S. Military," in *After Vietnam: Legacies of a Lost War*, ed. Charles E. Neu (Baltimore: Johns Hopkins University Press, 2000), 73–74; see also Appy, *American Reckoning*, particularly chapter 10, "No More Vietnams."

18. Herring, "'Vietnam Syndrome.'"

19. Evan Thomas et al., "No Vietnam," *Newsweek*, December 10, 1990, 24.

20. Charles Tustin Kamps, "Operation Eagle Claw: The Iran Hostage Rescue Mission," *Air & Space Power Journal International Edition—Spanish* 18 (Third Quarter 2006), http://www.airpower.maxwell.af.mil/apjinternational/apj-s/2006/3tri06/kampseng.html. See also Charles Cogan, "Desert One and Its Disorders," *Journal of Military History* 67 (January 2003): 201–216.

21. Coram, *Boyd*, 353. Cogan suggests in "Desert One and Its Disorders" that ten or twelve helicopters would have been enough.

22. Frank L. Jones, *A "Hollow Army" Reappraised: President Carter, Defense Budgets, and the Politics of Military Readiness* (Carlisle, PA: Strategic Studies Institute, US Army War College, 2012), 6–11, vii–ix.

23. *Congressional Record*, Senate, Extensions of Remarks, "Complex Technology Causing Military Readiness Problems," House of Representatives, May 29, 1980, 12752; the article Fazio cited was "U.S. Warplanes—a Giant Fleet of Lemons," by Patrick Oster.

24. Wheeler and Korb, *Military Reform*, 28.

25. Fallows, "Muscle-Bound," 62.

26. Christie interview notes, February 23, 2001, Coram Papers, box 8, folder 3; Boyd Date Books, 1980–1981, Boyd Papers, box 22; Kross, *Military Reform*, 210, nn6–7; Hammond, *Mind of War*, 111, n18.

27. Michael Getler, "Air Conflicts Used as Strategic Pattern," *Hartford (CT) Courant*, March 13, 1981, original article in *Washington Post*.

28. Henry Eason, "Mobility, Maneuver Concept Tossed at Traditional Pentagon Thinking," *Stevens Point (WI) Journal*, March 24, 1981, original article in *Atlanta Constitution*. The article was also reproduced in the *Washington Post*, although the claim to ace status was dropped, replaced with referring to Boyd simply as a "top-notch fighter pilot." See also "Veteran Fighter Pilot Does a Solo for the Military," *Asbury Park (NJ) Press*, May 3, 1981, original article in *Washington Post*.

29. Fallows, "America's High-Tech Weaponry," *Atlantic*, May 1981, 21–33.

30. Fallows, *National Defense* (New York: Random House, 1981), xiii–xv.

31. Fallows, *National Defense*, 42–47, 76–106.

32. Fallows, 171–173, 176–184.

33. Wheeler and Korb, *Military Reform*, 27.

34. Walter Kross, "Military Reform: Past and Present," *Air University Review* 32, no. 5 (July–August 1981): 101.

35. Kross, 102, 106.

36. Kross, 105, 107–108.

37. Quoted in James C. Slife, *Creech Blue: Gen Bill Creech and the Reformation of the Tactical Air Forces, 1978–1984* (Maxwell Air Force Base, AL: Air University Press, 2004), 67.

38. Slife, *Creech*, 67; James Fallows, "I Fly with the Eagles," *Atlantic*, November 1981.

39. Fallows, "I Fly."

40. Jeffrey Record, "The Military Reform Caucus," *Washington Quarterly* (Spring 1983): 125; Wheeler and Korb, *Military Reform*, 19, 38.

41. Timothy P. Malishenko, "Congressional Dynamics of the Military Reform Caucus," *National Contract Management Journal* 21 (Summer 1987): 23–26; Wheeler and Korb, *Military Reform*, 19, 33.

42. Wheeler and Korb, *Military Reform*, 19, n6.

43. Wheeler and Korb, 19–20; Malishenko, "Congressional Dynamics," 26–27; Record, "Military Reform Caucus," 125–129.

44. "Whitehurst Seeks Less Costly Weapons," *Daily Press* (Newport News, VA), August 12, 1981.

45. Michael McManus, "Support Growing for Better Defense Spending," *Democrat and Chronicle* (Rochester, NY), January 21, 1982; Wheeler and Korb, *Military Reform*, 33, n37.

46. McManus, "Support Growing."

47. Bruce Ingersoll, "Ace of the Fighter Pilots Has a New Theory of War," *Detroit Free Press*, May 5, 1982, original article in *Chicago Sun-Times*.

48. Ingersoll, "Ace."

49. "Weapons," *St. Louis Post-Dispatch*, June 10, 1982.

50. Sprey interview notes, February 24, 2001, Coram Papers, box 8, folder 3.

51. Jeffrey Barlow, ed., *Critical Issues: Reforming the Military* (Washington, DC: Heritage Foundation, 1981).

52. Bob Adams, "Fight Brewing over Complex, 'Goldplated' Arms," *St. Louis Post-Dispatch*, June 6, 1982.

53. Bob Adams, "'Cheap Hawks' Preach Reform," *St. Louis Post-Dispatch*, June 11, 1982.

54. Adams, "'Cheap Hawks.'"

55. Adams, "Fight Brewing."

56. Record, "Military Reform Caucus," 127; Malishenko, "Congressional Dynamics," 24; Wheeler and Korb, *Military Reform*, 33; Adams, "'Cheap Hawks'"; "Members—Military Reform Caucus," Coram Papers, box 8, folder 1.

57. Edwin Feulner, "Military Reform Important, but Not Hart's Plan," *Daily Reporter* (Greenfield, IN), July 6, 1983.

58. "Pentagon Worried by Military Reform Caucus," *Des Moines (IA) Register*, December 28, 1983.

59. Adams, "Fight Brewing"; Chiarelli and Gagnon, "Politics," 7; Henry Eason, "'Small Voice' Lobbies for Aggressive Defense," Cox News Service, *Palm Beach Post* (West Palm Beach, FL), July 11, 1982.

60. Moshe Schwartz, "The Nunn-McCurdy Act: Background, Analysis, and Issues for Congress," Congressional Research Service, 7–5700, R41293, June 21, 2010, https://fas.org/sgp/crs/misc/R41293.pdf.

61. Wheeler and Korb, *Military Reform*, 32–37; S. 675 (98th): Department of Defense Authorization Act, 1984, https://www.govtrack.us/congress/bills/98/s675/summary.

62. Charles Mohr, "Arms Numbers Decline as Costs Climb," *Daily Press* (Newport News, VA), October 24, 1982.

63. Adams, "Fight Brewing."

64. "Weapons," *St. Louis Post-Dispatch*; Kross, *Military Reform*, 174–179.

65. Kross, *Military Reform*, 204.

66. Christie interview notes, April 26, 2001, Coram Papers, box 8, folder 1.

67. Fred Reed, "Let's Reform the Military Reformers," *Washington Post*, October 11, 1987; Reed, "Reformers," *Air Force Magazine*, January 1, 1988.

68. Adams, "Fight Brewing."

69. "Weapons," *St. Louis Post-Dispatch*.

70. "Weapons," *St. Louis Post-Dispatch*.

71. See Glenn E. Bugos, *Engineering the F-4 Phantom II: Parts into Systems* (Annapolis, MD: Naval Institute Press, 1996); and Michael Hankins, "The Phantom Menace: The F-4 in Air Combat in Vietnam" (thesis, University of North Texas, 2013).

72. Tidal W. McCoy, "Arms Quality Is Vital Priority," *Chicago Tribune*, June 28, 1983.

73. Adams, "Fight Brewing."

74. An effective summary of these points can be found in Mohr, "Arms Numbers."

75. Burton interview notes, "76 Plus," Coram Papers, box 8, folder 1; Kross, *Military Reform*, 162–172; Wheeler and Korb, *Military Reform*, 25–26; Walter Isaacson, "The Winds of Reform," *Time*, March 7, 1983.

76. Floor statement by Senator Barry Goldwater, chairman, Subcommittee on Tactical Warfare, Senate Armed Services Committee, March 3, 1983, Boyd Papers, folder 7, box 24.

77. Robin Goldstein, "Courter: Watchdog of the Military," *Asbury Park (NJ) Press*, June 8, 1984; Lance Gay, "General Blames Rules for Loss of Several Copters in Grenada," *Pittsburgh Press*, June 23, 1984; Wheeler and Korb, *Military Reform*, 34.

78. Jeffrey Record, "Unprepared: Can U.S. Make War Even If It Wants To?," *Montgomery (AL) Advertiser*, February 2, 1984.

79. Transcript of General A. Slay's Remarks in Response to Pierre Sprey, Wilson Institute Proceedings, 1982, Coram Papers, box 9, folder 6.

80. Slay's Remarks.

81. "Pentagon Worried," Des Moines (IA) Register; "Members—Military Reform Caucus," Coram Papers, box 8, folder 1; Sprey interview notes, February 24, 2001, Coram Papers, box 8, folder 3; Wheeler and Korb, *Military Reform*, 17.

82. Hart and Lind, *America Can Win*, 134; Richard Halloran, "Hart Military Book Has '88 in Mind," *Detroit Free Press*, May 2, 1986.

83. Wayne Biddle, "Northrop F-20 Gets a Fighting Chance," *San Bernardino (CA) County Sun*, June 8, 1985; Jim Stewart, "Report: Disband Joint Chiefs," *Palm Beach Post* (West Palm Beach, FL), October 17, 1985.

84. Email, Wilbur Creech to Robert Coram, June 12, 2000; email, Wilbur Creech to Robert Coram, November 2, 2000; email, Wilbur Creech to Robert Coram, November 4, 2000; email, Chuck Spinney to Robert Coram, June 13, 2000; email, Chuck Spinney to Robert Coram, April 23, 2000; all in Coram Papers, box 8, folder 5. Slife, *Creech*, 69.

85. For examples see Fallows, *National Defense*, 37, 42–45, 100.

86. Coram, *Boyd*, 415–420.

87. Wheeler and Korb, *Military Reform*, 49–53.

88. Burton, *Pentagon Wars*, 237.

89. Celia Cohen, "An Unlikely Team: Bill Roth and Barbara Boxer: Delawarean, Californian Unite to Fight Defense Waste," *News Journal* (Wilmington, DE), May 14, 1989.

90. Cohen, "Unlikely Team."

91. Wheeler and Korb, *Military Reform*, 48.

92. Robert Becker, "Post–Cold War Crisis Challenges Defense Budget," *Daily Press* (Newport News, VA), August 9, 1990.

8. Kicking Vietnam Syndrome

Chapter epigraph quote in Keith Rosenkranz, *Vipers in the Storm: Diary of a Gulf War Fighter Pilot* (New York: McGraw Hill, 2002), 298.

1. Barry A. Turner, "The Organizational and Interorganizational Development of Disasters," *Administrative Science Quarterly* 21 (September 1976): 388.

2. John L. Romjue, "The Evolution of the AirLand Battle Concept," *Air University Review* 35, no. 4 (May–June 1984).

3. Burton, *Pentagon Wars*, 54.

4. Burton, 53; Coram, *Boyd*, 370.

5. Romjue, "Evolution."

6. Burton interview notes, "76 Plus," Coram Papers, box 8, folder 1.

7. Bruce Ingersoll, "Ace of the Fighter Pilots Has a New Theory of War," *Detroit Free Press*, May 5, 1982, original article in *Chicago Sun-Times*.

8. James Brooke, "Maj. Gen Donald Morelli, 51; Helped Design Strategic Plan," *New York Times*, July 4, 1984, http://www.nytimes.com/1984/07/04/obituaries/maj-gen-donald-morelli-51-helped-design-strategic-plan.html.

9. Burton, *Pentagon Wars*, 52.

10. Michael Getler, "Air Conflicts Used as Strategic Pattern," *Hartford (CT) Courant*, March 13, 1981, original article in *Washington Post*.

11. Coram, *Boyd*, 370–371; Burton, *Pentagon Wars*, 53.

12. Coram, *Boyd*, 371; Burton, *Pentagon Wars*, 243.

13. Burton, *Pentagon Wars*, 54–55, Burton mistakenly refers to the school as the "Infantry School"; Ian T. Brown, *A New Conception of War: John Boyd, the U.S. Marines, and Maneuver Warfare* (Quantico, VA: Marine Corps University Press, 2018), 158; Coram, *Boyd*, 376–381, 387–388.

14. Brown, *New Conception*, 150–172; *FMFM-1: Warfighting* (Washington, DC: Headquarters United States Marines Corps, 1989).

15. Coram, *Boyd*, 370.

16. Burton, *Pentagon Wars*, 51.

17. Michel, *Clashes*, 185–188; Getler, "Air Conflicts."

18. Herring, "Preparing," 69.

19. Laslie, *Air Force Way of War*; National Aeronautic Association, "Collier Trophy," accessed September 13, 2019, https://naa.aero/awards/awards-and-trophies/collier-trophy; see also Marshall L. Michel III, "The Revolt of the Majors: How the Air Force Changed after Vietnam" (PhD diss., Auburn University, 2006).

20. Quoted in John Andreas Olsen, *John Warden and the Renaissance of American Air Power* (Dulles, VA: Potomac Books, 2011), 4, 42.

21. John Warden, *The Air Campaign: Planning for Combat* (Washington, DC: National Defense University Press, 1988). Warden's work was frequently updated and revised in subsequent editions, some with significant changes. For more analysis of Warden's theories see Olsen, *Renaissance*, 64–82; David Mets, *The Air Campaign: John Warden and the Classical Airpower Theorists* (Maxwell Air Force Base, AL: Air University Press, 1998); Fadok, "John Boyd and John Warden."

22. Quoted in Olsen, *Renaissance*, 81.

23. Quoted in Olsen, 83.

24. Olsen, 88–96.

25. This case is made well in Mets, *Air Campaign*, 55–79.

26. Richard G. Davis, *On Target: Organizing and Executing the Strategic Air Campaign against Iraq* (Washington, DC: Air Force History and Museums Program, 2002), 58–59.

27. Davis, *On Target*, 66–67, 75–77, 82–91. See also Diane T. Putney, *Airpower Advantage: Planning the Gulf War Air Campaign, 1989–1991* (Washington, DC: Air Force History and Museums Program, 2004).

28. Thomas A. Keaney and Eliot A. Cohen, *Gulf War Air Power Survey Summary Report*, Washington, DC, 1993, 12–13 (hereafter cited as *GWAPS Summary Report*). See also Craig Brown, *Debrief: A Complete History of U.S. Aerial Engagements, 1981 to the Present* (Atglen, PA: Schiffer Military History, 2007).

29. Williamson Murray and Wayne W. Thompson, *Air War in the Persian Gulf* (Baltimore: Nautical and Aviation Publishing, 1997), 105, 130, 180, 193, 312.

30. "Operation Desert Storm: Evaluation of the Air Campaign," United States General Accounting Office Report to the Ranking Minority Member, Committee on Commerce, House of Representatives, June 1997, GAO/NSIAD-97-134, 172 (hereafter "Operation Desert Storm," GAO Report). The implication regarding the F-16 and the unverified Horner quote are from Winslow Wheeler, coauthor of the GAO report and a friend of Boyd's, from an email to the author.

31. *Gulf War Air Power Survey*, vol. 5, *A Statistical Compendium and Chronology*, Washington, DC, 1993, 637, 641, 653–654 (hereafter cited as *GWAPS* v5); "Intelligence Community Assessment of the Lieutenant Commander Speicher Case," March 27, 2001, FOIA Electronic Reading Room, CIA, September 10, 2006; "Aerial Victory Tables," US Air Force Historical Research Agency; Brown, *Debrief*.

32. Murray and Thompson, *Air War*, 67, 92.

33. Carlo Kopp, "Operation Desert Storm: The Electronic Battle Parts 1–3," Air Power Australia, 1993, accessed November 11, 2017, http://www.ausairpower.net/Analysis-ODS-EW.html; see also Murray and Thompson, *Air War*, 67–69.

34. Murray and Thompson, *Air War*, 122–123. Other missions totaled eighteen losses the first night, the majority on interdiction strikes: *GWAPS* v5, 642.

35. Brown, *Debrief*, 51–73; Murray and Thompson, *Air War*, 110–111, 162.

36. Murray and Thompson, *Air War*, 180.

37. Karl Mueller, "Strategies of Coercion: Denial, Punishment, and the Future of Air Power," *Security Studies* 7, no. 3 (1998): 212.

38. *GWAPS Summary Report*, 60; *GWAPS* v5, 653–654; Daniel Haulman, "No Contest: Aerial Combat in the 1990s," presentation, Society for Military History annual meeting, May 2001, 6; Brown, *Debrief*, 23–149.

39. Ian D'Costa, "The EF-111 Raven Managed to Take Down an Iraqi Mirage . . . without Ever Firing a Shot," Tactical Air Network, accessed November 11, 2017, https://tacairnet.com/2013/09/10/unarmed-kill/. Aviation analyst Tom Cooper has disputed this story, arguing that the Iraqi pilot escaped and later claimed the EF-111 as a kill of his own, although Cooper does not cite specific sources for the claim. See Tom Cooper, "In January 1991, Both Iraq and America Claimed Fictional Air-to-Air Victories," *War Is Boring*, September 28, 2017, http://warisboring.com/45910-2/.

40. For a brief overview of problems encountered see *GWAPS Summary Report*.

41. Correll, "Reformers," 44.

42. The literature discussing RMA is extensive. Two useful overviews and critiques of the concept include Stephen Biddle, *Military Power: Explaining Victory and Defeat in Modern Battle* (Princeton, NJ: Princeton University Press, 2006); and Thomas G. Mahnken, *Technology and the American Way of War since 1945* (New York: Columbia University Press, 2008).

43. Richard Hallion, *Storm over Iraq: Air Power and the Gulf War* (Washington, DC: Smithsonian Institution Press, 2002), 128, 146.

44. Burton, *Pentagon Wars*, 241, 242.

45. Werrell, *Chasing the Silver Bullet*, 99–119, 145–146.

46. *GWAPS* v5, 418; *GWAPS* "Summary Report," 142; Hallion, *Storm*, 211; Murray and Thompson, *Air War*, 297; "Operation Desert Storm," GAO Report, 26–27, 70–71.

47. "Operation Desert Storm," GAO Report, 1. The report's tally of "misses" also included many bomb strikes that had been counted as "hits" but lacked sufficient corroborating video or other proof, or strikes that lacked consistency in the criteria for determining a hit or miss. Many strikes included a "miss distance" for when a bomb was not perfectly on the aim point, and in some cases strikes recorded as hits or misses had similar miss distances. This could be the result of different target types and their vulnerabilities, although the report did not differentiate target vulnerability. See 128–132. Wheeler's comment is from an email to the author.

48. "Operation Desert Storm," GAO Report. Precision weapons are discussed throughout, with a summation on 193.

49. "Operation Desert Storm," GAO Report, 2, 35, 66.

50. Comments of Robert Coram, Marine Corps Air Station Beaufort, August 14, 2015, http://robertcoram.com/comments-of-robert-coram-marine-corps-air-station-beaufort-friday-14-august-2015/; Coram, *Boyd*, 422–425.

51. Dick Cheney interview notes, n.d., Coram Papers, box 8, folder 1.

52. Michael R. Gordon and Bernard E. Trainor, *The Generals' War: The Inside Story of the Conflict in the Gulf* (New York: Little, Brown, 1995), 124–153; see also Rick Atkinson, *Crusade: The Untold Story of the Persian Gulf War* (New York: Houghton Mifflin, 1993), 108–113; Gilbert E. Petrina, "An Agency Theory View of the Military Advisor" (thesis, School of Advanced Air and Space Studies, Air University, Maxwell Air Force Base, June 2005), 58.

53. James Burton, "Pushing Them out the Back Door," *Proceedings*, June 1993, 37–42; Burton, *Pentagon Wars*, 245–246.

54. Gordon and Trainor, *Generals' War*, 159, 290, 362, 377–432, 464; Atkinson, *Crusade*, 258–259, 400–407; Robert Citino, *Blitzkrieg to Desert Storm: The Evolution of*

Operational Warfare (Lawrence: University Press of Kansas, 2004), 285–287; See also Metz, "Boydmania," 105.

55. Mahnken, *Technology*, 132–133; Citino, *Blitzkrieg to Desert Storm*, 287; Gordon and Trainor, *Generals' War*, 408.

56. George (H. W.) Bush: "Remarks to the American Legislative Exchange Council," March 1, 1991, https://www.presidency.ucsb.edu/documents/remarks-the-american-legislative-exchange-council-0.

57. Tom Peters, "Don't Leap to Hasty Conclusions in the Wake of War," *Chicago Tribune*, March 25, 1991.

58. Fino, *Tiger Check*.

Conclusion

Chapter epigraph from Wilbur Creech email, forwarded to Thomas Christie, "Forthcoming Books on Boyd and His Discourse," March 24, 2001, Coram Papers, box 8, folder 4.

1. Ron Hutchinson, "F-16 Falcon Fights for Life," *Montgomery (AL) Advertiser*, October 23, 1991, original article in *Fort Worth Star-Telegram*.

2. Mistakenly reported as the prototype by Charles H. Bogino, "F-16 Gains Higher Stature at Langley, Monument Honors Role in Gulf War," *Daily Press* (Newport News, VA), October 25, 1991. The plane at Langley is the first delivered production model (serial 78-0001); see F-16.net, accessed October 8, 2020, http://www.f-16.net/aircraft-database/F-16/airframe-profile/11/.

3. "Problem Areas Are the Same," *Palm Beach Post* (West Palm Beach, FL), March 9, 1998.

4. Greg Schneider, "Leading an Assault on the Pentagon," *Baltimore Sun*, March 8, 1998.

5. Thomas Ricks, "Whatever Happened to . . . Pierre Sprey?," *Washington Post*, May 16, 2006, http://www.washingtonpost.com/wp-dyn/content/article/2006/05/15/AR2006051501518.html.

6. Winslow T. Wheeler, *The Wastrels of Defense: How Congress Sabotages U.S. Security* (New York: Naval Institute Press, 2004).

7. Winslow T. Wheeler, *The Pentagon Labyrinth: 10 Short Essays to Help You through It: From 10 Pentagon Insiders, Retired Military Officers and Specialists with over 400 Years of Defense Experience* (Washington, DC: Center for Defense Information, 2011).

8. Some colleagues in the late 1970s talked of Lind with apprehension; one described him as "a guest on the Joe Pyne show," a conservative talk show known for inviting extremists as guests; Fallows, "Muscle Bound," 62.

9. William Lind, "The Next Conservatism," Traditional Right, April 16, 2016, https://www.traditionalright.com/the-next-conservatism/; William Lind (under pen name Thomas Hobbes), *Victoria: A Novel of 4th Generation Warfare* (Kouvola, Finland: Castalia House, 2014). Excerpts of the book appear in Boyd Papers, box 23, folder 13, along with two other unattributed documents, box 24, folder 6, possibly written by Lind, that argue against Democratic liberalism and promote authoritarian systems and anti-Semitic conspiracy theories.

10. Richard Aboulafia, "Trump's Strange Fixation with the Super Hornet: Sorting the Fake from the Real," *Forbes*, September 11, 2017, https://www.forbes.com/sites/richardaboulafia/2017/09/11/trumps-super-hornet-assertions-sorting-fake-from-real/#5e79e6643254.

11. Ellen Mitchell, "Trump Wants 'Goddamned Steam' Catapults on New Aircraft Carriers," Hill, May 11, 2017, http://thehill.com/policy/defense/333040-trump-wants-goddamned-steam-catapults-on-new-aircraft-carriers.

12. Prine, "Q & A with Merrill 'Tony' McPeak."

13. For an example of the former see Burton, *Pentagon Wars*, 3; for the latter, tempered view, see Hammond, *Mind of War*, 77.

14. For example, Brown, *New Conception*, 140–144; Osinga, *Science, Strategy and War*, 6–9, 272–279; and "The Enemy as a Complex Adaptive System," 48–52; See also Fadok, "John Boyd and John Warden."

15. Osinga, *Science, Strategy, and War*, 5.

16. Tyson Wetzel, "Changing the USAF's Aerial 'Kill' Criteria," Balloons to Drones, June 26, 2017, https://balloonstodrones.wordpress.com/2017/06/26/changing-the-usafs-aerial-kill-criteria/; and Shawn Snow, "What Counts as an Aerial Victory? Drones Change the Face of Aerial Combat," *Air Force Times*, June 24, 2017, http://www.airforcetimes.com/articles/what-counts-as-an-aerial-victorydrones-change-the-face-of-aerial-combat; Oriana Pawlyk, "US F/A-18E Shoots Down Syrian Su-22 in Air-to-Air Kill," Military.com, June 18, 2017, https://www.military.com/daily-news/2017/06/18/us-navy-fa18e-shoots-down-su22-over-syria.html; Stephen Losey, "Air-to-Air Combat Is Back: How Will the Air Force Respond as the War over Syria Heats Up?," *Air Force Times*, June 26, 2017. https://www.airforcetimes.com/news/your-air-force/2017/06/26/air-to-air-combat-is-back-how-will-the-air-force-respond-as-the-war-over-syria-heats-up/.

17. The four pilots are Thomas Dietz, Robert Hehemann, Cesar Rodriguez, and Robert Wright. There have been four other victory credits due to guns, but not from fighter aircraft. Two are from B-52 gunners in 1972, and two from A-10s shooting down helicopters with the GAU-8 cannon in 1991. See Brown, *Debrief*; and Aerial Victory Tables, Air Force Historical Research Agency.

18. "Modern Warfare: The Evolution of the Aerial Dogfight," *Wall Street Journal*, August 7, 2019, https://www.wsj.com/video/modern-warfare-the-evolution-of-the-aerial-dogfight/DB02A933-F7FE-4BF8-9AE6-D73473BC3FCF.html.

19. All the chiefs of staff have also been men; no woman has ever served in that role. The appointment of Schwartz came in the context of scandals and institutional rivalries; the selection of someone with his background was likely intended to send a message to the services. See Tom Bowman, "New Chief Aims to Restore Air Force's Reputation," NPR, *All Things Considered*, August 26, 2008, https://www.npr.org/templates/story/story.php?storyId=93974973.

20. Williamson Murray and Mark Grimsley, "On Strategy," in *The Making of Strategy: Rulers, States, and War*, ed. Williamson Murray, Macgregor Knox, and Alvin Bernstein (New York: Cambridge University Press, 1994), 13.

21. Quoted in Scrogham, *Combat Relevant Task*, 67.

BIBLIOGRAPHY

Archival Sources

Air Force Historical Research Agency: Maxwell Air Force Base, AL

Greater St. Louis Air and Space Museum Archives

Marine Corps Archives and Records Division, Quantico, VA: John Boyd Personal Papers, Robert Coram Personal Papers

National Archives and Records Administration, College Park, MD

President Gerald Ford Presidential Library: White House Central Files Subject Files—ND 1 Aircraft 3/1/75–6/30/75, Martin R. Hoffmann Papers

Smithsonian National Air and Space Museum Archives

United States Air Force Academy, McDermott Library: Clark Special Collections Branch

University of Texas at Dallas, George H. Williams Jr. World War I Aviation Library: Ola Slater Collection, George H. Williams Collection, Henry Clay Papers, James Kerr Papers

Other Sources

Aboulafia, Richard. "Trump's Strange Fixation with the Super Hornet: Sorting the Fake from the Real." *Forbes*, September 11, 2017. https://www.forbes.com/sites/richardaboulafia/2017/09/11/trumps-super-hornet-assertions-sorting-fake-from-real/#5e79e6643254.

Adams, Bob. "'Cheap Hawks' Preach Reform." *St. Louis Post-Dispatch*, June 11, 1982.

Adams, Bob. "Fight Brewing over Complex, 'Goldplated' Arms." *St. Louis Post-Dispatch*, June 6, 1982.

Allard, Carl. *Command, Control, and the Common Defense*. New Haven, CT: Yale University Press, 1990.

Anderegg, C. R. *Sierra Hotel: Flying Air Force Fighters in the Decade after Vietnam*. Washington, DC: Air Force History and Museums Program, 2001.

Appy, Christian G. *American Reckoning: The Vietnam War and Our National Identity*. New York: Viking, 2015.

Arizona Republic (Phoenix). "Tactician Urges U.S. to Adopt Blitz Warfare." March 23, 1981.

Aronstein, David C., and Albert C. Piccirillo. "The F-16 Lightweight Fighter: A Case Study in Technology Transition." In *Technology and the Air Force: A Retrospective*

Assessment, edited by Jacob Neufeld, George M. Watson Jr., and David Che-noweth, 203–230. Washington, DC: Air Force History and Museums Program, 1997.

Aronstein, David C., and Albert C. Piccirillo. *The Lightweight Fighter Program: A Successful Approach to Fighter Technology Transition*. Reston, VA: American Institute of Aeronautics and Astronautics, 1997.

Asbury Park (NJ) Press. "Veteran Fighter Pilot Does a Solo for the Military." May 3, 1981. Original article in *Washington Post*.

Atkinson, Rick. *Crusade: The Untold Story of the Persian Gulf War*. New York: Houghton Mifflin, 1993.

Baker, Max B. "How the F-16 Fighter Jet Put Fort Worth on the Aerospace Map." *Fort Worth Star-Telegram*, November 24, 2017.

Barlow, Jeffrey G., ed. *Reforming the Military*. Washington, DC: Heritage Foundation, 1981.

Barrett, William E. "Squadron Parade: 90th Squadron." *Warbirds*, September 1934, 109–111.

Beard, Jim. "WonderCon 2012: Captain Marvel." Marvel.com, March 17, 2012. https://www.webcitation.org/6BjZkxz9A?url=http://marvel.com/news/story/18290/wondercon_2012_captain_marvel#.

Beaumont, Roger A. "On the Wehrmacht Mystique." *Military Review* 66 (July 1986): 44–56.

Becker, Robert. "Post–Cold War Crisis Challenges Defense Budget." *Daily Press* (Newport News, VA), August 9, 1990.

Biddle, Stephen. *Military Power: Explaining Victory and Defeat in Modern Battle*. Princeton, NJ: Princeton University Press, 2006.

Biddle, Wayne. "Northrop F-20 Gets a Fighting Chance." *San Bernardino County (CA) Sun*, June 8, 1985.

Bjorkman, Eileen. "The Outrageous Adolescence of the F-16." *Air & Space Magazine*, March 2014. https://www.airspacemag.com/military-aviation/outrageous-adolescence-f-16-180949491

Blesse, Frederick C. *"Check Six": A Fighter Pilot Looks Back*. New York: Ivy Books, 1987.

Bogino, Charles H. "F-16 Gains Higher Stature at Langley, Monument Honors Role in Gulf War." *Daily Press* (Newport News, VA), October 25, 1991.

Boyd, John R. *Aerial Attack Study*. Accessed December 26, 2017. http://www.ausair power.net/APA-Boyd-Papers.html.

Boyd, John R. *A Discourse on Winning and Losing*. Edited by Grant T. Hammond. Maxwell Air Force Base, AL: Air University Press, 2018.

Boyd, John R., Thomas P. Christie, and James E. Gibson. "Energy Maneuverability." Air Proving Ground Center Eglin Air Force Base. March 1966.

Boyne, Walter J. *Phantom in Combat*. Washington, DC: Smithsonian Institution Press, 1985.

Brandt, Thomas C., Howard E. Bethel, and Wallace B. Frank Jr. "Mission-Area Resource Allocation for Air Force R&D." *Defense Systems Management Review* 2 (Spring 1979): 77–92.

"Briefings—Colonel John R. Boyd, USAF." Boyd Papers collection. http://www.aus airpower.net/APA-Boyd-Papers.html.

"Brigadier General Garry A. Willard Jr." Biography. U.S. Air Force (website). Accessed June 4, 2017. http://www.af.mil/About-Us/Biographies/Display/Article/105256/brigadier-general-garry-a-willard-jr/.

Brooke, James. "Maj. Gen Donald Morelli, 51; Helped Design Strategic Plan." *New York Times*, July 4, 1984.

Brown, Craig. *Debrief: A Complete History of U.S. Aerial Engagements, 1981 to the Present.* Atglen, PA: Schiffer Military History, 2007.

Brown, Ian T. *A New Conception of War: John Boyd, the U.S. Marines, and Maneuver Warfare.* Quantico, VA: Marine Corps University Press, 2018.

Brown, Shannon A. *Providing the Means of War: Historical Perspectives on Defense Acquisition, 1945–2000.* Washington, DC: Government Printing Office, 2005.

Brownlow, Cecil. "Soviet Air Force Unveils Advanced Designs for Expanded Limited War Capability." *Aviation Week & Space Technology*, July 17, 1967, 21–39.

Bryson, A. E., and W. F. Denham. "A Steepest-Ascent Method for Solving Optimum Programming Problems." *Journal of Applied Mechanics* 29 (June 1962): 247–257.

Buckner, J. K., D. B. Benepe, and P. W. Hill. "Aerodynamic Design Evolution of the YF-16." American Institute of Aeronautics and Astronautics 6th Aircraft Design, Flight Test and Operations Meeting, August 12–14, 1974. Accessed September 14, 2019. https://doi.org/10.2514/6.1974-935.

Bugos, Glenn E. *Engineering the F-4 Phantom II: Parts into Systems.* Annapolis, MD: Naval Institute Press, 1996.

Builder, Carl H. *The Icarus Syndrome: The Role of Air Power Theory in the Evolution and Fate of the U.S. Air Force.* New York: Routledge, 2002. First published 1994 as a RAND report.

Builder, Carl H. *The Masks of War: American Military Styles in Strategy and Analysis.* Baltimore: Johns Hopkins University Press, 1989.

Burgon, Rob. *Piano Burning and Other Fighter Pilot Traditions.* Salt Lake City: Slipstream, 2016.

Burton, James. *The Pentagon Wars: Reformers Challenge the Old Guard.* Annapolis, MD: Naval Institute Press, 1993.

Burton, James. "Pushing Them out the Back Door." *Proceedings* (Naval Institute), June 1993, 37–42.

Busek, Joseph R. "A Historical Analysis of Total Package Procurement, Life Cycle Costing, and Design to Cost." Master's thesis, Air Force Institute of Technology, Air University, June 1976.

Bush, George (H. W.). "Remarks to the American Legislative Exchange Council." American Presidency Project. March 1, 1991. Online by Gerhard Peters and John T. Woolley. https://www.presidency.ucsb.edu/documents/remarks-the-american-legislative-exchange-council-0.

Cactus Air Force Wings and Wheels Museum. "EF-111A RAVEN." Accessed November 11, 2017. http://www.cactusairforce.com/inventory_item/ef-111a/.

Call, Steve. *Selling Air Power: Military Aviation and American Popular Culture after World War II.* College Station: Texas A&M University Press, 2009.

Chiarelli, Peter W., and Raymond C. Gagnon Jr. "The Politics of Military Reform." Center for Naval Warfare Studies Report 84–88. Newport, RI: Naval War College, June 1985.

Church, George, and Christopher Redman. "Pariah at the Pentagon." *Time*, March 7, 1983.

Citino, Robert. *Blitzkrieg to Desert Storm: The Evolution of Operational Warfare*. Lawrence: University Press of Kansas, 2004.

Citino, Robert. *The German Way of War: From the Thirty Years' War to the Third Reich*. Lawrence: University Press of Kansas, 2005.

Citino, Robert. *The Wehrmacht Retreats: Fighting a Lost War, 1943*. Lawrence: University Press of Kansas, 2012.

Clodfelter, Mark. *The Limits of Air Power: The American Bombing of North Vietnam*. Lincoln: University of Nebraska Press, 2006.

Code of Federal Regulations of the United States of America. Washington, DC: Government Printing Office. January 1, 1969, p. 63. https://books. google.com/books?id=POY6AAAAIAAJ&dq=%22Total%20Package%20 Procurement%22&pg=PA63.

Cogan, Charles. "Desert One and Its Disorders." *Journal of Military History* 67 (January 2003): 201–216.

Cohen, Celia. "An Unlikely Team: Bill Roth and Barbara Boxer: Delawarean, Californian Unite to Fight Defense Waste." *News Journal* (Wilmington, DE), May 14, 1989.

Collins, Michael D. "A Fear of Flying: Diagnosing Traumatic Neurosis among British Aviators of the Great War." *First World War Studies* 6 (July 2015): 187–202.

"Col. Richard R. Hallock Papers (MC284); Biographical Note." Columbia State University. Accessed September 24, 2017. https://archives.columbusstate.edu/ findingaids/mc284.php.

Congressional Record. Extensions of Remarks. "Complex Technology Causing Military Readiness Problems." House of Representatives, May 29, 1980, 12752.

Cooper, Tom. "In January 1991, Both Iraq and America Claimed Fictional Air-to-Air Victories." War Is Boring, September 28, 2017. http://warisboring. com/45910-2/.

Coram, Robert. *Boyd: The Fighter Pilot Who Changed the Art of War*. New York: Little, Brown, 2002.

Coram, Robert. "Comments of Robert Coram, Marine Corps Air Station Beaufort, 14 August 2015." http://robertcoram.com/comments-of-robert-coram-marine-corps-air-station-beaufort-friday-14-august-2015/.

Corn, Joseph. *The Winged Gospel: America's Romance with Aviation, 1900–1950*. Oxford: Oxford University Press, 1983.

Correll, John T. "A Brush with the Air Force." *Air Force Magazine*, July 2007, 42–49.

Correll, John T. "The Legend of Frank Luke." *Air Force Magazine*, August 1, 2009. https://www.airforcemag.com/article/0809luke/.

Correll, John T. "The Reformers." *Air Force Magazine*, February 2008, 40–44.

Correll, John T. "Up in the Air with Milton Caniff." *Air Force Magazine*, April 2013, 66–73.

Crane, Conrad C. *American Airpower Strategy in Korea, 1950–1953*. Lawrence: University Press of Kansas, 2000.

Crane, Conrad C. *Bombs, Cities, and Civilians: American Airpower Strategy in World War II*. Lawrence: University Press of Kansas, 1993.

Cunningham, Randy. *Fox Two: The Story of America's First Ace in Vietnam*. Mesa, AZ: Champlin Fighter Museum, 1984.

Daddis, Gregory. "The Importance of the Vietnam War's Tet Offensive." War on the Rocks, January 29, 2018. https://warontherocks.com/2018/01/importance-vietnam-wars-tet-offensive/.

Daily Press (Newport News, VA). "Whitehurst Seeks Less Costly Weapons." August 12, 1981.

Davis, Richard G. *On Target: Organizing and Executing the Strategic Air Campaign against Iraq*. Washington, DC: Air Force History and Museums Program, 2002.

D'Costa, Ian. "The EF-111 Raven Managed to Take Down an Iraqi Mirage . . . without Ever Firing a Shot." Tactical Air Network. Accessed November 11, 2017. https://tacairnet.com/2013/09/10/unarmed-kill/.

Deaile, Melvin G. *Always at War: Organizational Culture in Strategic Air Command, 1946–62*. Annapolis, MD: Naval Institute Press, 2018.

Des Moines (IA) Register. "Pentagon Worried by Military Reform Caucus." December 28, 1983.

Dildy, Douglas C., and Warren E. Thompson. *F-86 Sabre vs MiG-15: Korea 1950–1953*. Long Island City, NY: Osprey, 2013.

Dorr, Robert F. "Why the P-38 Flunked in Europe." *Aviation History* 24 (May 2014): 22.

Eason, Henry. "Mobility, Maneuver Concept Tossed at Traditional Pentagon Thinking." *Stevens Point (WI) Journal*, March 24, 1981. Original article in *Atlanta Constitution*.

Eason, Henry. "'Small Voice' Lobbies for Aggressive Defense." Cox News Service, in *Palm Beach Post* (West Palm Beach, FL), July 11, 1982.

Echevarria, Antulio. *After Clausewitz: German Military Thinkers before the Great War*. Lawrence: University Press of Kansas, 2000.

Echevarria, Antulio. *Reconsidering the American Way of War: US Military Practice from the Revolution to Afghanistan*. Washington, DC: Georgetown University Press, 2014.

Elliot, William. "The Development of Fly-by-Wire Control." *AFMC Historical Study 7*, December 1996.

Ethell, Jeff. *F-15 Eagle*. Shepperton, UK: Ian Allan, 1984.

"Extended Interview: Pierre Sprey." Fifth Estate, September 28, 2012. http://www.cbc.ca/fifth/blog/extended-interview-pierre-sprey.

Fadok, David S. "John Boyd and John Warden: Air Power's Quest for Strategic Paralysis." Thesis, School of Advanced Airpower Studies, Maxwell Air Force Base; Air University Press, 1995.

Fallows, James. "America's High-Tech Weaponry." *Atlantic*, May 1981, 21–33.

Fallows, James. "I Fly with the Eagles." *Atlantic*, November 1981, 70–77.

Fallows, James. "Muscle-Bound Superpower: The State of America's Defense." *Atlantic*, October 1979, 59–78.

Fallows, James. *National Defense*. New York: Random House, 1981.

Farnsworth, Clyde H. "Gen. Dynamics' 'Contract of the Century.'" Insert in "David S. Lewis Comments on Winning F-16 Contract." *St. Louis Post-Dispatch*, July 29, 1975.

Fehr, Ernst, and Urs Fischbacher. "The Nature of Human Altruism." *Nature* 425, no. 6960 (2003): 785.

"The F-15 Competition." *Armed Forces Journal* 107 (September 13, 1969): 14–24.

Feulner, Edwin. "Military Reform Important, but Not Hart's Plan." *Daily Reporter* (Greenfield, IN), July 6, 1983.

"The Fighter Aces." War Stories, Fox News. September 2009; interview conducted on unknown date in 2007, accessed November 18, 2017. Footage of the interview at https://www.youtube.com/watch?v=w0ezJLuUsdI. Information about the episode at http://www.foxnews.com/on-air/war-stories/2009/09/25/fighter-aces.

Fino, Steven A. "'All the Missiles Work': Technological Dislocations and Military Innovation." Drew Paper No. 12. Maxwell Air Force Base, AL: Air University Press, 2015.

Fino, Steven A. "Breaking the Trance: The Perils of Technological Exuberance in the U.S. Air Force Entering Vietnam." *Journal of Military History* 77 (Spring 2013): 625–655.

Fino, Steven A. "Doubling Down: AIMVAL-ACEVAL and US Air Force Investment in TacAir Post-Vietnam." *Vulcan* 2 (2014): 125–161.

Fino, Steven A. *Tiger Check: Automating the US Air Force Fighter Pilot in Air-to-Air Combat, 1950–1980.* Baltimore: Johns Hopkins University Press, 2017.

Fitzgerald, A. Ernest. *The High Priests of Waste.* New York: Norton, 1972.

Foreign Relations of the United States, 1969–1976. Vol. 1, *Foundations of Foreign Policy, 1969–1972.* Document 29. https://history.state.gov/historicaldocuments/frus1969-76v01/d29.

Frieser, Karl-Heinz. *The Blitzkrieg Legend: The 1940 Campaign in the West.* Annapolis, MD: Naval Institute Press, 2013.

Fritzsche, Peter. *A Nation of Fliers: German Aviation and the Popular Imagination.* Cambridge, MA: Harvard University Press, 1992.

Fussell, Paul. *The Great War and Modern Memory.* London: Oxford University Press, 1975.

Futrell, Robert F. *The United States Air Force in Korea, 1950–1953.* Washington, DC: Air Force History and Museums Program, 1983.

Gaddis, John Lewis. *Strategies of Containment: A Critical Appraisal of American National Security Policy during the Cold War.* Oxford: Oxford University Press, 2005.

Galland, Adolf. *The First and the Last: The Rise and Fall of the German Fighter Forces, 1938–1945.* Translated by Mervyn Savill. New York: Bantam, 1978; originally published New York: Henry Holt, 1954.

Garamond, Jack, and Jules Whitcover. "Butter and Guns Dilemma." *Chicago Sun-Times*, August 19, 1981.

Gay, Lance. "General Blames Rules for Loss of Several Copters in Greneda." *Pittsburgh Press*, June 23, 1984.

Gentile, Gian P. *How Effective Is Strategic Bombing? Lessons Learned from World War II and Kosovo.* New York: NYU Press, 2001.

Getler, Michael. "Air Conflicts Used as Strategic Pattern." *Hartford (CT) Courant*, March 13, 1981. Original article in *Washington Post*.

Gibbons, Floyd. "The Red Knight of Germany." *Liberty*, November 5, 1927, 61–65.

Gillespie, Daniel Mark. "Mission Emphasis and the Determination of Needs for New Weapon Systems." PhD diss., Massachusetts Institute of Technology, 2009.

Gintis, Herbert, Samuel Bowles, Robert Boyd, and Ernst Fehr. "Explaining Altruistic Behavior in Humans." *Evolution and Human Behavior* 24, no. 3 (2003): 153–172.

Gladysz, Thomas. "Now We're in the Air: The Silent Cinema and Aviation." SFGate, February 23, 2012. https://blog.sfgate.com/tgladysz/2012/02/23/now-were-in-the-air-the-silent-cinema-and-aviation/.

Goldstein, Robin. "Courter: Watchdog of the Military." *Asbury Park (NJ) Press*, June 8, 1984.

Good, Stephen. "F-16 Fighters Beginning to Roll off Production Line." *Morning News—Sunday News Journal* (Wilmington, DE), October 15, 1978. Original article in *Dallas Times Herald*.

Gordon, Michael R., and Bernard E. Trainor. *The Generals' War: The Inside Story of the Conflict in the Gulf*. New York: Little, Brown, 1995.

Gorn, Michael H. *Harnessing the Genie: Science and Technology Forecasting for the Air Force, 1944–1986*. Washington, DC: Office of Air Force History, US Air Force, 1989.

Grant, Tim, and Bas Kooter. "Comparing OODA and Other Models as Operational View C2 Architecture." 10th International Command and Control Research and Technology Symposium, 2005.

Grant, Zalin. *Over the Beach: The Air War in Vietnam*. New York: Pocket Books, 1986.

Gray, Colin. *Modern Strategy*. Oxford: Oxford University Press, 1999.

Greenhous, Brereton. "The Israeli Experience." In *Case Studies in the Achievement of Air Superiority*, edited by Benjamin Franklin Cooling, 563–601. Washington, DC: Air Force History and Museums Program, 1994.

Gulf War Air Power Survey. Vol. 5, *A Statistical Compendium and Chronology*. Washington, DC: Department of the Air Force, 1993.

Hagopian, Patrick. *The Vietnam War in American Memory: Veterans, Memorials, and the Politics of Healing*. Amherst: University of Massachusetts Press, 2012.

Hallion, Richard. *Storm over Iraq: Air Power and the Gulf War*. Washington, DC: Smithsonian Institution Press, 2002.

Halloran, Richard. "Hart Military Book Has '88 in Mind." *Detroit Free Press*, May 2, 1986.

Hamilton-Patterson, James. *Marked for Death: The First War in the Air*. New York: Pegasus Books, 2016.

Hammond, Grant. *The Mind of War: John Boyd and American Security*. Washington, DC: Smithsonian Books, 2001.

Hampton, Dan. *Viper Pilot: A Memoir of Air Combat*. New York: William Morrow, 2012.

Hankins, Michael. "The Phantom Menace: The F-4 in Air Combat in Vietnam." Thesis, University of North Texas, 2013.

Hankins, Michael. "The Teaball Solution: The Evolution of Air Combat Technology in Vietnam, 1968–1972." *Air Power History* 63 (Fall 2016): 7–24.

Hannah, Craig C. *Striving for Air Superiority: The Tactical Air Command in Vietnam*. College Station: Texas A&M University Press, 2002.

Hart, Gary, and William S. Lind. *America Can Win: The Case for Military Reform*. Bethesda, MD: Adler & Adler, 1986.

Hart, Peter. *Aces Falling: War above the Trenches, 1918*. London: Phoenix, 2008.

Hasík, James. "Beyond the Briefing: Theoretical and Practical Problems in the Works and Legacy of John Boyd." *Contemporary Security Policy* 34, no. 3 (2013): 583–599.

Hatch, Mary Jo, and Majken Schultz. "The Dynamics of Organizational Identity." *Human Relations* 55 (August 2002): 989–1018.

Haulman, Daniel. "No Contest: Aerial Combat in the 1990s." Presentation, Society for Military History annual meeting, May 2001.

Heatherly, Charles L. *Mandate for Leadership: Policy Management in a Conservative Administration.* Washington, DC: Heritage Foundation, 1981.

Herring, George C. "Preparing Not to Refight the Last War: The Impact of the Vietnam War on the U.S. Military." In *After Vietnam: Legacies of a Lost War*, edited by Charles E. Neu, 56–84. Baltimore: Johns Hopkins University Press, 2000.

Herring, George C. "The 'Vietnam Syndrome' and American Foreign Policy." *Virginia Quarterly Review* 57 (Autumn 1981): 594–612.

Hinton, Martin. "Producer's Perspective: Life and Times of Robin Olds." Fox News, July 6, 2007. http://www.foxnews.com/story/2007/07/06/producer-perspective-life-and-times-robin-olds.html.

"The History of SETP." Society of Experimental Test Pilots. Accessed June 14, 2017. http://www.setp.org/about-setp/history.html.

Hobson, Chris. *Vietnam Air Losses: United States Air Force, Navy, and Marine Corps Fixed-Wing Aircraft Losses in Southeast Asia, 1961–1973.* Hinkley, UK: Midland, 2001.

Holm, Jeanne. *Women in the Military: An Unfinished Revolution.* Rev. ed. Novato, CA: Presidio, 1993.

Holwill, Richard N. *Agenda '83.* Washington, DC: Heritage Foundation, 1983.

Honodel, David R. *The Phantom Vietnam War: An F-4 Pilot's Combat over Laos.* Denton: University of North Texas Press, 2018.

Hudson, James J. *Hostile Skies: A Combat History of the American Air Service in World War I.* Syracuse, NY: Syracuse University Press, 1968.

Hughes, Thomas P. *Networks of Power: Electrification in Western Society, 1880–1930.* Baltimore: Johns Hopkins University Press, 1983.

Hughes, Thomas P. "Technological Momentum." In *Does Technology Drive History? The Dilemma of Technological Determinism*, edited by Merritt Roe Smith and Leo Marx, 101–114. Cambridge, MA: MIT Press, 1994.

Hull, Isabel V. *Absolute Destruction: Military Culture and the Practices of War in Imperial Germany.* Ithaca, NY: Cornell University Press, 2005.

Hunter, James E. "Survivable Flight Control System Fly-by-Wire Development and Flight Test." Air Force Flight Dynamics Laboratory, August 1, 1976. NASA techdoc 19760024049.

Hutchinson, Herbert. *Inside History of the USAF Lightweight Fighters, 1900 to 1975.* Paso Robles, CA: Xlibris, 2018.

Hutchinson, Ron. "F-16 Falcon Fights for Life." *Montgomery (AL) Advertiser*, October 23, 1991. Original article in *Fort Worth Star-Telegram*.

Ingersoll, Bruce. "Ace of the Fighter Pilots Has a New Theory of War." *Detroit Free Press*, May 5, 1982. Original article in *Chicago Sun-Times*.

"Intelligence Community Assessment of the Lieutenant Commander Speicher Case." March 27, 2001. FOIA Electronic Reading Room, CIA. September 10, 2006.

"Interview Part I: Harry Hillaker: Father of the F-16." Code One, April 1991, 17–23.

"Interview Part II: Harry Hillaker: Father of the F-16." Code One, July 1991, 8–15.

Isaacson, Walter. "The Winds of Reform." Time, March 7, 1983.

"Jet Strategic Bombardment." Air University Review Quarterly 5 (Spring 1952): 17–38.

Johnsen, Frederick A. "Astronaut Armstrong Recalls the Origins of Test Pilot Society." NASA Public Affairs Office, October 1, 2005. https://www.nasa.gov/missions/research/armstrong_speech.html.

Jones, Frank L. A "Hollow Army" Reappraised: President Carter, Defense Budgets, and the Politics of Military Readiness. Carlisle, PA: Strategic Studies Institute, US Army War College, 2012.

Kahneman, Daniel. Thinking, Fast and Slow. New York: Farrar, Straus and Giroux, 2011.

Kamps, Charles Tustin. "Operation Eagle Claw: The Iran Hostage Rescue Mission." Air & Space Power Journal International Edition—Spanish 18 (Third Quarter 2006). http://www.airpower.maxwell.af.mil/apjinternational/apj-s/2006/3tri06/kamps.html.

Keaney, Thomas A., and Eliot A. Cohen. Gulf War Air Power Survey Summary Report. Washington, DC, 1993.

Kelley, Henry J. "Gradient Theory of Optimal Flight Paths." American Rocket Society Journal 30 (October 1960): 947–954.

Kelly, Shawna. Aviators in Early Hollywood. Charleston, SC: Arcadia, 2008.

Kennett, Lee. The First Air War: 1914–1918. New York: Free Press, 1991.

Kent, Glenn A. Thinking about America's Defense: An Analytical Memoir. Arlington, VA: RAND Corp., 2008.

Kilmann, Ralph H., Mary J. Saxton, Roy Serpa, et al., eds. Gaining Control of the Corporate Culture. San Francisco: Jossey-Bass, 1985.

"Knights of the Air." Literary Digest 49, no. 18 (October 31, 1914): 841–842.

Kolb, David A., and Ronald E. Fry. "Towards an Applied Theory of Experiential Learning." In Theories of Group Processes, edited by Cary L. Cooper, 33–58. New York: Wiley, 1975.

Kopp, Carlo. "Operation Desert Storm: The Electronic Battle Parts 1–3." Air Power Australia, 1993. Accessed November 11, 2017. http://www.ausairpower.net/Analysis-ODS-EW.html.

"Korean War 1950–1953 Teacher Resource Guide." National Museum of the United States Air Force. Undated (after 2010). Accessed February 10, 2018. http://www.nationalmuseum.af.mil/Portals/7/documents/education/teacher_resource_korean_war.pdf.

Koskinas, Ioannis. Black Hats and White Hats: The Effect of Organizational Culture and Institutional Identity on the Twenty-Third Air Force. CADRE Paper No. 24. Maxwell Air Force Base, AL: Air University Press, 2006.

Kross, Walter. "Military Reform: Past and Present." Air University Review 32 (July–August 1981): 101–108.

Kross, Walter. Military Reform: The High-Tech Debate in Tactical Air Forces. Fort McNair, Washington, DC: National Defense University Press, 1985.

Lambeth, Benjamin. The Transformation of American Air Power. Ithaca, NY: Cornell University Press, 2000.

Laslie, Brian D. *The Air Force Way of War: U.S. Tactics and Training after Vietnam.* Lexington: University Press of Kentucky, 2016.

Laslie, Brian D. *Architect of Air Power General Laurence S. Kuter and the Birth of the US Air Force.* Lexington: University Press of Kentucky, 2017.

Leahey, Michael J. "A History of Defense Reform since 1970." Master's thesis, Naval Postgraduate School, December 1989.

Lee, Wayne. *Barbarians and Brothers: Anglo-American Warfare, 1500–1865.* Oxford: Oxford University Press, 2011.

Lee, Wayne. "Mind and Matter—Cultural Analysis in American Military History: A Look at the State of the Field." *Journal of American History* 93 (March 2007): 1116–1142.

Lendon, J. E. *Soldiers and Ghosts: A History of Battle in Classical Antiquity.* New Haven, CT: Yale University Press, 2005.

Levin, Stuart. "F-15: The Teething of a Dogfighter." *Space/Aeronautics* 52 (December 1969): 36–47.

Lewis, Adrian. *The American Culture of War.* New York: Routledge, 2012.

Lewis, W. David. *Eddie Rickenbacker: An American Hero in the Twentieth Century.* Baltimore: Johns Hopkins University Press, 2005.

Lind, William. "The Next Conservatism." Traditional Right, April 16, 2016. https://www.traditionalright.com/the-next-conservatism/.

Longview (TX) News-Journal. "Warning to Reagan." August 23, 1982.

Lorell, Mark A., and Hugh P. Levaux. *The Cutting Edge: A Half Century of U.S. Fighter Aircraft R&D.* Washington, DC: RAND Corp., 1998.

Losey, Stephen. "Air-to-Air Combat Is Back: How Will the Air Force Respond as the War over Syria Heats Up?" *Air Force Times,* June 26, 2017. https://www.airforcetimes.com/news/your-air-force/2017/06/26/air-to-air-combat-is-back-how-will-the-air-force-respond-as-the-war-over-syria-heats-up/.

Losey, Stephen. "Top USAF General Sitting Out This Mustache March." *Air Force Times,* March 3, 2015. https://www.airforcetimes.com/news/your-air-force/2015/03/03/top-usaf-general-sitting-out-this-mustache-march/.

Lowery, John. "Have Doughnut." *Air Force Magazine,* June 2010, 64–67.

Lupack, Barbara Tepa. *Richard E. Norman and Race Filmmaking.* Bloomington: Indiana University Press, 2014.

Mahnken, Thomas G. *Technology and the American Way of War since 1945.* New York: Columbia University Press, 2008.

Malishenko, Timothy P. "Congressional Dynamics of the Military Reform Caucus." *National Contract Management Journal* 21 (Summer 1987): 23–33.

McCoy, Tidal W. "Arms Quality Is Vital Priority." *Chicago Tribune,* June 28, 1983.

McFarland, Stephen Lee. *America's Pursuit of Precision Bombing, 1910–1945.* Tuscaloosa: University of Alabama Press, 2008.

McGowan, William. "Cost Analyst Blew Whistle on Air Force." *Pensacola (FL) News Journal,* November 5, 1984.

McManus, John C. *Deadly Sky: The American Combat Airman in World War II.* New York: NAL Caliber, 2000.

McManus, Michael. "Support Growing for Better Defense Spending." *Democrat and Chronicle* (Rochester, NY), January 21, 1982.

McPeak, Merrill A. *Hangar Flying.* Lake Oswego, OR: Lost Wingman, 2012.

Meilinger, Phillip S. *Bomber: The Formation and Early Years of Strategic Air Command.* Maxwell Air Force Base, AL: Air University Press, 2012.

Mets, David. *The Air Campaign: John Warden and the Classical Airpower Theorists.* Maxwell Air Force Base, AL: Air University Press, 1998.

Mets, David. "Boydmania." *Air and Space Power Journal* 18 (Fall 2004): 98–108.

Michel, Marshall. *Clashes: Air Combat over North Vietnam: 1965–1972.* Annapolis, MD: Naval Institute Press, 1997.

Michel, Marshall. "The Revolt of the Majors: How the Air Force Changed after Vietnam." PhD diss., Auburn University, 2006.

Miller, Jay. "F-16 Design Origins." Code One, February 4, 2014. http://www.codeo nemagazine.com/article.html?item_id=131.

Miller, Jay. *The General Dynamics F-16 Fighting Falcon.* Austin, TX: Aerofax, 1982.

Millet, Allan R., and Peter Maslowski. *For the Common Defense: A Military History of the United States of America.* New York: Free Press, 1984.

Minis, Margaret. "High Flying: A World War I Flying Ace Remembers His Exploits with War and the Ladies." *Georgia Gazette and Journal Record* (Savannah), May 28, 1979.

Minutaglio, Bill. "Tales of the Fighter Mafia." *Dallas Life Magazine*, May 3, 1987, 9–30.

Mitchell, Ellen. "Trump Wants 'Goddamned Steam' Catapults on New Aircraft Carriers." Hill, May 11, 2017. http://thehill.com/policy/defense/333040-trump-wants-goddamned-steam-catapults-on-new-aircraft-carriers.

Mohr, Charles. "Arms Numbers Decline as Costs Climb." *Daily Press* (Newport News, VA), October 24, 1982.

Mohr, Charles. "Pentagon Budget Planning Criticized by 2 Studies." *New York Times*, January 12, 1983.

Molter, Bennett. *Knights of the Air.* New York: D. Appleton, 1918.

Momyer, William W. *Air Power in Three Wars: WWII, Korea, Vietnam.* Washington, DC: Office of Air Force History, 1978.

Morris, Craig. *The Origins of American Strategic Bombing Theory.* Annapolis, MD: Naval Institute Press, 2017.

Mrozek, Donald J. *The US Air Force after Vietnam: Postwar Challenges and Potential for Responses.* Maxwell Air Force Base, AL: Air University Press, 1988.

Mueller, Karl. "Strategies of Coercion: Denial, Punishment, and the Future of Air Power." *Security Studies* 7, no. 3 (1998): 182–228.

Mumford, Alan, ed. *Action Learning at Work.* Brookfield, VT: Gower, 1997.

Murphy, T. B. *Kiffin Rockwell, the Lafayette Escadrille and the Birth of the United States Air Force.* Jefferson, NC: McFarland, 2016.

Murray, Williamson, and Mark Grimsley. "On Strategy." In *The Making of Strategy: Rulers, States, and War*, edited by Williamson Murray, Macgregor Knox, and Alvin Bernstein, 1–23. New York: Cambridge University Press, 1994.

Murray, Williamson, and Wayne W. Thompson. *Air War in the Persian Gulf.* Baltimore: Nautical and Aviation Publishing, 1997.

Murrow, John. "The First World War, 1914–1919." In *A History of Air Warfare*, edited by John Andreas Olsen, 3–26. Dulles, VA: Potomac Books, 2010.

National Aeronautic Association. "Collier Trophy." Accessed September 13, 2019. https://naa.aero/awards/awards-and-trophies/collier-trophy.

Neufeld, Jacob. "The F-15 Eagle: Origins and Development, 1964–1972." Washington, DC: Office of Air Force History, November 1974.

Newman, Rick, and Don Shepperd. *Bury Us Upside Down: The Misty Pilots and the Secret Battle for the Ho Chi Minh Trail*. New York: Ballantine Books, 2006.

New York Times. "U.S. Decision in 'Fighter-Plane Sweepstakes' Is Due Jan. 15." December 26, 1974.

Nowak, Martin A. "Five Rules for the Evolution of Cooperation." *Science* 314, no. 5805 (2006): 1560–1563.

Nye, David. *America as Second Creation: Technology and Narratives of New Beginnings*. Cambridge, MA: MIT Press, 2004.

Nye, David. *Technology Matters: Questions to Live With*. Cambridge, MA: MIT Press, 2007.

Odessa (TX) American. "Military Reformer Fired from Project." March 27, 1982. Original article in *Chicago Sun-Times*.

Olds, Robin, with Christina Olds and Ed Rasimus. *Fighter Pilot: The Memoirs of Legendary Ace Robin Olds*. New York: St. Martin's, 2010.

Olsen, John Andreas. "Boyd Revisited: A Great Mind with a Touch of Madness." *Air Power History*, Winter 2016, 7–16.

Olsen, John Andreas. *John Warden and the Renaissance of American Air Power*. Dulles, VA: Potomac Books, 2011.

Orr, George. *Combat Operations C3I: Fundamentals and Interactions*. Maxwell Air Force Base, AL: Air University Press, 1983.

Osinga, Frans P. B. "The Enemy as a Complex Adaptive System: John Boyd and Airpower in the Postmodern Era." In *Airpower Reborn: The Strategic Concepts of John Warden and John Boyd*, edited by John Andreas Olsen, 48–92. Annapolis, MD: Naval Institute Press, 2015.

Osinga, Frans P. B. *Science, Strategy and War: The Strategic Theory of John Boyd*. Netherlands: Eburon Academic, 2005.

Palm Beach Post (West Palm Beach, FL). Obituary for John Henry Axley. April 4, 2015. http://www.legacy.com/obituaries/palmbeachpost/obituary.aspx?pid=174575094.

Palm Beach Post (West Palm Beach, FL). "Problem Areas Are the Same." March 9, 1998.

Pawlyk, Oriana. "US F/A-18E Shoots Down Syrian Su-22 in Air-to-Air Kill." Military.com, June 18, 2017. https://www.military.com/daily-news/2017/06/18/us-navy-fa18e-shoots-down-su22-over-syria.html.

Peacock, Lindsay. *On Falcon Wings: The F-16 Story*. Fairford, UK: Royal Air Force Benevolent Fund Enterprises, 1997.

Peck, Gaillard R., Jr. *America's Secret MiG Squadron: The Red Eagles of Project Constant Peg*. Long Island City, NY: Osprey, 2012.

Pendo, Stephen. *Aviation in the Cinema*. Metuchen, NJ: Scarecrow, 1985.

Peters, Tom. "Don't Leap to Hasty Conclusions in the Wake of War." *Chicago Tribune*, March 25, 1991.

Petrina, Gilbert E. "An Agency Theory View of the Military Advisor." Thesis, School of Advanced Air and Space Studies, Air University, Maxwell Air Force Base, June 2005.

Poncar, Jerry V., and James R. Johnston III. "History and Analysis of the C-5A Program: An Application of the Total Package Procurement Concept." Thesis, Wright-Patterson Air Force Base, Air Force Institute of Technology, October 1970.

Poole, Walter S. *Adapting to Flexible Response, 1960–1968*. Washington, DC: Historical Office, Office of the Secretary of Defense, 2013.

Prine, Carl. "Q & A with Merrill 'Tony' McPeak." *San Diego Union Tribune*, November 23, 2017. http://www.sandiegouniontribune.com/military/sd-me-mcpeak-speaks-20171113-story.html.

Putney, Diane T. *Airpower Advantage: Planning the Gulf War Air Campaign, 1989–1991*. Washington, DC: Air Force History and Museums Program, 2004.

Rasimus, Ed. *Palace Cobra: A Fighter Pilot in the Vietnam Air War*. New York: St. Martin's, 2006.

Rasor, Dina. *The Pentagon Underground*. New York: Times Books, 1985.

Record, Jeffrey. "Has America's Military Lost Its Fighting Effectiveness?" *Age* (Melbourne, Australia), June 4, 1984. Original article in *Washington Post*.

Record, Jeffrey. "The Military Reform Caucus." *Washington Quarterly*, Spring 1983, 125–129.

Record, Jeffrey. "Unprepared: Can U.S. Make War Even If It Wants To?" *Montgomery (AL) Advertiser*, February 2, 1984.

Reed, Fred. "Let's Reform the Military Reformers." *Washington Post*, October 11, 1987.

Reed, Fred. "Reformers." *Air Force Magazine*, January 1, 1988.

Riccioni, Everest E. "The Air Superiority Fighter: A Modern Analysis." FR 39919. Research Report, Air War College, Air University, Maxwell Air Force Base, AL, April 1968.

Ricks, Thomas. "Whatever Happened to . . . Pierre Sprey?" *Washington Post*, May 16, 2006.

Rider, James G. "YF-16 Pilot Report." *Air Force Magazine*, October 1976, 32–37.

Riley, Jonathan. *At the Fulcrum of Air Force Identity: Balancing the Internal and External Pressures of Image and Culture*. Drew Paper No. 11. Maxwell Air Force Base, AL: Air University Press, 2014.

Ringle, William. "Caucus Wants Answers on Defense Windfall." *Pensacola (FL) News Journal*, May 24, 1985.

Ringle, William. "Conservative GOP'ers Lead Team That Stamps Out Government Abuse." *Florida Today* (Cocoa), June 3, 1986.

Robertson, Linda R. *The Dream of Civilized Warfare: World War I Flying Aces and the American Imagination*. Minneapolis: University of Minnesota Press, 2003.

Romjue, John L. "The Evolution of the Airland Battle Concept." *Air University Review* 35, no. 4 (May–June 1984): 52–55.

Rosenkranz, Keith. *Vipers in the Storm: Diary of a Gulf War Fighter Pilot*. New York: McGraw-Hill, 2002.

Rutowski, Edward S. "Energy Approach to the General Aircraft Performance Problem." *Journal of the Aeronautical Sciences* 21 (March 1954): 187–195.

Schneider, Greg. "Leading an Assault on the Pentagon." *Baltimore Sun*, March 8, 1998.

Schultz, Timothy. *The Problem with Pilots: How Physicians, Engineers, and Airpower Enthusiasts Redefined Flight.* Baltimore: Johns Hopkins University Press, 2018.

Schwartz, Moshe. "The Nunn-McCurdy Act: Background, Analysis, and Issues for Congress." Congressional Research Service, 7-5700, R41293. June 21, 2010. https://fas.org/sgp/crs/misc/R41293.pdf.

Scrogham, Wade A. *Combat Relevant Task: The Test and Evaluation of the Lightweight Fighter Prototypes.* Edwards Air Force Base, CA: Air Force Test Center History Office, 2014.

Seligman, Lara. "Podcast: F-35 in the Crossfire, Part 1." *Aviation Week*, July 20, 2017. http://aviationweek.com/combat-aircraft/podcast-f-35-crossfire-part-1?page=1.

Shepperd, Don, ed. *Misty: First Person Stories of the F-100 Mist Fast FACs in the Vietnam War.* Don Shepperd, 2002.

Sherry, Michael. *The Rise of American Air Power: The Creation of Armageddon.* New Haven, CT: Yale University Press, 1987.

Sherwood, John Darrell. *Fast Movers: Jet Pilots and the Vietnam Experience.* New York: Free Press, 1999.

Sherwood, John Darrell. *Officers in Flight Suits: The Story of American Air Force Fighter Pilots in the Korean War.* New York: NYU Press, 1996.

Slife, James C. *Creech Blue: Gen Bill Creech and the Reformation of the Tactical Air Forces, 1978–1984.* Maxwell Air Force Base, AL: Air University Press, 2004.

Smith, Frederick H. "Current Practice in Air Defense." *Air University Review* 6 (Spring 1953): 31–39.

Smith, G. K., et al. *The Use of Prototypes in Weapon Systems Development.* RAND Project Air Force Report, number R-2345-AF, March 1981.

Smith, Perry McCoy. *The Air Force Plans for Peace, 1943–1945.* Baltimore: Johns Hopkins University Press, 1970.

Snow, Shawn. "What Counts as an Aerial Victory? Drones Change the Face of Aerial Combat." *Air Force Times*, June 24, 2017. https://www.airforcetimes.com/articles/what-counts-as-an-aerial-victory-drones-change-the-face-of-aerial-combat.

Spangenberg, George. Oral History of George Spangenberg. February 21, 1990. https://www.docdroid.net/x9czNLE/george-spangenberg-oral-history.pdf.

Spick, Mike. *The Ace Factor: Air Combat and the Role of Situational Awareness.* Shrewsbury, UK: Airlife, 1988.

Spinney, Franklin C. "Defense Facts of Life." Office of the Secretary of Defense. December 5, 1980. http://pogoarchives.org/labyrinth/defense-facts-of-life-1980.pdf.

Spinney, Franklin C. "Genghis John." *Proceedings of the U.S. Naval Institute*, July 1997, 42–47.

Sprey, Pierre. "The Case for More Effective, Less Expensive Weapons Systems." United States Military Academy Senior Conference XX: "The Military Reform Debate: Directions for the Defense Establishment for the Remainder of the Century." June 1982. http://pogoarchives.org/labyrinth/11/12.pdf.

Statesman Journal (Salem, OR). "Military Reform Caucus Criticizes Inflation Figures." May 24, 1985.

Stephens, Alan. "The Air War in Korea, 1950–1953." In *A History of Air Warfare*, edited by John Andreas Olsen, 85–106. Washington, DC: Potomac Books, 2010.

Stevenson, James. *McDonnell Douglas F-15 Eagle*. Fallbrook, CA: Aero, 1978.

Stewart, Jim. "Report: Disband Joint Chiefs." *Palm Beach Post* (West Palm Beach, FL), October 17, 1985.

St. Louis Post-Dispatch. "General Dynamics' F-16 Selected as Air Force's New Jet Fighter." January 14, 1975.

St. Louis Post-Dispatch. "Weapons." June 10, 1982.

Storr, Jim. "Neither Art nor Science—towards a Discipline of Warfare." *RUSI Journal* 146 (April 2001): 39–45.

Sutherland, J. P. "Fly-by-Wire Control Systems." Air Force Flight Dynamics Laboratory, Wright-Patterson Air Force Base, OH. AD 679 158, September 3, 1968.

31st Fighter Wing Public Affairs Office. "555th Fighter Squadron 'Triple Nickel.'" Fact sheet. Accessed November 18, 2017. https://web.archive.org/web/2013 1217184107/http://www.aviano.af.mil/library/factsheets/factsheet.asp?id= 4353.

Thomas, Evan, John Barry, Amm McDaniel, and Douglas Waller. "No Vietnam." *Newsweek*, December 10, 1990.

Thompson, Wayne. *To Hanoi and Back: The United States Air Force and North Vietnam, 1966–1973*. Washington, DC: Smithsonian Institution Press, 2000.

Thornborough, Anthony M. *The Phantom Story*. New York: Arms and Armour, 1994.

Thornborough, Anthony M. *USAF Phantoms: Tactics, Training, and Weapons*. New York: Arms and Armour, 1988.

Tilford, Earl H. *Crosswinds: The Air Force's Setup in Vietnam*. College Station: Texas A&M University Press, 1993.

Tomayko, James E. "Blind Faith: The United States Air Force and the Development of Fly-by-Wire Technology." In *Technology and the Air Force: A Retrospective Assessment*, edited by Jacob Neufeld, George M. Watson Jr., and David Chenoweth, 167–177. Washington, DC: Air Force History and Museums Program, 1997.

Turner, Barry A. "The Organizational and Interorganizational Development of Disasters." *Administrative Science Quarterly* 21 (September 1976): 378–397.

Tuso, Joseph F. *Singing the Vietnam Blues: Songs of the Air Force in Southeast Asia*. College Station: Texas A&M University Press, 1990.

Tyler, Rick. "Newt Gingrich Is a Military Expert." *Chicago Tribune*, March 6, 2006.

United States General Accounting Office. *Operation Desert Storm: Evaluation of the Air Campaign*. GAO Report to the Ranking Minority Member, Committee on Commerce, House of Representatives, June 1997. GAO/NSIAD-97-134.

United States Marine Corps. *FMFM-1: Warfighting*. Washington, DC: Headquarters United States Marines Corps, 1989.

Van Staaveren, Jacob. *Gradual Failure: The Air War over North Vietnam*. Washington, DC: Air Force History and Museums Program, 2002.

Vlahos, Kelley Beaucar. "40 Years of the 'Fighter Mafia.'" *American Conservative*, September 20, 2013. http://www.theamericanconservative.com/articles/ 40-years-of-the-fighter-mafia/.

Warden, John A. *The Air Campaign: Planning for Combat*. Washington, DC: National Defense University Press, 1988.

Weapons System Evaluation Group Report 116: Air-to-Air Encounters in Southeast Asia (also known as the "Red Baron Report"). Vol. 1. Arlington, VA: Institute for Defense Analyses Systems Evaluation Division, October 1967.

Weigley, Russell. *The American Way of War: A History of United States Military Strategy and Policy.* New York: Macmillan, 1973.

Weigley, Russell. "Response to Brian McAllister Linn." *Journal of Military History* 66, no. 2 (April 2002): 531–533.

Werrell, Kenneth P. *Chasing the Silver Bullet: U.S. Air Force Weapons Development from Vietnam to Desert Storm.* Washington, DC: Smithsonian Books, 2003.

Werrell, Kenneth P. *Sabres over MiG Alley: The F-86 and the Battle for Air Supremacy in Korea.* Annapolis, MD: Naval Institute Press, 2005.

Wette, Wolfram. *The Wehrmacht: History, Myth, Reality.* Cambridge, MA: Harvard University Press, 2007.

Wetzel, Tyson. "Changing the USAF's Aerial 'Kill' Criteria." Balloons to Drones, June 26, 2017. https://balloonstodrones.wordpress.com/2017/06/26/changing-the-usafs-aerial-kill-criteria/.

Wheeler, Winslow T. *The Pentagon Labyrinth: 10 Short Essays to Help You through It: From 10 Pentagon Insiders, Retired Military Officers and Specialists with over 400 Years of Defense Experience.* Washington, DC: Center for Defense Information, 2011.

Wheeler, Winslow T. *The Wastrels of Defense: How Congress Sabotages U.S. Security.* New York: Naval Institute Press, 2013.

Wheeler, Winslow T., and Lawrence J. Korb. *Military Reform: An Uneven History and an Uncertain Future.* Stanford, CA: Stanford University Press, 2007.

Wilcox, Robert K. *Scream of Eagles: The Dramatic Account of the U.S. Navy's Top Gun Fighter Pilots and How They Took Back the Skies over Vietnam.* New York: Pocket Star Books, 1990.

Williams, Amy E. *The American Fighter Plane.* New York: Barnes & Noble Books, 2004.

Wohl, Robert. *A Passion for Wings: Aviation and the Western Imagination, 1908–1918.* New Haven, CT: Yale University Press, 1996.

Wolk, Herman. *The Struggle for Air Force Independence, 1943–1947.* Washington, DC: Air Force History and Museums Program, 1997.

Worden, Mike. *Rise of the Fighter Generals: The Problem of Air Force Leadership, 1945–1982.* Maxwell Air Force Base, AL: Air University Press, 1988.

Yeager, Chuck, and Leo Janos. *Yeager: An Autobiography.* Toronto: Bantam Books, 1986.

Ziemke, Caroline F. "In the Shadow of the Giant: USAF Tactical Air Command in the Era of Strategic Bombing, 1945–1955." PhD diss., Ohio State University, 1989.

Index

www.ingramcontent.com/pod-product-compliance
Ingram Content Group UK Ltd.
Pitfield, Milton Keynes, MK11 3LW, UK
UKHW040900140325
456137UK00014B/96/J

9 781501 760655